W9-BWE-754

PROFITABLE CANDLESTICK TRADING

PROFITABLE CANDLESTICK TRADING

Pinpointing Market Opportunities to Maximize Profits

Stephen Bigalow

John Wiley & Sons, Inc.

New York • Chichester • Weinheim • Brisbane • Singapore • Toronto

Published by John Wiley & Sons, Inc.
Published simultaneously in Canada.

Library of Congress Cataloging-in-Publication Data:

Bigalow, Stephen.
Profitable candlestick trading: pinpointing market opportunities to maximize profits / Stephen Bigalow.
p. cm. -- (Wiley trading)
Includes index.
ISBN 0-471-02466-X (cloth: alk. paper)
1. Stocks--Charts, diagrams, etc. 2. Investment analysis. 3. Stocks--Prices--Japan--Charts, diagrams, etc. I. Title. II. Series.

HG4638 .B54 2002
332.63'222'021--dc21 2001046563

Printed in the United States of America.

10 9 8

ACKNOWLEDGMENTS

This book was made possible through the influences and inspiration of many people. It is hard to decide who to mention first due to the integral input of all during the process of writing this book.

My first and foremost thanks goes to my mother June Bigalow who has always been there to support my endeavors. I am also blessed with a great and supportive brother and sister, along with their families. Their support through this effort has been greatly appreciated.

I am forever grateful for the encouragement from friends and business acquaintances, who have since become good friends, for their parts in advancing the progress of this book. Drew and Dee Dee Vickers, Dan Dubose, Daryl and Barbara Thompson have been great inspirers. Wally and Rose Ann Peckham provided great coaching as well as a refuge to clear the mind for the next go-round of typing. Mark Storey has been a constant source of innovative ideas and procedures through the years for the development of investment programs. Ken Melber has patiently gone through the experience of actual trading programs, sorting out the good and bad, and finally benefiting from the establishment of trading rules. Dave Goddard lent his genius in statistical analysis whenever was requested.

Professor Abbie Smith, of Chicago University, receives my thanks for being the initial inspiration for writing this book. Mike Harper, President of the Houston chapter of the Market Technicians Association, has been a great help with his extensive background in Elliot Wave analysis.

Mike Roberts has my heartfelt thanks for the work he did way above the call of duty. His many hours of editing and format suggestions will never be forgotten. I don't know what I would have done without his gracious assistance. Vince Kaminski and Gary Hickerson contributed invaluable access to functional trading concepts and research integration along with intellectual encouragement.

Many thanks go to my Cornell University, DU fraternity buddies for their encouragement and insights. Their inspiration to put my best foot forward acted as a goal for me throughout my many hours of hunt-and-peck typing.

Many thanks go to my Cornell University, DU fraternity buddies for their encouragement and insights. Their inspiration to put my best foot forward acted as a goal for me throughout my many hours of hunt-and-peck typing.

Thanks to the CQG Company for providing clear and easy to work with charts. Also thanks to TC2000 for providing an efficient search software program.

A special acknowledgment goes to Steve Nison. His books *Japanese Candlestick Charting Techniques* and *Beyond Candlesticks* were instrumental in my initial interest in candlesticks. His extensive research into candlestick methodology provided an excellent reference source.

A special thanks goes out to my agent, Robert G. Deforio of D4EO Literary Agency, for his guidance in working with publishers. And I feel fortunate to have worked with Claudio Campuzano and Pamela van Giessen at John Wiley & Sons, Inc. Their counseling and guidance has made the experience of publishing this book a pleasant one. Marie Garcarz is greatly appreciated for her valued advice and direction.

To keep from possibly blemishing any reputations associated with those acknowledged as providing something toward the completion of this book, it should be noted that any factual errors or omissions found within this book are solely my responsibility.

Greg Morris needs to be acknowledged for his excellent writing on the candlestick signals. Six or eight of the high-profit signals in this book were from his developments. It is highly recommended that Greg Morris' books be read for further education in candlesticks.

CONTENTS

PREFACE

Japanese Candlestick charting and analysis is one of the most effective technical methodologies in the universe of technical analysis. This bold statement is consistent with the same statements that were made one to two decades ago in books written about Candlesticks when they were first introduced into the United States. The exact same problems that appeared to keep the Candlestick method out of the limelight back then have persisted to make Candlesticks still a fairly underused method today. Through the years, the number of people who have become proficient users of Candlestick analysis has been minimal. Nearly two decades of using the signals have produced two basic revelations: the signals are extremely accurate, and it is unusual that more people have not become advocates of the technique.

One of the most powerful investment techniques has been sitting in front of the U.S. investment community, yet it has not exploded in popularity as one would expect. Years of informal surveys have reached this conclusion. There is a definite perception about Candlestick trading. It is seen as requiring a long time to learn and become proficient at it. That is the major reason the majority of investors have stayed away from Candlesticks. That misconception is what spurred the writing of this book. Other books on the topic were written nearly a decade ago. Those books were informational and well written, however, they were published in somewhat of a vacuum. Once the books were read, each investor was out there on his or her own. The number of people to confer with after first becoming exposed to the Candlestick method was minimal. The ideas were new in the United States and there were few places to turn to for guidance.

For the past two decades, most investors have been aware of Candlesticks. The most common statement is, "They know about Candlesticks; they just don't know how they work." An extremely high percentage of chart followers have the Candlestick formations on their charts versus the standard bar charts. This is due to the favorable visual impact. The illustrative properties of the Candlestick chart make viewing much easier.

Four hundred years of research by profitable Japanese rice traders was the inception of statistical analysis. What may take computers one afternoon to perform, the Japanese rice traders assembled over centuries of time. However, there is a definite benefit involved with human interpretation of these signals. The Japanese traders were able to describe the investor sentiment behind the formation of the signals. This becomes an extremely powerful asset for exploiting profits from markets that involve human emotions.

Being thoroughly convinced that Candlestick analysis surpasses all other technical analysis induced me to eliminate the misperceptions. Japanese Candlesticks is definitely not a passing fad. It is here stay and effectively extract profits from the trading markets—profits for those who take the little time required to become acquainted with the Candlestick thinking process.

Not only does the knowledge of what a signal looks like benefit the candlestick educated investor, but learning the common-sense psychology that formed the signal provides the investor with a whole new perspective into successful investing. Somebody is making huge profits in the markets. It is not the conventional wisdom advocates, buy and hold. The big winners are those who have developed successful methods for interpreting when to buy and sell. Candlestick analysis is that method. Read this book and your investment abilities will be forever improved, improved to the point of not just constantly exceeding market averages, but being able to exploit the indications of the signals to amass extraordinary profits.

Once you learn the Japanese Candlestick technique, your understanding of how investment markets work will dramatically alter your investment psychology. The probabilities of producing magnificent profits will always be in your favor. Learn Candlesticks and reap the knowledge that has led to centuries of successful trading.

Stephen W. Bigalow
Houston, Texas

Chapter 1

INTRODUCTION

The learning of books, that you do not make your own wisdom, is money in the hands of another in time of need. Japanese Proverb

Japanese Candlestick analysis is a highly effective, but under-used investment decision-making technique. Most people in the United States' investment community are aware of Candlestick analysis, but few understand how or why it actually works. Candlestick charts reveal many insights using well-recognized Japanese candlestick formations, yet few people understand the ramifications or significance of the signals that are clearly and reliably displayed.

This book was written to educate investors on how to use the Japanese Candlestick technique profitably. The easy-to-follow procedures detailed in this book provide the reader with profit-making techniques that can be learned quickly. More importantly, learning the principles of market psychology underlying the Candlestick methodology will revolutionize the reader's overall investment psyche forever. While this may sound bold and far-fetched, fortunes have been made using the Japanese Candlestick techniques. Knowing how to use the candlesticks and why they work will immediately improve the reader's investment profitability and permanently alter overall investment perceptions. This newly acquired perception will produce consistent profits along with an associated mental re-programming designed to maximize investment returns. Once an investor becomes convinced of the reliability of the Candlestick methodology, that investor also acquires a pre-programmed investment discipline. As a result, Candlesticks add a whole new dimension to enhancing the investor's profit-making abilities.

Most readers will be surprised at how the knowledge gained from a close reading of this book dramatically enhances investment abilities across all investment vehicles and over all trading timeframes. More than 400 years of refined reversal-identification and trend continuity projection is now at the reader's disposal. Mastering the Candlestick methodology will be the next major step for maximizing investment returns.

Why aren't the Candlestick signals used more? Why, if the signals demonstrate such a high degree of accuracy, are there not many more investors, whether institutional or individual, using these signals? The answer is that the Candlestick technique in the past has been too labor-intensive and required a long and steep learning curve before the investor gained proficiency. This book was written to provide the reader with an easy and fast training program to circumvent those obstacles.

The Benefits from the Candlestick System

Japanese Candlestick signals possess one major attribute that is not present in other technical systems: The signals are created by the change in investor sentiment. This point is the crux of the success of Candlestick analysis. Again, to emphasize the importance of what you have just read: *The signals are created by the change in investor sentiment.* Understanding this truism will make it easier to acclimate your investment psychology to this successful trading discipline.

The secrets of the effectiveness of the signals can be learned in a fast and easy process. An investor does not need to be knowledgeable about technical charting to take immediate advantage of the signals. The graphical formation of a signal makes reversals immediately visible. A Candlestick formation provides a visual graphic of investor psychology during a specific time period. For the purpose of illustration in this book, the standard timeframe is one day, and the trading entity is stock—equity as opposed to commodity. Investment strategies can be structured, of course, for whatever time period is suited for your trading style: minute-to-minute or monthly. Applicable trading instruments include any vehicle that has the key elements of investor fear and greed.

The graphics of a Candlestick chart have greater appeal than Western charts (commonly known as *bar charts*). The amount of data displayed is exactly the same, but the ease of visual interpretation is dramatically different. The immediate representative depiction of price movement as the result of investor sentiment is visually in front of you. Recognizing the change in investor sentiment is made easier when the graphics are clear and easy to understand.

Once you become accustomed to the Candlestick charts, all other charting will seem diminished in terms of effectiveness. That is not to say that other charting techniques cannot be used as "alert" functions. Candlestick signals, incorporated with other types of charts, fine-tune the reversal identification process. Watch your profits soar by simply combining Candlesticks with basic technical charting methods.

A Successful History

Knowing the history of the formations inevitably imparts confidence in the Japanese Candlestick technique. Japanese rice traders developed the system over a 400-year period. Logic dictates that a system that has persevered that long must have credible features. The history of the rice traders that developed the signals reinforces that assumption. With its 400 years of development, the Candlestick methodology got its major refinement in the mid-1700s.

Kosaku Kato (1716–1803) was born in the city of Sakata (now Tamagata Prefecture) during the Tokugawa Period (Eighth Shogunate). Adopted by the Honma family, he became known as Sokuta Honma. His successful interpretation of the candlestick formations made him the most feared and respected rice trader in Japan, and the wealth he produced for his family became legendary.

Success is a ladder that cannot be climbed with your hands in your pockets. Japanese Proverb

Songs were written about the Honma family's untouchable wealth, as reflected in the lyric, "Nobody could ever be a Honma, but everybody would like to be at least a lord." Their mastery of the rice market price movements was popularized in verses such as, "When it shines in Sakata, it's cloudy in Dojima. And in Edo (Tokyo), it rains." In other words, when there is good weather in Sakata (the growing region), the prices fall on the Dojima exchange and rice prices plummet in Tokyo.

Honma's methods are divided into two categories: the Market Sanmi No Den and Sakata's Method. The Market Sanmi No Den rules can be summarized as:

A. Without being too greedy, analyze the time and price ratio by reviewing its past movements.
B. Aim at selling at the ceiling and purchasing at the bottom.
C. Increase the position after a rise of 100 bags from the bottom or 100 bags from the top. (The price stayed the same; the volume measured in bags changed in those days.)
D. If a trade is not working, analyze it as fast as possible. Once it is discovered to be a bad trade, liquidate it immediately and rest before putting on the next trade.
E. Liquidate 70 to 80 percent of a profitable trade, liquidating the remainder after the price has indicated a top or bottom.

The Market Sanmi No Den rules A, B, and C require that the investor study charts. Rules D and E represent investing philosophies.

Sakata's Method is the first verifiable beginning of pattern recognition.

Although, Honma did not originate Candlestick analysis, his rules and philosophies gave the technique credibility. When in his early 50s, Honma wrote 160 rules that became the cornerstone of Japanese Candlestick analysis, as well as the basis for Japanese investment disciplines. His use of three-period patterns is the foundation for Japanese charting, along with other Western charting practices.

Through Candlestick recognition, the name Sokyu Honma is associated with successful investing in Japan, as the name Bill Gates is associated with successful computer program marketing in the United States. Learning to "consult" the market, as Honma did a few hundred years ago, will greatly enhance your investing probabilities in the markets today, as you will see in the next section.

Consult the Market about the Market

When analyzing the market, pay attention to the market movement itself—in other words, *consult the market about the market.* The would-be investor has to follow the market movement like the cat that wishes to catch the mouse. Charts reflect the past. Theoretically, it is not possible to predict the market's future; yet, analyzing identifiable patterns as a prelude to a high probability result is as close as an investor can get. Repeating patterns are not 100 percent accurate, but visually verifiable probabilities can adjust the odds immensely in your favor. Identification of certain events provides a basis for predicting an occurrence. Otherwise, admonitions such as "Red skies at night, sailor's delight" would not be in existence. Hundreds of years of weather observations produced a high probability for a reliable prediction about tomorrow's weather. The same historical observations have made Candlestick signals highly accurate.

Candlestick Charts Versus Bar Charts

After using the Candlestick charts, you will find that bar charts do not provide the same clarity. Despite the fact that the exact same information is being conveyed, the Candlestick charts, through greater visual appeal, provide information that is more communicative than bar charts. Candlestick patterns allow the investor to identify pertinent information in a relatively fast and unencumbered manner.

Bar Charts

A vertical line, seen here in Figure 1.1, represents the daily price movement on a bar chart. The top of the line is the high of the daily trading range; the bottom is the low of the day. A notch to the right side of the line represents the closing price. In more recent years, a notch has been added to the left side of the line to designate the opening price. Opening prices have not been as readily available in stock transactions until a few years back. Futures and commodity charts have had access to this information for a longer period of time.

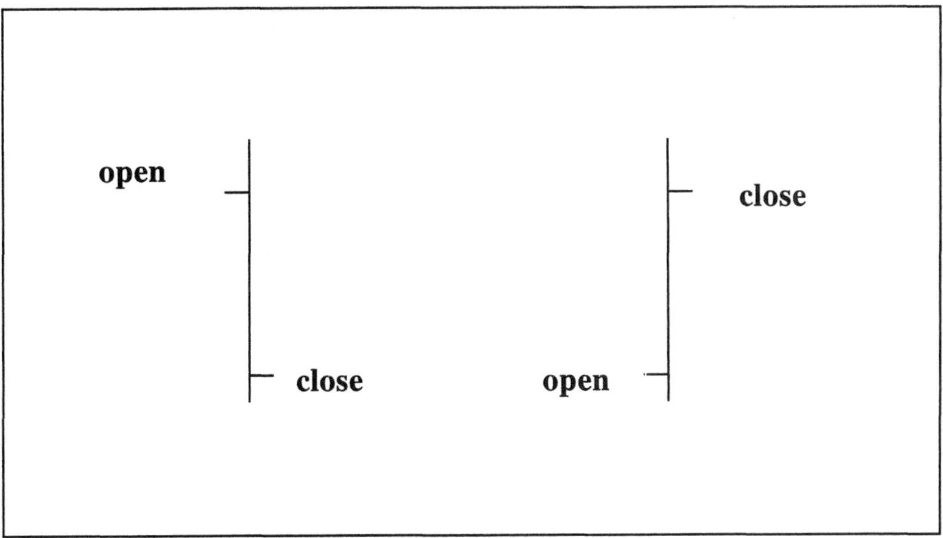

Figure 1.1 Daily price movement.

Internet charting services and software vendors provide a large number of additional technical indicators along with the charts. Fortunately, we are living in a time when software packages are constantly being developed to provide more and more technical information. This is mentioned to illustrate the benefits of technology that can be applied to better enhance the investor's evaluations. Upon becoming accustomed to the Candlestick charts, an individual can fine-tune the probabilities of successful trades many times greater than what the capabilities would have been just a few short years ago.

Candlestick Charts

Using the same information provided in a bar chart, Japanese Candlestick charts provide immensely more illustrative graphics. As in bar charts, the open, close, high, and low are all that is required. Yet, the manner in which they are depicted provides a great amount of information to the Candlestick analyst.

Forming the Candlesticks

Horizontal lines represent the open and the close. (See Figure 1.2.) Once both lines are added to the chart, they are boxed. This box is called the BODY. If the close is higher than the open, the body is white or empty. If the close is lower than the open, the body is black or filled. Keep in mind, this does not necessarily mean that a white body represents that the price was up for the

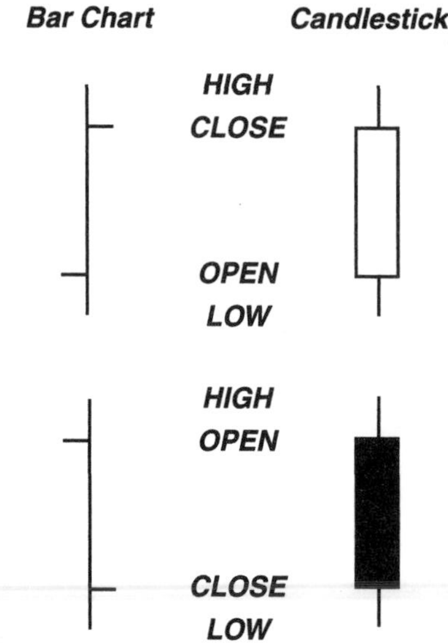

Figure 1.2 Forming the Candlesticks.

day or that a black body represents that the price was down for the day. The body color only illustrates where the close was compared to the open.

The contrasting colors of the bodies provide for rapid visual interpretations. A declining column of dark candles interrupted by the appearance of a white candle attracts the attention of the eye immediately. This is something that would not occur when viewing conventional bar charts.

The lines extending from the body represent the extremes of the price movement during the day. These are known as the *shadows*. The shadow above the body is known as the *upper shadow*. In some Japanese analytical circles, the upper shadow is also described as the hair. The shadow below the body is known as the *lower shadow* or the tail. The length of the shadows has important implications to the strength of reversal moves.

The bodies with shadows look much like candles—thus the name Candlesticks. But don't let the unsophisticated name throw you. The information provided by the formations puts the Candlestick analyst giant leaps ahead of other technical analysts.

The colors of the boxes are not important. For visual clarity, white and black easily show contrast. Some computer software uses green for up and red for down. The purpose of the chart is to provide a clear indication of what signals are being formed.

Figures 1.3 and 1.4 are included for comparison purposes. Once you have become accustomed to the candlestick charts, the visual aspects of the candlestick charts will make all other charting techniques seem obsolete.

Figure 1.3 Bar chart.

Figure 1.4 Candlestick chart.

Contrasts between the information conveyed by Figure 1.4 and that conveyed by Figure 1.3 will become dramatically apparent by the time you finish studying this book.

Exploiting Reason while Eliminating Emotion

Japanese Candlesticks perform a dual function. Investor fear and greed create the signals. Knowing this information creates a frame of mind to anticipate how formations might be developing. What is the glib response to the question, "How do you make money in the stock market?" Buy low and sell high! That simple. Yet reality reveals over and over that John Q. Public is going to buy a stock *after* it has already made a major move upwards. This decision is based on greed. You can see the evidence for yourself as the daily price range expands and the volume increases at the top of up moves.

Conversely, rational investment decisions are overpowered by fear when prices reach the lower end of their decline. When prices are getting lower, common sense says to be buying. However, the same expansion of daily volatility and volume can be seen as investors get panicky. It is at these stages that the Candlestick signals will enable you to make inordinate profits. Observing uniquely accurate Candlestick signals will provide you with a much more positive investment frame of mind. Doubt and fear will give way to confidence. Knowing that a signal creates a high probability occurrence allows you to make rational, not emotional decisions about your portfolio.

> **There is a time to take counsel of your fears, and there is a time to never listen to any fear. General George S. Patton, United States Army**

The logic conveyed by the Candlestick formations is simple. For a quick illustration (also seen later in this book in the section describing "windows" or "gaps"), consider the common investor psychology when a stock has been going down steadily for the past eight trading days. Each day the stock price goes lower and lower. Finally, everybody just wants out of the stock at any price. They can't stand it anymore. Fear now takes control. The stock price gaps down the next day on big volume. Investors are finally relieved of the pain and fear of holding that stock any longer.

Note after the long decline (shown in Figure 1.5), the fear gets so painful, that the price gaps down. The first question that should come up is, "Who was buying all that stock to relieve everybody's pain?" In other words, who was using the concept of buying low? Candlestick analysis allows investors to be prepared and profit from these moves.

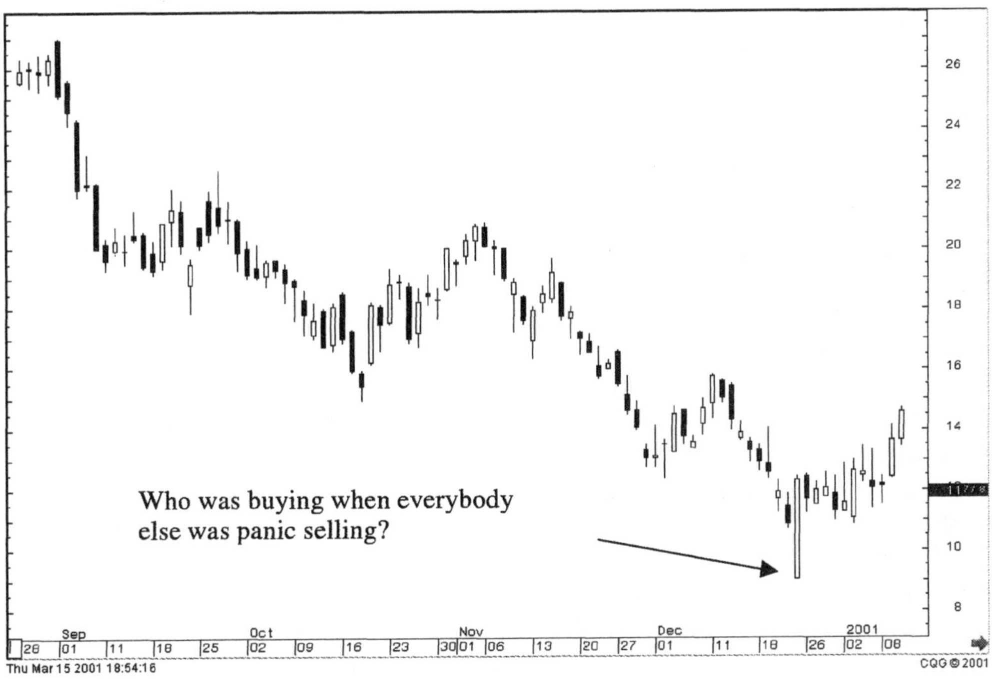

Figure 1.5 After an extensive decline, prices gap down when the pain is too great.

Improve Investment Skills Permanently

Japanese Candlestick analysis will improve your investment skills permanently. Knowing how investors react to price movements provides the Candlestick analyst with powerful advantages. First, the knowledge of what bottoming signals look like keeps the investor from grabbing for the falling knife. Patience is essential while waiting for a signal. Secondly, Candlestick investors now have an investment platform for buying at the bottom and selling at the top. Knowing that bottoming signals occur with a high degree of accuracy takes the emotion out of getting into or out of a position. Looking for signals to occur at the low end of a trading range creates an unemotional discipline. The risk factors are greatly diminished when buying at the bottoms and selling at the tops. Yet this practice is not taught at any institution of learning.

The experience most investors obtain to become reasonably proficient investors, unfortunately comes from the school of hard knocks. Apparently, some people get a handle on good discipline much easier than others do. Otherwise, everybody would be doing well in the markets. But for those who require a stronger framework for establishing a good investment regimen, the

Japanese Candlestick method has those qualities. Not only does the methodology direct you to buy at the bottoms and sell at the tops, it gives you the background psychology that makes you understand why a reversal is occurring. Buying the "hot tips" becomes much more controlled by being able to analyze when the first buying waves came into the " hot stock's" most recent move.

Becoming a Profitable Candlestick Investor

Most investors do not have an investment plan. This is simple to confirm. Ask friends and associates how they find their investment picks. The answers will range across the board: a tip from a friend of a friend, an article about a company in a magazine, a news clip about a firm or product on CNBC, the number one stock pick from an investment newsletter. On top of it all, it is usually a combination of these and many other mishmash approaches. The performance is inconsistent. To make matters worse, if the performance is decent, there usually is no way to measure the successful sources. This book will provide you with strategies that will dramatically increase your investment returns. You will be exposed to techniques that teach you how to remember and utilize the signals, quickly.

The descriptions of the signals in this book will be provided in a "condensed" version. Again, the point is to educate you in an efficient, yet expeditious manner. There are other books on the market that will be recommended for your full learning process. Those books will be more descriptive in how the signals were named and the psychology behind their formation. The primary value of this book to you is learning how to produce consistent profits from the signals.

This book is divided into two sections. The first section is oriented towards

- Learning the signals.
- Evaluating the most profitable trades quickly.
- Learning what confirming indicators are the most effective.

The implementation of this information will be used to eliminate "false signals." Search results will be quantified for harvesting the trades with the greatest potential.

The second section focuses on how to maximize profits. This includes trading strategies that minimize the downside risk. You will learn how to close out losing trades with minimal loses and no emotional attachment. At the same time, profit maximization procedures and philosophies will be demonstrated when closing out profitable trades.

Creating Maximum Trade Probabilities

The Candlestick methodology focuses on the investor's main objective: How do I maximize profitability? There are always rationalizations that move away from this vital outlook. Common investment counseling states, "Long term investing is the only way to make good returns: you can't time the market." Or, "Find a strong fundamentally sound company and it will grow." These reasons are heard all the time. But that is usually the advice for a person who doesn't want to or can't focus on maximizing the returns with the minimum of risk—the point of investing.

Whether one is managing money for others or whether they are managing their own funds, the same basic question should arise each time an investment decision is required: "Is this the best possible place for my investment funds to maximize returns, based upon my risk tolerances?" The use of the Candlestick method keeps the investor focused on that question. The cultivation process is directed to finding the *best* place for investment funds. This step-by-step procedure (explained in Chapter 9) builds in a self-directing discipline for maintaining profit maximization.

To enhance those probabilities, you will have the benefit of reading about subtle signal variations that will keep you from losing money. You will be exposed to common mistakes that can be avoided when producing a profit maximization program. This book introduces you to software programs with excellent search capabilities. You will be exposed to search formulas that produce highly profitable trade situations in a matter of minutes. Step-by-step trade implementation procedures describe how to place all the probabilities in your favor. This is a powerful, common sense trading process that the signals create for the candlestick-educated investor. Not only does Candlestick analysis provide a mechanical investment game plan, it produces a blueprint for establishing a non-emotional investment procedure.

Fundamental Analysis Versus Technical Analysis

Fundamental analysis influences 90 percent of all investment decisions. For the long-term investor, it is the reasonable basis for committing long-term funds. Yet, is it the way to maximize returns? Consider what is involved when analyzing the future potential of a stock price. Projecting the future of a company's capabilities has hundreds of different variables. Is the management capable? Is the product line sustainable? What are their competitors doing? How are government regulations affecting this industry? Any one of many fundamental elements can change at any time, creating a reversal in the growth potential of a company.

Most financial "experts" advise buying the good quality company and hanging on to it for the long term. The stock market has averaged approximately an 11 percent return annually over the course of history. These statistics have been skewed during the past four years. Until 1997, the market never had more than two years in a row of double-digit growth. Most investors today have not experienced a severe bear market. A bear market does not give a hoot about fundamentals. When the market tide goes down, all corporate ships are lowered. Conversely, the worst stocks in the world can get a boost when the markets are skyrocketing.

Perception — The Major Investment Truism

One truism about making money in any market is that *perception overpowers reality.* Even during periods of great economic growth, holding on to the stock of fundamentally sound companies may not make you any richer. If investors perceive that better profits can be made elsewhere, that is where the money is going to go. Evidence of this is apparent in the titles "old economy" and "new economy." The returns on stock of fundamentally sound companies over the past few years have paled next to the returns produced by owning a "new economy" stock—at least prior to the bursting of the technology stock bubble in March, 2000. It may be true that you make more money by holding a good fundamentally sound stock for the long term, provided that the only alternative is to hold non-fundamentally sound stocks for the same timeframe.

If your intent is to maximize portfolio growth, the logical method of investing includes buying what has the most upside potential today. That brings us back to investor perception. The Candlestick signals identify where investor funds are going today, this week, this month. The Candlestick signals pinpoint the turns in investor sentiment. Using this knowledge produces trading strategies that minimize downside and maximize upside probabilities.

Buy on the Rumor

If it is obvious, it is obviously wrong. Joseph Granville

How often have we witnessed a company announcing good earnings or a beneficial contract or disclosing information that would appear to be advantageous for the stock price, yet the price of the stock immediately declines? "Buy the rumor, sell the news" is an oft-repeated Wall Street adage. Unless you are positioned in the "in-the-know" Wall Street crowd, how can you possibly know the scuttlebutt on each and every company followed in the investment arena? A major advantage of identifying Candlestick signals is the lack of need to maintain expansive information networks.

A Candlestick buy signal provides you with the knowledge of when the buyers are stepping into a stock. You do not need to know why that is occurring. The only fact that should concern an investor is what stocks are going up and what stocks are going down. If there is a rumor that implies that a company's earnings are going to be good or that they are going to be bought out, who cares? A Candlestick buy signal represents the probability that this stock is positioned to make you money. Your identification of the buying in a particular stock presents a favorable probability of being in positions that eventually announce good "surprise" news. If something good is happening to a company, the people "in-the-know" will be accumulating the stock before the announcement. The Candlestick signals identify that action.

"Buy the rumor, sell the news." Quite often, this is the correct investment strategy. But how do you determine whether the news is more or less of a surprise as to what was anticipated? That can be easily determined by the candlestick that is formed, putting you days, sometimes weeks, ahead of the rest of the investment community. A gap down, at the bottom of a trend resulting from bad news, may *not* indicate the time to buy. A black-bodied candle formation that day means something completely different than a white-bodied candle. This will be dealt with in detail in Chapter 9.

Where Do We Learn How to Invest?

Where did you learn how to invest? Where does anybody learn how to invest? There are no official courses that are taught to investors. In school, we are taught about the different investment vehicles and strategies. But there are few forums for teaching the actual psychology of a professional investor. Even if there were a qualified investment education program, teaching the emotional disciplines may be nearly impossible. *Experience* is the major factor when becoming successful in most investment disciplines. Experience is the only education for developing the proper mental process. This is the most difficult hurdle in the path to proficient investing practices.

A person who has had a bull by the tail once has learned 60 to 70 times as much as a person who hasn't. Mark Twain

Putting one's own money on the line creates new dynamics. Investing and love are in the same category: Despite any amount of logical reasoning, intellectual analysis, and preplanning in a decision involving either, emotion takes over as the dominant component. The power of investment discipline can be harnessed. Investment rationale, which is the foundation of Candlestick formations, is implemented in a sensible and logical methodology. Reading this book will expose you to highly defined pattern recognition techniques. With this knowledge, an investor—whether a beginner or vastly experienced—can employ the basics of investment logic in a calculated program.

So where *do* we learn how to invest? Was there a point in *your* investment life where you decided to make a study of the most successful investment programs? If so, did you sit down and consciously investigate strategies and learn how to use specific trading philosophies? Unfortunately, most investors start their investment programs because they have a little money to invest. Where do they turn for investment advice? A stockbroker, banker, parent, friend, investment newsletter service, or a multitude of sources, some of whom probably started out the same way they did. Beginning investors are looking for somebody to direct them about where to find a good investment, not a good investment strategy.

And once you've begun investing, who do you turn to when you have permitted fear to scare you out at the bottom or greed suck you in at the top *again*? Who do you blame when you sell out of your profitable positions too early because you are afraid they will pull back and turn into losses? Or you hang on to your losing positions as they ratchet down, each little up-tick giving you hope, but finally sell out at the bottom because the pain is too great? This syndrome is described as "eating like a bird and pooping like an elephant."

Identifying the Candlestick signals puts you in control of your investment program. Emotion is eliminated. You will not have to "hope" that the last trade you put on will work. This book will put you in the position of feeling confident that the vast majority of your investment positions will work. You will be able to sleep well every night. You will learn to quickly identify the trade that is not working, immediately liquidate it, and then put those funds into the next position where the probabilities are greatly in your favor.

Learn How to Fish

Many people spend more time and energy on buying a car than they do in researching how to build their financial wealth. And there is a good explanation for that. The experience of buying a car—the haggling with salespeople and then hoping nobody finds out that you could have negotiated a $600 better price if you knew what you were doing—occurs every three, five, or seven years. Buying a car, even finding out that you paid too much for it, ends with the decision process. You own it. You paid too much for it. Too bad! Now life goes on.

The investment decision has a constant decision-making aspect to it. Each month, week, day, or minute has the potential for making another decision. The decision-making process required for producing good returns on your portfolio is a constant and scutinizable activity, one that can have many embarrassing throwbacks, such as buying at the peak, selling out at the bottom, picking the wrong company in an industry, selling too early, or selling too late. Without the use of a definable investment strategy, most investors go through life hoping that their investment decisions are going to work out. They had no game plan going in; they usually have no game plan for exiting. Fortunately, the markets overall growth, in general, has "raised all boats" over the years.

The Candlestick signals work equally well on both sides of a trade. They are as accurate for showing when selling comes into a stock price as they are for showing when buying comes into a position, thereby enabling investors to control their entry and exit strategies.

Human Emotion

Why do most investors repeatedly make the same trade mistakes? That great bugaboo *emotion*. Investment logic and investment emotions create a vast decision-making divergence. Have you ever analyzed a stock situation, whether fundamentally or technically, and planned your entrance and exit strategies thoroughly before putting on the trade? Once the trade is on, the circumstances that you analyzed occur, but all the preplanning for the establishment of the trade now disappear. You don't follow through with your game plan. Why? This phenomenon is a common occurrence among investors—easily explained, but hard to overcome: human ego! We all think we are intelligent. We analyze an investment situation and put our stamp of intellectual prowess on the line. Buying a stock position immediately declares that, with the same investment criteria available to everybody else, we have made a statement, subconsciously, that our analytical abilities are better than the average investor. Of course, when a stock price moves against us, that is just a temporary misreading of the market factors.

Man who toot in church sit in his own phew. Proverb??

Ego—Our Investing Hurdle

Part of our minds—our egos—assure us that our assessments were correct and everybody else will eventually see this stock price moving in the direction that we first anticipated. Unlike making a decision to buy a car, a book, a vacuum cleaner, or anything else that required a one-time decision about the expenditure of funds, investments have an additional emotionally debilitating element. The decision process continues each tick after the initial purchase.

You buy a stock and the price immediately goes down. Do you sell it here or is it at the bottom? It keeps going down, the same question occurs every day, every tick. Conversely, the stock price is going up. Is it time to take profits? How embarrassing it would be if it went back down to where you bought it. Or worse, if after it was up at this price, you eventually sold the position for a loss. Each position becomes an emotional conquest—your intellect versus the rest of the market players.

Man is the only kind of varmint that sets his own trap, baits it, and then steps in it. John Steinbeck

Candlestick formations take the emotional factors out of investing. In Chapter 7, you will learn how to take the emotion out of owning each individual position. The signals provide a discipline that can be inherently adhered to. If you follow the signals, the percentage of correct trades becomes more evident as you invest. If you trade against what the signals are indicating, common sense or investment pain will readily illustrate that you need to follow the signals. The percentage of correct trade results, produced from properly analyzed signals, will reinforce a trading platform that you will learn to follow faithfully.

What is the optimal trading system? Isn't that the "golden goose" we are all looking for? What trading program will eliminate the flaws that we each have in our investment psyche? How can we find the investments that will produce profits NOW? When do we get in? When do we get out?

Ultimate Criteria for the Optimal Trading Program

- Proven and tested results.
- Easy to identify reversal indicators.
- Elimination of emotional decision-making aspects.

Using any trading discipline will produce greater returns than the normal non-structured investment approach. Using the Candlestick signals, however, will produce a greater profit-potential investment strategy than you can imagine. Hundreds of years of honing the visual identification process —the initial form of statistical analysis—provide a well-founded investment stratagem. You can reasonably assume that the percentage of positive results from Candlestick signals is significantly worthwhile. Otherwise, those signals would not be in existence today.

Additionally, it is extremely useful to implement a trading strategy that can be documented and analyzed. Each new trade provides an analytical tool. What went right with this trade? What went wrong with this trade? The post trade results can be compared to existing results produced by similar signal formations. An investor should be able to evaluate each trade in order to better the results of the next trade. Being able to identify the potential of a high-probability trade, days ahead of the other market participants, has obvious advantages. The downside risk is reduced. The signals alert you to the first change in investor sentiment. You get into and out of positions before the masses. Upside potential is enhanced, exploiting the next round of buying by the investment analysts.

"Why isn't everybody using Candlesticks?" You will be asking that same question when you finish this book. Candlesticks provide all of the elements needed for successful investing:

- They identify where the buying or selling is occurring.
- They are accurate enough to still be in use 400 years after their beginning.
- They eliminate emotion and instill discipline.
- They enhance existing technical methods.
- They tell you when to get into and out of a trade.

Once you finish this book, your mental investment procedures will be radically altered. Mastery of the Candlestick technique will provide the mindset of a successful professional investor. You will also gain valuable insights into human nature. You will be able to cash in on low-risk, high-potential opportunities overlooked by the common investor. The inherent nature of the signals instills common sense disciplines. You are about to be exposed to the most refined signal generating system in all of financial history. Hundreds of years of observation have produced results with a system that has thrived through the centuries.

Are you tired of settling for mediocre returns? Does the rationale of losing less than what the indexes lost not impress you anymore? Do recommendations from major Wall Street brokerage firms appear to have lukewarm potential by the time they are presented to you? Why settle for watered down investment programs when you can pinpoint exact bottoms and tops? Why forego profit potential that can be extracted from the markets directly into your pocket? The effort required to master the Candlestick technique is minimal when going about it in a structured manner. Practical insights derived from the visual aspects of the signals will point out the real profit potential of investing.

The following chapters explain the formations, the psychology behind the formations, and give illustrations of the signals. Read these sections at your own pace. It is not necessary to remember each signal and the psychology behind it to a high degree. Learning how the signal is created aids in remembering the signal, but it is not required for making profits. Of the 40 or so signals, there are approximately ten major signals. Become familiar with what the signals look like. Later chapters outline the process for learning the signals easily and rapidly.

Chapter 2

THE REVERSAL PATTERNS

Change is the law of life. And those who look only to the past or the present are certain to miss the future. John F. Kennedy

The most valuable aspect of technical analysis is the recognition of reversal points. This is the "golden goose" of any successful trading program. Japanese Candlestick analysis puts the probabilities on your side. To drive the point home, the signals are the results of hundreds of years of visual recognition of successful reversals. The ability to identify technical clues that put the probabilities in your favor is the ultimate function of technical analysis.

Western charting has patterns that indicate reversals of major trends. Head and shoulders, double tops or double bottoms, and island reversals are formations that have exhibited high degrees of accuracy for identifying change in the current trends.

Candlestick analysis enhances an investor's ability to prepare for trend changes. Being familiar with the psychology behind specific candle formations provides immense advantages. Candle signals can identify a trend reversal in one day. More often, the Candlestick signals can forewarn when a trend is preparing to change.

Using the analogy of a steam locomotive as a trend, most trends do not reverse on a dime. If a train has to reverse direction, there are logical indications. First may be a whistle, then the rhythm of the wheels can be heard to slow down. Steam may shoot out the sides as the brakes are applied. The wheels start squealing on the rails. All these signs give you the belief that the train is coming to a stop. The Candlestick signals give investors similar indications.

A major trend will probably not have a one-day reversal. It may take a few days or weeks for the force (psychology of investors) to expend itself and reverse direction. The appearance of a reversal signal alerts the investor that a change of investor sentiment is occurring or is about to occur. Viewing a sell signal at the top of a long uptrend should inform you that the trend might now be losing stream. Will the trend continue up from here? Probably. But not with the same potential as putting your investment funds elsewhere. The

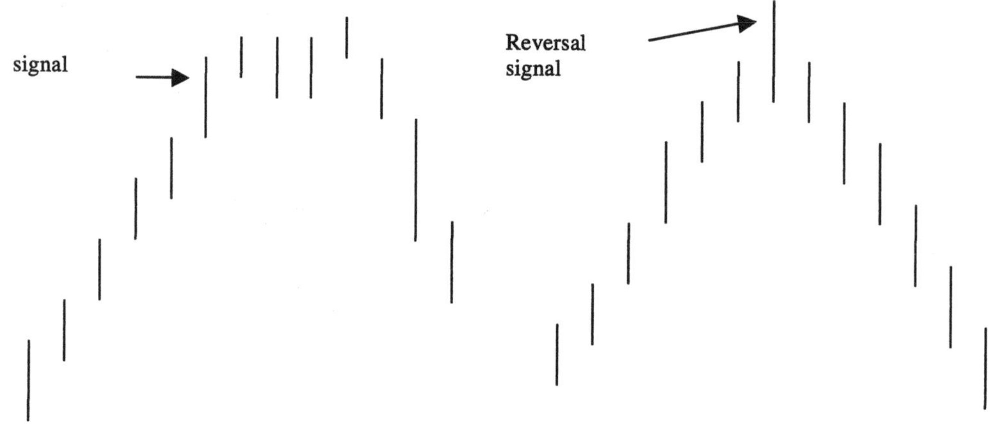

Figure 2.1 Reversal signals can occur prior to the actual top.

signal should have told you that sellers were stepping in at these levels. The force of the trend may still take prices higher. However, with the indications that the sellers may be stepping in, the strength of the uptrend should be greatly diminished. The investor can now be preparing for the appearance of the next sell signal.

Will the trend reverse and go back the other direction? That will take more signals to confirm. (See Figure 2.1.) The trend may go flat for a while. Or waffle in a range. You will want to monitor the situation, looking for a strong sell signal. In the meantime, you have dozens of other excellent Candlestick potentials to shift money into on any given day.

With these principles in mind, review the rest of this chapter. The signals themselves are to be learned by simple visual remembrance. Do not be greatly concerned with trying to learn each and every one. Chapter 5 demonstrates techniques that will help you learn and remember the signals. The first 8 or 10 signals produce the majority of trade potentials. Just those signals alone provide most investors with more trade opportunities than what they can use each day.

Keep in mind that these signals are the results of hundreds of years of cultivation for the most important aspect—PROFITS!

Candlestick Formations

Japanese Candlestick charting dramatically increases the depth of information conveyed for visual analysis. Each formation or series of formations can clearly illustrate the change of investor sentiment. This process is not apparent in standard bar chart interpretation. Each candle formation has a unique name. Some have Japanese names; others have English names. When possible in this book, the English name and Japanese name are given. The Japanese names are shown in Romanji writing so that English-speaking people can say the names.

Single candles are often referred to as yin and yang lines. These terms are actually Chinese, but are used by Western analysts to account for opposites: in/out, up/down, and over/under. Inn and yoh are the Japanese equivalents. Yin is bearish. Yang is bullish. There are nine basic yin and yang lines in Candlestick analysis. These are expanded to 15 to cover all possibilities clearly. The combination of most patterns can be reduced to one of these patterns.

Long Days

The long day (shown in Figure 2.2) represents a large price move from open to close. Long represents the length of the candle body. What qualifies a candle body to be considered long? That is a question that has to be answered relative to the chart being analyzed. The recent price action of a stock determines whether a long candle has been formed. Analysis of the previous two or three weeks of trading should be a current representative sample of the price action.

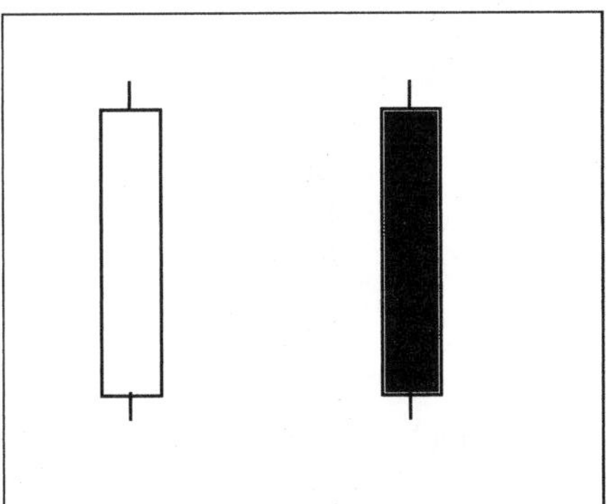

Figure 2.2 Long-day formations.

Short Days

Short days (shown in Figure 2.3) can be interpreted by the same analytical process as used with the long candles. There is a large percentage of trading days that do not fall into either of these two categories.

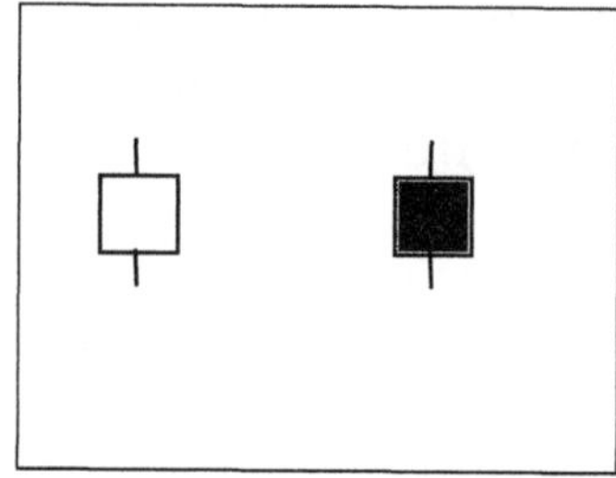

Figure 2.3 Short-day formations.

Marubozu

In Japanese, Marubozu means close-cropped or close-cut. Bald or Shaven Head is more commonly used in Candlestick analysis. Its meaning reflects the fact that there are no shadows extending from either end of the body.

Black Marubozu

The long black body with no shadows at either end (shown in Figure 2.4) is known as a Black Marubozu. It is considered a weak indicator. It is often identified in a bearish continuation or bullish reversal pattern, especially if it occurs during a downtrend. A long black candle could represent the final sell off, making it an alert to a bullish reversal setting up. The Japanese often call it the Major Yin or Marubozu of Yin.

Figure 2.4 Black Marubozu—no shadows at either end.

White Marubozu

The White Marubozu (shown in Figure 2.5) is a long white body with no shadows on either end. This is an extremely strong pattern. Consider how it is formed. It opens on the low and immediately heads up. It continues upward until it closes, on its high. Counter to the Black Marubozu, it is often the first part of a bullish continuation pattern or bearish reversal pattern. It is called a Major Yang or Marubozu of Yang.

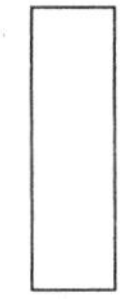

Figure 2.5 White Marubozu—no shadows at either end.

Closing Marubozu

The Closing Marubozu (shown in Figure 2.6) has no shadow at its closing end. A white body does not have a shadow at the top. A black body does not have a shadow at the bottom. In both cases, these are strong signals corresponding to the direction that they each represent.

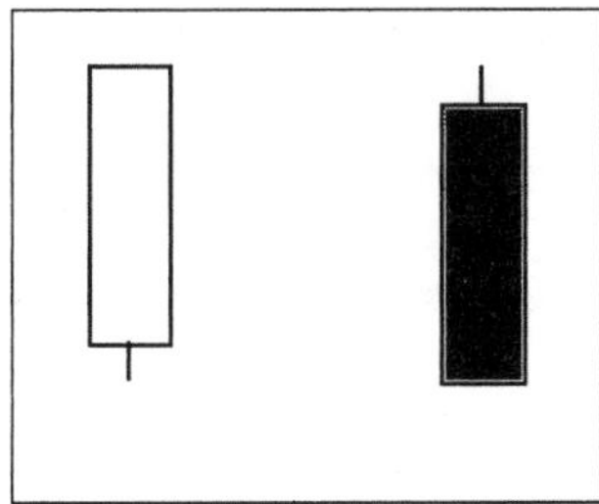

Figure 2.6 Closing Marubozu—no shadow at the closing end.

Opening Marubozu

The Opening Marubozu (shown in Figure 2.7) has no shadows extending from the open price end of the body. A white body would not have a shadow at the bottom end; the black candle would not have a shadow at its top end. Though these are strong signals, they are not as strong as the Closing Marubozu.

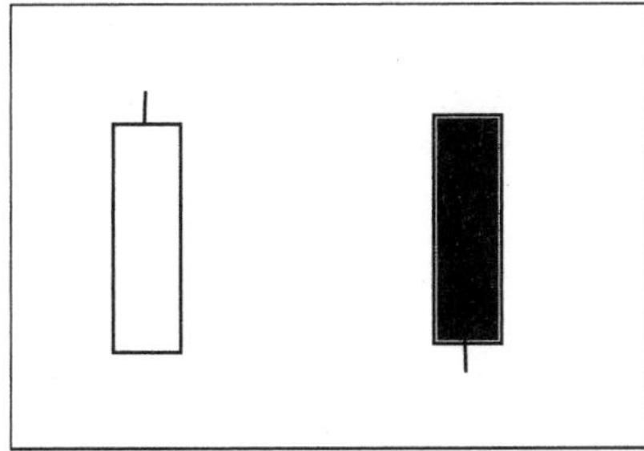

Figure 2.7 Opening Marubozu—no shadow at the opening range.

Spinning Top

Spinning Tops (as seen in Figure 2.8) are depicted with small bodies relative to the shadows. This demonstrates some indecision on the part of the bulls and the bears. They are considered neutral when trading in a sideways market. However, in a trending or oscillating market, a relatively good rule of thumb is that the next day's trading will probably move in the direction of the opening price. The size of the shadow is not as important as the size of the body for forming a Spinning Top.

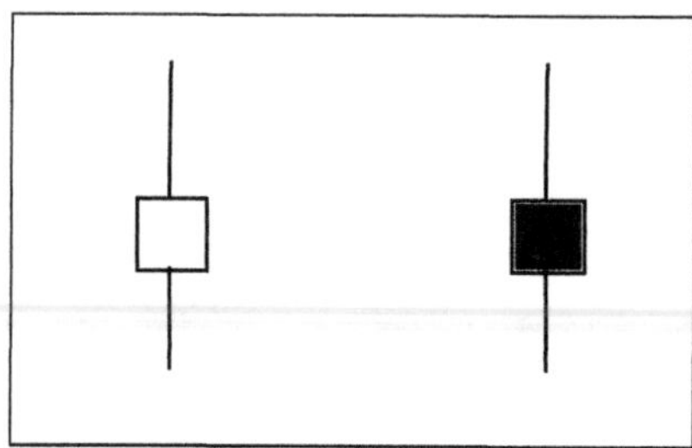

Figure 2.8 Spinning Top—small body with shadows at both ends.

Doji

The Doji (shown in Figure 2.9) is one of the most important signals in Candlestick analysis. It is formed when the open and the close are the same or nearly the same. The lengths of the shadows can vary. The longer the shadows are, the more significant the Doji becomes. More will be explained about the Doji in the next few pages. ALWAYS pay attention to the Doji.

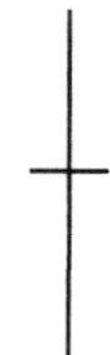

Figure 2.9 Doji—open and close are the same.

Stochastics

Before going into the description of the signals, an explanation of stochastics is in order. The effectiveness of Candlestick signals is greatly enhanced when buy signals occur in oversold situations and sell signals appear in overbought situations. The best indicators for establishing overbought and oversold criteria are the stochastics. Stochastics were developed many years ago by George Lane. They are oscillators that measure the relative position of the closing price compared to the daily trading range. Simply stated, where is the close relative to the range of prices over the last x trading periods?

Stochastics are a function of some simple observations. Closing prices have a tendency to close near the higher end of a daily trading range as an uptrend gains strength. Conversely, closing prices close near the lower end of a daily trading range as a decline picks up strength. At market turns, for example, when a trend is about to reverse, going from up to down, the daily highs get higher but the closing price settles near the lower end of the day's trading range. This makes stochastics unique from most oscillators. Most oscillators are normalized representations of relative strength, the difference between the close and the current trend.

As will be explained later, %D is calculated by applying a simple three-day moving average of the %K. Stochastics, as a straight trading indicator, are most effective when %D and %K cross, preferably in the extreme areas on a grid of 0 to 100 (overbought is 80 or higher, oversold is 20 or lower). However, when used in combination with the Candlestick signals, the signal will be viable when the stochastics are in the extreme ranges. %D and %K crossing is more effective, but the signal itself pinpoints when the turn has occurred.

Stochastics Formula

%K is considered the RAW stochastic or the FAST stochastic. It is the more sensitive between the two, %K and %D. The %K formula is

$$\frac{(\text{Close}) - (\text{Low of N})}{(\text{High of N}) - (\text{Low of N})} \times 100 = \%\text{K}$$

Close = current price
Low of P = low of the range during the period used
High of P = high of the range during the period being used

Major Signals

To expedite the learning process, it is important to realize that a full-blown memorizing procedure is not required. The function of the chart patterns is to provide a clear visual signal. As you read through this section, try to remember the physical attributes of the signals. This is what you will use when analyzing charts.

The following section will be broken down into two segments: the major signals and minor signals. The difference between the two is a combination of the frequency that they appear and the reversal-probabilities produced by their appearance.

THE MAJOR SIGNALS

- THE DOJI
- BULLISH ENGULFING
- BEARISH ENGULFING
- HAMMERS
- HANGING MAN
- PIERCING PATTERN
- DARK CLOUD
- HARAMI—BULLISH
- HARAMI—BEARISH
- MORNING STAR
- EVENING STAR
- KICKER SIGNAL
- SHOOTING STAR
- INVERTED HAMMER

THE DOJI
(Doji Bike)

DOJI STAR

Description

The Doji is comprised of one candle. The Japanese say when a Doji occurs, one should always take notice. It is one of the most important Candlestick signals. (See Figure 2.10.) The formation is created when the opening price and closing price are the same. This forms a horizontal line. The implication is that the bulls and the bears are in a state of indecision. It is an important alert at both the top and bottom of trends. At the top of a trend, the Doji signals a reversal without needing confirmation. The rule of thumb is that you should close a long or go short immediately.

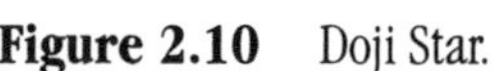

Figure 2.10 Doji Star.

However, the Doji occurring during the downtrend requires a bullish day to confirm the Doji day. The Japanese explanation is that the weight of the market can still force the trend downwards.

The Doji is an excellent example of the Candlestick method having superior attributes compared to the Western bar charting method. The deterioration of a trend is not going to be as apparent when viewing standard bar charts.

Criteria

1. The open and the close are the same or nearly the same.
2. The length of the shadows should not be excessively long, especially when viewed at the end of a bullish trend.

Signal Enhancements

1. A gap away from the previous day's close sets up for a stronger reversal move.
2. Large volume on the signal day increases the chances that a blowoff day has occurred although it is not a necessity.

3. It is more effective after a long candle body, usually an exaggerated daily move compared to the normal daily trading range seen in the majority of the trend.

Pattern Psychology

After an uptrend or a downtrend has been in effect, the Doji, immediately reveals that there is now indecision in the bull's and the bear's camp. (See Figure 2.11.) After the trend move and the price opens at a level, the bulls and the bears move the price up and down during the day. By the end of the day, the price closes at or close to the level that it opened. This state of equilibrium now has the controlling group in some doubt. The opposite group builds up confidence that the trend has lost steam.

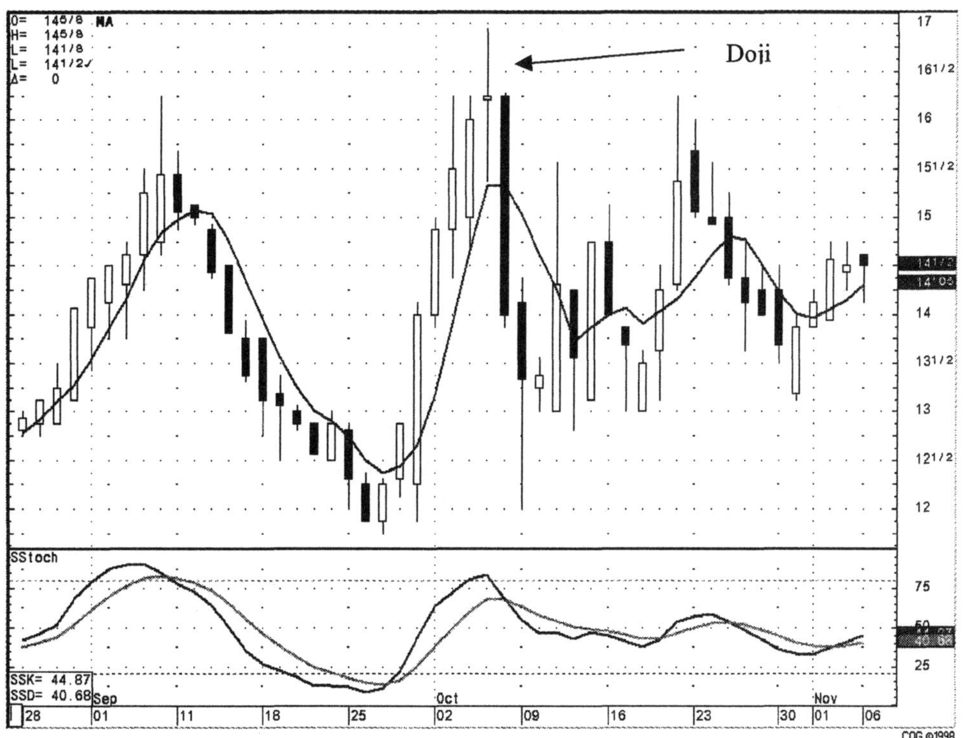

Figure 2.11 The Doji is a sign of indecision, watch for major changes in investor sentiment.

THE DOJIS
(Doji Bike)

THE LONG LEGGED DOJI (JUJI)

The Long Legged Doji (as shown in Figure 2.12) is comprised of long upper and lower shadows. The price opened and closed in the middle of the trading range. Throughout the day, the price moved up and down dramatically before it closed at or near the opening price. This reflects the great indecision that exists between the bulls and the bears. Juji means "cross."

Figure 2.12 Long Legged Doji.

GRAVESTONE DOJI (TOHBA)

The Gravestone Doji (as shown in Figure 2.13) is formed by the open and the close being at the low of the trading range. The price opens at the low of the day and rallies from there, but by the close the price is beaten back down to the opening price. The Japanese analogy is that it represents those who have died in battle. The victories of the day are all lost by the end of the day. A Gravestone Doji, at the top of the trend, is a specific version of the Shooting Star. At the bottom, it is a variation of the Inverted Hammer. The Japanese

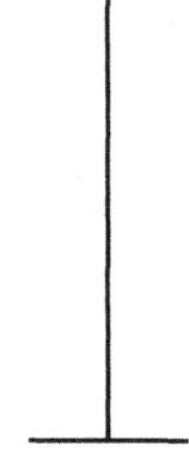

Figure 2.13 Gravestone Doji.

sources claim that the Gravestone Doji can occur only on the ground, not in the air. This implication is that it works much better to show a bottom reversal than a top reversal. However, a Doji shows indecision no matter where it is found.

THE DOJI'S DRAGONFLY DOJI (TONBO)

The Dragonfly Doji (in Figure 2.14) occurs when trading opens, trades lower, and then closes at the open price that is the high of the day. At the top of the market, it becomes a variation of the Hanging Man. At the bottom of a trend, it becomes a specific Hammer. An extensively long shadow on a Dragonfly Doji at the bottom of a trend is very bullish.

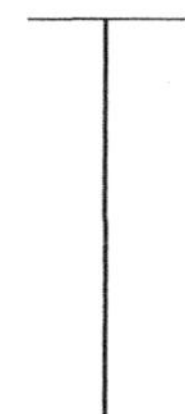

Figure 2.14 Dragonfly Doji.

Dojis that occur in multiday patterns make those signals more convincing reversal signals. (See Figures 2.15 through 2.20.)

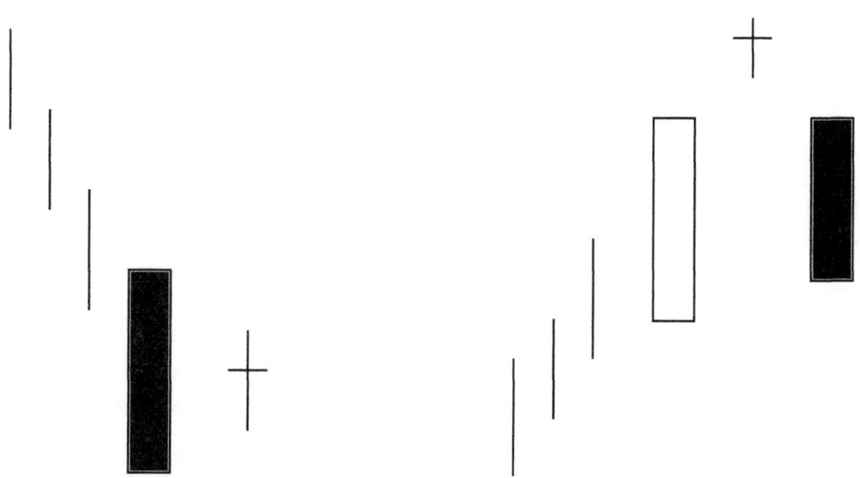

Figure 2.15 Harami—Doji.

Figure 2.16 Evening Star—Abandoned Baby.

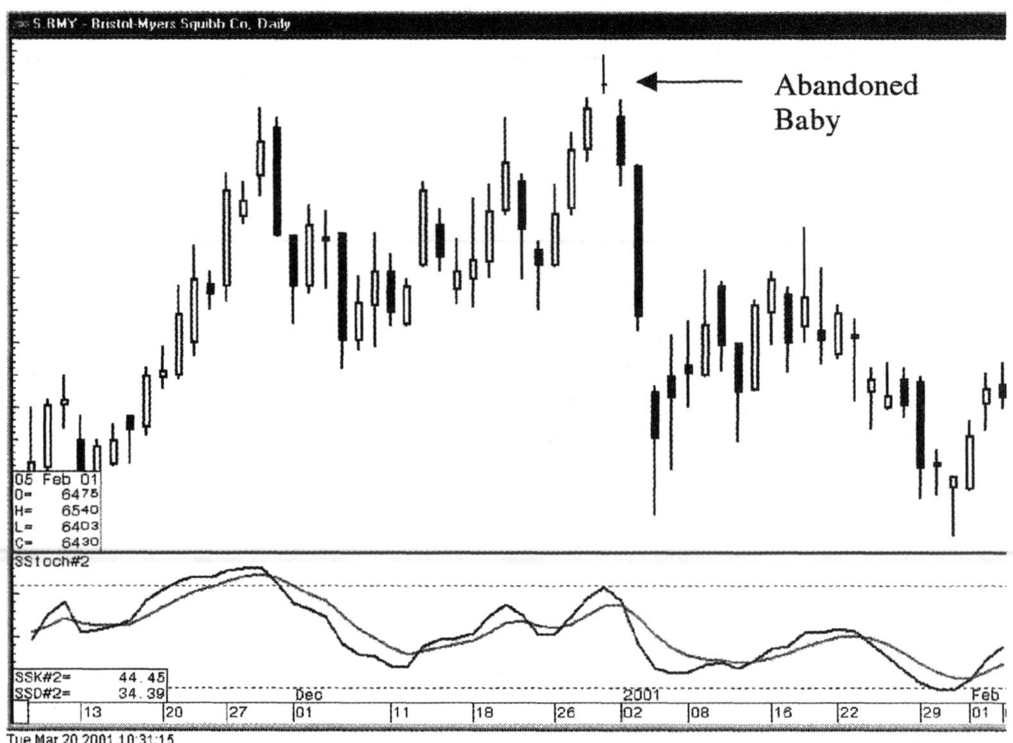

Figure 2.17 BMY reversed on a powerful Abandoned Baby pattern, a strong reversal signal.

Figure 2.18 Compuware Corp.'s rally started and ended with Doji's.

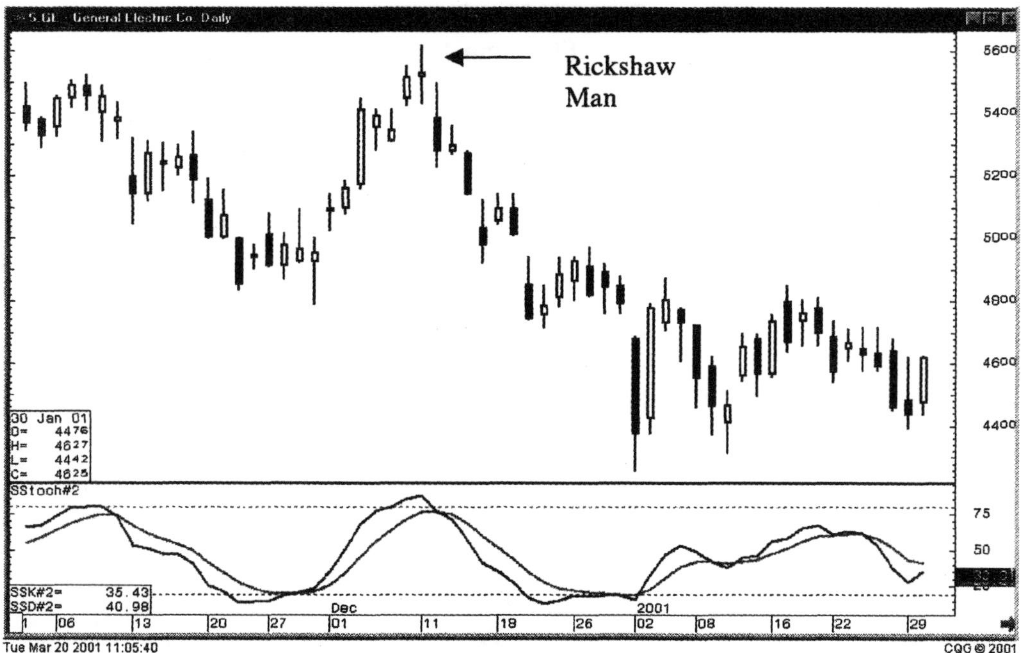

Figure 2.19 GE Corp. starts a downtrend with the appearance of a Rickshaw Man.

Figure 2.20 The Doji/Harami stopped Metromedia Fiber Network's downtrend.

ENGULFING PATTERNS
(Tsutsumi)

BULLISH ENGULFING

Description

The Engulfing Pattern is a major reversal pattern comprised of two opposite colored bodies. The bullish Engulfing Pattern (Figure 2.21) is formed after a downtrend. It opens lower than the previous day's close and closes higher than the previous day's open. Thus, the white candle completely engulfs the previous day's black candle. Engulfing can include either the open or the close being equal to the open or close of the previous day but not both.

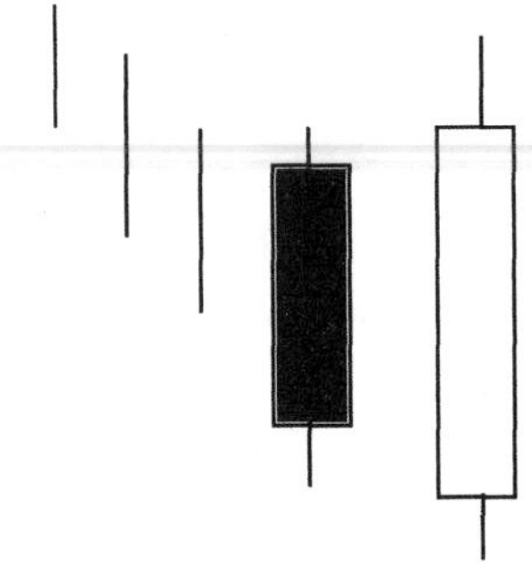

Figure 2.21 Bullish Engulfing pattern.

Criteria

1. The body of the second day completely engulfs the body of the first day. Shadows are not a consideration.
2. Prices have been in a definable downtrend, even if it has been short term.
3. The body of the second candle is opposite color of the first candle, the first candle being the color of the previous trend. The exception to this rule is when the engulfed body is a Doji or an extremely small body.

Signal Enhancements

1. A large body engulfing a small body. The previous day was showing the trend was running out of steam. The large body shows that the new direction has started with good force.
2. When the Engulfing Pattern occurs after a fast move down, there will be less stock to slow down the reversal move.
3. Large volume on the engulfing day increases the chances that a blowoff day has occurred.

4. The engulfing body engulfing more than one previous body demonstrates power in the reversal.
5. If the engulfing body engulfs the body and the shadows of the previous day, the reversal has a greater probability of working.
6. The greater the open gaps down from the previous close, the greater the probability of a strong reversal.

Pattern Psychology

After a downtrend has been in effect, the price opens lower than where it closed the previous day. (See Figure 2.22.) Before the end of the day, the buyers have taken over and moved the price above where it opened the day before. The emotional psychology of the trend has now been altered.

Figure 2.22 Bullish Engulfing pattern—a definite change of investor sentiment.

ENGULFING PATTERNS
(tsutsumi)

BEARISH ENGULFING

Description

The Bearish Engulfing Pattern in Figure 2.23 is a major reversal pattern comprised of two opposite-colored bodies. The Bearish Engulfing Pattern is formed after an uptrend. It opens higher than the previous day's close and closes lower than the previous day's open. Thus, the black candle completely engulfs the previous day's white candle. Engulfing can include either the open or the close be equal to the open or close of the previous day but not both.

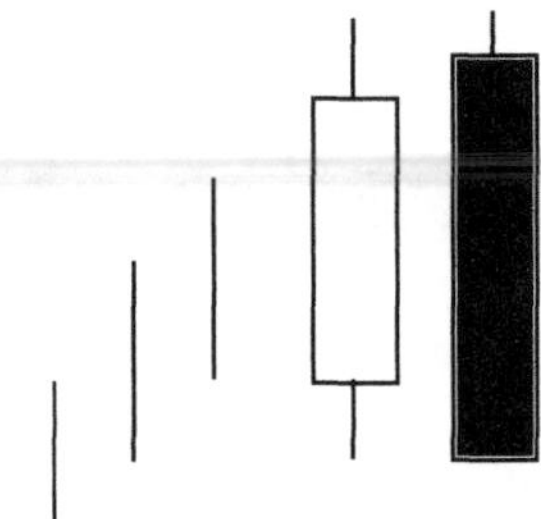

Figure 2.23 Bearish Engulfing pattern.

Criteria

1. The body of the second day completely engulfs the body of the first day. Shadows are not a consideration.
2. Prices have been in a definable uptrend, even if it has been short term.
3. The body of the second candle is opposite color of the first candle, the first candle being the color of the previous trend. The exception to this rule is when the engulfed body is a Doji or an extremely small body.

Signal Enhancements

1. A large body engulfing a small body. The previous day was showing the trend was running out of steam. The large body shows that the new direction has started with good force.
2. When the Engulfing Pattern occurs after a fast spike up, there will be less supply of stock to slow down the reversal move. A fast move makes a stock price over-extended and increases the potential for profit taking and a meaningful pullback.
3. Large volume on the engulfing day increases the chances that a blowoff day has occurred.

4. The engulfing body engulfing more than one previous body demonstrates power in the reversal.
5. If the engulfing body engulfs the body and the shadows of the previous day, the reversal has a greater probability of working.
6. The greater the open gaps down from the previous close, the greater the probability of a strong reversal.

Pattern Psychology

After a downtrend has been in effect, the price opens lower than where it closed the previous day. (See Figure 2.22.) Before the end of the day, the buyers have taken over and moved the price above where it opened the day before. The emotional psychology of the trend has now been altered.

Figure 2.22 Bullish Engulfing pattern—a definite change of investor sentiment.

ENGULFING PATTERNS
(tsutsumi)

BEARISH ENGULFING

Description

The Bearish Engulfing Pattern in Figure 2.23 is a major reversal pattern comprised of two opposite-colored bodies. The Bearish Engulfing Pattern is formed after an uptrend. It opens higher than the previous day's close and closes lower than the previous day's open. Thus, the black candle completely engulfs the previous day's white candle. Engulfing can include either the open or the close be equal to the open or close of the previous day but not both.

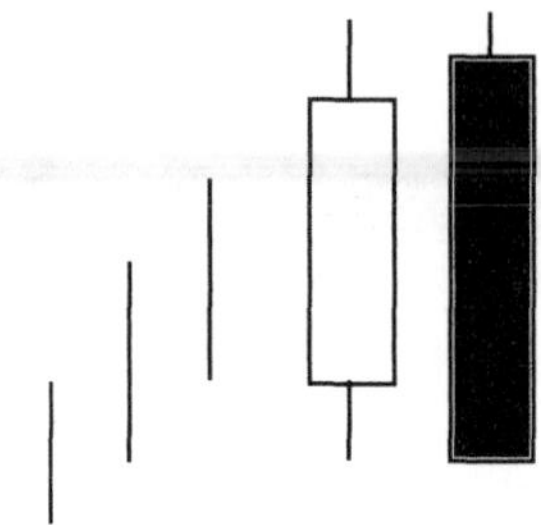

Figure 2.23 Bearish Engulfing pattern.

Criteria

1. The body of the second day completely engulfs the body of the first day. Shadows are not a consideration.
2. Prices have been in a definable uptrend, even if it has been short term.
3. The body of the second candle is opposite color of the first candle, the first candle being the color of the previous trend. The exception to this rule is when the engulfed body is a Doji or an extremely small body.

Signal Enhancements

1. A large body engulfing a small body. The previous day was showing the trend was running out of steam. The large body shows that the new direction has started with good force.
2. When the Engulfing Pattern occurs after a fast spike up, there will be less supply of stock to slow down the reversal move. A fast move makes a stock price over-extended and increases the potential for profit taking and a meaningful pullback.
3. Large volume on the engulfing day increases the chances that a blowoff day has occurred.

4. The engulfing body engulfing more than one previous body demonstrates power in the reversal.
5. If the engulfing body engulfs the body and the shadows of the previous day, the reversal has a greater probability of working.
6. The greater the open gaps up from the previous close, the greater the probability of a strong reversal.

Pattern Psychology

After an uptrend has been in effect, the price opens higher than where it closed the previous day. Before the end of the day, the sellers have taken over and moved the price below where it opened the day before. The emotional psychology of the trend has now been reversed. (See Figure 2.24.)

Figure 2.24 Bearish Engulfing pattern, a clear ominous pattern.

HAMMERS AND HANGING MAN
Paper Umbrella (karakasa)

HAMMERS

(TAKURI)

Description

The Hammer in Figure 2.25 is comprised of one candle. It is easily identified by the presence of a small body with a shadow at least two times greater than the body. Found at the bottom of a downtrend, this shows evidence that the bulls started to step in. The color of the small body is not important but a white candle has slightly more bullish implications than the black body. A positive day is required the following day to confirm this signal.

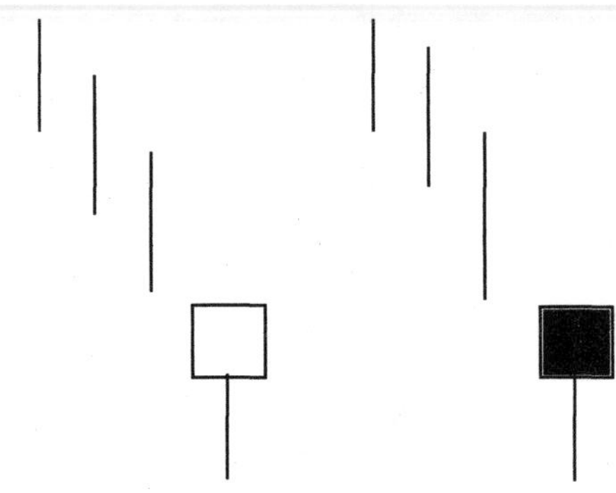

Figure 2.25 Hammers.

Criteria

1. The lower shadow should be at least two times the length of the body.
2. The real body is at the upper end of the trading range. The color of the body is not important although a white body should have slightly more bullish implications.
3. There should be no upper shadow or a very small upper shadow.
4. The following day needs to confirm the Hammer signal with a strong bullish day.

Signal Enhancements

1. The longer the lower shadow, the higher the potential of a reversal occurring.
2. A gap down from the previous day's close sets up for a stronger reversal move provided the day after the Hammer signal opens higher.

3. Large volume on the Hammer day increases the chances that a blowoff day has occurred.

Pattern Psychology

After a downtrend has been in effect, the atmosphere is extremely bearish. The price opens and starts to trade lower. The bears are still in control. The bulls then step in. They start bringing the price back up towards the top of the trading range. This creates a small body with a large lower shadow. This represents that the bears could not maintain control. The long lower shadow now has the bears questioning whether the decline is still intact. A higher open the next day would confirm that the bulls had taken control. (See Figure 2.26.)

Figure 2.26 Hammers, hammering out the bottom.

HAMMERS AND HANGING MAN
Paper Umbrella (Karakasa)

HANGING MAN

Description

The Hanging Man in Figure 2.27 is also comprised of one candle. It is easily identified by the presence of a small body with a shadow at least two times greater than the body. It is found at the top of an uptrend. The Japanese named this pattern because it looks like a head with the feet dangling down.

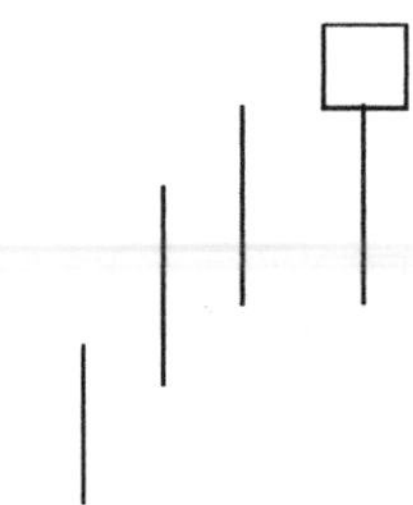

Figure 2.27 Hanging Man.

Criteria

1. The lower shadow should be at least two times the length of the body.
2. The real body is at the upper end of the trading range. The color of the body is not important although a black body should have slightly more bearish implications.
3. There should be no upper shadow or a very small upper shadow.
4. The following day needs to confirm the Hanging Man signal with a black candle or, better yet, a gap down with a lower close.

Signal Enhancements

1. The longer the lower shadow, the higher the potential of a reversal occurring.
2. A gap up from the previous day's close sets up for a stronger reversal move provided the day after the Hanging Man signal trades lower.
3. Large volume on the signal day increases the chances that a blowoff day has occurred although it is not a necessity.

Pattern Psychology

After a strong uptrend has been in effect, the atmosphere is bullish. The price opens higher but starts to move lower. The bears take control. But before the end of the day, the bulls step in and take the price back up to the higher end of the trading range, creating a small body for the day. This could indicate that the bulls still have control if analyzing a Western bar chart. However, the long lower shadow represents that sellers had started stepping in at these levels. Even though the bulls may have been able to keep the price positive by the end of the day, the evidence of the selling was apparent. A lower open or a black candle the next day reinforces the fact that selling is going on. (See Figure 2.28.)

Figure 2.28 A Hanging Man indicates the lack of buying at the top.

PIERCING PATTERN
(Kirikomi)

PIERCING PATTERN

Description

The Piercing Pattern in Figure 2.29 is composed of a two-candle formation in a downtrending market. The first candle is black, a continuation of the existing trend. The second candle is formed by opening below the low of the previous day. It closes more than midway up the black candle, near or at the high for the day.

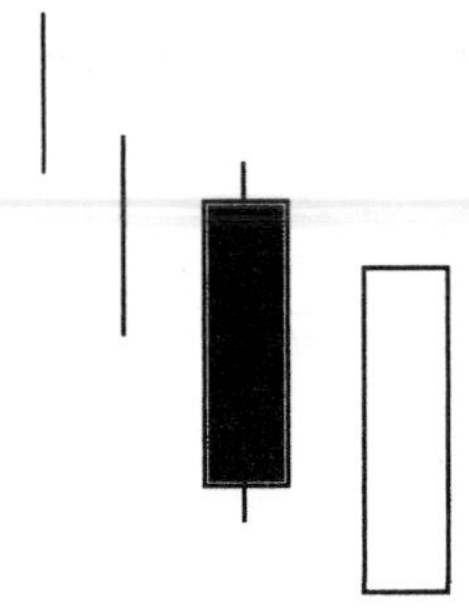

Figure 2.29 Piercing pattern.

Criteria

1. The body of the first candle is black; the body of the second candle is white.
2. The downtrend has been evident for a good period. A long black candle occurs at the end of the trend.
3. The second day opens lower than the trading of the prior day.
4. The white candle closes more than halfway up the black candle.

Signal Enhancements

1. The longer the black candle and the white candle, the more forceful the reversal.
2. The greater the gap down from the previous days close, the more pronounced the reversal.
3. The higher the white candle closes into the black candle, the stronger the reversal.
4. Large volume during these two trading days is a significant confirmation.

Pattern Psychology

After a strong downtrend has been in effect, the atmosphere is bearish. Fear becomes more predominant. The prices gap down. The bears may even push the prices down further. But before the end of the day, the bulls step in and dramatically turn prices around. They finish near the high of the day. The move has almost negated the price decline of the previous day. This now has the bears concerned. More buying the next day will confirm the move. (See Figure 2.30.)

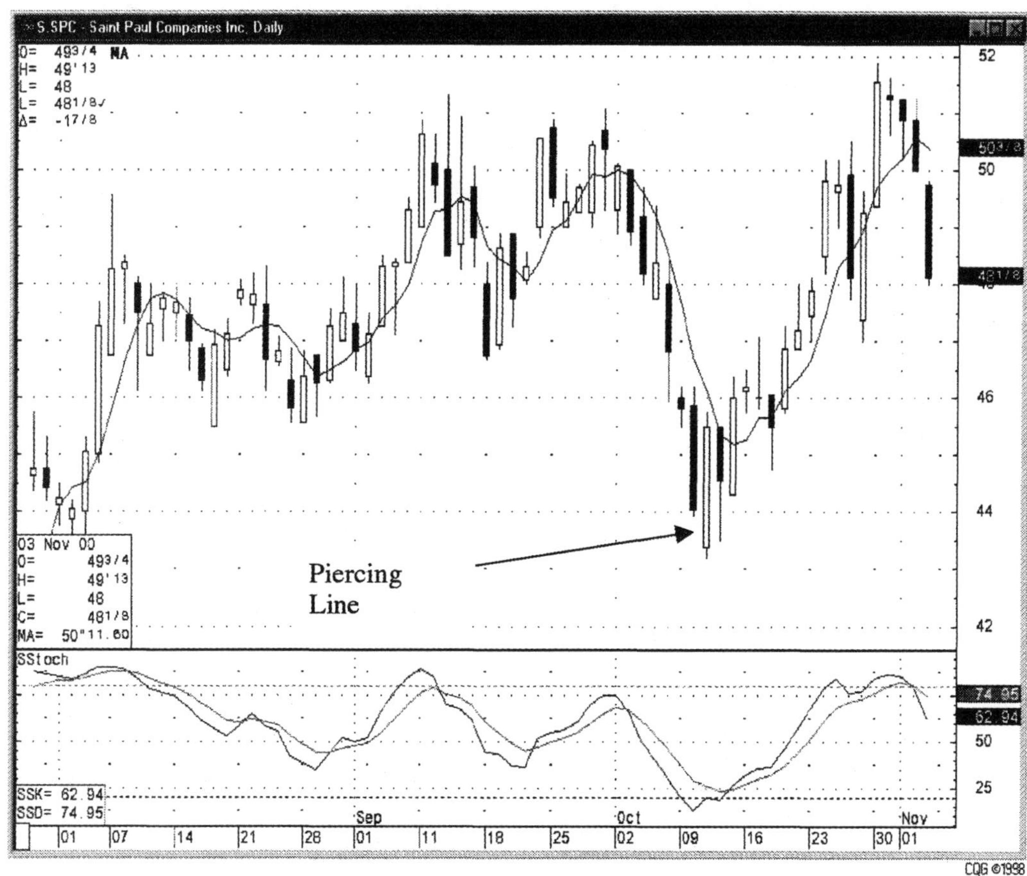

Figure 2.30 A Piercing pattern shows a surge in buying.

DARK CLOUD COVER
(Kabuse)

DARK CLOUD COVER

Description

The Dark Cloud Cover in Figure 2.31 is the bearish counterpart to the Piercing Pattern. The first day of the pattern is a long white candle at the top end of a trend. The second day's open is higher than the high of the previous day. It closes at least one-half way down the previous day candle, the further down the white candle, the more convincing the reversal. Remember that a close at or below the previous day's open turns this pattern into a Bearish Engulfing Pattern. *Kabuse* means to get covered or to hang over.

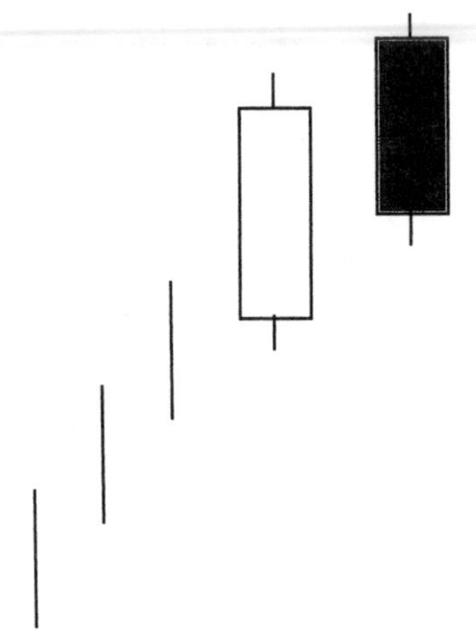

Figure 2.31 Dark Cloud Cover.

Criteria

1. The body of the first candle is white; the body of the second candle is black.
2. The uptrend has been evident for a good period. A long white candle occurs at the top of the trend.
3. The second day opens higher than the trading of the prior day.
4. The black candle closes more than halfway down the white candle.

Signal Enhancements

1. The longer the white candle and the black candle, the more forceful the reversal.

2. The higher the gap up from the previous days close, the more pronounced the reversal.
3. The lower the black candle closes into the white candle, the stronger the reversal.
4. Large volume during these two trading days is a significant confirmation.

Pattern Psychology

After a strong uptrend has been in effect, the atmosphere is bullish. Exuberance sets in. They gap the price up. The bears start to show up and push the price back down. It finally closes at or near the lows for the day. The close has negated most of the previous day's gains. The bulls are now concerned. They obviously see that the uptrend may have stopped. This signal makes for a good short, with a stop being the high of the black candle day. Notice that if the Dark Cloud Cover were to close lower, below the open of the previous day, it becomes a Bearish Engulfing pattern. The bearish Engulfing Pattern has slightly stronger bearish implications. (See Figure 2.32.)

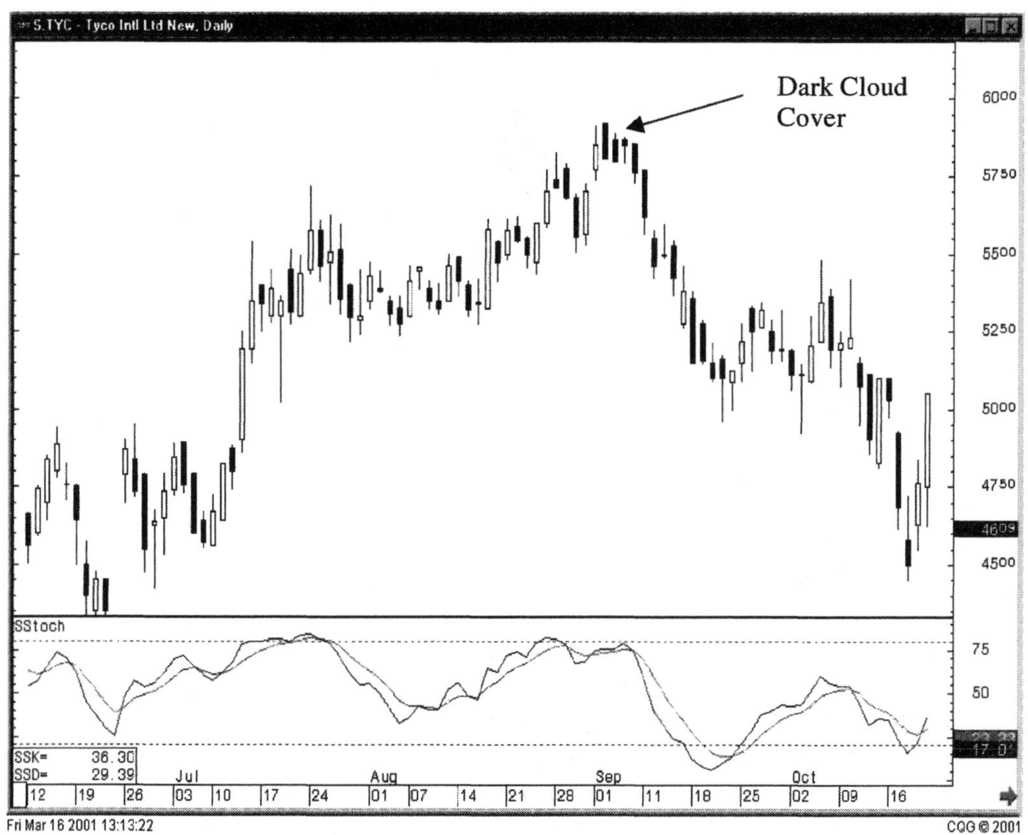

Figure 2.32 The Dark Cloud Cover signal looks ominous at the end of an uptrend.

HARAMI
(Harami)

BULLISH HARAMI

Description

The Harami is an often seen formation. The pattern is composed of a two-candle formation in a downtrending market. The body of the first candle is the same color as the current trend. The first body of the pattern is a long body; the second body is smaller. The open and the close occur inside the open and the close of the previous day. Its presence indicates that the trend is over.

The Japanese definition for Harami is pregnant woman or body within. The first candle is black, a continuation of the existing trend. The second candle, the little belly sticking out, is usually white, but that is not always the case (see Homing Pigeon). The location and size of the second candle will influence the magnitude of the reversal.

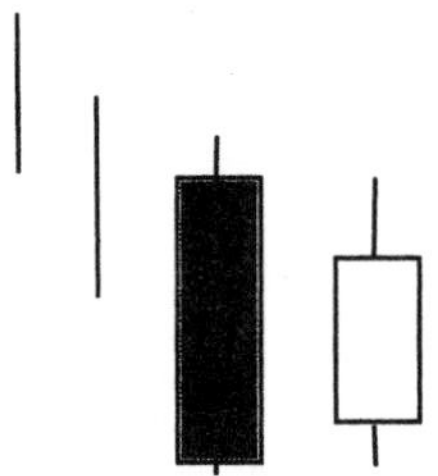

Figure 2.33 Harami, the selling has stopped.

Criteria

1. The body of the first candle is black; the body of the second candle is white.
2. The downtrend has been evident for a good period. A long black candle occurs at the end of the trend.
3. The second day opens higher than the close of the previous day and closes lower than the open of the prior day.
4. Unlike the Western Inside Day, just the body needs to remain in the previous day's body, where as the Inside Day requires both the body and the shadows to remain inside the previous day's body.
5. For a reversal signal, further confirmation is required to indicate that the trend is now moving up.

Signal Enhancements

1. The longer the black candle and the white candle, the more forceful the reversal.
2. The higher the white candle closes up on the black candle, the more convincing that a reversal has occurred despite the size of the white candle.

Pattern Psychology

After a strong downtrend has been in effect and after a selling day, the bulls open the price higher than the previous close. The shorts get concerned and start covering. The price finishes higher for the day. This is enough support to have the short sellers take notice that the trend has been violated. A strong day after that would convince everybody that the trend was reversing. Usually the volume is above the recent norm due to the unwinding of short positions. (See Figure 2.34.)

Figure 2.34 The Bullish Harami reveals buying.

HARAMI
(Harami)

BEARISH HARAMI

Description

The Bearish Harami (shown in Figure 2.35) is the exact opposite of the Bullish Harami. Again, the pattern is composed of a two-candle formation. The body of the first candle is the same color as the current trend. The first body of the pattern is a long body; the second body is smaller. The open and the close occur inside the open and the close of the previous day. Its presence indicates that the trend is over.

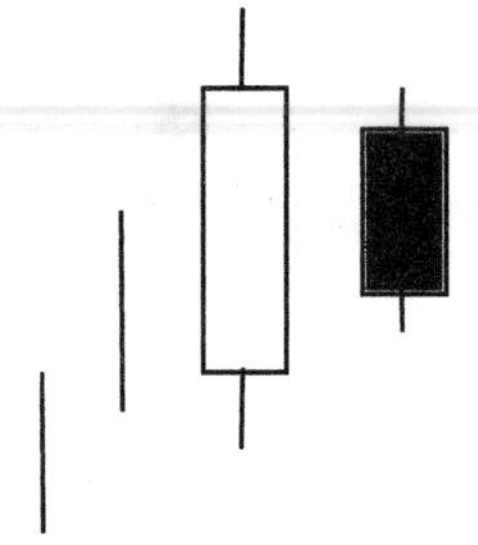

Figure 2.35 Bearish Harami.

Criteria

1. The body of the first candle is white; the body of the second candle is black.
2. The uptrend has been apparent. A long white candle occurs at the end of the trend.
3. The second day opens lower than the close of the previous day and closes higher than the open of the prior day.
4. For a reversal signal, confirmation is needed. The next day should show weakness.

Signal Enhancements

1. The longer the white candle and the black candle, the more forceful the reversal.

2. The lower the black candle closes down on the white candle, the more convincing that a reversal has occurred, despite the size of the black candle.

Pattern Psychology

After a strong uptrend has been in effect and after a long white candle day, the bears open the price lower than the previous close. The longs get concerned and start profit taking. The price finishes lower for the day. The bulls are now concerned as the price closes lower. It is becoming evident that the trend has been violated. A weak day after that would convince everybody that the trend was reversing. Volume increases due to the profit taking and the addition of short sales. (See Figure 2.36.)

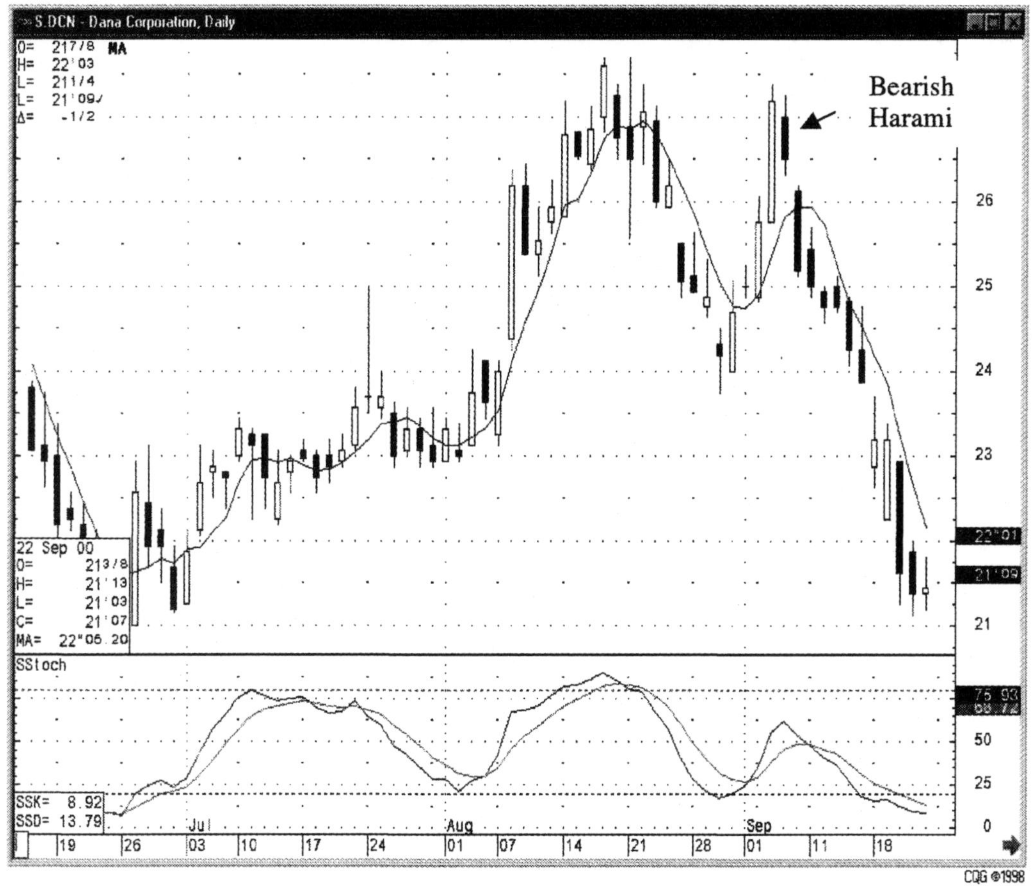

Figure 2.36 A bearish Harami shows that the buying had stopped.

MORNING STAR

(Sankawa Ake No Myojyo)

MORNING STAR

Description

The Morning Star in Figure 2.37 is a bottom reversal signal. Like the planet Mercury, the morning star, it foretells that brighter things—sunrise, is about to occur, or that prices are going to go higher. It is formed after an obvious downtrend. It is made by a long black body, usually one of the fear-induced days at the bottom of a long decline. The following day gaps down. However, the magnitude of the trading range remains small for the day. This is the star of the formation. The third day is a white candle day. And represents the fact that the bulls have now stepped in and seized control. The optimal Morning Star signal would have a gap before and after the star day.

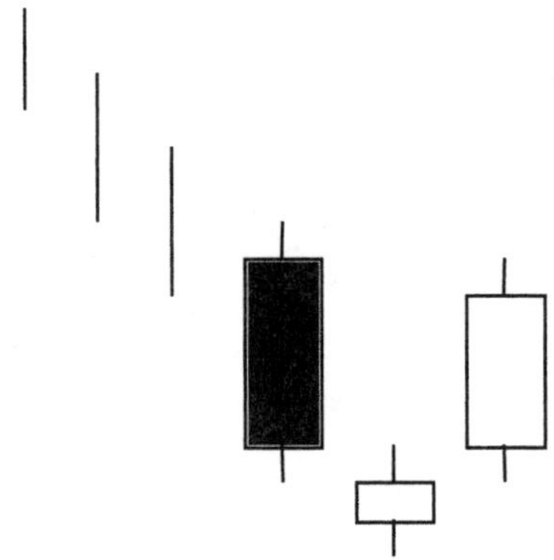

Figure 2.37 Morning Star.

The make-up of the star, an indecision formation, can consist of a number of candle formations. The important factor is to witness the confirmation of the bulls taking over the next day. That candle should consist of a closing that is at least halfway up the black candle of two days prior.

Identifying the Morning Star signal is relatively easy. It is visually apparent to the eye.

Criteria

1. The downtrend has been apparent.
2. The body of the first candle is black, continuing the current trend. The second candle is an indecision formation.
3. The third day shows evidence that the bulls have stepped in. That candle should close at least halfway up the black candle.

Signal Enhancements

1. The longer the black candle and the white candle, the more forceful the reversal.
2. The more indecision that the star day illustrates, the better probabilities that a reversal will occur.
3. A gap between the first day and the second day adds to the probability that a reversal is occurring.
4. A gap before and after the star day is even more desirable.
5. The magnitude, that the third day comes up into the black candle of the first day, indicates the strength of the reversal.

Pattern Psychology

A strong downtrend has been in effect. The sellers start getting panicky. There is a large sell-off day. The next day as the selling continues, bulls are stepping in at the low prices. If there is big volume during these days, it shows that the ownership has dramatically changed hands. The second day does not have a large trading range. The third day the bears start to lose conviction as the bulls increase their buying. When the price starts moving back into the trading range of the first day, the sellers diminish and the buyers seize control. (See Figure 2.38.)

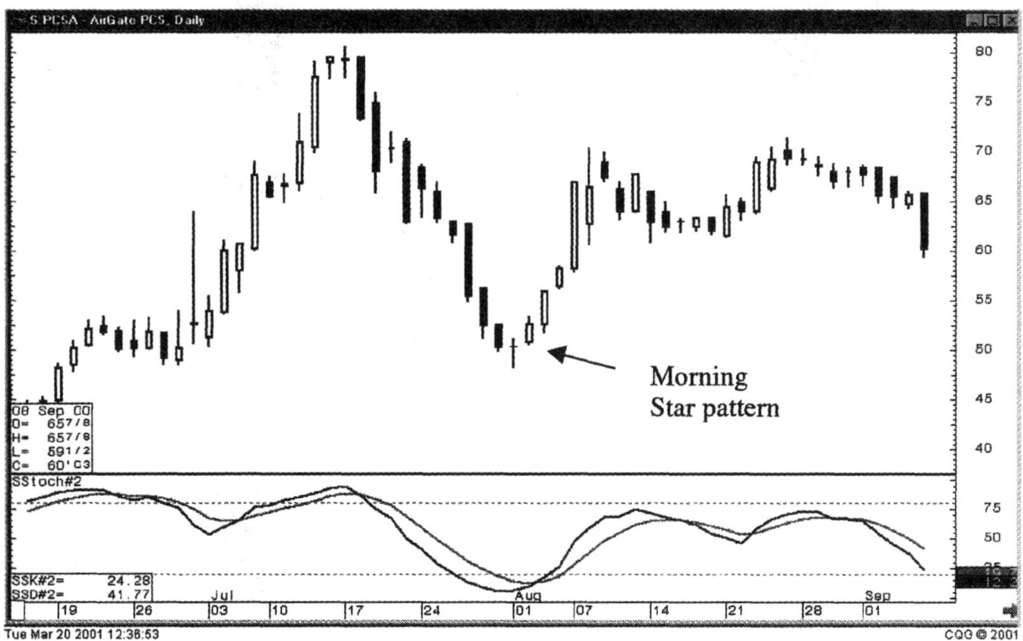

Figure 2.38 A Morning Star pattern has a symmetry that illustrates a change in investors' sentiment.

MORNING STAR DERIVATIVES

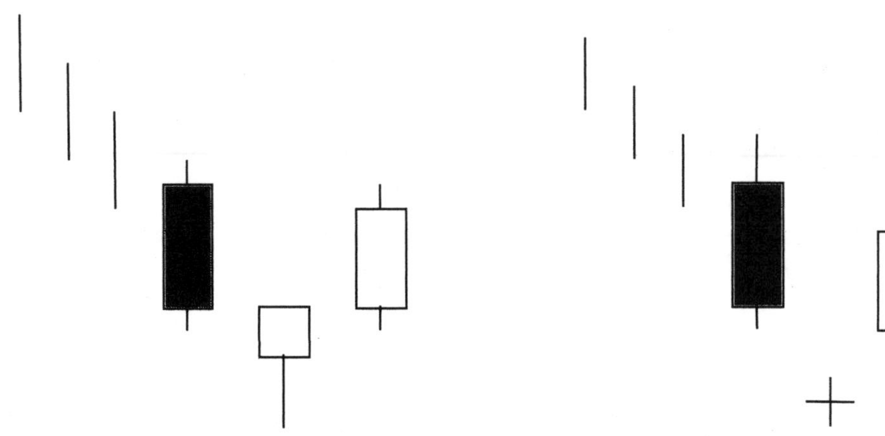

Figure 2.38a Hammer.

Figure 2.38b Abandoned Baby.

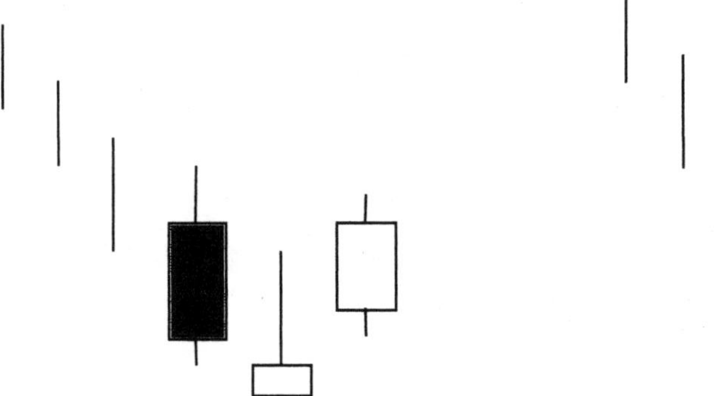

Figure 2.38c Reverse Hammer.

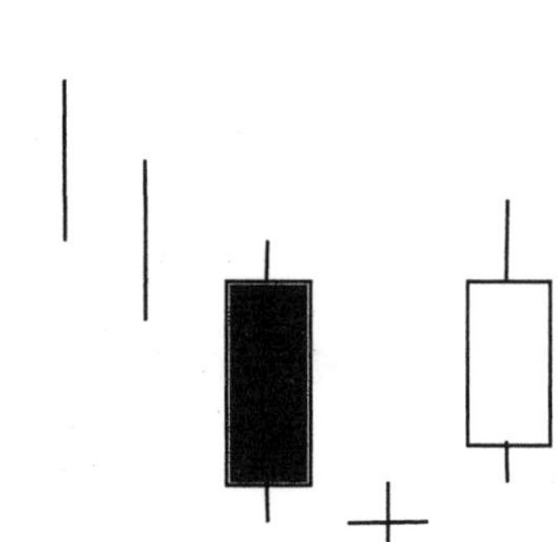

Figure 2.38d Doji Star.

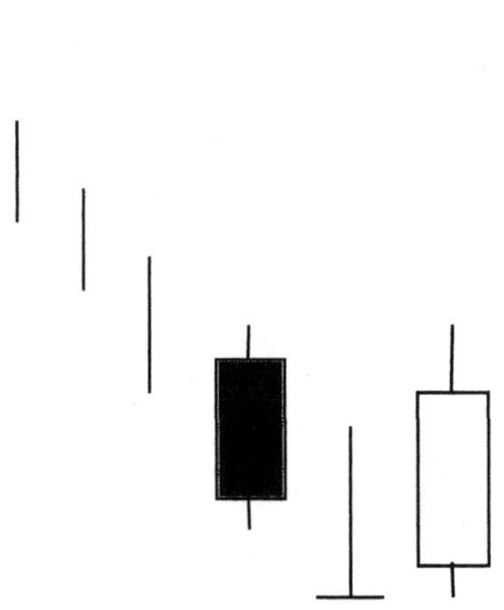

Figure 2.38e Gravestone Doji.

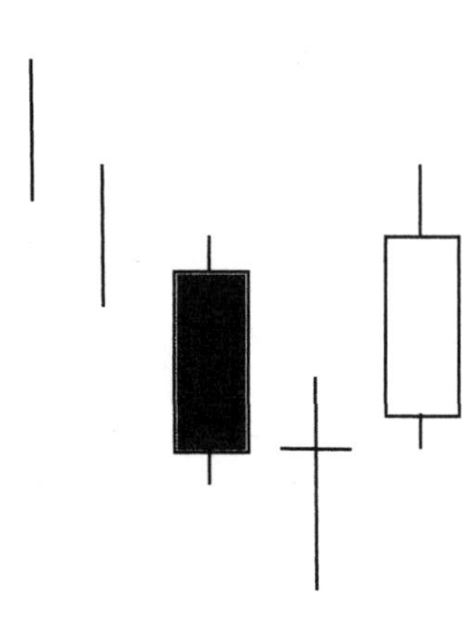

Figure 2.38f Doji Cross.

MORNING STARS

Using the Morning Star definition liberally, it is a three-day pattern that can be visually identified at the bottom of a trend (see Figures 2.38a through 2.38f). The black candle is usually an exaggerated long body after a series of black candled dominated trend. That should be the telltale sign that fear and panic is overweighing rational analysis. This alerts the Candlestick Analyst to watch for an indecision day. The third day up move confirms that the trend has reversed. (See Figures 2.39 and 2.40.)

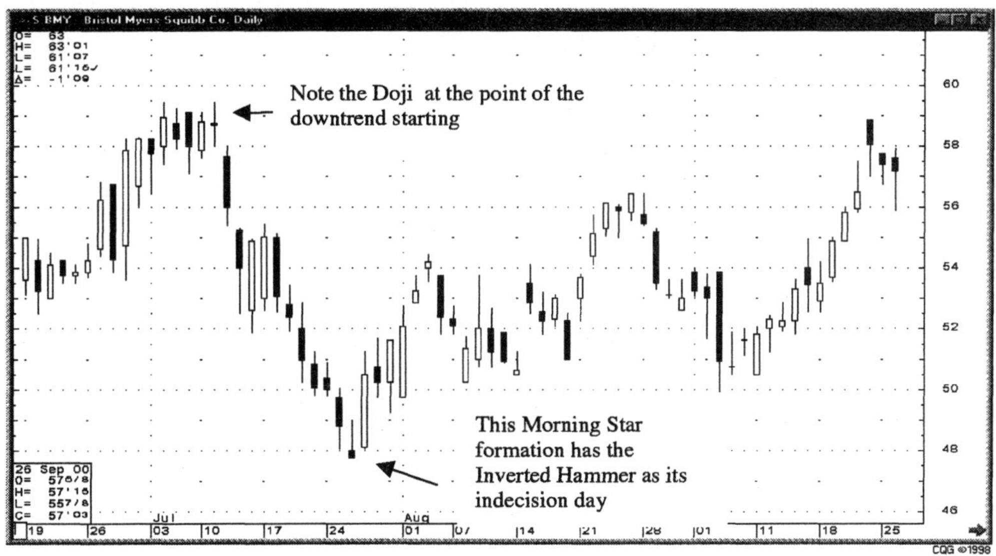

Figure 2.39 The Reverse Hammer is the indecision signal.

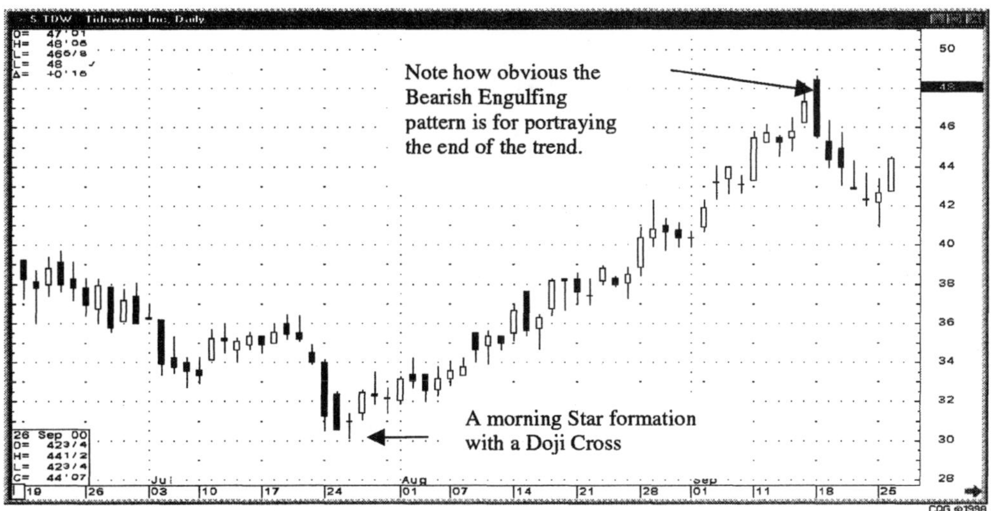

Figure 2.40 A Doji with a gap up the third day.

EVENING STAR
(Sankawa Yoi No Myojyo)

EVENING STAR

Description

The Evening Star in Figure 2.41 is a top reversal signal. It is exactly opposite the Morning Star signal. Like the planet Venus, the evening star, it foretells that darkness is about to set or that prices are going to go lower. It is formed after an obvious uptrend. It is made by a long white body occurring at the end of an uptrend., usually when the confidence has finally built up. The following day gaps up, yet the trading range remains small for the day. Again, this is the star of the formation. The third day is a black candle day. And represents the fact that the bears have now seized control. That candle should consist of a closing that is at least halfway down the white candle of two days prior. The optimal Evening Star signal would have a gap before and after the star day.

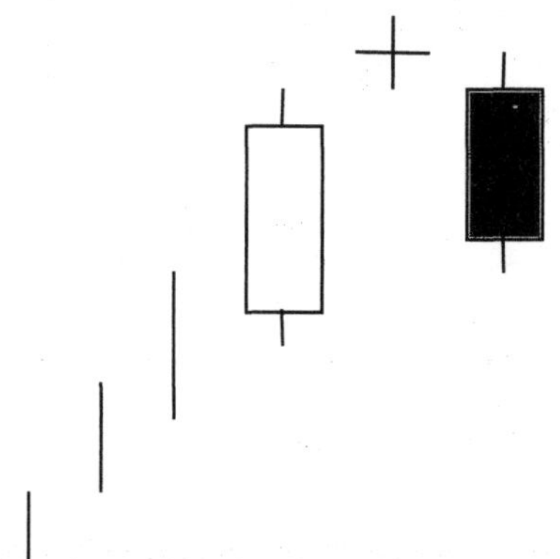

Figure 2.41 Evening Star.

Criteria

1. The uptrend has been apparent.
2. The body of the first candle is white, continuing the current trend. The second candle is an indecision formation.
3. The third day shows evidence that the bears have stepped in. That candle should close at least halfway down the white candle.

Signal Enhancements

1. The longer the white candle and the black candle, the more forceful the reversal.

2. The more indecision that the star day illustrates, the better probabilities that a reversal will occur.
3. A gap between the first day and the second day adds to the probability that a reversal is occurring.
4. A gap before and after the star day is even more desirable. The magnitude, that the third day comes down into the white candle of the first day, indicates the strength of the reversal.

Pattern Psychology

A strong uptrend has been in effect. The buyers can't imagine anything going wrong and they are piling in. However, it has now reached the prices where sellers start taking profits or think the price is fairly valued. The next day all the buying is being met with the selling, causing for a small trading range. The bulls get concerned and the bears start taking over. The third day is a large sell-off day. If there is big volume during these days, it shows that the ownership has dramatically changed hands. The change of direction is immediately seen in the color of the bodies. (See Figure 2.42.)

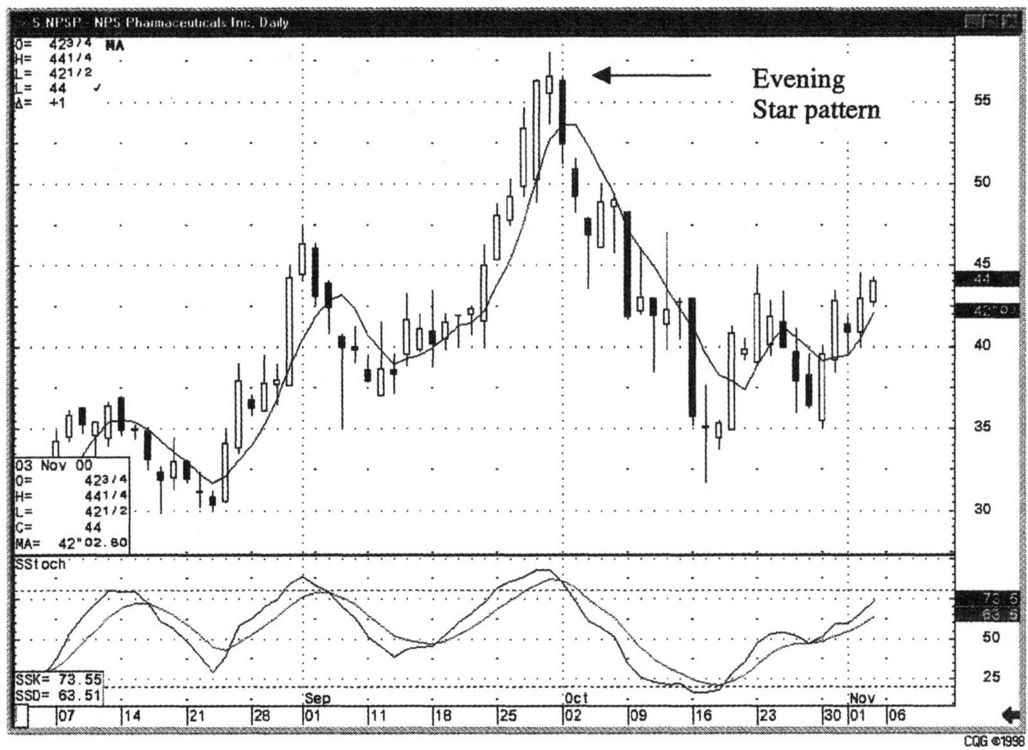

Figure 2.42 The Evening Star shows an obvious change of direction.

KICKER SIGNAL
(Keri Ashi)

KICKER

Description

The Kicker Signal in Figure 2.43 is the most powerful signal of all. It works equally well in both directions. Its relevance is magnified when occurring in the overbought or oversold area. It is formed by two candles. The first candle opens and moves in the direction of the current trend. The second candle opens at the same open of the previous day, a gap open, and heads in the opposite direction of the previous day's candle. The bodies of the candles are opposite colors. This formation is indicative of a dramatic change in investor sentiment. The Candlesticks visually depict the magnitude of the change.

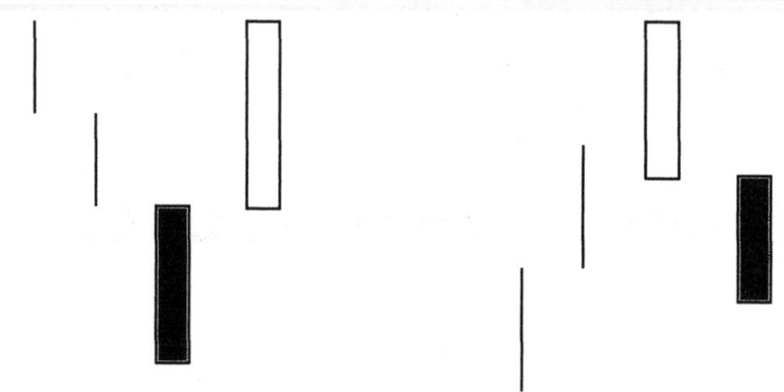

Figure 2.43 Bullish and Bearish Kicker signals.

Criteria

1. The first day's open and the second day's open are the same. The price movement is in opposite directions from the opening price.
2. The trend has no relevance in a kicker situation.
3. The signal is usually formed by surprise news before or after market hours.
4. The price never retraces into the previous days trading range.

Signal Enhancements

1. The longer the candles, the more dramatic the price reversal.
2. Opening from yesterday's close to yesterday's open already is a gap. However, gapping away from the previous day's open further enhances the reversal.

Pattern Psychology

The Kicker Signal demonstrates a dramatic change in the investor sentiment. Something has occurred to violently change the direction of the price. Usually a surprise news item is the cause of this type of move. The signal illustrates such a change in the current direction that the new direction will persist with strength for a good while.

There is one caveat to this signal. If the next day prices gap back in the same direction as the original trend, liquidate the trade immediately. This does not happen often, but when it does, get out immediately. (See Figure 2.44.)

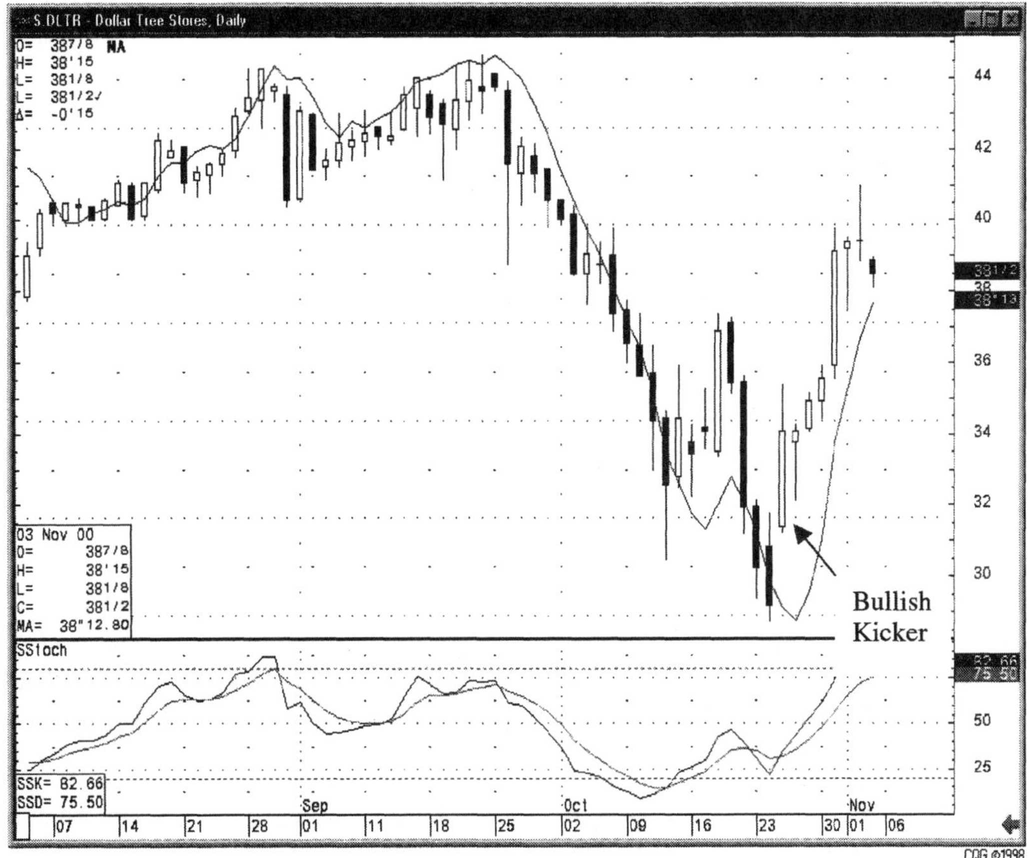

Figure 2.44 A bullish Kicker signal reveals very strong buying.

SHOOTING STAR AND INVERTED HAMMER
SHOOTING STAR

(Nagare Boshi)

Description

The Shooting Star in Figure 2.45 is also comprised of one candle. It is easily identified by the presence of a small body with a shadow at least two times greater than the body. It is found at the top of an uptrend. The Japanese named this pattern because it looks like a shooting star falling from the sky with the tail trailing it.

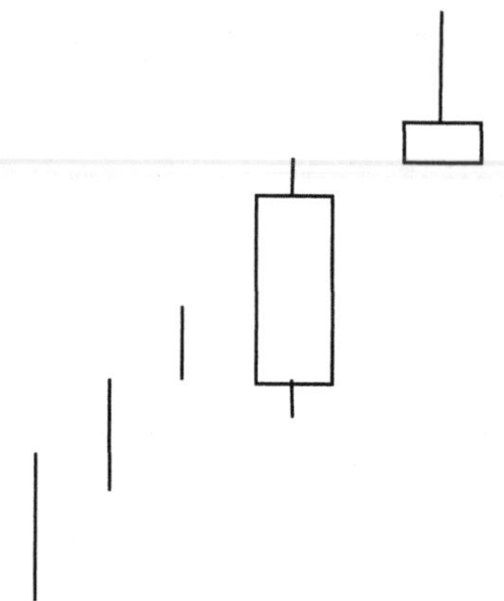

Figure 2.45 Shooting Star.

Criteria

1. The upper shadow should be at least two times the length of the body.
2. The real body is at the lower end of the trading range. The color of the body is not important although a black body should have slightly more bearish implications.
3. There should be no lower shadow or a small lower shadow.
4. The following day needs to confirm the Shooting Star signal with a black candle or better yet, a gap down with a lower close.

Signal Enhancements

1. The longer the upper shadow, the higher the potential of a reversal occurring.
2. A gap up from the previous days close sets up for a stronger reversal move provided.

3. The day after the Shooting Star signal opens lower.
4. Large volume on the Shooting Star day increases the chances that a blowoff day has occurred although it is not a necessity.

Pattern Psychology

After a strong uptrend has been in effect, the atmosphere is bullish. The price opens and trades higher. The bulls are in control. But before the end of the day, the bears step in and take the price back down to the lower end of the trading range, creating a small body for the day. This could indicate that the bulls still have control if analyzing a Western bar chart. However, the long upper shadow represents that sellers had started stepping in at these levels. Even though the bulls may have been able to keep the price positive by the end of the day, the evidence of the selling was apparent. A lower open or a black candle the next day reinforces the fact that selling is going on. (See Figure 2.46.)

Figure 2.46 A Shooting Star reveals that the bulls are not in control anymore.

INVERTED HAMMERS

(Tohba)

Description

The Inverted Hammer in Figure 2.47 is comprised of one candle. It is easily identified by the presence of a small body with a shadow at least two times greater than the body. Found at the bottom of a downtrend, this shows evidence that the bulls started to step in, but that the selling was still going on. The color of the small body is not important but a white candle has slightly more bullish implications than the black body. A positive day is required the following day to confirm this signal.

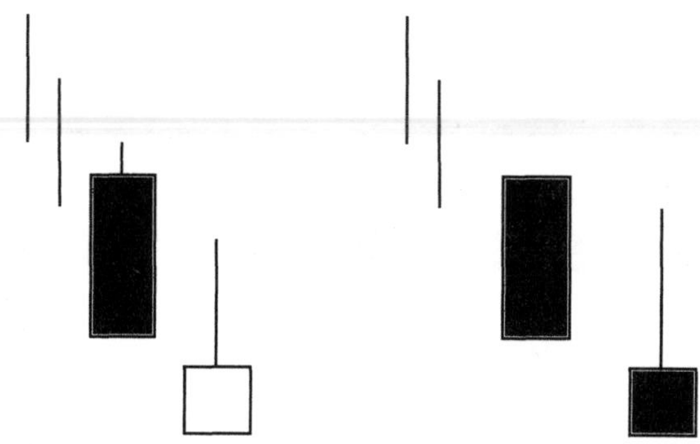

Figure 2.47 Inverted Hammer.

Criteria

1. The upper shadow should be at least two times the length of the body.
2. The real body is at the lower end of the trading range. The color of the body is not important although a white body should have slightly more bullish implications.
3. There should be no lower shadow or a very small lower shadow.
4. The following day needs to confirm the Inverted Hammer signal with a strong bullish day.

Signal Enhancements

1. The longer the upper shadow, the higher the potential of a reversal occurring.
2. A gap down from the previous day's close sets up for a stronger reversal move provided.
3. The day after the hammer signal opens higher.

4. Large volume on the Reverse Hammer day increases the chances that a blowoff day has occurred.

Pattern Psychology

After a downtrend has been in effect, the atmosphere is quite bearish. The price opens and starts to trade higher. The bulls have stepped in, but they can't maintain the strength. The existing sellers knock the price back down to the lower end of the trading range. The bears are still in control. This is an unusual signal. It has the aspects of being a bearish signal. But the next day, the bulls step in and take the price move back up without major resistance from the bears. They had used up their resources during the previous day's selling. If the price remains strong after the Inverted Hammer day, that confirms the signal. (See Figure 2.48.)

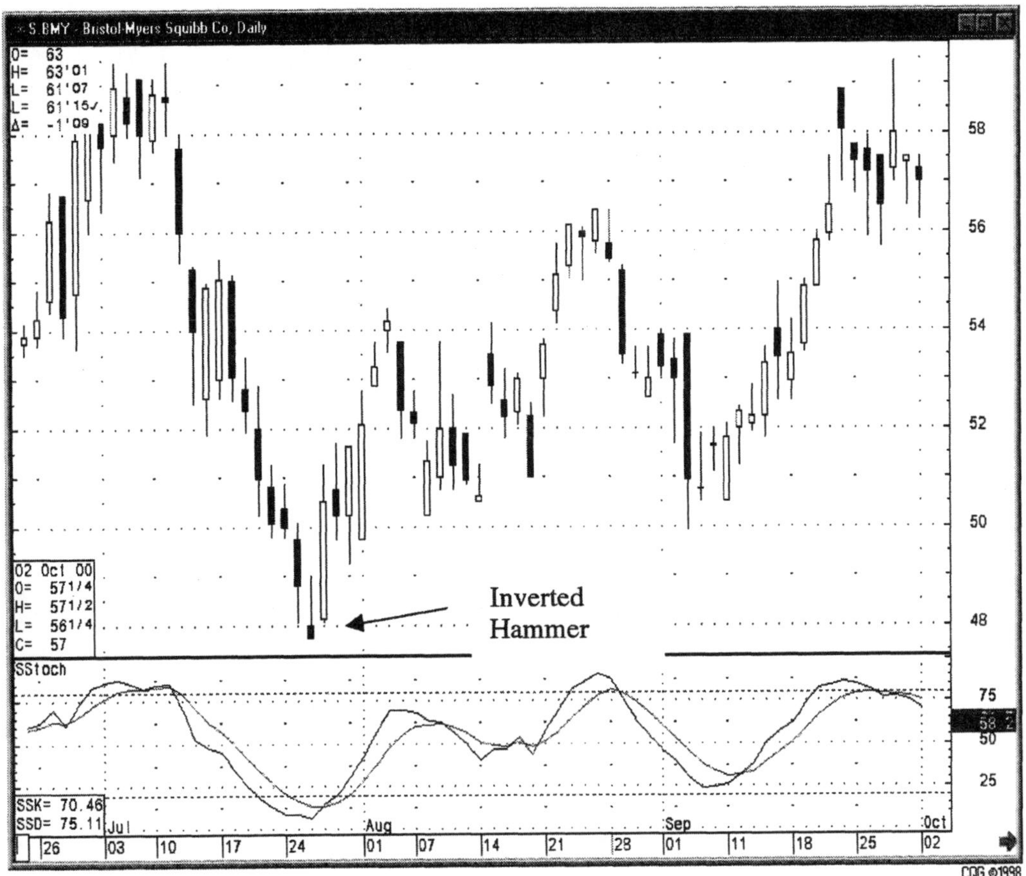

Figure 2.48 An Inverted Hammer shows that the buyers were stepping in.

THE SECONDARY SIGNALS

The following signals are less significant in the fact that they do not appear as frequently as the major signals. That does not negate the effectiveness or their importance for identifying reversal points. Despite the infrequency of the occurrence of some of these formations, their appearance produces highly profitable trades.

The speed of computer search programs produces more highly profitable trade potentials than most investors need. This supply comes just from the major signals. However, being aware of what the secondary signals look like will provide the investor with additional opportunities during the course of investing.

SECONDARY SIGNALS

- THE TRI STAR
- THREE BLACK CROWS
- THREE IDENTICAL CROWS
- TWO CROWS
- UPSIDE GAP TWO CROWS
- MEETING LINES
- BELT HOLD
- UNIQUE THREE RIVER BOTTOM
- THE BREAKAWAY
- THREE INSIDE UP & THREE INSIDE DOWN
- THREE STARS IN THE SOUTH
- THREE WHITE SOLDIERS
- ADVANCE BLOCK
- DELIBERATION
- CONCEALING BABY SWALLOW
- STICK SANDWICH
- HOMING PIGEON
- LADDER BOTTOM
- MATCHING LOW

THE TRI STAR
(Santen Boshi)

TRI STAR

Description

The Tri Star pattern in Figure 2.49 is relatively rare; however, it is a significant reversal indicator. It is comprised of three Dojis. The three-day period illustrates indecision of a period of days.

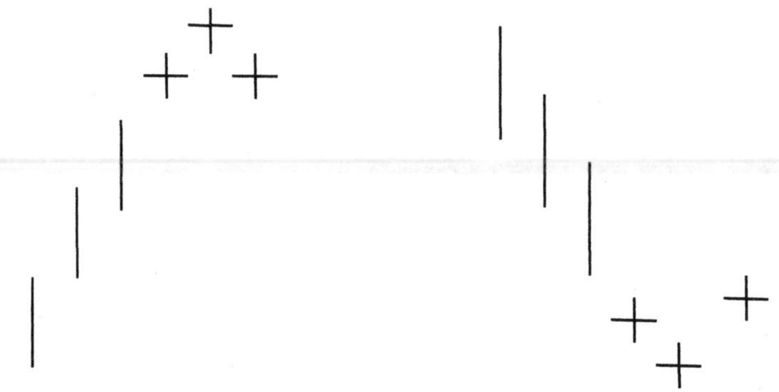

Figure 2.49 Bullish and Bearish TriStar signals. Confirmation is needed.

Criteria

1. All three days are Dojis.
2. The middle day gaps above or below the first and third day. The length of the shadow should not be excessively long, especially when viewed at the end of a bullish trend.

Signal Enhancements

1. The greater the gap, away from the previous day's close, sets up for a stronger reversal move.
2. Large volume on one of the signal days increases the chances that a significant reversal is taking place.

Pattern Psychology

After an uptrend or a downtrend has been in effect, the appearance of the first Doji reveals that there is now indecision in the bull's and the bear's camp. The next day gaps in the same direction as the existing trend and forms the second Doji. This reveals that no certainty for either direction has become apparent. The third day opens opposite the previous trends direction and forms another Doji that day. The final Doji is the last gasp. Any investors who had any conviction are now reversing their position. Because of the rarity of this pattern, double-check the data source to confirm that the Dojis are not bad data. (See Figure 2.50.)

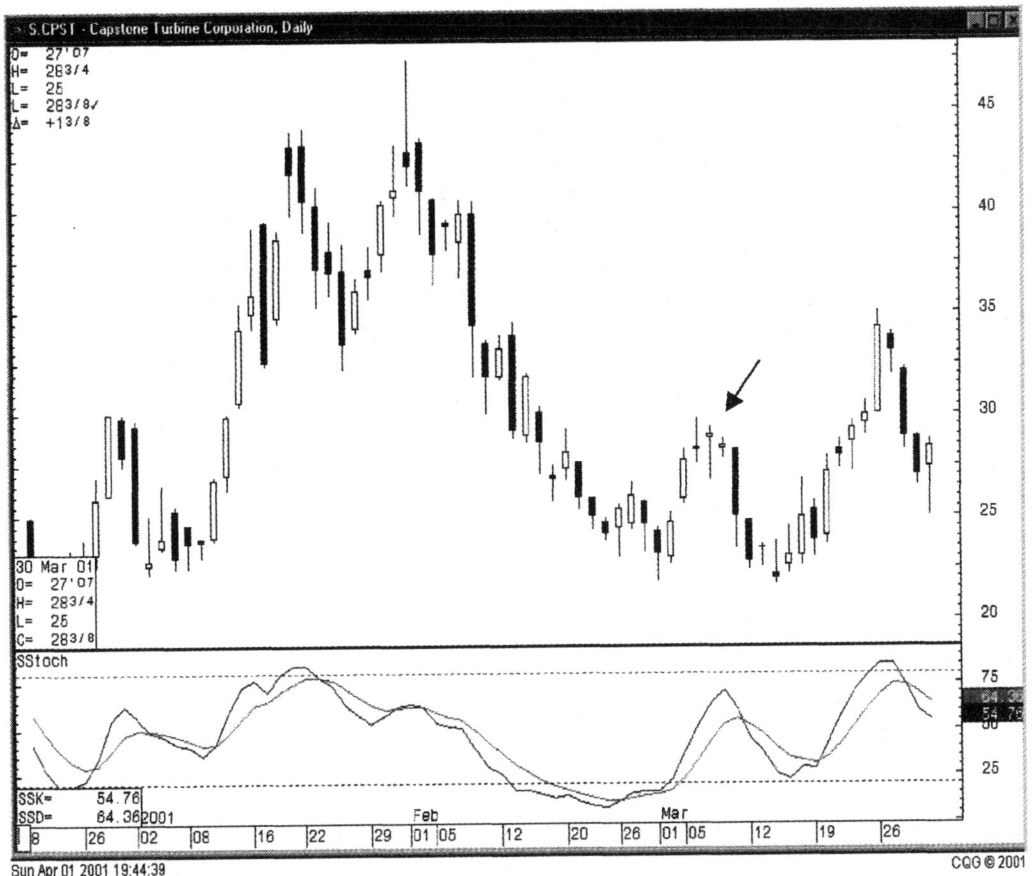

Figure 2.50 A bearish Tri Star pattern reveals major indecision.

THREE BLACK CROWS
(Sanba Garasu)

Three Black Crows

Description

As illustrated in Figure 2.51, the Three Black Crows got their name from the resemblance of three crows looking down from their perch in a tree. This signal, occurring after a strong uptrend, indicates the crows looking down or lower prices are to come. Each of these candles should close very near the low for the day. This pattern, as will be seen, is the opposite of the Three White Soldiers.

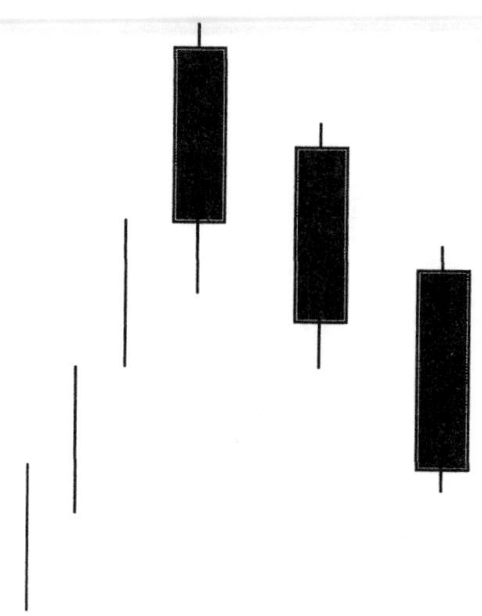

Figure 2.51 Three Black Crows.

Criteria

1. Three long black bodies occur, all of close to equal length.
2. The prior trend should have been up.
3. Each day opens within the body of the previous day.
4. Each day closes near its low.

Pattern Psychology

After an uptrend a long black candle forms. The uptrend has now reached levels where the sellers have started to step in. The first long black candle body is followed by two more long black bodies. Each having opened in the previous days body indicates that buying was occurring early each day but the bears kept forcing prices down by the end of the day. This more consistent process of selling provides a stronger downtrend potential versus a rapid overselling period. (See Figure 2.52.)

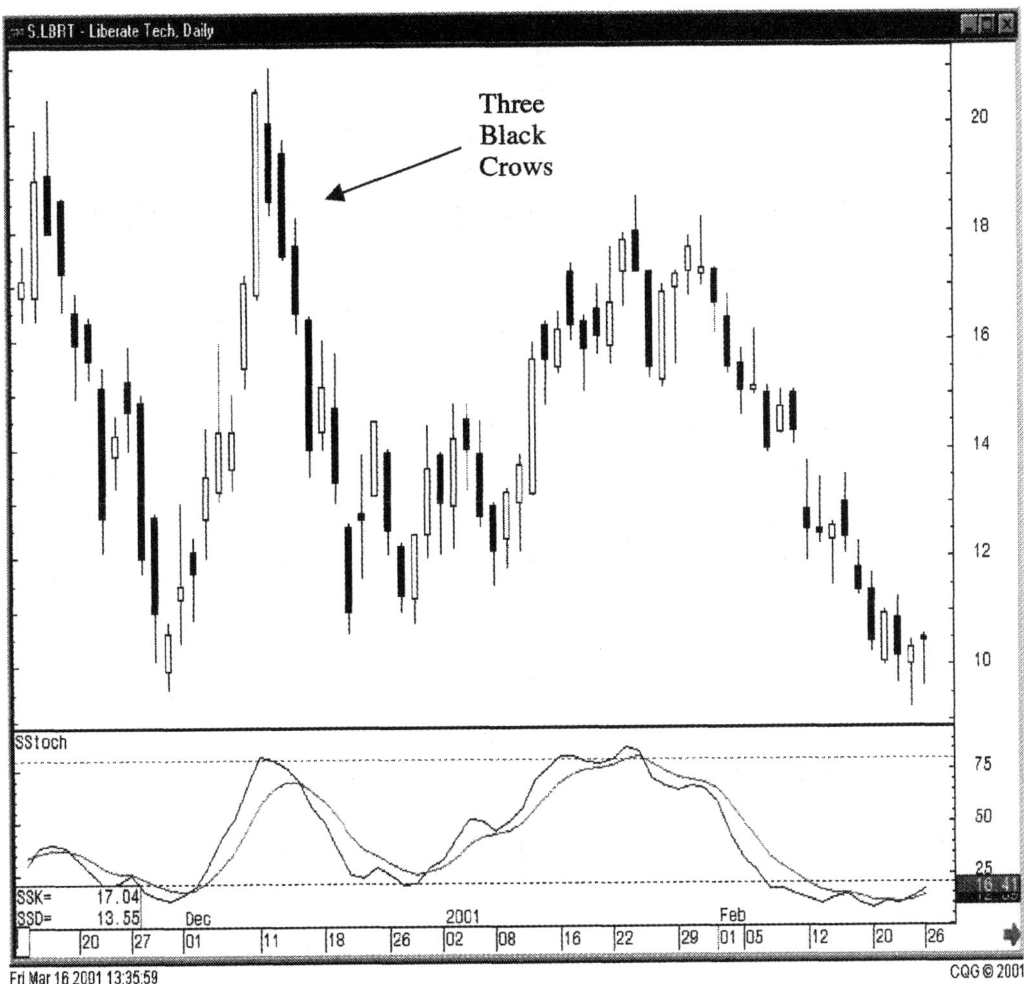

Figure 2.52 Three Black Crows is a negative appearing signal.

THREE IDENTICAL CROWS
(Doji Sanba Garasu)

Description

The Three Identical Crows in Figure 2.53 have the same criteria as the Three Black Crows. The difference is that the opens are at the previous day's close.

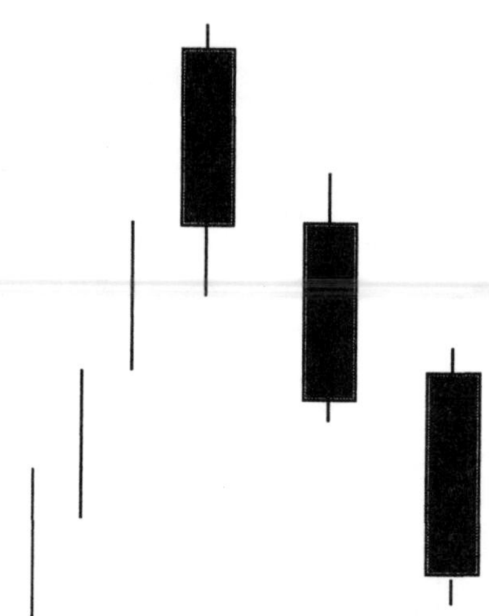

Figure 2.53 Three identical Crows. No confirmation needed.

Criteria

1. Three long black bodies occur, all of close to equal lengths.
2. The prior trend should have been up.
3. Each day opens at the close of the previous day.
4. Each day closes near its low.

Pattern Psychology

After an uptrend a long black candle forms. However, the selling is more severe. There do not appear to be any buyers at the next day's open. The long black candles, having a stair-stepping pattern to them, indicates a much greater motivation to get out of the position. (See Figure 2.54.)

Figure 2.54 Three Identical Crows demonstrates more anxious selling than the Three Black Crows pattern.

TWO CROWS
(Niwa Garasu)

Two Crows

Bearish reversal pattern.

Description

The Two Crows in Figure 2.55 is a three-day pattern. It is only a top-reversal pattern. Like the Upside Gap Two Crows, a gap is created between the long white candle at the top of an uptrend and the small black candle of the second day. The black candle gaps open and pulls back before the end of the day. Even though it has pulled back, it did not fill the gap. The third day opens in the body of the small black candle. The bears maintain the control and move it lower. They are able to fill the gap and close the price within the white candle body. The gap being filled so quickly eliminates any expectations from the bulls.

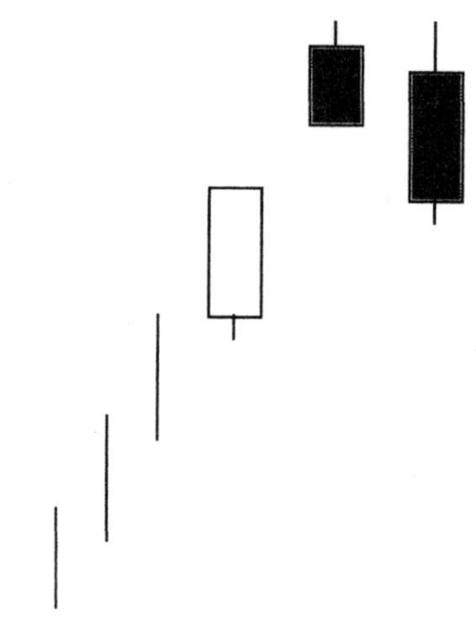

Figure 2.55 Two Crows. Needs confirmation.

Criteria

1. A long white candle continues the uptrend.
2. The real body of the next day is black while gapping up and not filling the gap.
3. The third day opens within than the second day's body and closes within the white candle's body. This produces a black candle that filled in the gap.

Signal Enhancements

1. If the third day was to close more than halfway down the white candle, it would form an Evening Star pattern.

Pattern Psychology

After a strong uptrend has been in effect, the atmosphere is bullish. The price gap opens but cannot hold the gains. Before the end of the day, the bears step in and take the price back down. However, the gap up from the white candle was not filled. The next day, the price opens slightly higher, within the body of the previous black candle. The bulls aren't as boisterous and cannot keep the momentum going. Prices head lower and closes in the white candle range. The gap up from the bullish exuberance of the previous day is very quickly wiped away. The further the third day closes into the white candle body, the more bearish it is. (See Figure 2.56.)

Figure 2.56 Two Crows show the disappearance of buying.

UPSIDE GAP TWO CROWS
(Shita Banare Niwa Garasu)

Upside Gap Two Crows

Description

The Upside Gap Two Crows in Figure 2.57 is a three-day pattern. The upside gap is created between the long white candle at the top of an uptrend and the small black candle of the second day. The black candle gaps open and pulls back before the end of the day. Even though it has pulled back, it did not fill the gap. The third day opens above where the first black candle opened. It can not hold at these levels and pulls back before the end of the day. Closing lower than the previous day, it has engulfed the small black candle's body. However, it still did not close the gap from the white candle.

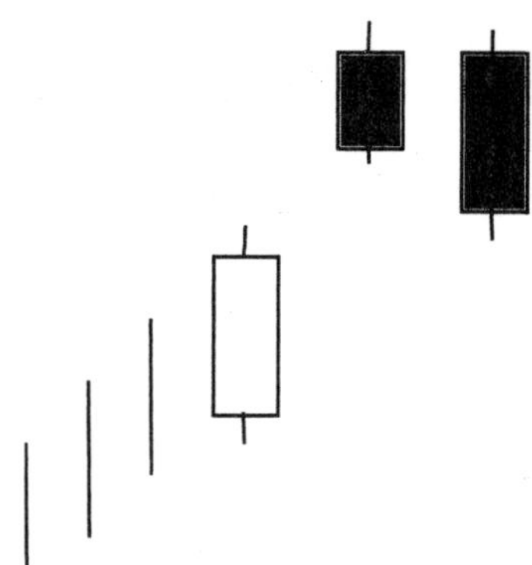

Figure 2.57 Bearish reversal, confirmation is required. Upside Gap Two Crows.

Criteria

1. A long white candle continues the uptrend.
2. The real body of the next day is black while gapping up and not filling the gap.
3. The third day opens higher than the second day's open and closes below the second day's close. This produces a black candle that completely engulfs the small black candle.
4. The close of the third day is still above the close of the last white candle.

Signal Enhancements

1. If the third day were to close within the white candle, it would become Two Crows.

(See Two Crows)

Pattern Psychology

After a strong uptrend has been in effect, the atmosphere is bullish. The price gap opens but cannot hold the gains. Before the end of the day, the bears step in and take the price back down. However, the gap up from the white candle was not filled. The next day, the bulls try again; they open the price higher than the open of the previous day. Again, they cannot hold the price up. It backs off and closes lower than the previous day. This now has taken all the steam out of the bulls. At this point, you will want to see the bears really stepping in the next day to confirm the reversal. This pattern is not as bearish as the Two Crow pattern. (See Figure 2.58.)

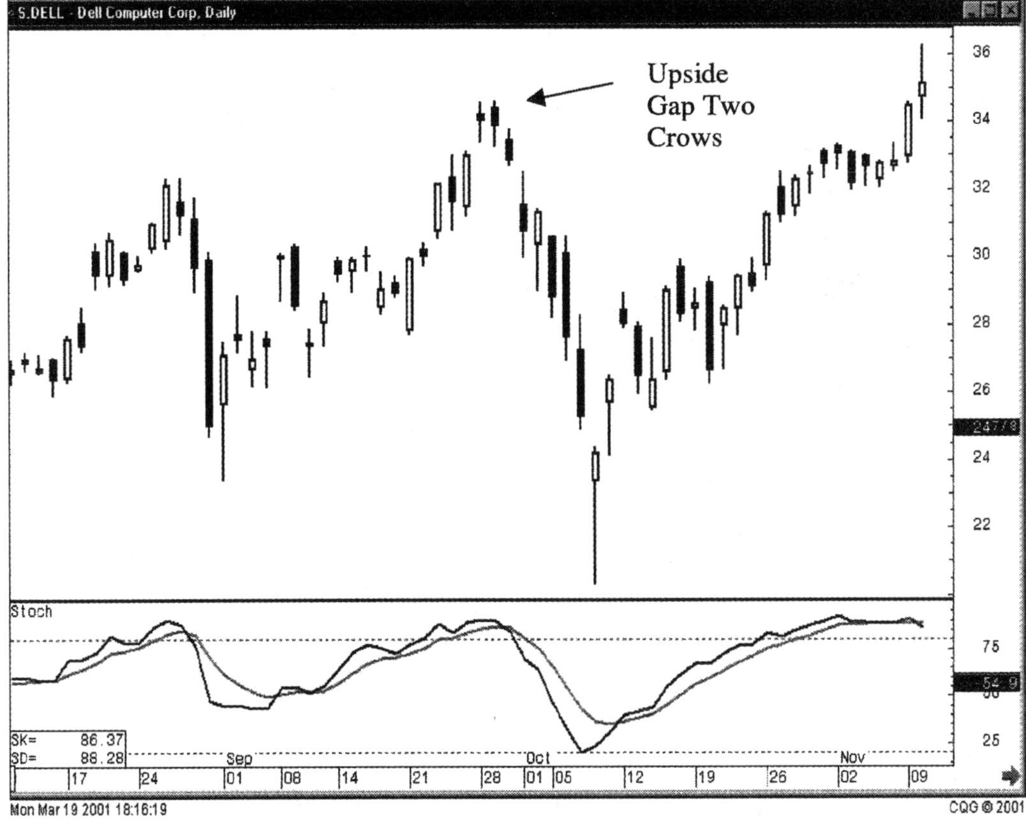

Figure 2.58 The upside gap Two Crows is the last gasp of an uptrend.

MEETING LINES (Deaisen)

Counterattack lines

(gyakushusen)

Description

Meeting Lines (Deaisen) in Figure 2.59 or Counterattack Lines (Gyakushu) in Figure 2.60 are formed when opposite colored bodies have the same closing price. The first Candlestick body is the same color as the current trend. The second body is formed by a gap open in the same direction as the trend. However, by the close, it has come back to the previous days close. The bullish Meeting Line has the same criteria as the Piercing Line except that it closes where it closed the previous day and not up into the body. Likewise, the bearish Meeting Line is the same as the Dark Cloud pattern, but it does not close down into the body of the previous day.

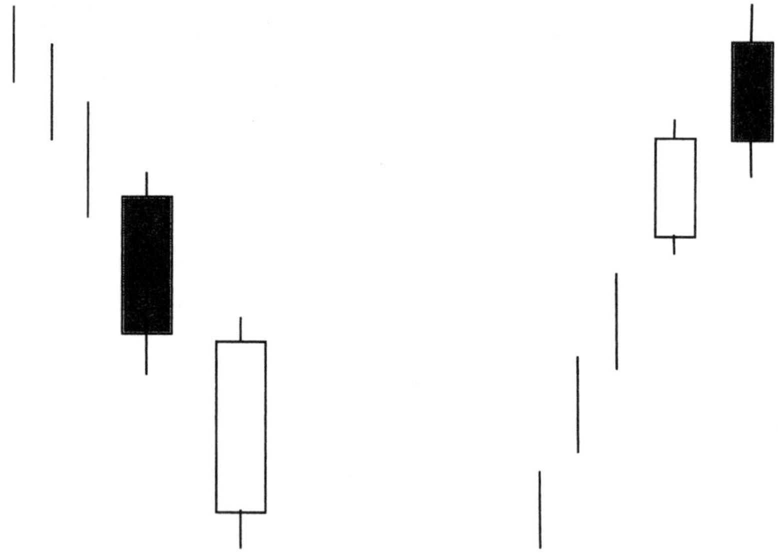

Figure 2.59 Bullish Meeting Line.

Figure 2.60 Bearish Meeting Line.

Criteria

1. The first Candlestick body should continue the prevailing trend.
2. The second Candlestick gaps open continuing the trend.
3. The real body of the second day closes at the close of the first day.

4. The body of the second day is opposite color of the first day.
5. Both days should be long candle days.

Signal Enhancements

1. The longer the bodies, the more significant the reversal pattern.

Pattern Psychology

After a strong trend has been in effect, the trend is further promoted by a long body day. The exuberance is increased the second day with a gap in the same direction. But before the end of the day, the price has come back to the same closing price of the previous day. This indicates that the other side of the market has now stepped in. Another day, opposite of the predominant trend is required to demonstrate that the trend has reversed. The opposite colored body does not need to be as long as the first body. In every case, a confirmation day is going to be needed. The pattern has more strength if the are no shadows at the meeting point. (See Figure 2.61.)

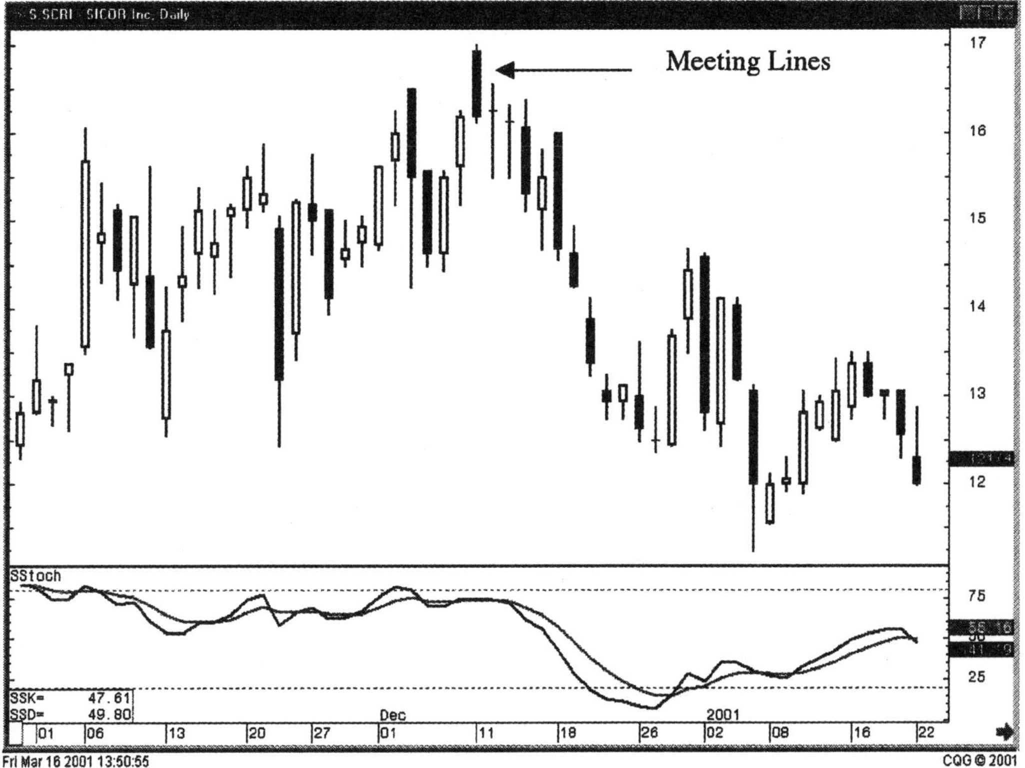

Figure 2.61 The Meeting line pattern reveals a complete change in investor sentiment.

BELT HOLD
(Yorikiri)

Belt Hold

Description

The Belt Hold lines in Figure 2.62 are formed by single Candlesticks. The Bullish Belt Hold is a long white candle that has gapped down in a downtrend. From it's opening point, it moved higher for the rest of the day. This is called a White Opening Shaven Bottom or White Opening Marubozu. The bearish Belt Hold is just the opposite. It is formed with a severe gap away from the existing uptrend. It opens at its high and immediately backs off for the rest of the day. It is known as a Black Opening Shaven head or Black Opening Maruboza. Yorikiri, a sumo wrestling term, means pushing your opponent out of the ring while holding onto his belt. The longer the body of the Belt Hold, the more significant the reversal. (See Figures 2.62 and 2.63.)

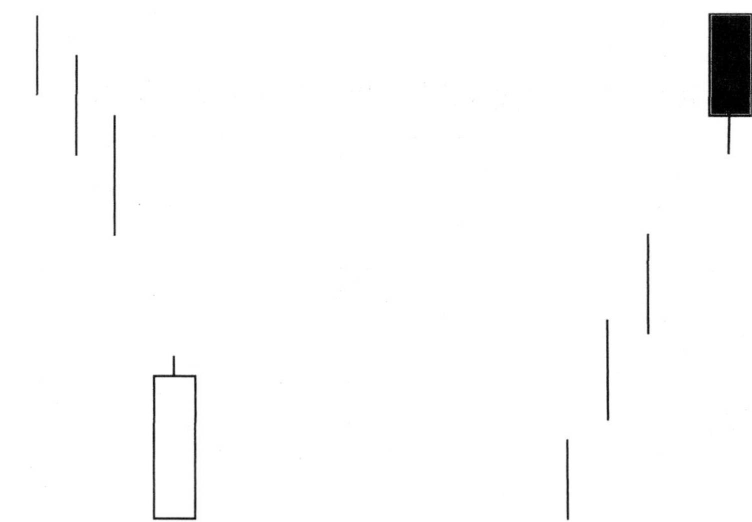

Figure 2.62 Bullish belt Hold.

Figure 2.63 Bearish Belt Hold.

Criteria

1. The Candlestick body should be the opposite color of the prevailing trend.
2. It significantly gaps open, continuing the trend.

3. The real body of the Candlestick has no shadow at the open end. The open is the high or low of that trend.
4. The length of the body should be a long body. The greater the length, the more significant the reversal signal.

Signal Enhancements

1. The longer the body, the more significant the reversal pattern.

Pattern Psychology After a strong trend has been in effect, the trend is further promoted by a gap open, usually a large gap. The opening price becomes the point where the price immediately moves back in the direction of the previous close. This makes the opening price the high or the low for the trend. This causes concern. Investors start to cover shorts or selling outright. This starts to accentuate the move, thus reversing the existing trend. (See Figure 2.64.)

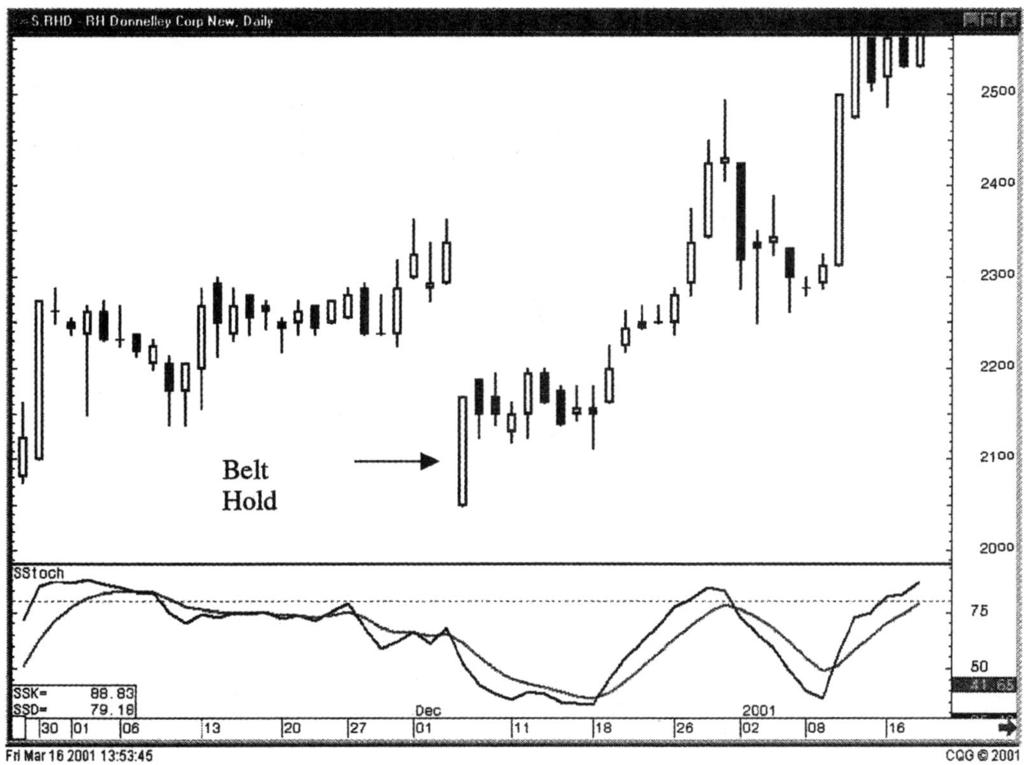

Figure 2.64 A bullish Belt Hold reveals immediate buying after a severe drop in price.

UNIQUE THREE RIVER BOTTOM (Sankawa Soko Zukae)

Unique Three

Description

The Unique Three River Bottom in Figure 2.65 is a bullish pattern, somewhat characteristic of the Morning Star Pattern. It is formed with three candles. At the end of a downtrend, a long black body is produced. The second day opens higher, drops down to new lows, and then closes near the top of the trading range. This is a Hammer-type formation. The third day opens lower but not below the low of the previous day. It closes higher, producing a white candle. But it doesn't close higher than the previous day's close. This pattern is rare.

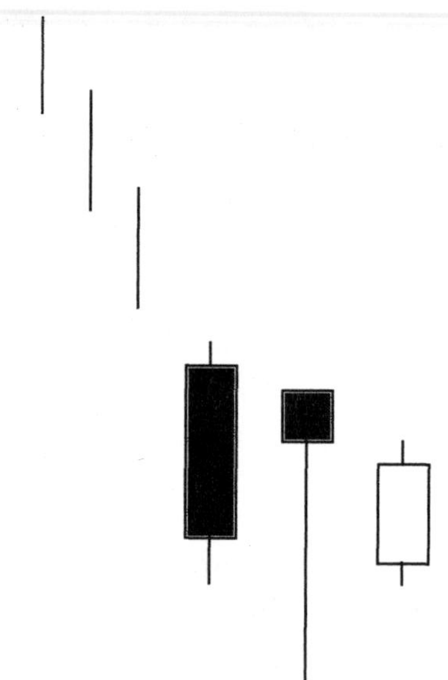

Figure 2.65 Unique Three River Bottom.

Criteria

1. The Candlestick body of the first day is a long black candle, consistent with the prevailing trend.
2. The second day does a Harami/Hammer. It also has a black body.
3. The second day's shadow has set a new low.

4. The third day opens lower, but not below the lowest point of the previous day. It closes higher but below yesterday's close.

Signal Enhancements

1. The longer the shadow of the second day, the probability of a successful reversal becomes greater.

Pattern Psychology

After a strong downtrend has been in effect, the trend is further promoted by a long body black candle. The next day prices open higher but the bears are able to take prices down to new lows. Before the end of the day, the bulls bring it back up the top end of the trading range. The third day, the bears try to take it down again, but the bulls maintain control. If the following day sees prices going up to new highs, the trend has confirmed a reversal. (See Figure 2.66.)

Figure 2.66 The Unique Three River Bottom demonstrates buying at the end of a downtrend.

THE BREAKAWAY (Hanare Sante No Shinte Zukae)

Breakaways

Description

If a trend has been evident, the breakaway pattern (see Figures 2.67 and 2.68), whether bullish or bearish initially indicates the acceleration of that trend. The pattern starts with a long candle representing the current trend. The next candle gaps away from the long candle with the color of that candle the same as the long candle. The third day can be either color. It will not show a change in the trend. The fourth day continues the trend, having the same color as the trend. The fifth day reverses the trend. It opens slightly opposite of the way the trend has been running. From there, it continues in the same direction to where it closes in the gap area.

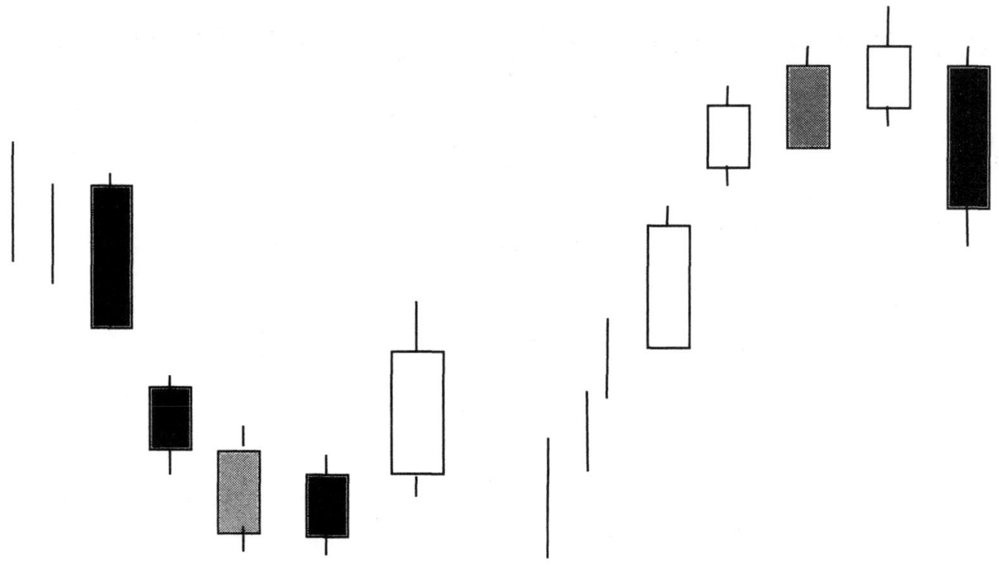

Figure 2.67 Bullish breakaway.

Figure 2.68 Bearish breakaway.

Criteria

1. The first day is a long-body day and has the color of the existing trend.
2. The second day gaps away from the previous close. It has the same color as the first day candle.
3. Days three and four have closes that continue the trend.
4. The last day is an opposite color day that closes in the gap area between day one and day two.

Pattern Psychology

After a trend, usually in an overbought or oversold area, a long candle forms. The next day they gap the price further. That day has the same color as the trend. For the next two days, the bulls and/or bears keep the trend going in the same direction, but with less conviction. The final day, the move goes opposite the existing trend with enough force to close in the gap area between day one and day two. This day completely erases the move of the previous three days. (See Figure 2.69.)

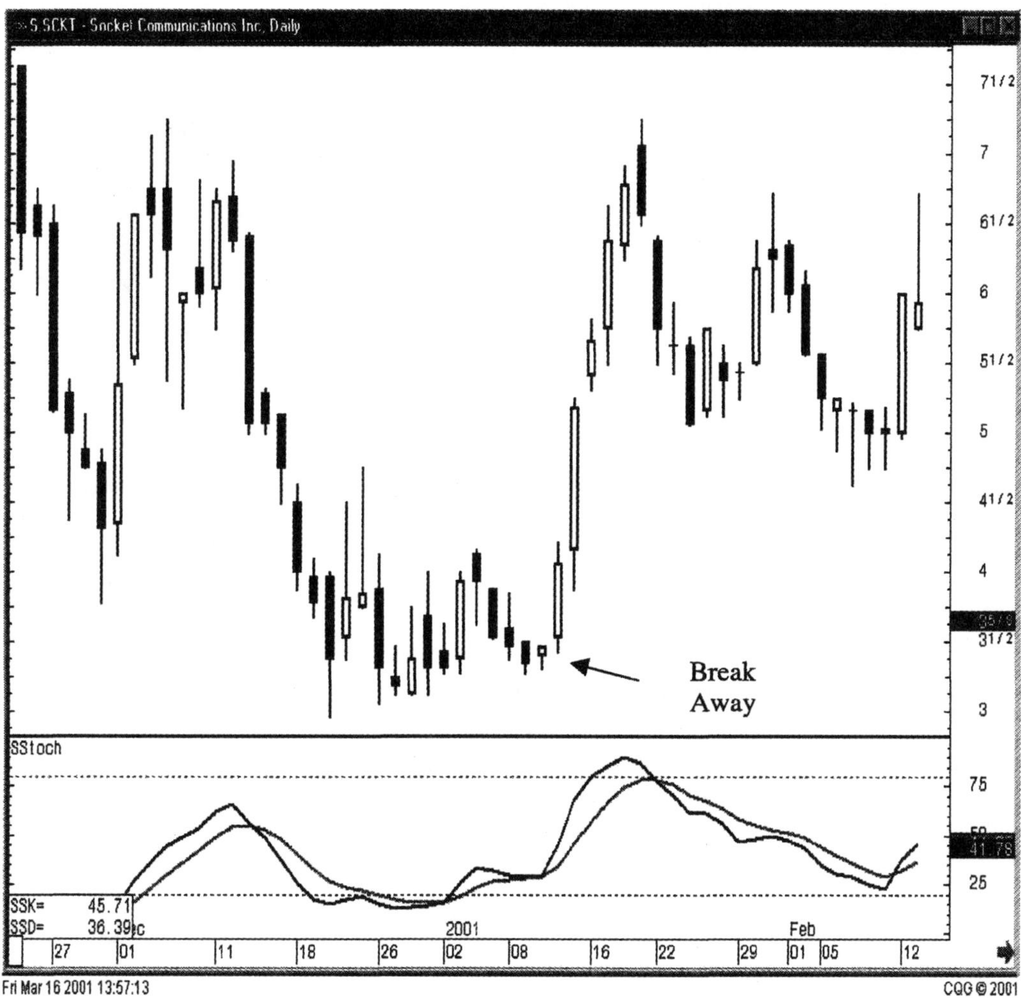

Figure 2.69 The slight gap up in the Bullish Breakaway pattern is the indication that buying is occurring with strength.

THREE INSIDE UP and THREE INSIDE DOWN (Harami Age and Harami Sage)

Description

Note that after the long candle day that is in the same direction of the trend that the Harami pattern occurs. (See Figures 2.70 and 2.71.) The Harami is the first indication that they trend has stopped. The third day confirms that the Harami has indicated correctly. The three-day pattern is a modern era confirmation of the Harami pattern.

Figure 2.70 Three Inside Up. **Figure 2.71** Three Inside Down.

Criteria

1. The Harami pattern is the overriding signal component of this pattern.
2. The harami body should be the opposite color of the long candle day.
3. Day three has a close that is higher than the open of day one. Or lower than day one in the bearish indicator.

Pattern Psychology

After a trend and the occurrence of a long body day that extends that trend, the Harami pattern shows that the trend has stopped. A factor that helps identify the strength of the reversal is how big the Harami is compared to the previous day's body. A body that is relatively large indicates more strength in the opposite direction. Additionally, the magnitude of the strength in day three adds to the potency of the reversal. (See Figures 2.72.)

Figure 2.72 The Three Inside Up pattern demonstrates the presence of buyers.

THREE STARS in the SOUTH
(Kyoku No Santen Boshi)

Description

The slow down of the trend is visually obvious (see Figure 2.73). The opposite signal pattern is the Advance Block pattern. The long black body at the end of a downtrend is the first portion of this pattern. The shadow indicates that some buying had presented itself. The next day reveals a deterioration of the selling. The third day is a Marubozu, no shadows. A bullish day following this pattern is good confirmation that the downtrend fizzled and reversed.

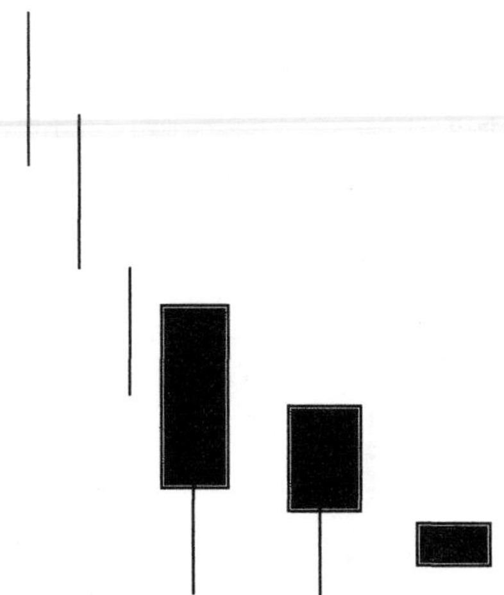

Figure 2.73 Three Stars in the South. Bullish reversal pattern. Confirmation needed.

Criteria

1. The first black candle day has a lower shadow that indicates buying stepping in—almost a Hammer but not quite.
2. The second day is like the first but on a smaller scale.
3. Day three should be a Marubozu with no shadows. It is within the previous day's trading range.

Pattern Psychology

After a downtrend, the daily formations start indicating that buyers are becoming evident. The second day indicates the same message on a small scale. Day three brings movement to a slow process. The bears should now be concerned about their positions. New lows are diminishing rapidly. This gives enough time for the short sellers to start covering their positions. (See Figure 2.74.)

Figure 2.74 The Three Stars in the South shows a waning of selling, then the buying stepping in.

THREE WHITE SOLDIERS
(Aka Sanpei)

Three White Soldiers

Description

The Advancing Three White Soldiers in Figure 2.75 (commonly known as Three White Soldiers) is a healthy market reversal pattern. It consists of three white candles, the second and third candles opening lower than the previous close but closing at a new high.

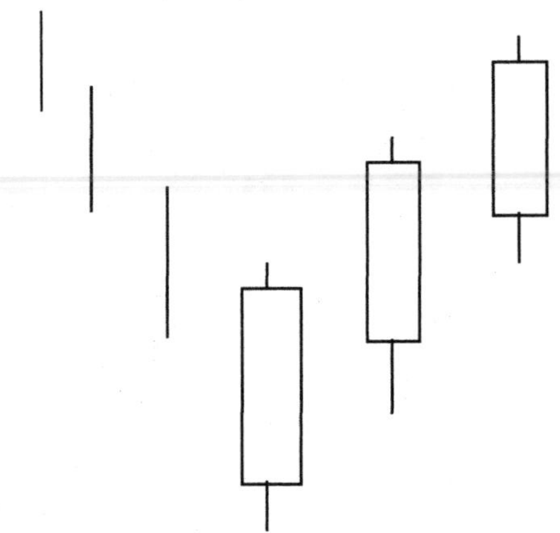

Figure 2.75 Three White Soldiers. Bullish reversal pattern. Needs no confirmation.

Criteria

1. Each consecutive long candle closes with a higher close.
2. The second and third Candlesticks open in the previous day's body.
3. Each day should close very near its high for the day.
4. The opens should be within the top half of the previous day's body.

Pattern Psychology

After a downtrend or a flat period, the presence of this formation suggests a healthy rally to be occurring. The strength of this formation consists of the fact that each day, the lower open suggests that sellers are present. By the end of each day, the buying has overcome the early sellers. This represents that a healthy continued rally has selling occurring as it is happening. As in any rally, too much buying with little selling can be dangerous. (See Figure 2.76.)

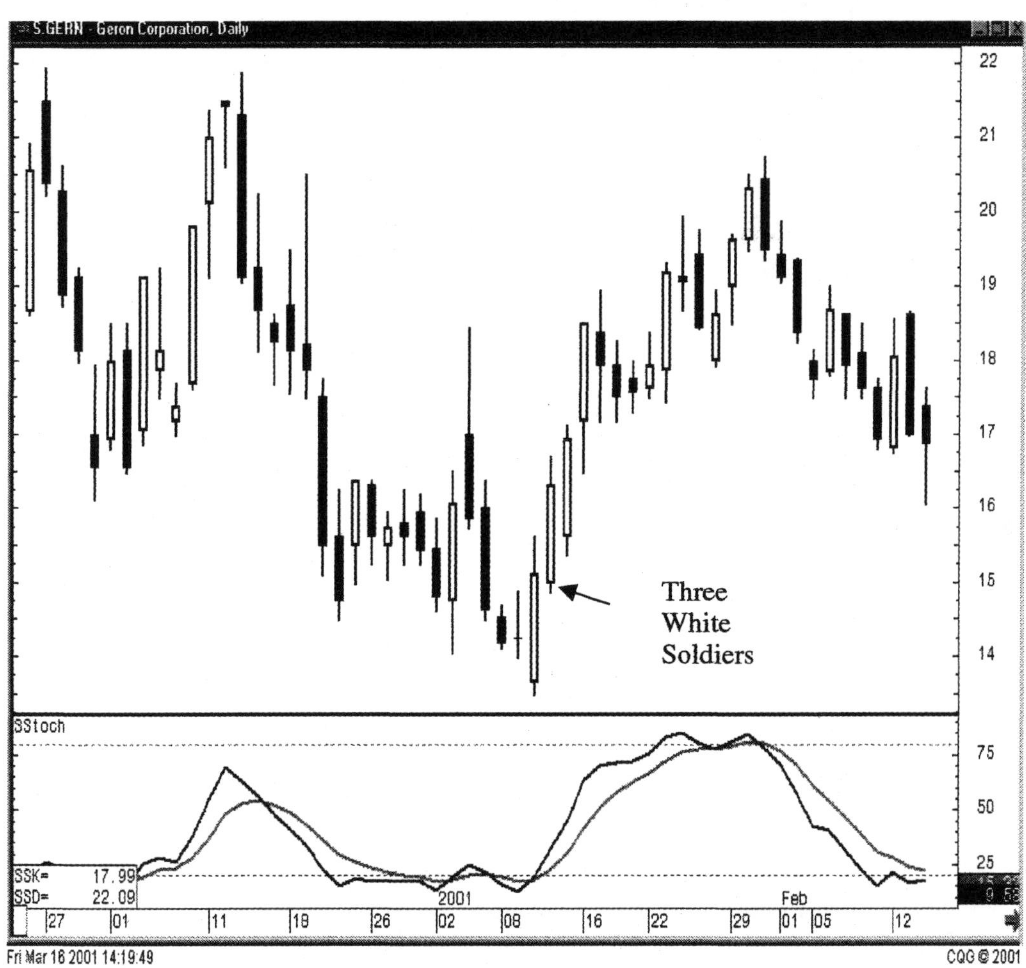

Figure 2.76 Three White Soldiers is an obvious pattern of buying.

ADVANCE BLOCK
(Saki Zumarii)

Advance Block

Description

The Advance Block in Figure 2.77 is somewhat indicative as the Three White Soldiers but it is a bearish signal. Unlike the Three White Soldiers, having consistent long candles, the Advance Block shows signs of weakness. The bodies are diminishing as prices rise and the upper shadows becoming longer indicate that the bulls are getting more resistance from the bears. This pattern is going to occur in an uptrend or occurs during a bounce up in a downtrend. It is visually obvious that the rise is losing its power.

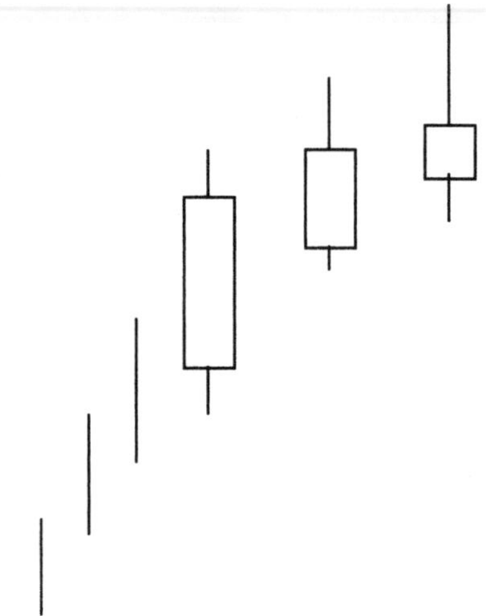

Figure 2.77 Advance Block. Bearish reversal pattern. Confirmation is suggested.

Criteria

1. Each white candle occurs with higher closes.
2. The opens occur in the previous day's body.
3. The bodies are getting smaller and/or the upper shadows are getting longer.

Pattern Psychology

After an uptrend or a bounce up during a long downtrend, the Advance Block will show itself with an initial strong white candle day. However, unlike the Three White Soldiers, each proceeding day becomes less strong. If the bulls try to take the prices up, the bears step in and take them back down. After three days of waning strength, the bears should confirm the reversal with further deterioration. (See Figure 2.78.)

Figure 2.78 The Advance Block reveals a slowing of the buying.

DELIBERATION
(Aka Sansei Shian Boshi)

Stalled pattern

Description

Another pattern close to the Three White Soldiers pattern is the Deliberation pattern as seen in Figure 2.79. It is formed by two long white bodies. These are followed by a small white candle. This last candle may have opened at or near the previous day's close or it may have gapped up. The Japanese say that this is the time for deliberation. The slow down in the advance is time for the bulls to get out.

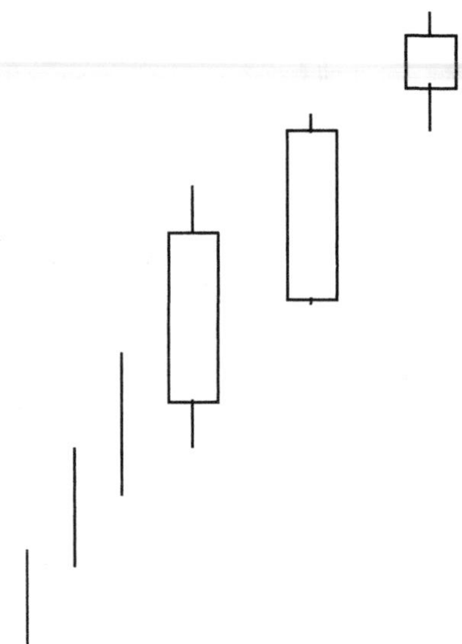

Figure 2.79 Deliberation. Bearish reversal pattern. Confirmation is suggested.

Criteria

1. The first two white candles are relatively equal long candles.
2. The third day is a small body.
3. The small body opened at or very near the previous day's close. Or it may have gapped up slightly.

Pattern Psychology

After an uptrend or a bounce up during a long downtrend, the deliberation signal can occur. Like the Advance Block signal, this pattern also represents buyer weakness. In this case, it shows the weakness in one day. This pattern is slightly more difficult to recognize than the Advance Block Pattern. (See Figure 2.80.)

Figure 2.80 The Deliberation pattern shows the buying diminishing.

CONCEALING BABY SWALLOW (Kotsubame Tsutsumi)

Bullish Reversal Pattern

CONCEALING BABY SWALLOW

Description

The first two days of the signal, two Black Marubozus demonstrate the continuation of the downtrend (see Figure 2.81). The third day, the Reverse Hammer illustrates that the downtrend is losing steam. Notice that it gapped down on the open, then traded up into the previous days trading range. This demonstrated buying strength. The last day opens higher and closes below the previous days close. It completely engulfs the whole trading range of the prior day. Although the trading ended at the trends low point, the magnitude of the downtrend had deteriorated significantly. Expect buying to show itself at these levels. This is a very rare signal.

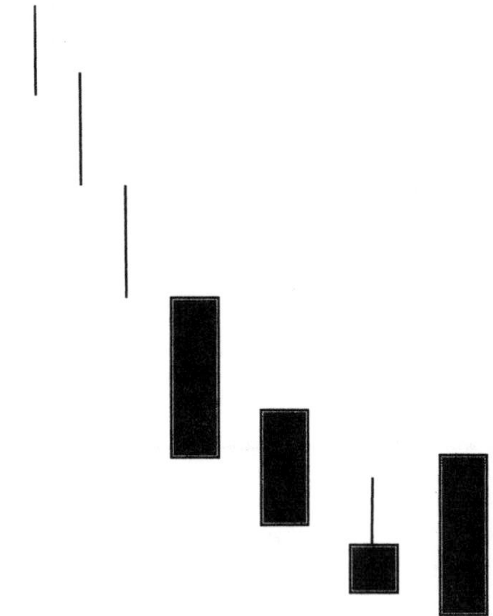

Figure 2.81 Concealing Baby Swallow. Confirmation not needed.

Criteria

1. Two large Black Marubozus make up the beginning of this pattern.
2. The third day is a Reverse Hammer formation. It gaps down from the previous day's close.
3. The final day completely engulfs the third day, including the shadow.

Pattern Psychology

The bears have been in control for awhile. At the end of a downtrend, two Black Marubozu days appear. The third day gaps down at its low, and then trades up into the trading range of the previous day. This buying is then negated by the sellers stepping back in. However, the bears have taken notice of the buying that occurred. The final day opens higher, again causing much concern for the sellers. As it sells off for the rest of the day, the concerned shorts have time to cover their positions. The new closing low is not of the same magnitude of the previous down days of the trend. The buyers do not run into very much selling resistance from here. There is no chart to illustrate this pattern.

STICK SANDWICH
(Gyakusashi Niten Zoko)

Stick Sandwich Pattern

Description

The Stick Sandwich in Figure 2.82 looks somewhat like an ice cream sandwich. It consists of two dark candles with a white candle in between. The closing prices of the two black candles are equal. This demonstrates an obvious support price. The probability of a reversal in the trend is high from this area.

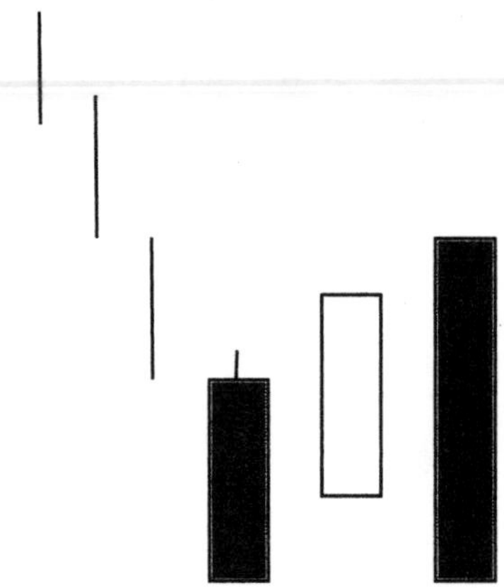

Figure 2.82 Stick Sandwich pattern. Bullish reversal pattern. Confirmation is suggested.

Criteria

1. A downtrend is concluded with a large black candle followed by a white candle. The white candle opens above the black candle close and closes above the black candles open.
2. The final day completely engulfs the white candle and closes at the same level as the previous black candle.

Pattern Psychology

The bears have been in control for awhile. At the end of the downtrend, the last black candle is followed by a large white candle. The white candle opens higher than the close of the last black candle. It trades up for the rest of the day, closing above where the previous day opened. This action makes apparent to the bears that the downtrend may be coming to an end. The next day opens higher but trades down for the rest of the day. It cannot close lower than the previous low close of two days prior. The shorts take notice and start covering upon any buying strength over the next couple of days. (See Figure 2.83.)

Figure 2.83 The Stick Sandwich pattern reveals the last gasp of the sellers.

HOMING PIGEON
(Shita Banare Kobato Gaeshi)

HOMING PIGEON

Description

The Homing Pigeon in Figure 2.84 is the same as the Harami except for the color of the second day's body. The pattern is composed of a two-candle formation in a downtrending market. Both candles are the same color as the current trend. The first body of the pattern is a long body, the second body is smaller. The open and the close of the second day occurs inside the open and the close of the previous day. Its presence indicates that the trend is over.

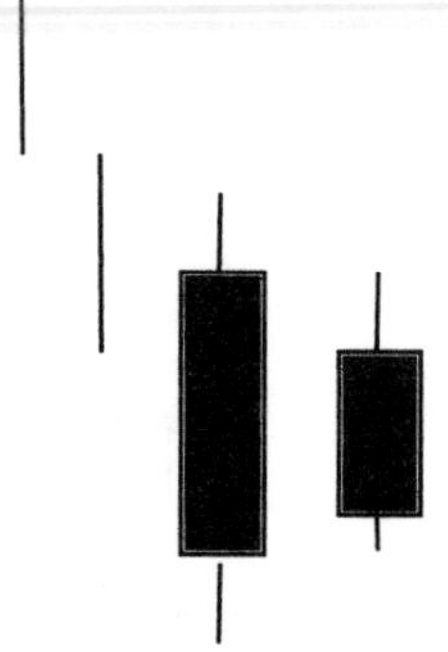

Figure 2.84 Homing Pigeon.

Criteria

1. The body of the first candle is black, the body of the second candle is black.
2. The downtrend has been evident for a good period. A long black candle occurs at the end of the trend.
3. The second day opens higher than the close of the previous day and closes lower than the open but above the closing price of the prior day.
4. Unlike the Western Inside Day, just the body needs to remain in the previous day's body, where as the Inside Day requires both the body and the shadows to remain inside the previous day's body.
5. For a reversal signal, further confirmation is required to indicate that the trend is moving up.

Signal Enhancements

1. The higher the second candle closes up on the first black candle, the more convincing that a reversal has occurred.

Pattern Psychology

After a strong downtrend has been in effect and after a long black candle, the bulls open the price higher than the previous close. The shorts get concerned and start covering. The price finishes lower for the day but not as low as the previous day. This is enough support to have the short sellers take notice that the trend has been violated. A strong day after that would convince everybody that the trend was reversing. Usually the volume is above the recent norm due to the unwinding of short positions. (See Figure 2.85.)

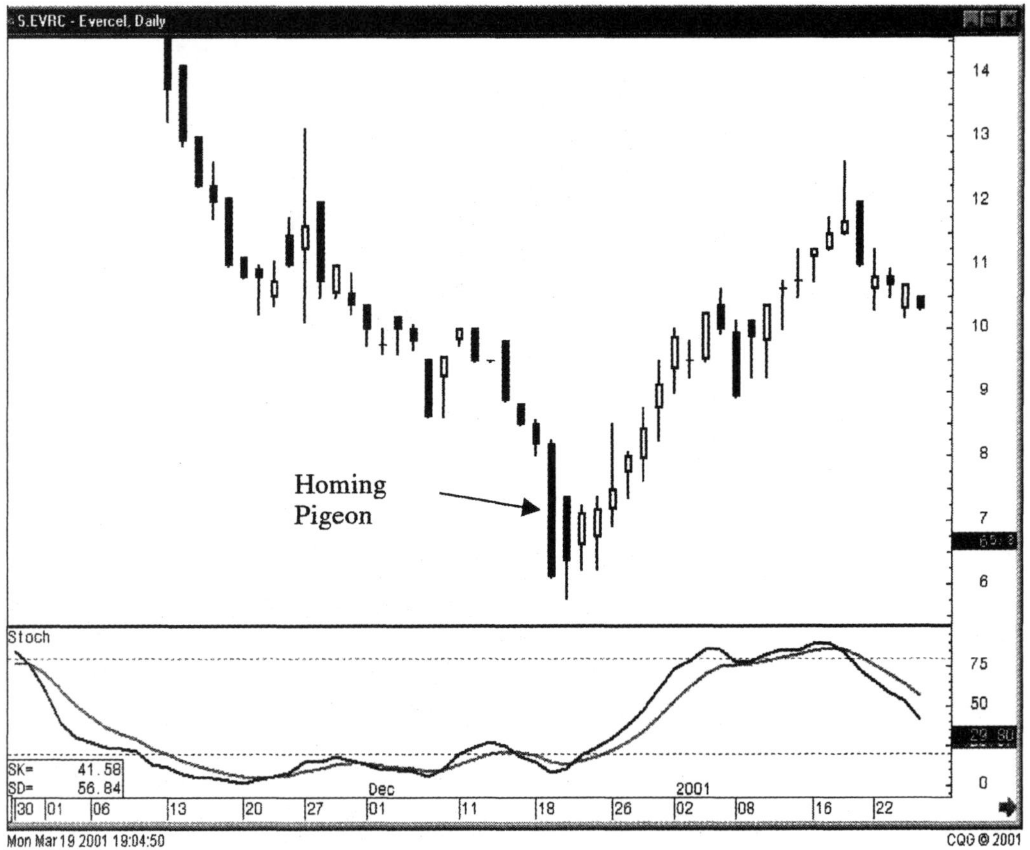

Figure 2.85 The Homing pigeon reveals diminishing selling pressure.

LADDER BOTTOM
(Hashigo Gaeshi)

LADDER BOTTOM

Description

The downtrend shown in Figure 2.86 is finishing with four consecutive black candles, each closing lower than the previous day. The fourth day is different. It opens and trades higher during the day, even though it closes the day on the low. The next day opens higher than the open of the previous day, a gap up, and continues to head up all day. The final day of the signal closes higher than the trading range of the past three days.

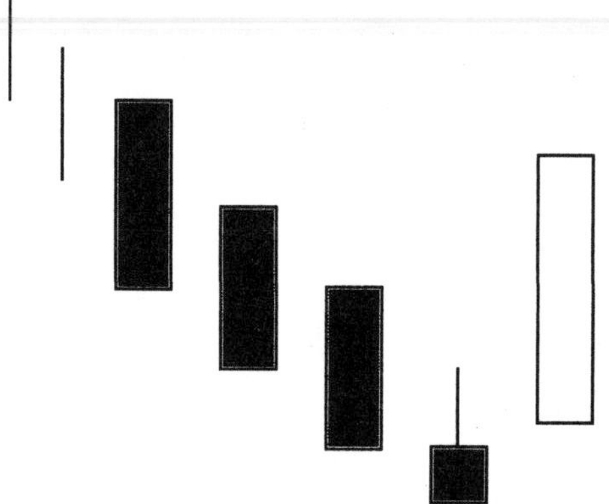

Figure 2.86 Bullish Reversal Pattern. Ladder Bottom. Confirmation is suggested.

Criteria

1. Like the Three Black Crows pattern, the beginning of the signal has three black candle days, each with lower opens and closes of the previous day.
2. The fourth day resembles a reverse hammer, opening, then trading up during the day before closing on its low.
3. The final day opens above the open of the previous day open, a gap up and continues upward for the rest the day, a Kicker-type pattern. It finally closes above the trading range of the previous three days.

Pattern Psychology

After a strong downtrend has been in effect for a while, there is a day when prices try to climb back up to the previous day's high. This gets the bears attention even though in closes on the low that day. When it opens up much higher the next day, the bears start scrambling to cover and the bulls start taking control. If volume increases noticeably on the final day, that will be a good indication that the bulls and the bears have exchanged their positioning. (See Figure 2.87.)

Figure 2.87 The Ladder Bottom is a slowing down of selling, then the buyers taking over.

MATCHING LOW
(Niten Zoko/Kenuki)

LOW

Description

The Matching Low pattern in Figure 2.88 is similar to the Homing Pigeon pattern, the exception being that the two days of the pattern close on their lows, at the same level. After a long downtrend, recognizing that the price has closed at the same level without going through is an indication to the bears that the bottom has been hit.

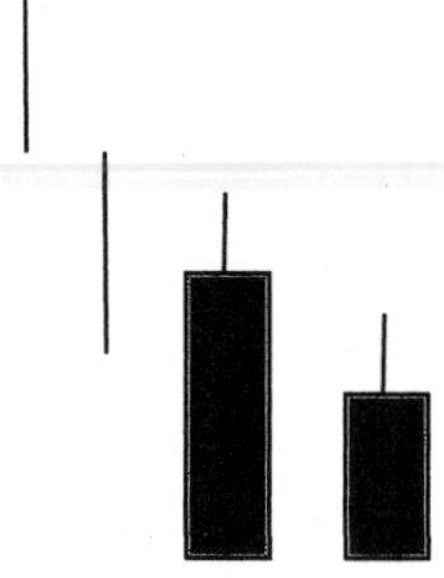

Figure 2.88 Matching Low.

Criteria

1. The body of the first candle is black; the body of the second candle is black.
2. The downtrend has been evident for a good period. A long black candle occurs at the end of the trend.
3. The second day opens higher than the close of the previous day and closes at the same close as the prior day.
4. For a reversal signal, further confirmation is required to indicate that the trend is moving up.

Pattern Psychology

After a strong downtrend has been in effect and after a long black candle, the bulls open the price higher than the previous close. The shorts get concerned and start covering. However, the bears still have enough control to close the price at the low of the day, the low being the same as the close of the previous day. The psychological impact for the bears is that it couldn't close below the previous close, thus causing concern that this is a support level. (See Figure 2.89.)

Figure 2.89 The Matching Low pattern establishes the closing prices as a support level.

Chapter 3

CONTINUATION PATTERNS

Most Candlestick signals are reversal patterns; however, there are periods of trends that represent rest. The Japanese insight is, "There are times to buy, times to sell, and times to rest." Once a pattern is recognized, it is suggesting a direction for future price movement. Continuation patterns help with the decision-making process. Whatever the pattern, a decision has to be made—even if the decision is to do nothing.

For easier reference, continuation patterns have a chapter of their own. The continuation patterns included in this chapter are:

- UPSIDE TASUKI GAP
- DOWNSIDE TASUKI GAP
- ON NECK LINE
- IN NECK LINE
- THRUSTING
- RISING THREE METHOD
- FALLING THREE METHOD
- SIDE-BY-SIDE WHITE LINES
- SEPARATING LINES
- MAT HOLD
- THREE-LINE STRIKE
- UPSIDE GAP THREE METHOD

UPSIDE TASUKI GAP
(uwa banare tasuki)

Description

The Upside Tasuki Gap is found in a rising trend. A white candle forms after gapping up from the previous white candle, as shown in Figure 3.1. The next day opens lower and closes lower than the previous day. If the gap is not filled, the bulls have maintained control. If the gap was filled, then the bullish momentum has come to an end. If the gap is not filled, it is time to go long if not long already. The definition of Tasuki is a sash that holds up one's sleeve.

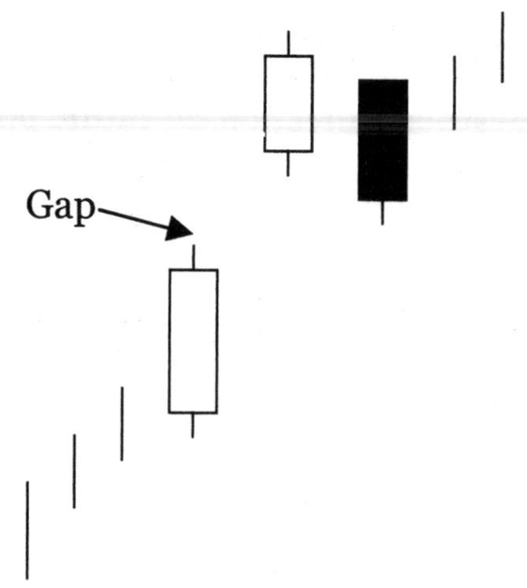

Figure 3.1 Upside Tasuki Gap. Confirmation is required.

Criteria

1. An uptrend is in progress. A gap occurs between two candles of the same color.
2. The color of the first two candles is the same as the prevailing trend.
3. The third day, an opposite color candlestick opens within the previous candle and closes below the previous open.

4. The third day close does not fill the gap between the two white candles.
5. The last two candles, opposite colors, are usually about the same size.

Pattern Psychology

Explaining the Tasuki Gap is simple. The Japanese place significance on gaps. When one appears in the middle of the trend and is not able to fill itself on weakness the next day, the strength is still in the uptrend. The pullback day is now construed as being a profit-taking day. (See Figure 3.2.)

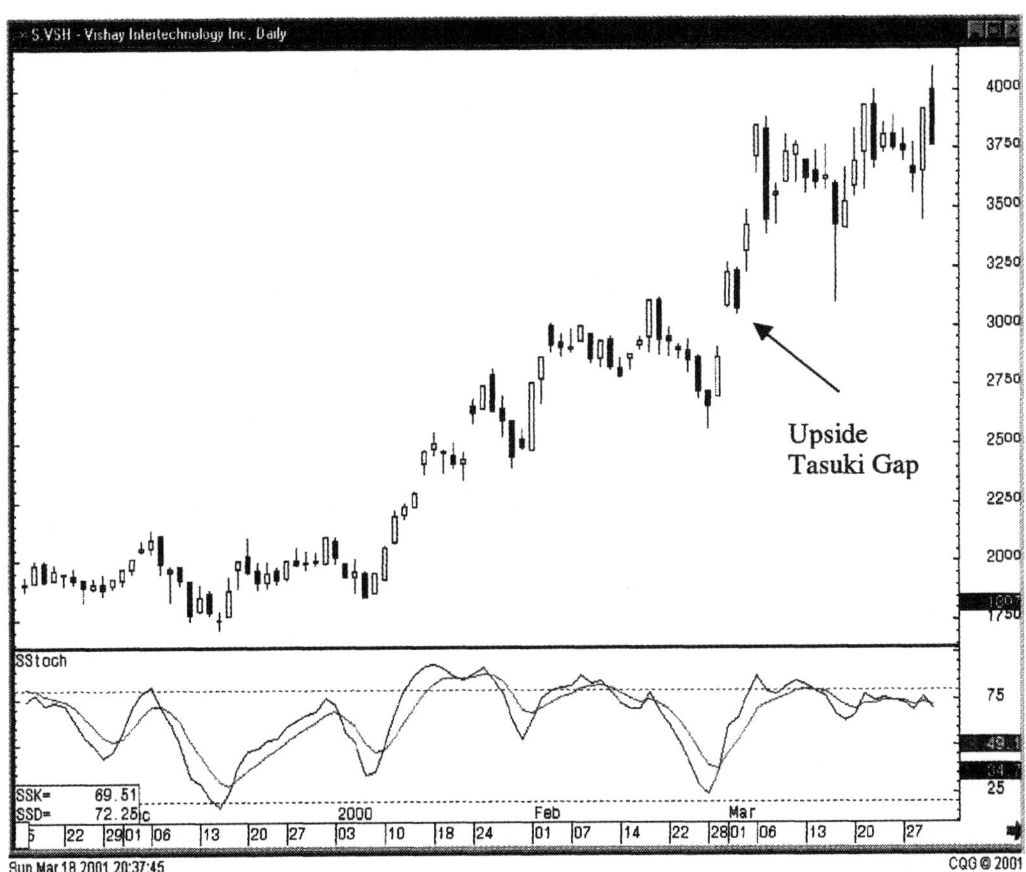

Figure 3.2 Upside Tasuki Gap.

DOWNSIDE TASUKI GAP
(SHITA banare tasuki)

Description

The Downside Tasuki Gap is found during a declining trend. A black candle forms after gapping down from the previous black candle. The next day opens higher and closes higher than the previous day's open. If the gap is not filled, the bears have maintained control. If the gap was filled, then the bearish momentum has come to an end. If the gap is not filled, it is time to go short if not short already. You will find the Tasuki pattern more often in the Upside pattern than the Downside pattern. (See Figure 3.3.)

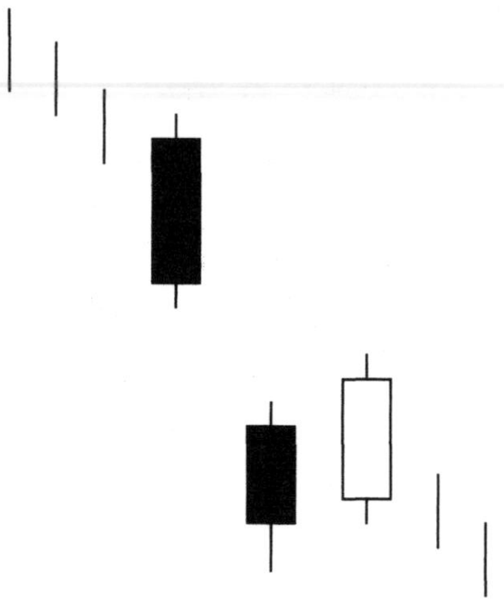

Figure 3.3 Confirmation is required.

Criteria

1. A downtrend is in progress. A gap occurs between two candles of the same color.
2. The color of the first two candles is the same as the prevailing trend.
3. The third day, an opposite color candlestick opens within the previous candle and closes below the previous open.
4. The third day close does not fill the gap between the two black candles.
5. The last two candles, opposite colors, are usually about the same size.

Pattern Psychology

Just the opposite as the Upward Tasuki, explaining the Tasuki gap is simple. The Japanese put significance into gaps. When one appears in the middle of the trend and is not able to fill itself on strength the next day, the momentum is still in the downtrend. The bounceup day should be construed as being a short-covering day. After the short covering disappears, the selling continues. (See Figure 3.4.)

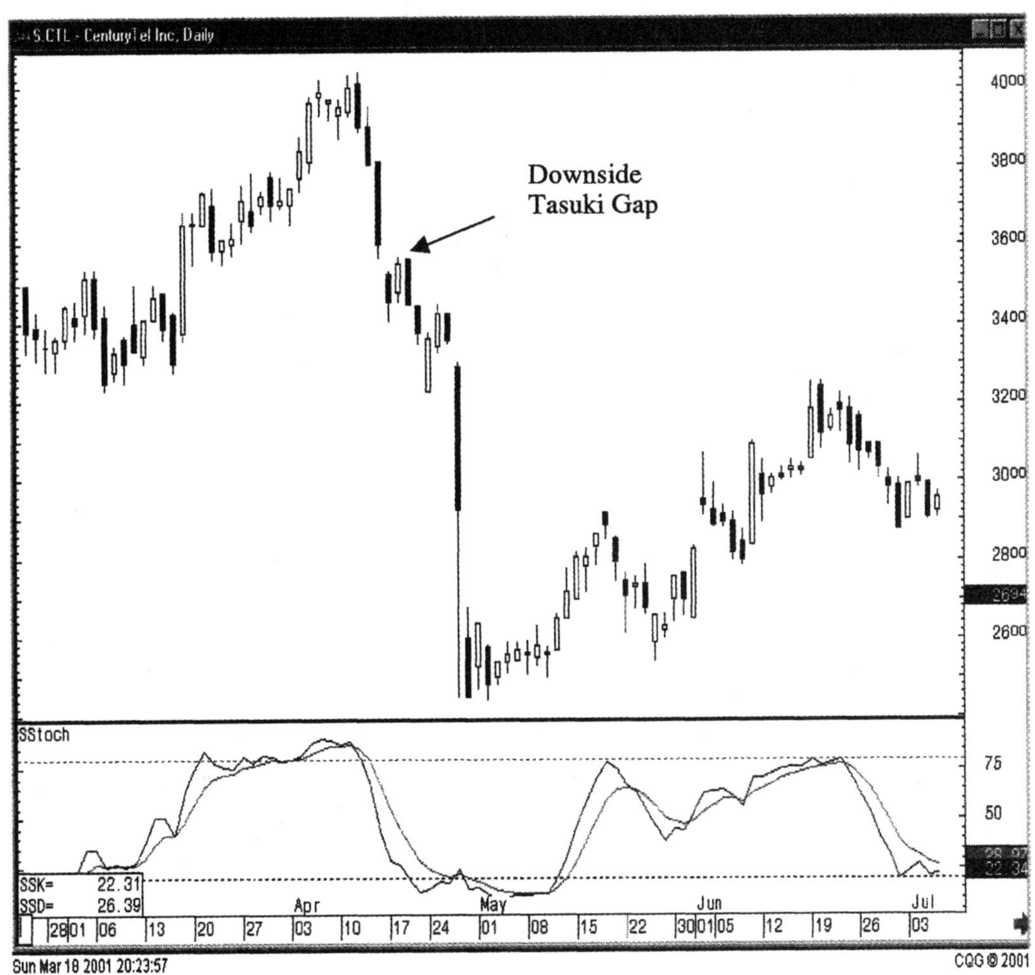

Figure 3.4 Downside Tasuki Gap.

ON NECK LINE
(ate kubi)

Description

The On Neck pattern is almost a Meeting Line pattern, but the critical term is almost. The On Neck pattern does not reach the previous day's close; it only reaches the previous day's low. (See Figure 3.5.)

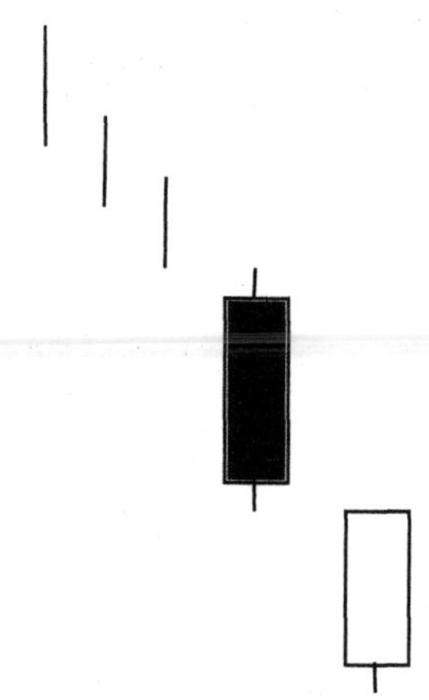

Figure 3.5 Confirmation is suggested. Bearish continuation pattern.

Criteria

1. A long black candle forms in a downtrend.
2. The next day gaps down from the previous day's close; however, the body is usually smaller than one seen in the Meeting Line pattern.
3. The second day closes at the low of the previous day.

Pattern Psychology

After a market has been moving in a downward direction, a long black candle enhances the downtrend. The next day opens lower, a small gap down, but the trend is halted by a move back up to the previous day's low. The buyers in this upmove should be uncomfortable that there was not more strength in the upmove. The sellers step back in the next day to continue the downtrend. (See Figure 3.6.)

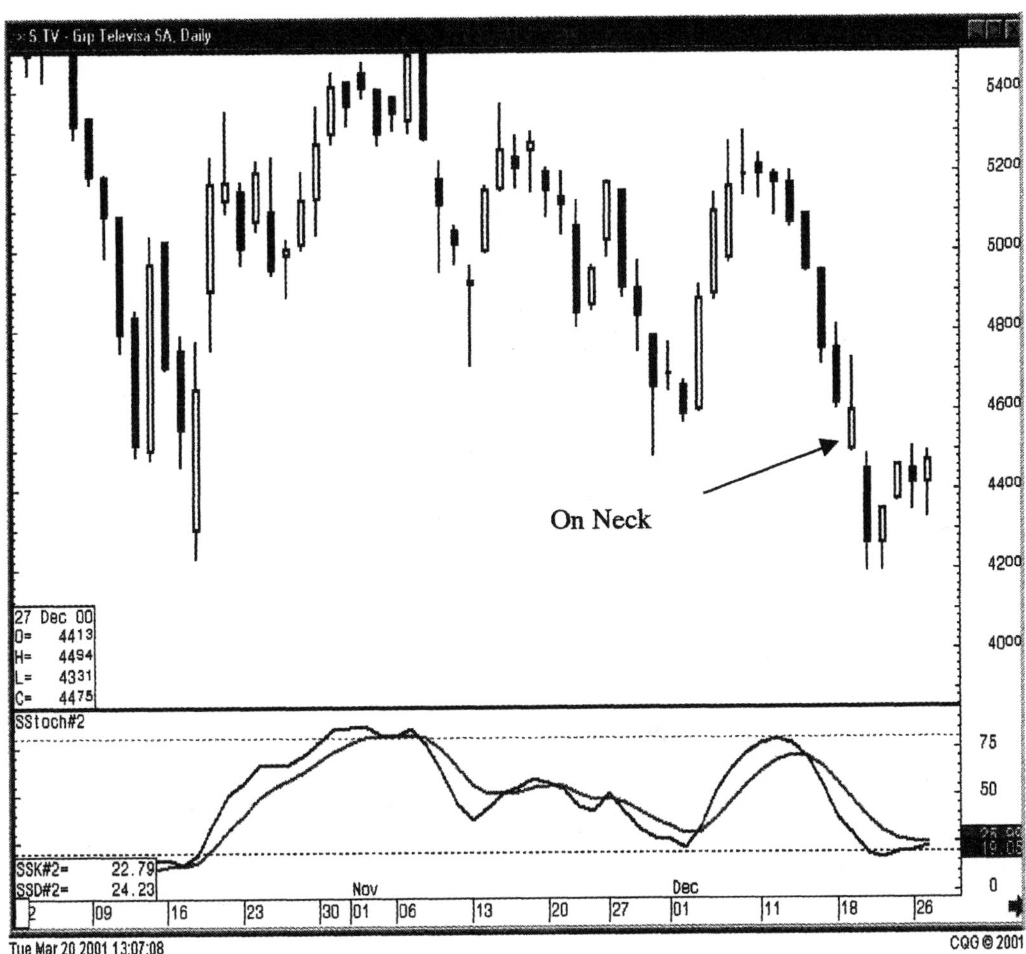

Figure 3.6 On Neck.

IN NECK LINE
(iri kubi)

Description

The In Neck pattern, shown in Figure 3.7, is almost a Meeting Line pattern also. It has the same description as the On Neck pattern except that it closes at or slightly above the previous day's close.

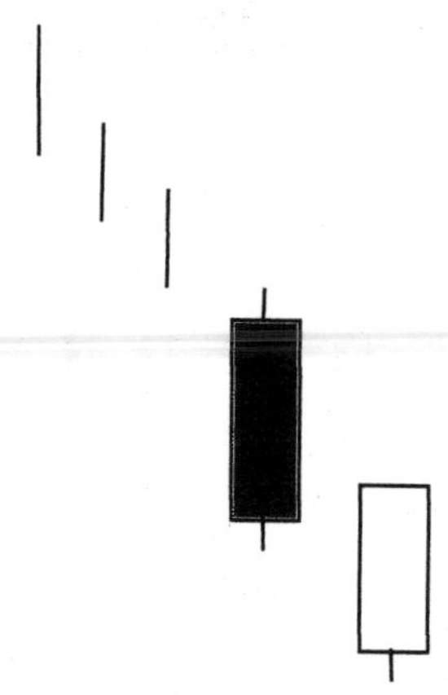

Figure 3.7 Confirmation is suggested. Bearish continuation pattern.

Criteria

1. A long black candle forms in a downtrend.
2. The next day gaps down from the previous day's close; however, the body is usually smaller than one seen in the Meeting Line pattern.
3. The second day closes at the close or just slightly above the close of the previous day.

Pattern Psychology

This is the same scenario as the On Neck pattern. After a market has been moving in a downward direction, a long black candle enhances the downtrend. The next day opens lower, a small gap down, but the trend is halted by a move back up to the previous day's low. The buyers in this upmove should be uncomfortable that there was not more strength in the upmove. The sellers step back in the next day to continue the downtrend. (See Figure 3.8.)

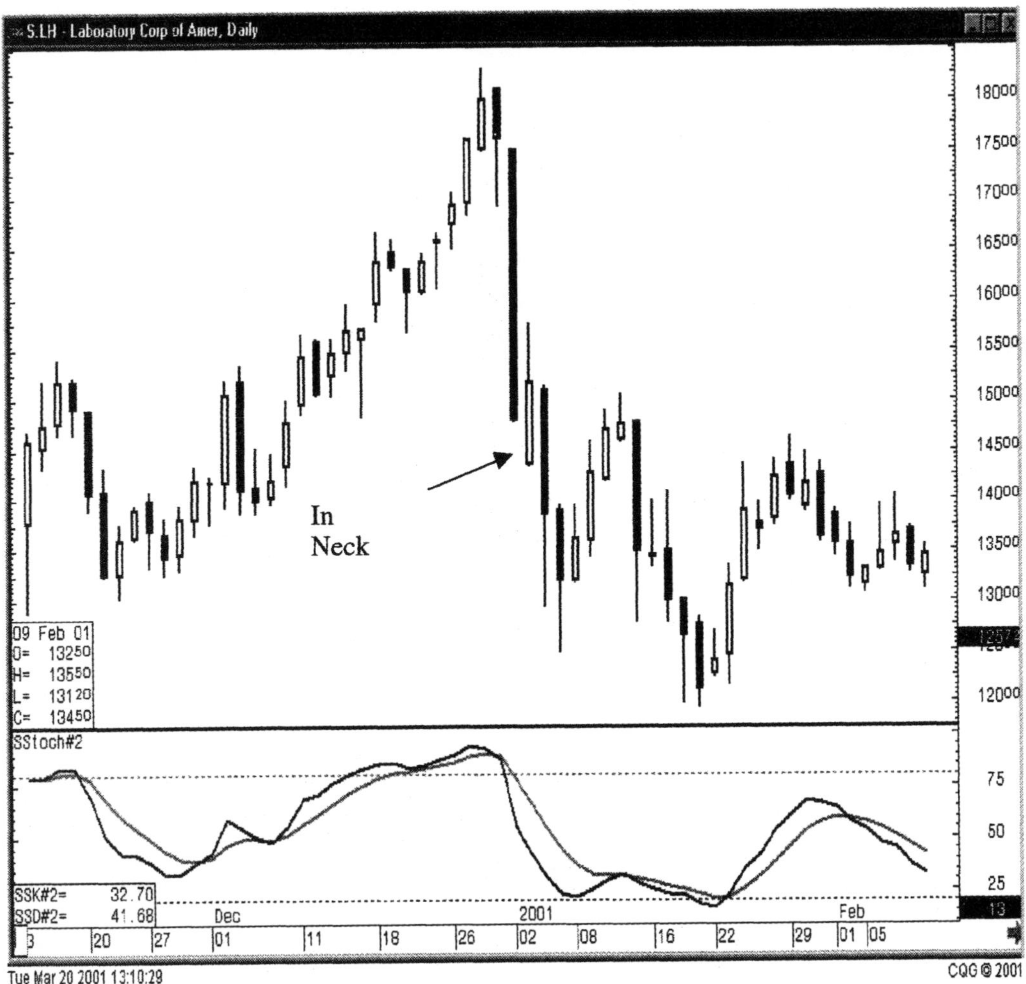

Figure 3.8 In Neck Line indicates some short covering, but not a change in trend direction.

THRUSTING
(sashikomi)

Description

The Thrusting pattern, seen in Figure 3.9, is almost an On Neck or an In Neck pattern and resembles the Meeting Line pattern, also. It has the same description as the On Neck pattern except that it closes near, but slightly below the midpoint of the previous day's black body.

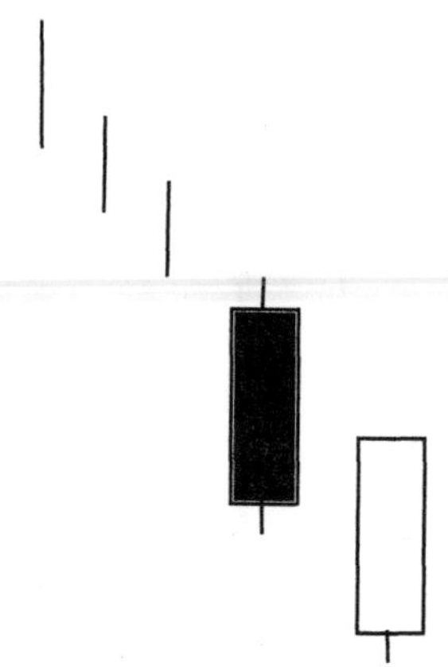

Figure 3.9 Confirmation is suggested. Bearish continuation pattern.

Criteria

1. A long black candle forms in a downtrend.
2. The next day gaps down from the previous day's close; however, the body is usually bigger than the ones found in the On Neck and In Neck patterns.
3. The second day closes just slightly below the midpoint of the previous day's candle.

Pattern Psychology

This is the same scenario as the On Neck pattern. After a market has been moving in a downward direction, a long black candle enhances the downtrend. The next day opens lower, a small gap down, but the trend is halted by a move back up to the previous day's low. The buyers in this upmove should be uncomfortable that there was not more strength in the upmove. The sellers step back in the next day to continue the downtrend. It is a little stronger than the On Neck and In Neck patterns, but not quite as strong as a Piercing Line pattern. (See Figure 3.10.)

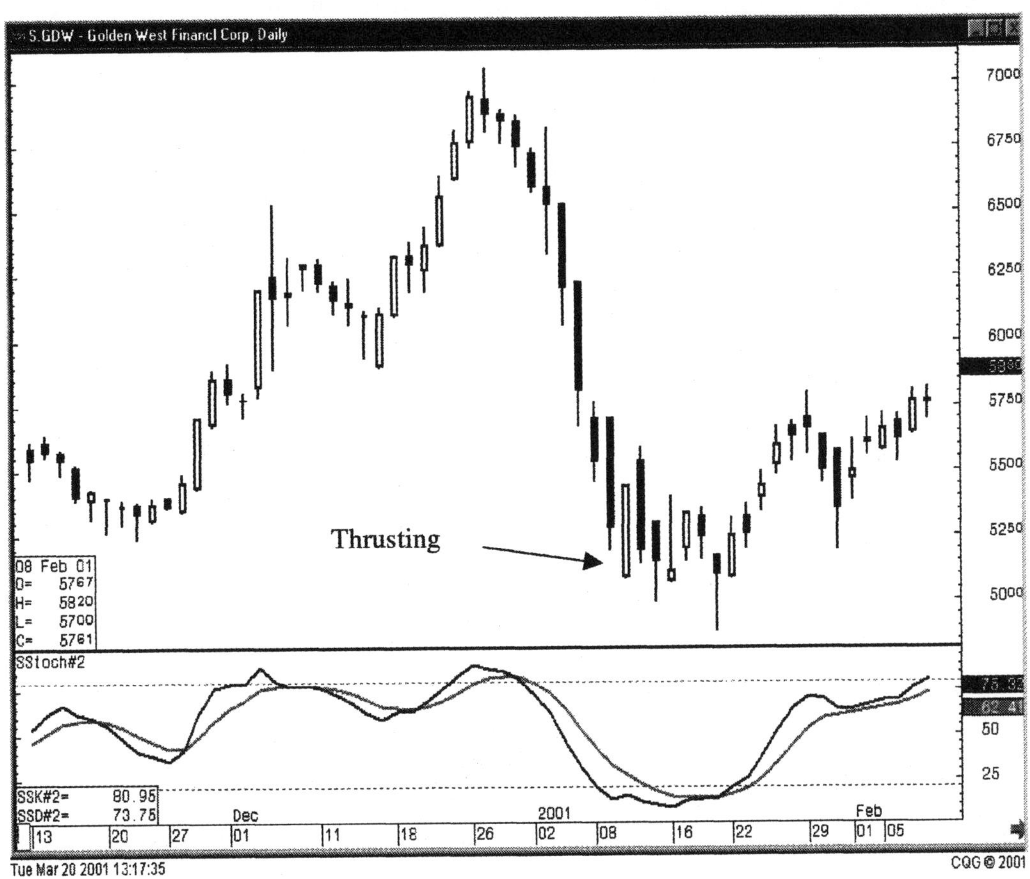

Figure 3.10 Thrusting.

RISING THREE METHOD
(uwa banare sanpoo ohdatekomi)

Description

The Rising Three Method is an easy pattern to see during uptrends. A long, white candle forms. It is then followed by a series of small candles, each consecutively getting lower. The optimal number of pull-back days should be three. Two or four or five pull-back days can also be observed. The important factor is that they do not close below the open of the big white candle. It is also preferred that the shadows do not go below the white candle's open. The final day of the formation should open up in the body of the last pull-back day and close higher than the first big white candle. (See Figure 3.11.)

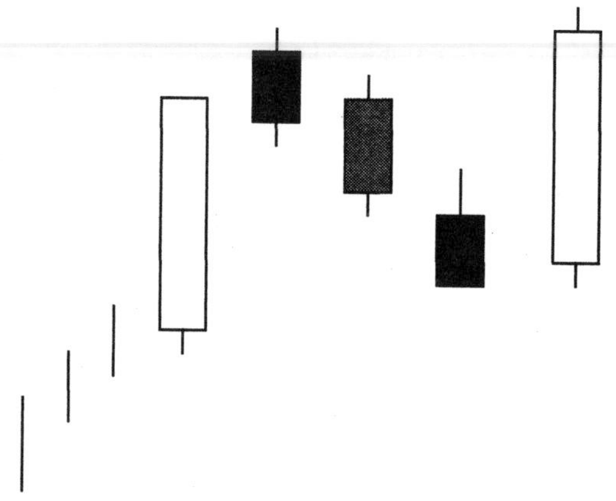

Figure 3.11 Confirmation is not required.

Criteria

1. An uptrend is in progress. A long white candle forms.
2. A group of small-bodied candles follow, preferably black bodies.
3. The close of any of the pull-back days does not close lower than the open of the big white candle.
4. The final day opens up into the body of the last pull-back day and proceeds to close above the close of the first big white candle day.

Pattern Psychology

The Rising Three Method, seen in Figure 3.12, is considered a rest in the trend or, in Japanese terms, a rest from battle. The concept is that the first black candle day brings some doubt into the bull camp. The next day does the same. By the third day, the bulls are now convinced that the bears do not have the strength to push prices down anymore. The bulls get their courage back and start stepping in. The pattern resembles the Western bull flag or pennant formation, however, the concept was originally developed in the 1700s. In modern terms, the market was just "taking a breather."

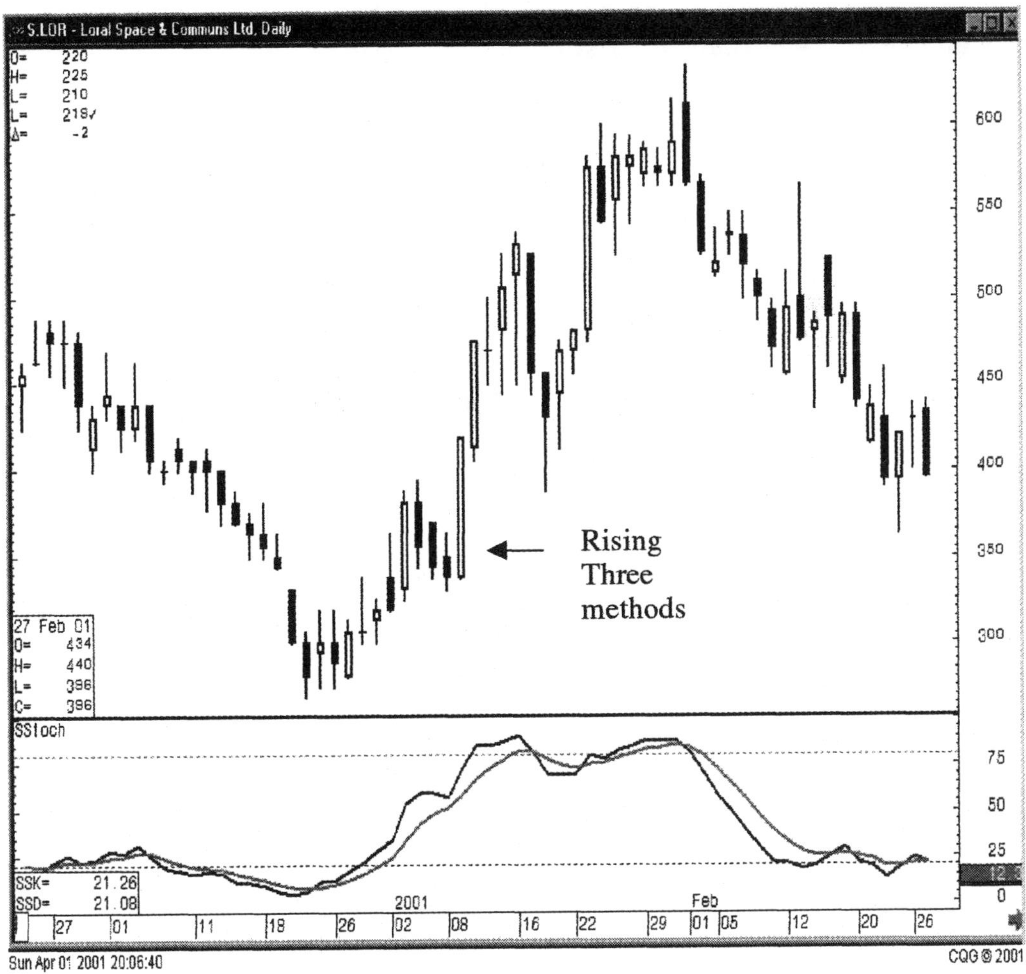

Figure 3.12 Rising Three Method shows the lack of bearish conviction.

FALLING THREE METHOD
(shita banare sanpoo ohdatekomi)

Description

The Falling Three Method, seen in Figure 3.13, is basically the opposite of the Rising Three Method. The market has been in a downtrend. A long black candle forms. It is then followed by a series of small candles, each consecutively getting higher. The optimal number of uptrending days should be three. Again, two or four or five counter trend days can be observed. The important factors are that they do not close above the open of the big black candle and that the shadows do not go above the black candle's open. The final day of the formation should open down in the body of the last uptrend day and close lower than the first big black candle's close.

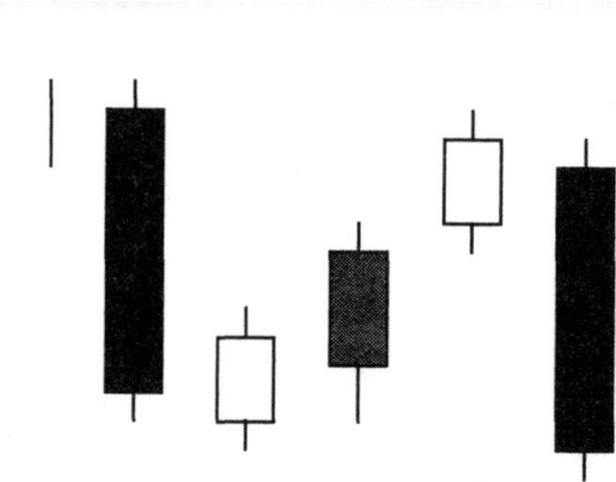

Figure 3.13 Falling Three Method. Confirmation is not required.

Criteria

1. A downtrend is in progress. A long black candle forms.
2. A group of small-bodied candles follow, preferably white bodied.
3. The close of any of the uptrend days does not close higher than the open of the big white candle.
4. The final day opens up into the body of the last uptrend day and proceeds to close below the close of the first big black candle day.

Pattern Psychology

The Falling Three Method is considered a rest in the downtrend. Just like the Rising Three Method, the appearance of the white candle unnerves the bears. But as they see the bulls unable to take the prices higher, the bears gain their confidence back and resume their selling. The concept is that the first black candle day brings some doubt into the bull camp. The next day does the same. By the third day, the bears are now convinced that the bulls do not have the strength to push prices up anymore. The bulls get their courage back and start stepping in. (See Figure 3.14.)

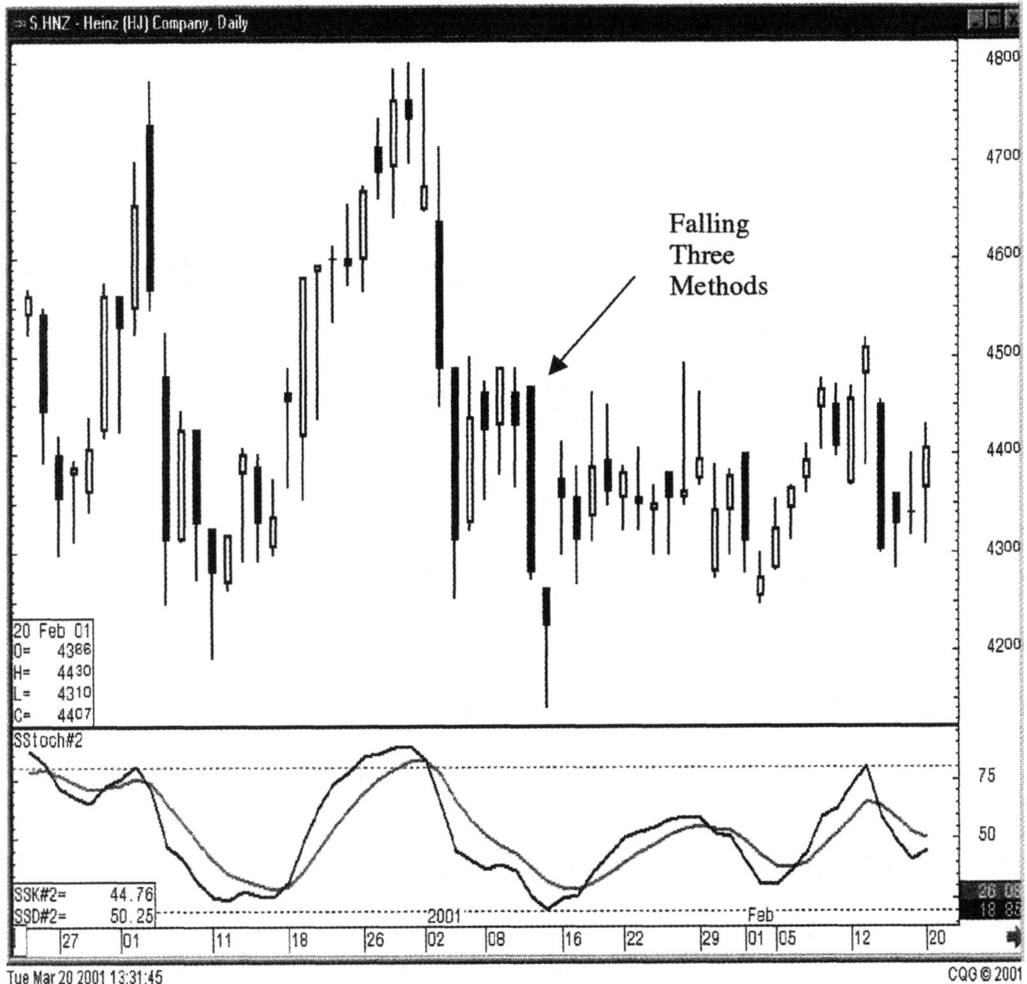

Figure 3.14 Falling Three Method shows that the bulls did not have enough power to move prices up.

SIDE-BY-SIDE WHITE LINES
(narabi aka)

Description

Side-by-Side White Lines are found in uptrends. Two white candles form side-by-side after gapping up from the previous white candle. Narabi in Japanese means "in a row." *Narabi aka* means "whites in a row," Side-by-Side Lines, black or white, indicate a pause or stalemate when they are observed by themselves. In this case, they have a different meaning because they occur after a gap in the trend's direction. (See Figure 3.15.)

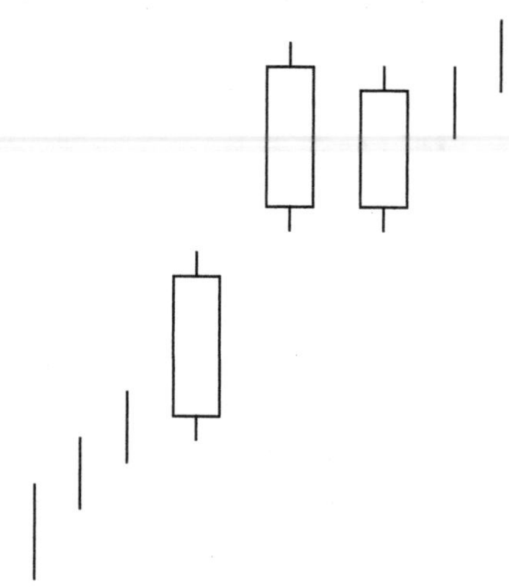

Figure 3.15 Side-by-Side White Lines. Confirmation is not required.

Criteria

1. An uptrend is in progress. A gap occurs between two candles of the same color.
2. The color of the first two candles is the same as the prevailing trend.
3. The third day, a candle opens at the same or near the open price of the previous day.
4. The third day closes near the close of the previous day.

Pattern Psychology

During a downtrend, a white candle gaps up from the white candle of the previous day. The next day opens at the open of the gap up; yet, it persists in maintaining the upward move again. This indicates that the bears were making a try to turn the trend around, but lost to the bulls almost immediately. These patterns are somewhat rare, but at least you will know what is happening when you see this formation. (See Figure 3.16.)

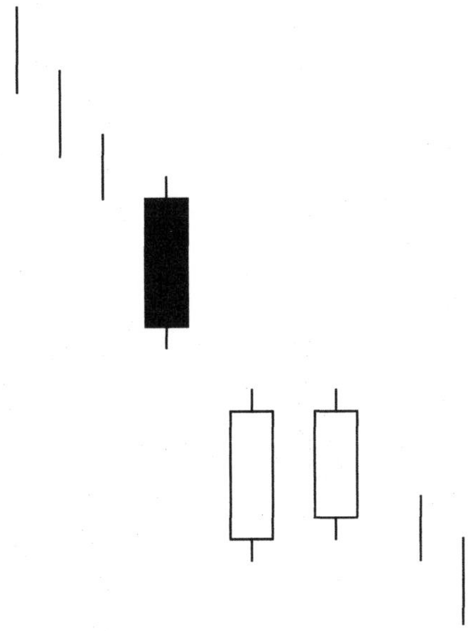

Figure 3.16 White candles during an uptrend.

The bearish Side-by-Side Line pattern is more rare than the bullish Side-by-Side. It represents short covering occurring. When the sellers step in again, more short covering occurs. Finally when the short covering is over, the downtrend continues.

SEPARATING LINES
(iki chigai sen)

Description

Iki chigai sen is defined as "lines that move in opposite directions." The market is in an uptrend when there is a pull-back, exhibited by a long black candle, as seen in Figure 3.17. However, the next day opens back up at the level that it opened the prior day. The Separating Line Pattern has the same open and is the opposite colors. This is the exact reverse of the Meeting Line Pattern. In other Japanese circles, this is also known as *Furiwake* or Dividing Lines.

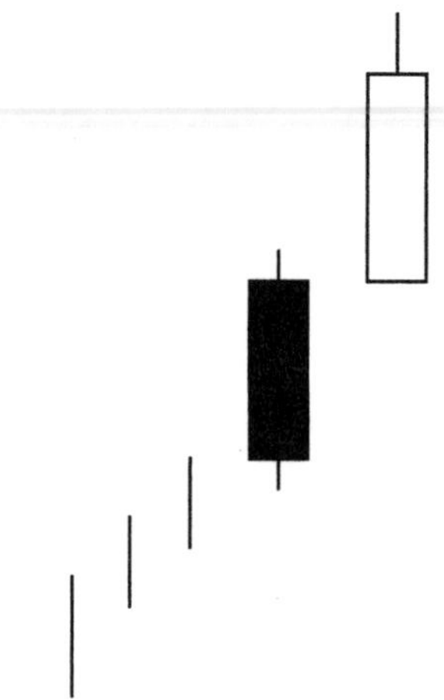

Figure 3.17 Separating Lines. Confirmation is required.

Criteria

1. An uptrend is in progress. Then a day occurs that is the opposite color of the current trend.
2. The second day opens at the open of the previous day.
3. The second day, should open on its low for the day and proceed to go higher.

Pattern Psychology

During the uptrend, a black body occurs. This causes some concern to the bulls. But the next day the prices gap back up to the previous day's open. This gives the bulls confidence that the trend still has life in it. They jump back in and move prices higher. Confidence is renewed and the trend continues. The bearish Separating Line works the exact same way in the opposite direction. (See Figure 3.18.)

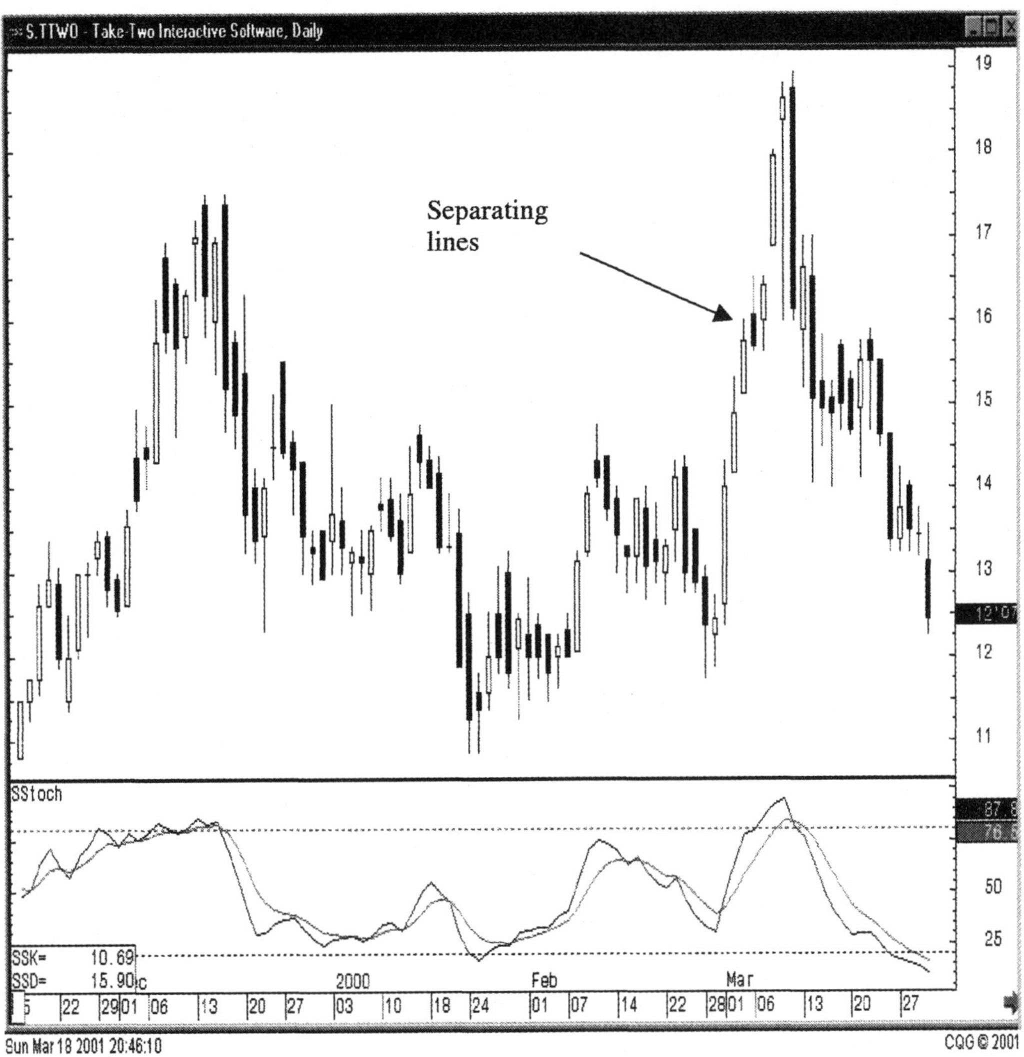

Figure 3.18 Separating Lines give the foresight of a trend continuing.

MAT HOLD
(uwa banare sante oshi)

Description

The Mat Hold pattern, shown in Figure 3.19, is similar to the Rising Three Method. It has the look of the Upside Gap Two Crows except that the second black body (third day) dips into the body of the large white candle. It is followed by another small black body that dips a little further into the white candle body. The final day gaps to the upside. It continues its upward move to close higher than the trading range of any of the previous days. The implication is that the trend has not been stalled. This is a good point to add to positions. The Mat Hold pattern is a stronger continuation pattern than the Rising Three Method. During the days of "rest," unlike the Rising Three Method, the price stays close to the top of the white candle's upper range.

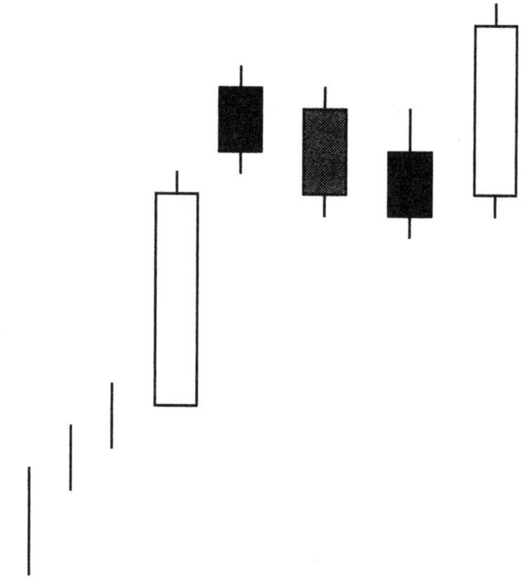

Figure 3.19 Mat Hold. Confirmation is not required.

Criteria

1. An uptrend is in progress. A long white candle forms.
2. A gap up day that closes lower than its open creates a small black candle.

3. The next two days form small candles somewhat like the Rising Three Method.
4. The final day gaps up and closes above the trading ranges of the previous four days.

Pattern Psychology

The Rising Three Method is considered a rest in the trend, whereas the Mat Hold pattern does not fall back as far. The Mat Hold is easier to identify. The pull-back days are less concerning. The relatively flat rest period does not create the concern that the Rising Three Method does. After three days of the bears not being able to knock the price down to any great degree, the bulls step back in with confidence. (See Figure 3.20.)

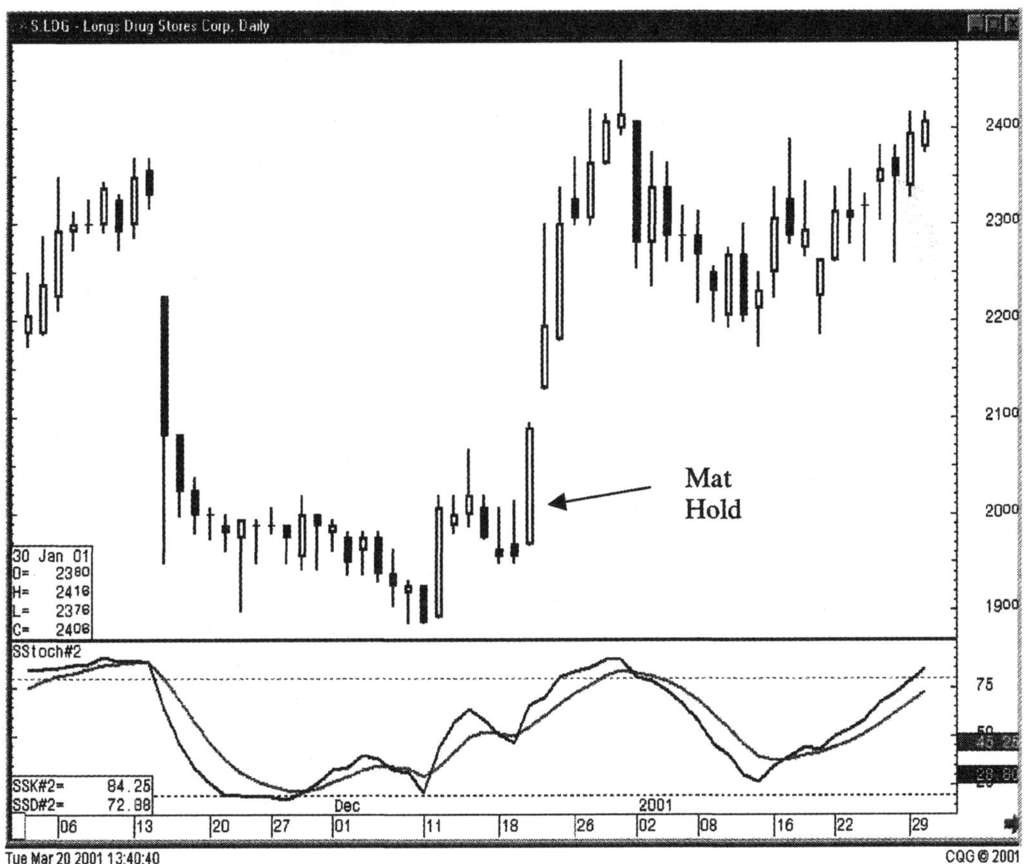

Figure 3.20 Mat Hold patterns demonstrate that the bears could not push prices down.

THREE-LINE STRIKE
(sante uchi karasu no bake sen)

Description

Three Line Strike, also known as the Fooling Three Soldiers, is a four-line pattern that occurs during a defined trend (see Figure 3.21). This pattern represents a resting period, but unlike most resting periods, this one occurs all in one day. It ends up as an extended Three White Soldiers pattern.

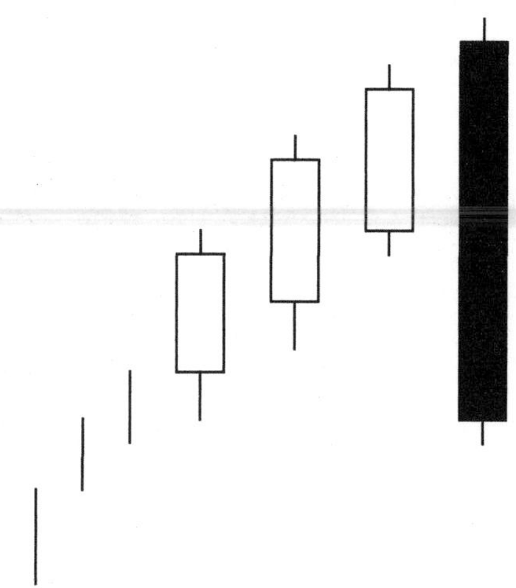

Figure 3.21 Three-Line Strike. Confirmation is not required.

Criteria

1. Three White Soldiers, three white candles, are continuing an uptrend.
2. The fourth day opens higher, but then pulls back to close below the open of the first white candle.

Pattern Psychology

The Three White Soldiers indicate the trend is continuing. The fourth day opens in a manner that resembles the previous days; however, profit taking sets in. It continues until the close is below the open of the first white candle. The black candle body completely negates the rise of the past three days, but it has gotten the short-term pull-back sentiment out of the way. The uptrend continues from this point.

UPSIDE GAP THREE METHOD
(uwa banare sanpoo hatsu oshi)

Description

The Upside Gap Three Method, shown in Figure 3.22, is a simplistic pattern, similar to the Upside Tasuki Gap, occurring in a strong trending market. In an uptrend, a gap occurs between two white candles. The final day opens within the top white body and closes in the lower white body, filling the gap between them.

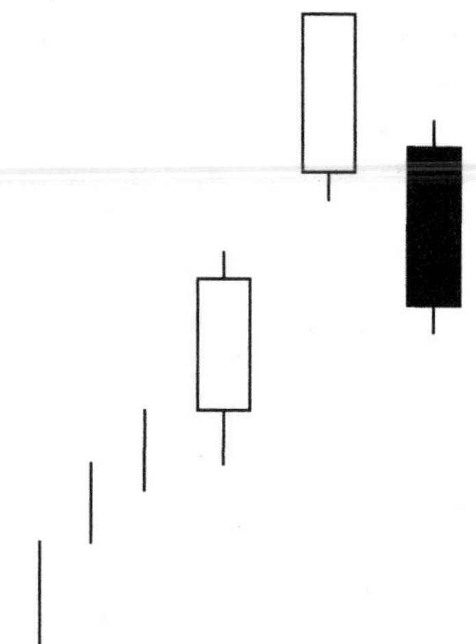

Figure 3.22 Upside Gap Three Method. Confirmation is suggested.

Criteria

1. In an uptrend, two white candles form, having the second one gapping above the first.
2. The third day opens lower, in the body of the top white candle and closes in the body of the first white candle.

Pattern Psychology

A market has been moving in a direction, then a gap appears between two white candles. Gaps have significance in that they eventually have to be filled. The fact that it becomes filled immediately leads investors to think that the pull-back is just a profit-taking pull-back. The trend should resume immediately after the gap filling is satisfied.

Learning the Signals and Continuation Patterns

Hopefully you have read through the signals with relative speed, not getting bogged down with a memorization project. Chapter 5 explains how to remember the signals using fast and efficient methods. But before you get to that section, Chapter 4 spells out the investor psychology that was influential in forming the major signals. Knowing what makes a reversal signal brings invaluable perceptions into an investor's mental arsenal. Knowing why the masses invest the way they do yields eye-opening truths.

Learning the continuation patterns has important features. In some cases, differences between reversal patterns and the continuation of a trend can be subtle. The knowledge of how minor price variations can affect the direction of a trend can lead to enhancement of profits. As the charts are studied, recognizing the differences will greatly alter investment strategies.

Chapter 4

MAJOR SIGNALS EXPLAINED

However much thou art read in theory, if thou hast no practice thou art ignorant. Sa'di Gulistan

This section is devoted to the further description of the major signals. The purpose is to better familiarize you with the important signals and to gain more insight on how and when to use these signals. The better your understanding of the development of each formation, the better prepared you will be for implementing profitable trades. It is good practice to review this section from time to time. Being reminded of the ramifications of specific formations will increase the probabilities of making the correct trades.

As mentioned previously, the major signals will produce the vast majority of the trade opportunities. Some of the secondary signals are seen so rarely, they are not worth spending much memorization time. On a day where you thought that a secondary signal may have occurred, there will be a supply of major signals to choose from. The secondary signals are important only if no major signals occur on a particular day. If you had to put a position on that day, maybe a secondary signal appeared. However, with the capabilities of today's search software, it is almost impossible not to have a handful of excellent trade "potentials" every day.

For that reason, further explanation will be directed at the signals that are going to produce the major portion of your profits. The Doji, due to its importance for signaling a potential direction change, is a good starting point.

The Doji

The true Doji occurs when the open and the close are exactly the same. However, an open and close that is close, but not exact, can be construed as a Doji. For example, if a stock has a trading range of four dollars during a trading day and the open and close are three-eighths of a point apart, that can be viewed as a Doji. The message conveyed by that trading day is that the bulls and the bears were not decisive about the direction. This flexibility in definition also is a function of how lengthy the shadows were that day.

Spinning Tops bear close resemblance to the Doji. The decision to call a signal a Doji or a Spinning Top does not matter that greatly. Both signify indecision. Both would warrant watching for the next day's price action. You will come across low-volume charts where Dojis occur often. If many Dojis are observed on a chart, then the appearance of a new Doji will not carry that much weight.

As one of the Candlestick's most important signals, The Doji should always be heeded. The Japanese say that the psychology behind the Doji's formation always warrant analysis. They feel that it provides a significant warning. It is better to attend a false signal than to ignore a real one. With all its inherent implications, it is dangerous to ignore a Doji at anytime.

Dojis at the Top

Dojis occurring at the top of a trend have major implications and even more relevance occurring after a long white candle. Remember that the Doji represents indecision on the part of the bulls and the bears. After a long uptrend, the price level (the Doji) has now demonstrated indecision and uncertainty on the bulls' part. For a rally to continue, the bulls need the conviction of sustained buying. The presence of the Doji could mean that the conviction has deteriorated. This pattern appears to be so correct that the Japanese advise getting out immediately when a Doji occurs at the top.

Note that in Figure 4.1, IBM had flattened out in its trading for a couple of weeks. During that time, the stochastics had been drifting down. However, the downtrend did not start until the Doji occurred. It finally illustrated a level of indecision at the top. Notice how the Doji indicated more indecision at the top of the next rally on the way down.

Figure 4.2 shows the Doji as the final top formation after a major price rise of Openware Systems, Inc. A few days prior, a Shooting Star Pattern appeared. This would have gotten the longs out or at least warned that the top was near.

The stochastics were in the over-bought range. This should have alerted the bulls to start watching for another sell signal in the near future. Also, notice the high close back on December 8. The Doji forming at this level should provide a good indication that the bulls were not strong enough to close at a new high. The following day, the dark candle illustrates that the bears had then moved in.

Dojis do not have as much credence in identifying reversals in a downtrend. The reason, as the Japanese explain, is that the weight of the market can still move the market down after the appearance of a Doji. A Doji in a downtrend requires evidence from the next day to confirm the change of direction.

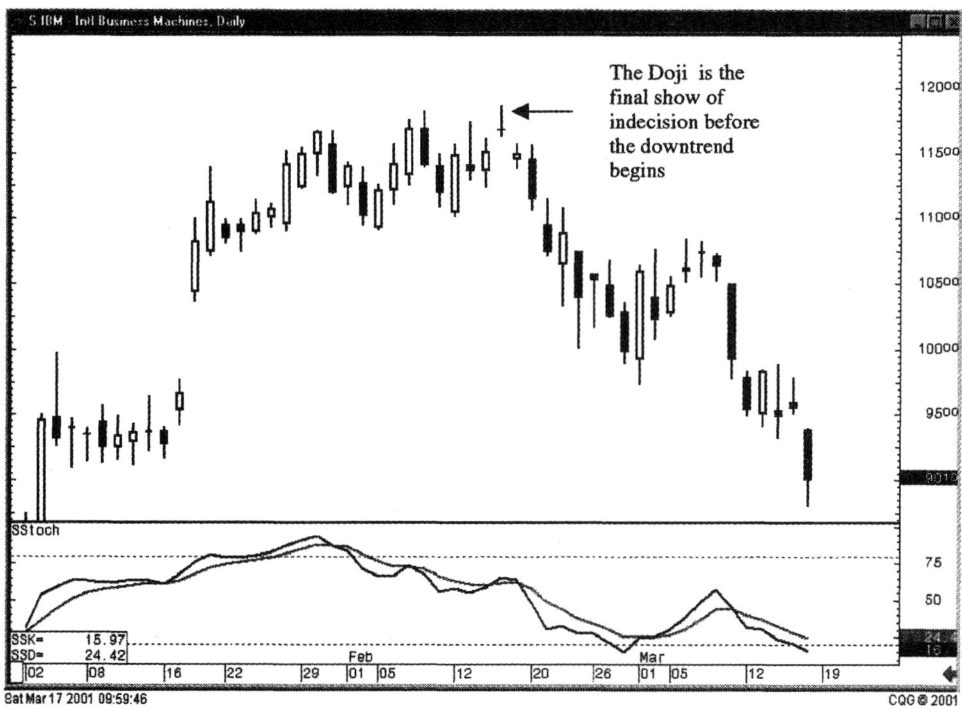

Figure 4.1 IBM doesn't turn down until the Doji appeared.

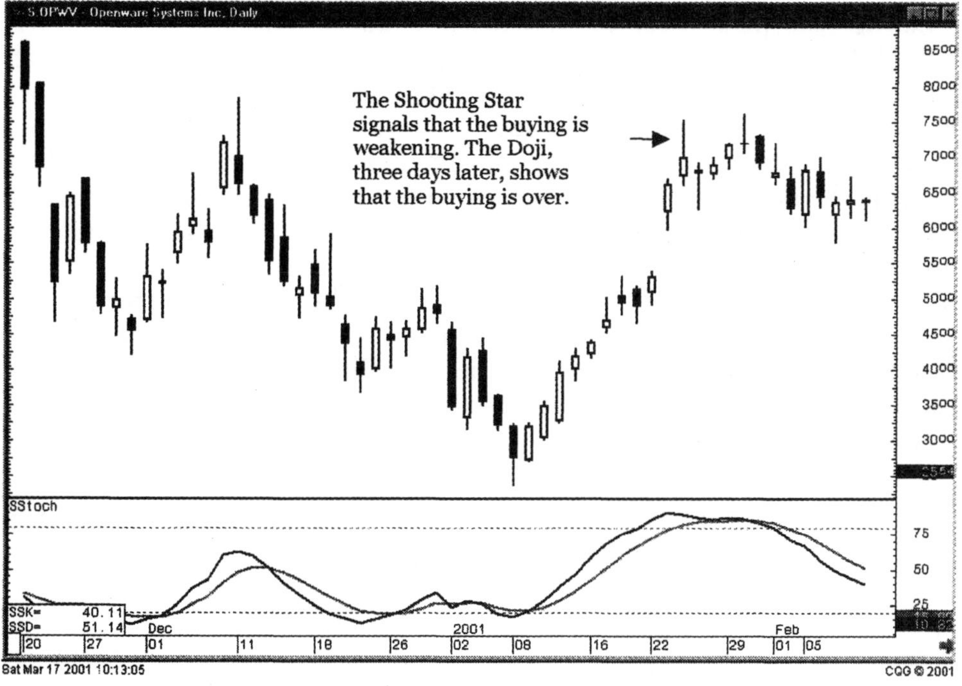

Figure 4.2 The Doji is the strongest signal for indicating that the trend is heading in a new direction.

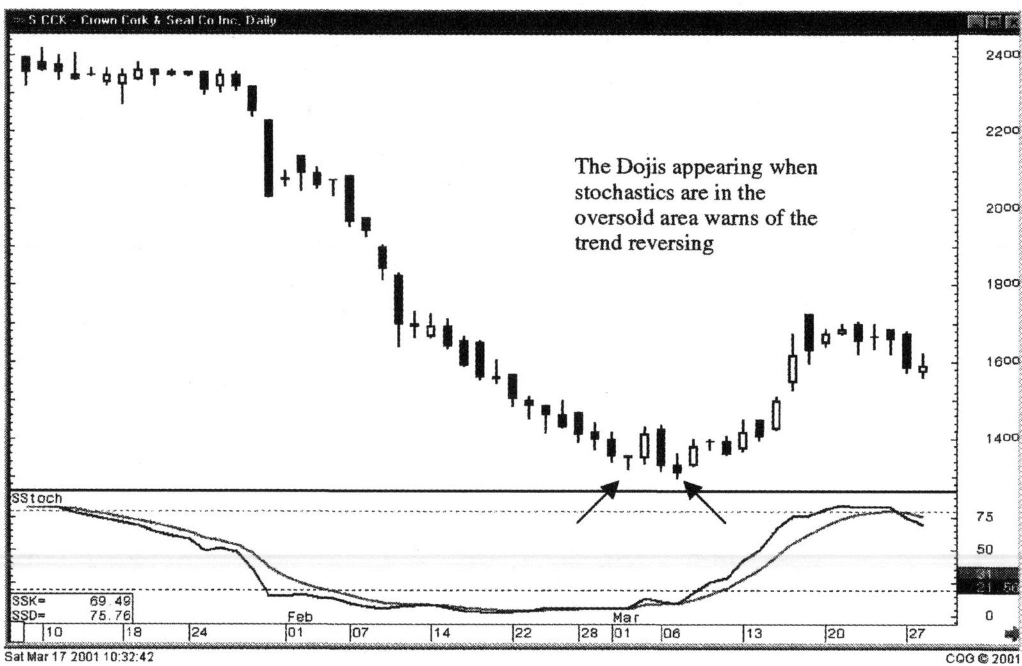

Figure 4.3 A multiple number of Doji's in an oversold area should alert investors that a turn is coming.

During the price decline in Crown Cork & Seal Co. Inc., shown in Figure 4.3, a couple of Dojis appeared, yet there was no follow-through to make significant buy signals. The first Doji, forming a Harami, did not follow through the next day. It opened much lower. This was clearly not the sign of buyers stepping in. The second signal did not have strong candle days following the Doji. A Spinning Top, showing indecision, and a Shooting Star, reflecting selling into the upmove, would not have enticed the commitment of investment funds. However, it should have indicated that the bottom was not too far away and that buyers were making themselves present.

The final Doji was confirmed the next day. The bullish candle closed more than 50 percent up the dark-bodied candle of two days before. The stochastics curled up and came up through the 20 level.

A good rule of thumb upon witnessing a Doji is that the direction will be dictated by the open of the next day. The indecision represented by the Doji can either be a consolidation after a big price move of the previous day, or it can be the change of fundamental occurrences during a price trend.

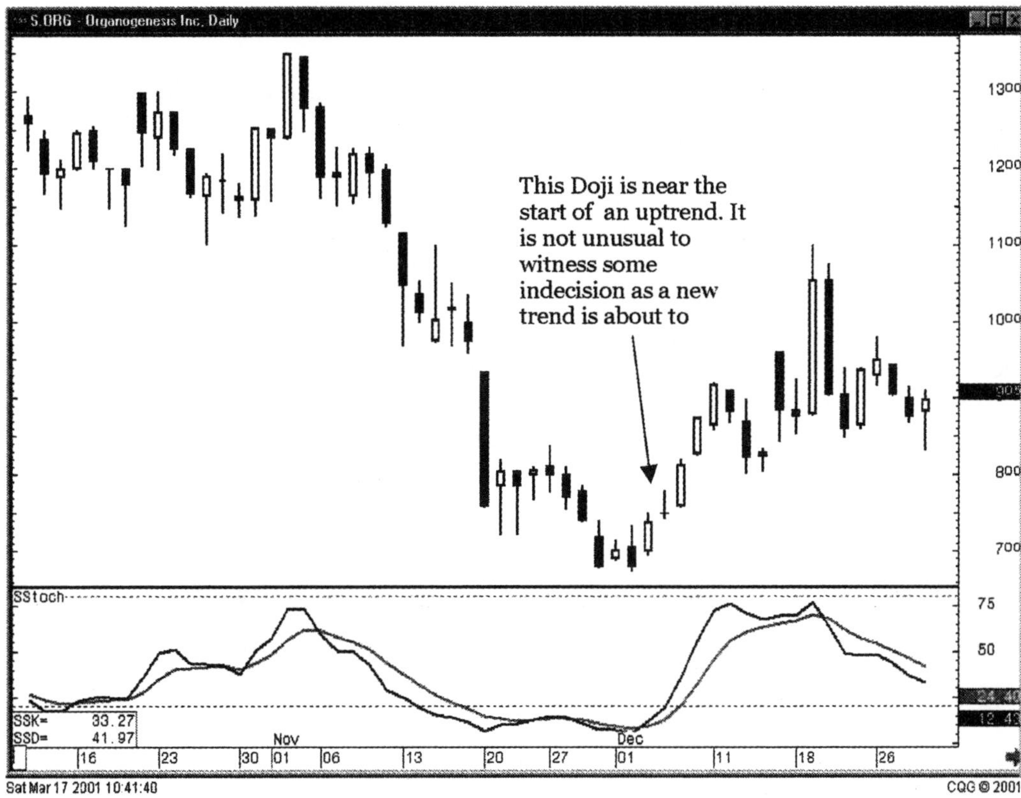

Figure 4.4 A Doji near the start of a trend indicates that the last of the sellers are getting out. Watch for how the price opens the next day.

In the Organogenesis Inc. chart shown in Figure 4.4, note the upmove, started by a Kicker type formation. The next day a Doji formed. Keep in mind that this stock had been in a major downtrend for the past three weeks. The buyers started to step in. After the first strong up day, it is not unusual to see the sellers still getting out of their position, now that they can get a little better price than the past few days. That last batch of selling is sopped up by the new buyers coming into the stock. This produces a day of price equalizing. After that, the bears realize that whoever is buying has a strong taste for owning the stock at these levels. They may start backing away. This allows the bulls to take over.

The Long-Legged Doji (Rickshaw Man)

The Long-Legged Doji is a valuable signal at trend tops. The excessive length of the shadows indicates massive indecision. If the open and close are near the center of the trading range, the formation is known as the Rickshaw Man. A formation with a small body and long upper and/or lower shadows is called a high-wave candlestick. When the exceedingly long shadows appear, the Japanese say that the trend has "lost its sense of direction."

Extended Systems Inc. produced a clear illustration of Long-Legged Dojis at the top of a trend, as shown in Figure 4.5. The first formation easily demonstrates that the buying was being counter-acted by the bears bringing prices back down by the end of the day. The following day, the Rickshaw Man formation showed "definite indecision." These were the days to be exiting this trade. The stochastics confirmed the overbought conditions.

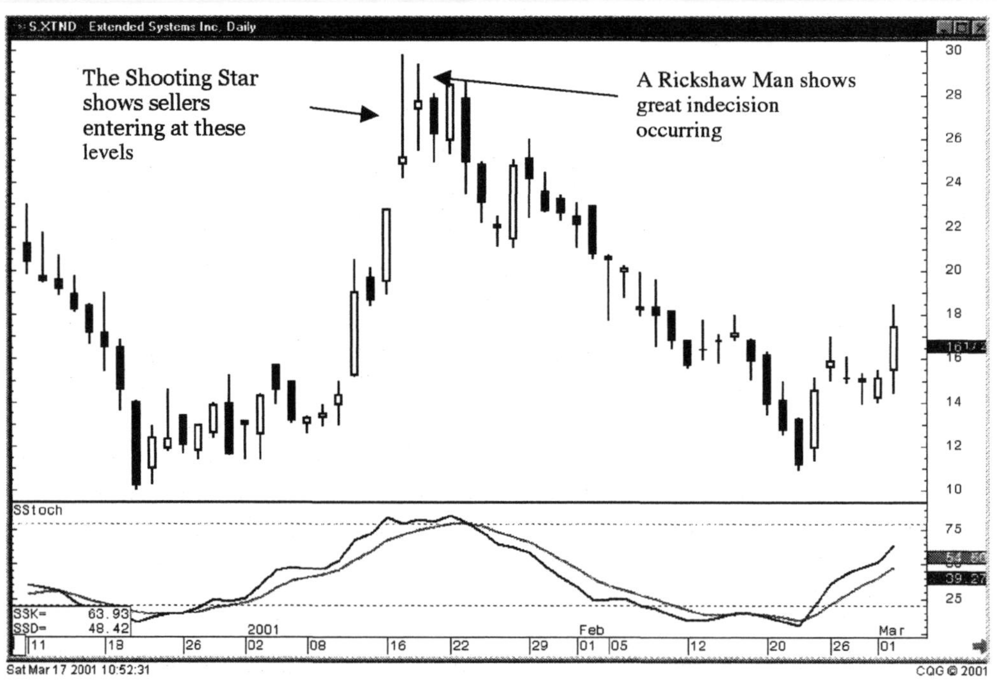

Figure 4.5 Extensive shadows with small bodies infer great indecision. Watch for a change of direction.

High-Wave Pattern

A series of high-wave signals, called the High-Wave Pattern indicates a significant reversal about to occur. The accumulation of indecision is the prelude to investor sentiment getting ready to change dramatically.

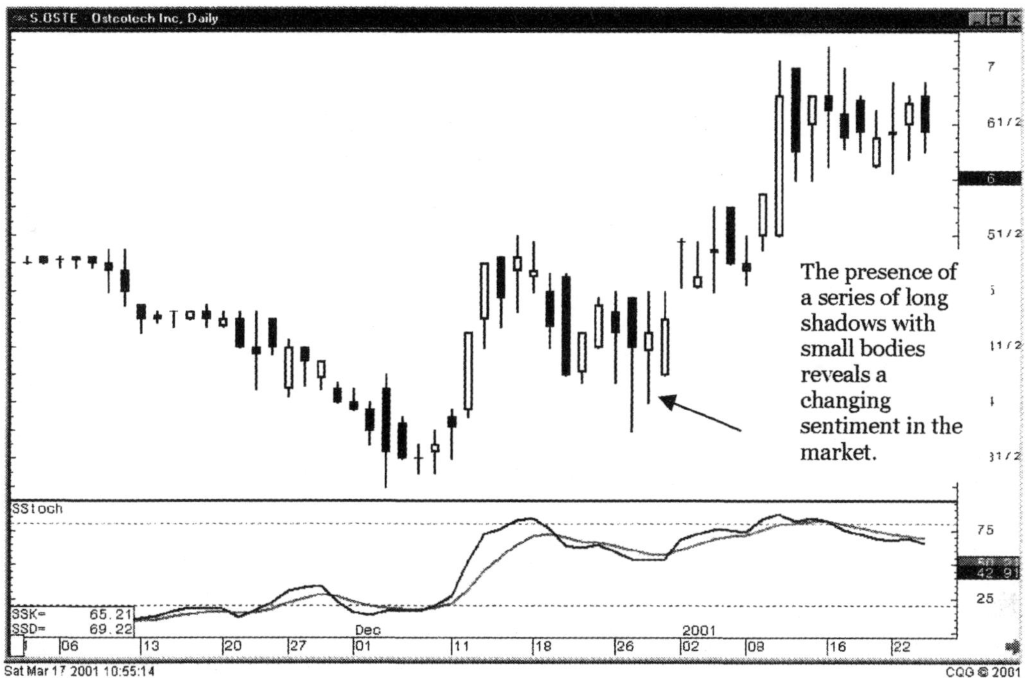

Figure 4.6 Long shadows are the forewarning of a major direction change.

Osteotech Inc. has a High-Wave Pattern forming in a trading area where investors would not have projected a turn to occur, as shown in Figure 4.6. The stochastics had shown a mild downward bias. Three days in a row showing long shadows should have alerted the Candlestick analyst that major indecisiveness was going on toward this stock and to watch for a big move in the opposite direction. There was no indication that any change of direction was happening except for the presence of the shadows.

The Gravestone Doji

The Gravestone Doji (a variation of the Inverted Hammer) can be found at the bottom of trends, but its strong point is calling the tops. Logic is simple in this case. After an uptrend, the bulls open the price and immediately continue its rally. It moves up to and exceeds the recent highs. But before the end of the day, the bears step in and drive the price back down to the opening price and the low of the day. That should warn the bulls that their strength has gone out of the rally.

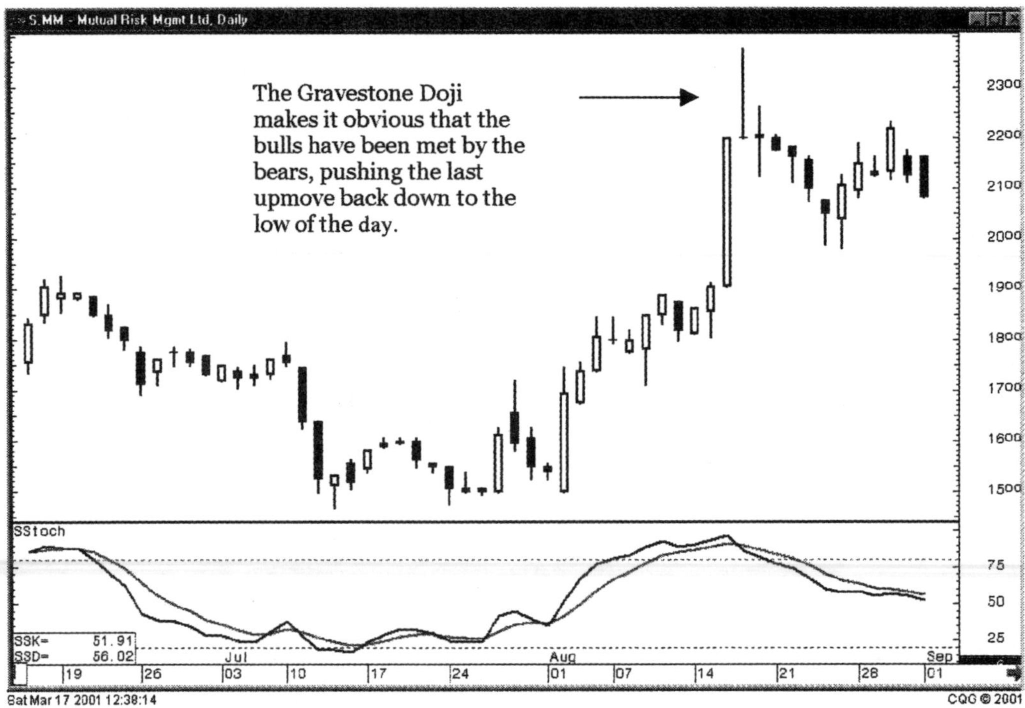

Figure 4.7 The obvious large upper shadow reveals that the bulls have run out of steam.

Note that in Figure 4.7, representing Mutual Risk Mgmt Ltd., the Gravestone Doji at the top has obvious visual implications. It is a more forceful illustration than the Shooting Star. The bigger the upper shadow, the more dramatic the reversal potential. The same can be said about the Gravestone Doji at the bottom. It acts as a more powerful Inverted Hammer. Keep in mind that the Inverted Hammer and the Hanging Man are the two formations that act contrary to the common sense of the signals. The explanation is that they are the evidence of new buying and/or selling coming into a trend. Although, they were overcome by the participants of the current trend before the end of the day, the fact that they altered the direction of the trend for a portion of the day creates doubt in the minds of the trend participants. A new batch of buying, in the case of a Gravestone Doji or an Inverted Hammer at the bottom, makes the sellers aware that the current downward trend might be over. They start backing out of the way as more buying comes into the stock, giving it more impetus to the upside.

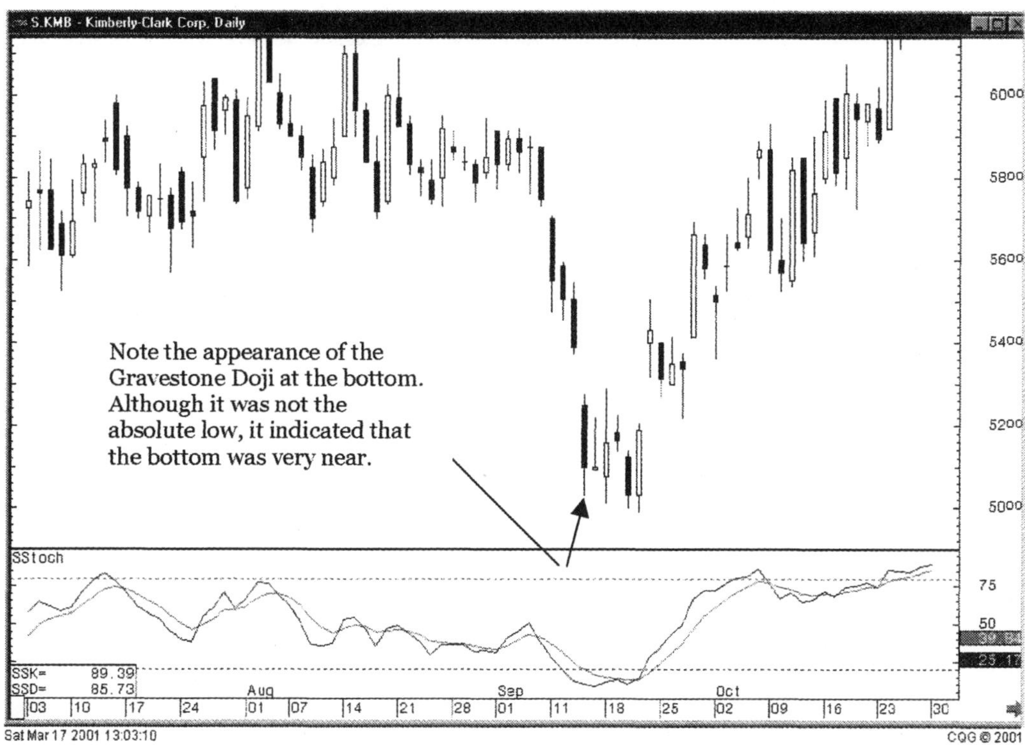

Figure 4.8 A Gravestone Doji showing the bottom.

The Gravestone Doji shown in Figure 4.8, Kimberly Clark Corp., brought the severe down-draught to a halt. This was the first indication that the bulls were making themselves present, even though the stock price closed on the low of the day.

Tri-Star Pattern

The Tri-Star Pattern illustrates the same sentiment as seen in the High-Wave Pattern. There is an accumulation of indecision occurring over the span of a few days. This projects a major change occurring in investor sentiment. The appearance of three indecisive days, as in the Broadcom Corp. chart (shown in Figure 4.9), indicates that the bulls and the bears are really tussling for control. The location of the stochastics adds to the probability that the steam

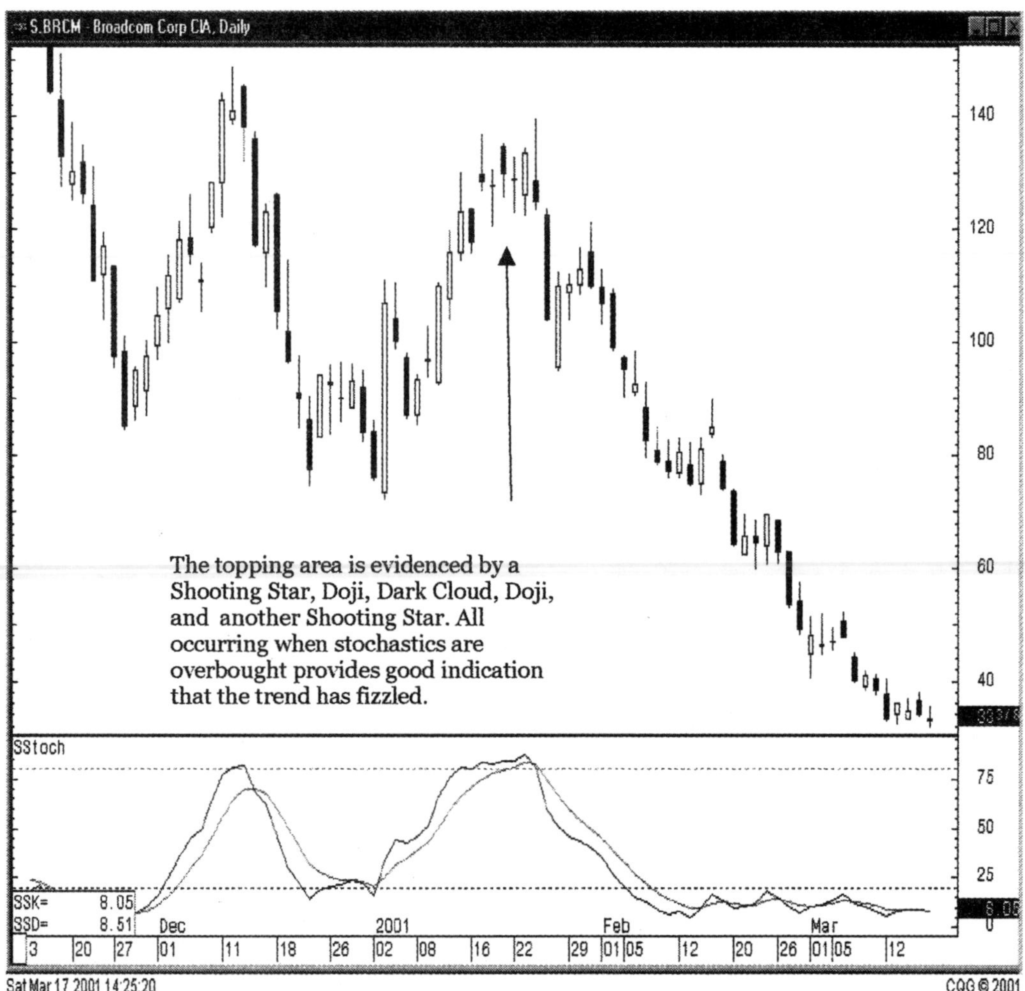

Figure 4.9 A group of Dojis reveal great indecision at these levels, watch for a trend reversal.

is running out of the trend. Despite the fact that all three days were not Dojis, those three days still showed that the bulls and bears were not letting the price move in either direction. This provides a good opportunity for investors to exit the trade and go find trades with much better upside potential.

Once more, common sense would tell you that after a strong run up, indecision at these levels indicates that the bears consider these prices as a good area to start selling. Why fight in this squabble? Take profits and find a trade that does not have the probabilities stacked-up against it.

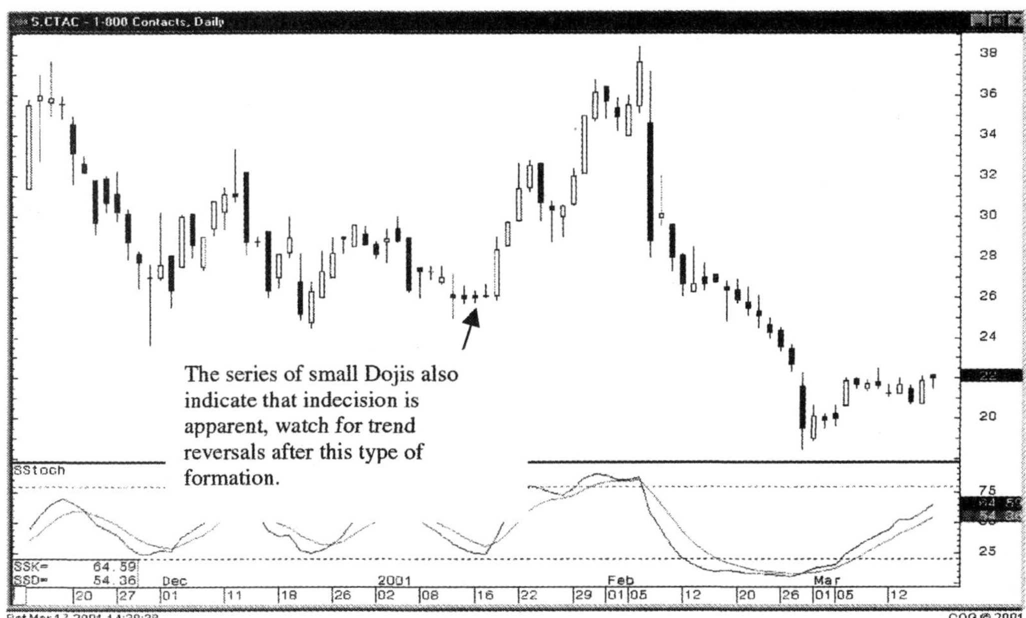

Figure 4.10 Dojis, indecision for a number of days in a row alerts of a change coming.

Figure 4.10 illustrates a trend reversal at a point that would not suggest a reversal. The stochastics were not in the oversold area. No major trendlines were apparent. The only warning of the trend changing was the presence of three small Doji indecision days.

Dojis in Combination

Dojis will occur in combination with other signals. A Harami with a Doji as the second day of the formation will produce a more powerful reversal. As seen in Figure 4.11, representing Superior Energy Services Inc., the bottom Doji/Harami was confirmed the next day with a good solid white candle. The three previous days, the Doji/Harami did not have any follow-up strength to confirm that the selling stopped. Also, note that the first Doji/Harami occurred before the stochastics had gotten down into the oversold area.

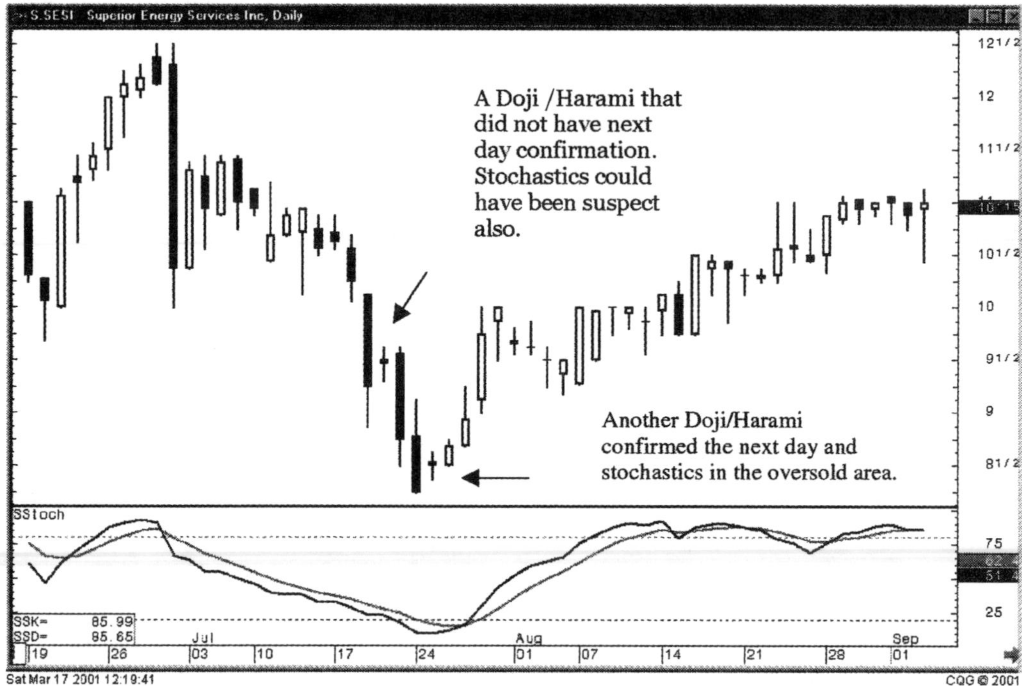

Figure 4.11 A Harami signal with a Doji is usually a strong reversal signal.

The important point that should be clear is the magnitude of strength demonstrated after the Doji/Harami was confirmed. A Harami tells you that the selling should have stopped. That does not always mean that the buyers will step in. The presence of the Doji reveals that there was indecision between the bulls and the bears, especially when the Doji was creating the Harami signal. This is a sign that the bulls are going to act more aggressively.

Remember, anytime the Doji appears, you should take immediate notice. The fact that the Doji has powerful implications and it is so easily identified, makes it one of your best signals for producing profits.

The Hammers

The Hammer is a major signal—not only in importance but also in the frequency it occurs. The Hammer only requires common sense to understand. After a downtrend, the bears open the price and continue to push the prices lower. Finally, it reaches a level where the bulls decide to start stepping in.

Before the end of the day, the bulls have brought the price back up toward the top of the trading range. A good Hammer formation should have a shadow at least twice as long as the body. The Japanese say that the bears have now "hammered out the bottom." The evidence of the long lower shadow indicates that the prices could not be held down. Whenever the shadows are apparent in one direction or the other, expect to see the trend move in the opposite direction in the near future.

In the following Lightbridge Inc. example, it becomes apparent that the lower the prices, the more the buyers stepped in before the end of the day. Note in the chart shown in Figure 4.12, the series of days with lower shadows. This clearly illustrates that every time the bears knocked the price down, the bulls stepped back in. After a few days of this interaction, with the bulls maintaining control, the bears eventually step out of the way and allow the bulls to completely control.

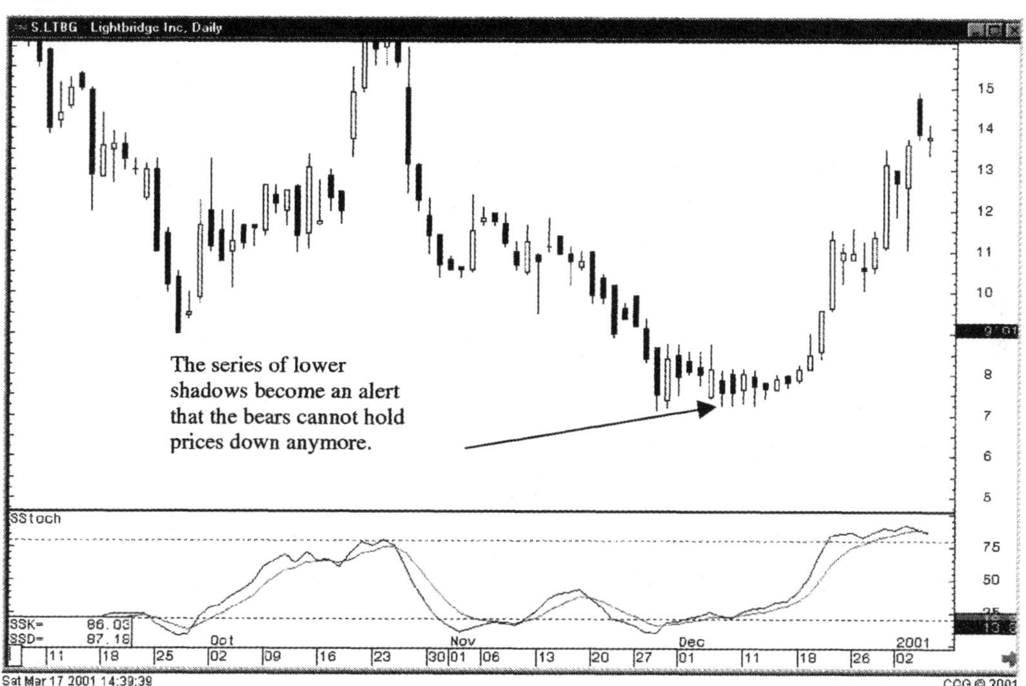

Figure 4.12 A series of tails to the downside demonstrate that the bears can move prices lower.

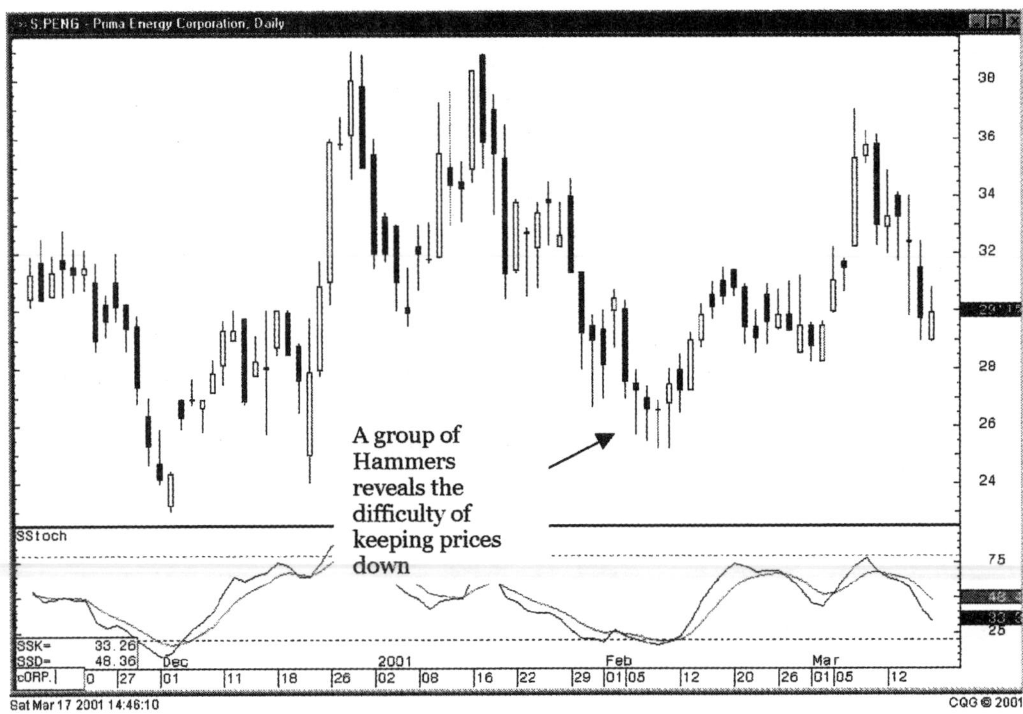

Figure 4.13 The longer the tails, the more compelling that a reversal will occur.

The Prima Energy Corporations chart, shown in Figure 4.13, is another illustration of the Hammers. It becomes apparent that the bears could not keep the prices down over a period of four days. Each day, the bulls would bring the price back up to the higher end of the trading range.

These indications are much more evident on a Candlestick chart than a bar chart. The fact that the bulls keep fighting back gives the investor an alert that the bears could weaken soon, leading to the bulls being able to take control. These are not high-tech observations. The long lower shadows, with small bodies at the top, provide the information visually.

The Shooting Star

Conversely, when the shadows occur above the bodies, the bulls are being overpowered by the bears before the end of the day (see Figure 4.14). When the bulls try to advance the price, the bears move in and knock it back down. This should forewarn the investor that the price is getting weak at these levels.

Figure 4.14 Long upper shadows indicate bullish sentiment dispelling.

Remember where the stochastics are. At the top of a prolonged trend, a Shooting Star is relevant. Even part way into the uptrending stochastics, a gap up Shooting Star, followed by a gap down black candle day makes for an easy read. The bears have taken over. Or a cluster of days that can not get above a certain level, leaving upside shadows as evidence, should warn the Candlestick analyst that the bulls are being overpowered. Use these obvious signs to your advantage.

A man, though wise, should never be ashamed of learning more, and unbend his mind. Sophocles

Again, common sense is required in every aspect of Candlestick analysis. The interpretation of what you are seeing produces a clear understanding of what is happening.

The Shooting Star in Figure 4.15, representing TIBCO Software, dramatically illustrates how the bulls could not maintain the rally. The bears brought prices back down to the lower range of that day's trading. This is a

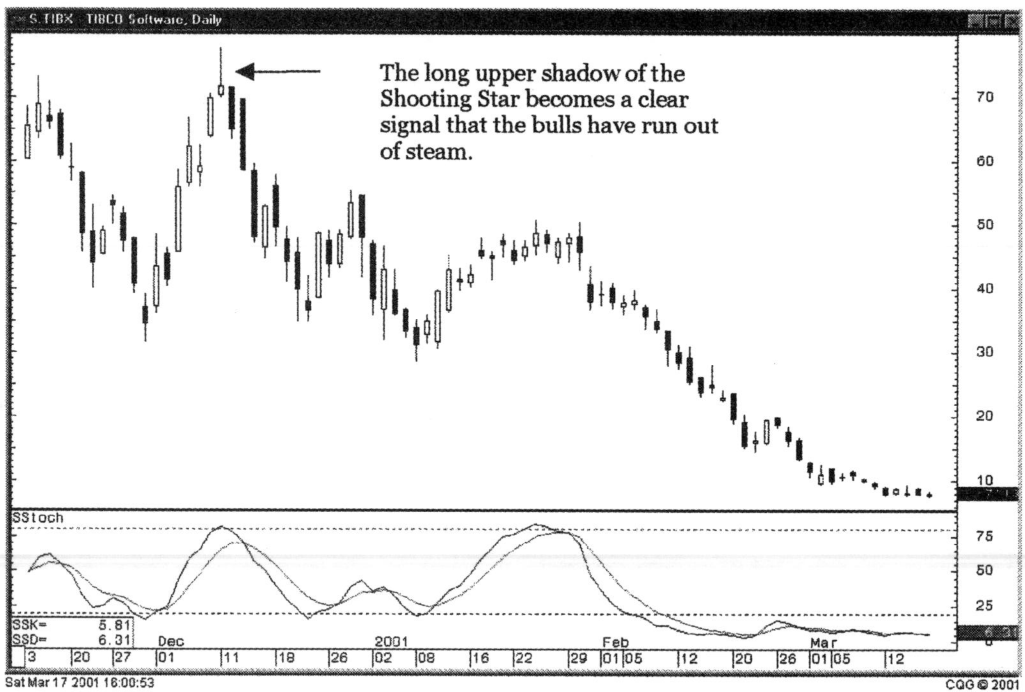

Figure 4.15 A Shooting Star, part of the Evening Star pattern dramatizes the fact that the uptrend is over and a downtrend should be starting.

clear message. The rally is over. When the selling continues into the next day, creating an Evening Star formation, this permits the Candlestick-educated investor to start putting on short positions well ahead of the conventional technical analyst.

As for probabilities, the signal, aligned with overbought stochastics, produces an extremely high-probability trade situation. In Figure 4.15, the next seven trading days produce over a 50-percent profit—and Candlestick analysts knew that the probabilities were in our favor.

Engulfing Patterns

Being able to see the obvious reversals in investor sentiment is like finding free money. It's like seeing that white gleaming golf ball in the rough that somebody else hit there. You know other people have been in the area, but your eyes caught sight of the ball. It's yours. Free. Or imagine spotting that valuable collector's item at a garage sale. You know it's worth hundreds or thousands of times more than the few dollars that the owner is asking. There have been hundreds of people looking at it before you got there and they all passed it up. Your eyes spot it and it seems to jump out at you. Knowing the Candlestick signals and seeing them occur will give you the same exhilaration when you realize the extremely high potential of putting money in your pocket.

The Engulfing Patterns produce that type of visual excitement. It will shine at you. The visual aspect of the signal makes it so obvious, you can't wait to get into the position. As illustrated in Exhibit 4.16, the contrast between the previous trend and the new Engulfing Pattern signal is blatantly observed. When the stochastics and the signal appear in conjunction, it feels like finding free money. It is obvious that a dramatic change has occurred.

Is this 100-percent foolproof? Certainly not. But the odds of making money from this signal are so great, there shouldn't be any reason not to commit funds each and every time a strong Engulfing Pattern occurs. The true Engulfing Pattern gives the investor a great opportunity to establish a low-risk trade.

Understanding the emotional process of how the Engulfing Pattern develops provides the Candlestick investor with a gigantic advantage. You have been following the price of a stock or group of stocks. The stochastics indicate that they are in the oversold area. You recognize the panic setting in to the stock price. (See Chapter 9 for more on using signals.) The price gaps in

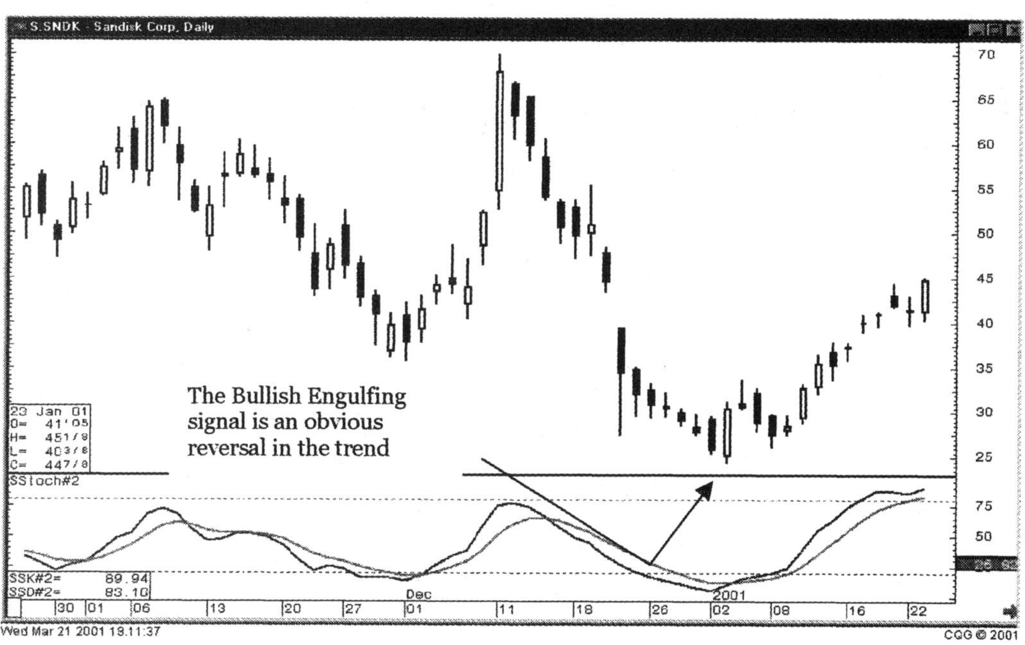

Figure 4.16 Bullish Engulfing Pattern.

the same direction as the trend—people wanting to get out in a downtrend and wanting to get in during the uptrend. After the first few minutes of trading, it becomes apparent that they opened the price at the extreme of the day.

In the case of a downtrend reversal, the open gaps down and shows no signs of trading lower. It starts to move up. Conversely, in an uptrend, the stock price has built up so much confidence with day after day of going higher, the investment public now has the confidence to get in, no matter what the cost. They gap it open to the upside, but no more buying appears. The price starts to back off, as shown in Figure 4.17.

The bearish Engulfing Pattern is easy to see. It is an obviously ominous signal. A big black candle, opening higher than the previous day's close, maybe opening higher than the previous day's trading range, and closing below the previous day's open. There is a definite change in investor sentiment. Liquidate longs and go short.

If you had been long before the bearish Engulfing Pattern occurred, you do not have to let the pattern play out before liquidating. Some of your profits can be saved by visualizing what could occur. For example, if prices open higher at the top of a trend and start to pull back, use the halfway point of

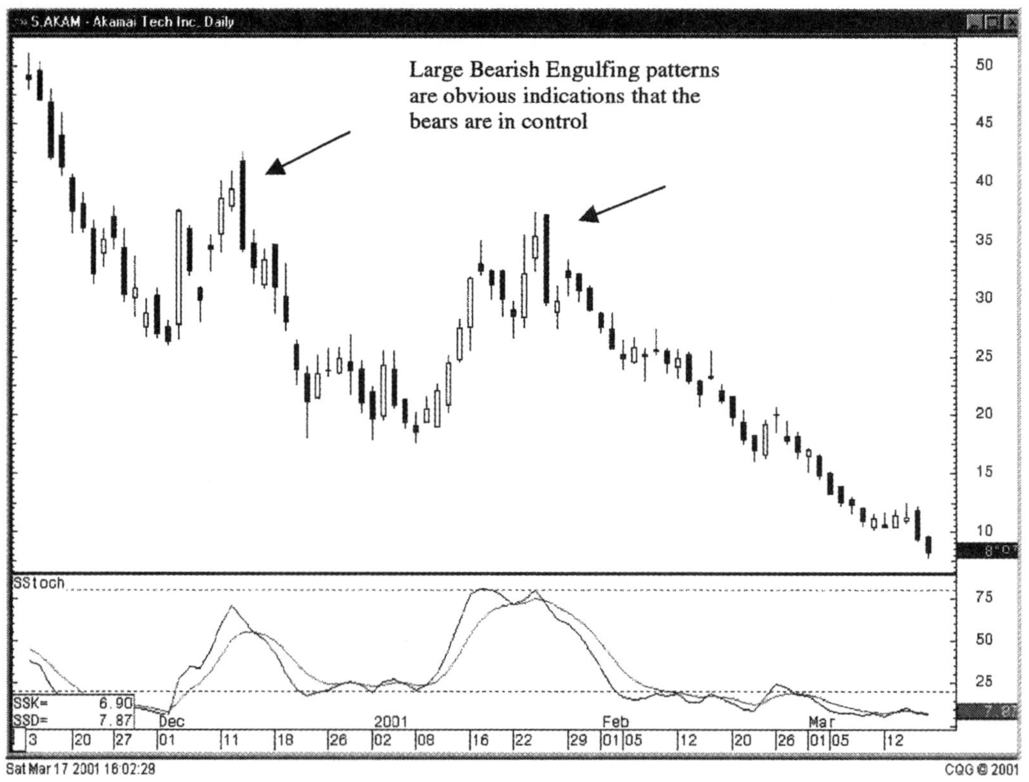

Figure 4.17 A Bearish Engulfing pattern looks ominous, a strong sell signal.

the previous white candle as your stop. If prices come back down to that level during the day, it is going to take a big rally from that point to *not* form a weak signal. At best, the price could come back up to where it opened that day, or maybe a little higher. If so, it will still have formed a Hanging Man. This would be a bearish signal. You would be liquidating regardless of any other factors or signs. If there is any doubt, get out. If you have good profits because you bought at the low end of the trend, move your money to a better spot. Why stay in a risky trade? Take the profits and find a low risk/high profit potential trade. If, at the end of the day, you see that a good sell signal has been formed, short the position and ride it back down.

The Harami Pattern

The Harami Pattern is useful in determining both a reversal in a trend and a stall of a trend. As described earlier, a Harami is an open and close inside the previous day's open and close. It indicates that the trend has stopped. It also can be used to determine how fast a new direction will take hold. As seen in Figure 4.18, representing the Sprint Group PCS Group., there are two Haramis at the bottom. The first one is relatively strong, but still has the momentum of the downtrend that outweighs a move upward. The second

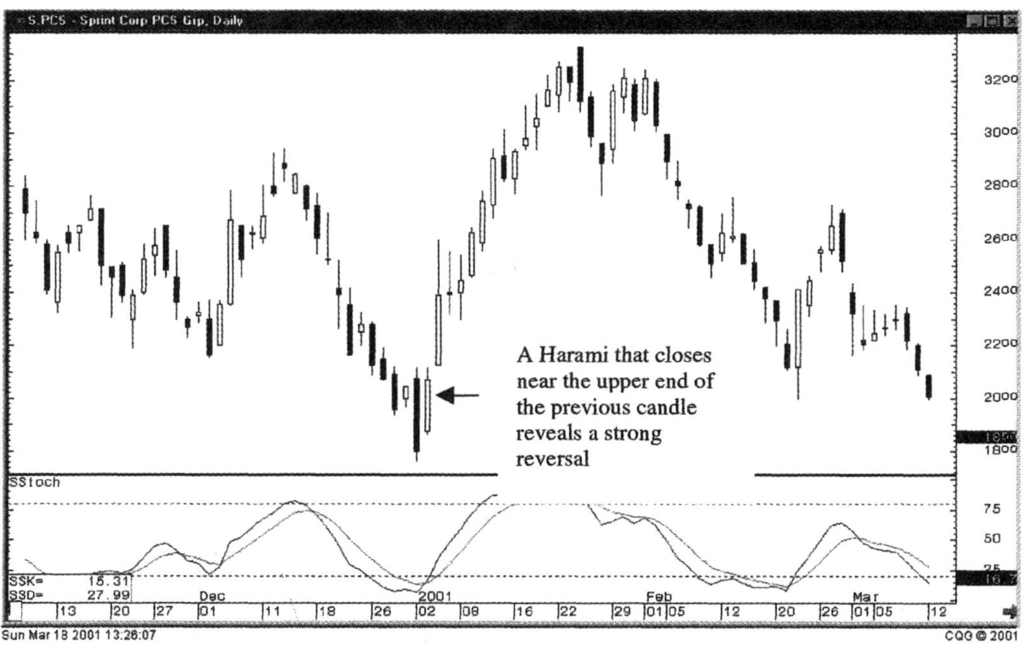

Figure 4.18 Harami closing at the high end of the previous candle shows good strength.

Harami, closing at the top of the last long black candle, demonstrates a high probability that the bulls are trying to take back control.

The Harami can be used as a fairly efficient barometer. The size and the level that it closes in the previous day's body give an accurate projection of how fast or slow the reversal will occur. This can aid in pinpointing when funds should be allocated to a position. Illustrated in Figure 4.18 is a strong Harami. Figure 4.19 represents a weak Harami signal. Note that after a weak Harami, it takes a few days to finally get the trend to turn positive.

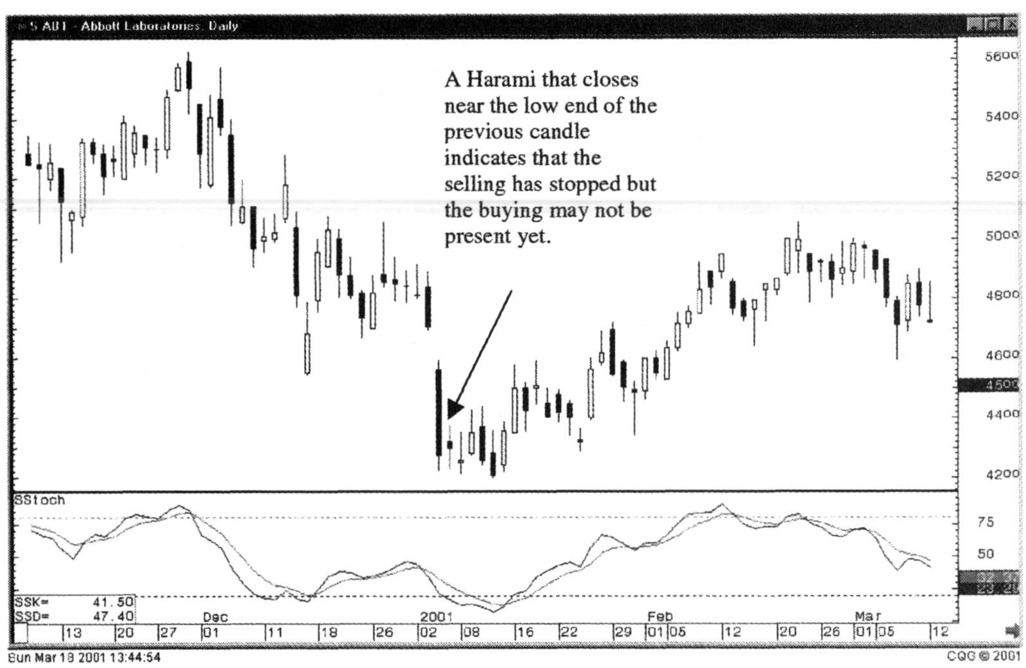

Figure 4.19 A weak Harami means it takes the trend a few days to get going.

The Harami barometer also works in situations after the trend is in progress. It can be an indicator of how long a "rest" in a trend will last. Review At Home Corporation's chart in Figure 4.20. A Harami forms about one-quarter down into the previous days long white body. The long white body was the confirmation that the trend had turned. But the location of the Harami implies that there will be two to four days of consolidation. A Harami forming more than one-half way down that candle would show consolidation of five to seven days before the trend moved up. A Harami forming at the lower end of the white body would immediately demonstrate that the bulls did not take over. In the last case, if a position was put on the previous day, it should be liquidated and the funds moved to another situation.

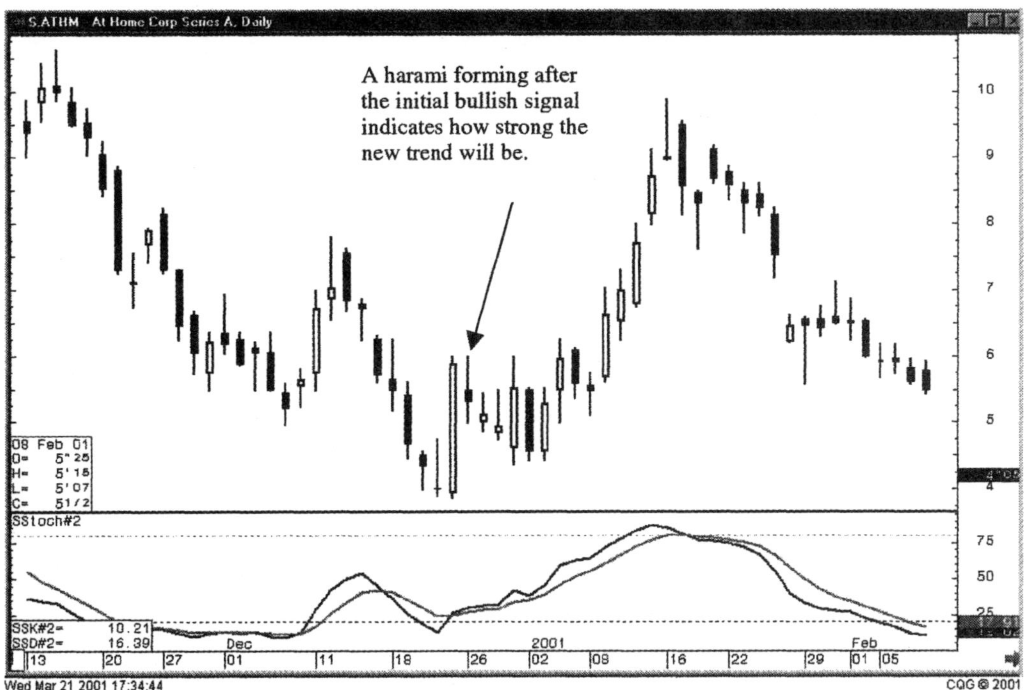

Figure 4.20 A Harami forming after a strong initial move indicates that there will be a few days of flat trading before the trend resumes.

A Harami forming at the top of a white candle should imply a day or two of consolidation. This would not be unexpected after a long downtrend with a recent big reversal. There will still be some sellers hanging around, thinking that the bounce up is a good place to finally get out.

The same criteria can be implemented for the top of trends. A Harami Pattern can demonstrate the strength of the reversal by its location in the previous body. Note in Figure 4.21, representing Exfo Electrol-Optical Engineering. Inc., the Doji/Harami is at the top. A Doji at the top should always invoke selling a position. A week later, the Shooting Star/Harami, closing about a quarter of the way down the previous white candle, should tell the Candlestick investor that the downtrend is intact, but it could be two to four days for it to get full-blown.

Having insight into the effect of Haramis provides investors with the opportunity to maximize returns. If all your investment funds are being fully used, a Harami may reveal that one of the positions you own has stalled for a few days. The aggressive trader may want to move those funds to a better potential trade, and then come back after a few days to reinvest in the same position when it is moving again.

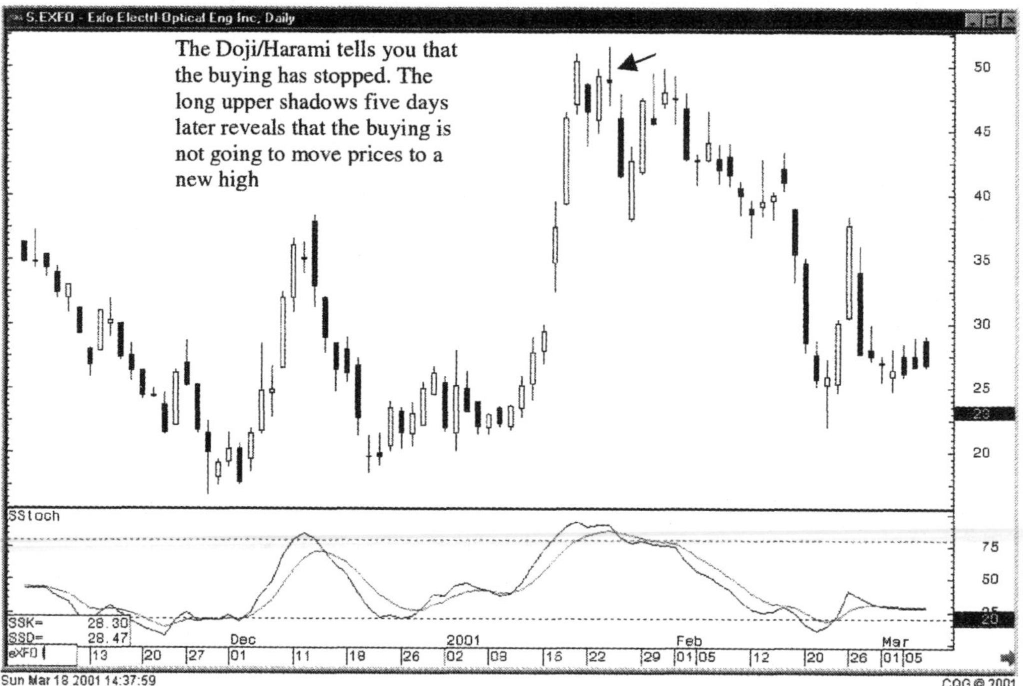

Figure 4.21 A Harami at the extreme top of a trend reveals that the buying has come to an end.

The Kicker Signal

One of the most important signals that needs to be addressed is the Kicker Signal. As discussed in the signals chapter, the Kicker Signal is the most powerful reversal signal. Its chart easily depicts a dramatic change in investor sentiment. As suggested for the Doji, its presence should always be heeded. The fact that the price gaps back to the previous open is part of the evidence of a change of investor sentiment. The change is further heightened by the trading continuing in the same direction, the opposite direction of the previous day's trading. This reveals clear and dramatic evidence that the investing mood is nowhere near the same as the day before. Ninety-nine percent of the time this signal will produce excellent returns. Even after a day or two of consolidation after the Kicker Signal appears, the probabilities remain extremely high that the force that caused the reversal will still be exhibited in the price move. If the price does consolidate after the initial signal, keep a close eye of the trading. If new buying becomes evident within a few days, this will be a good opportunity to add to the position.

There is one condition under which you would not follow the indications of a Kicker signal and it's a rare occasion. If the day following the Kicker signal opens below the opening price again, going back the opposite direction, liquidate the position immediately. Something has gone wrong, usually the news that created the signal in the first place is discovered to be incorrect. Get out and go to another trade situation.

Summary

The 8 or 10 major signals will usually provide more trade potentials than most investors require each day or week or whatever time period that is being considered. The analysis of the best potential chart patterns is simplified by knowing the strengths of each signal. The supply of trades is not a problem. This enables investors to consistently fine-tune their portfolio. Major reversal patterns are occurring every day. Once found, the investor has the benefit of replacing any doubtful positions with good probability positions. The searches, analysis and position placements can be reduced to less than 20 minutes a day. Allocation of that amount of time in an investor's daily schedule can reap better returns than those provided by most investment programs.

The procedure for learning how to recognize the signals quickly and how to create searches for the best trades available is described in the following chapter.

Chapter 5

FINDING AND LEARNING THE SIGNALS MADE EASY

To learn is a natural pleasure, not confined to philosophers, but common to all men. Aristotle

The impression that learning the Candlestick patterns is difficult has been the biggest deterrent for the method to be widely used in the United States. The stigma of trying to memorize all the signal patterns may have had some basis in fact until recently. The advent of the computer has made the learning process simple, and experienced tutors are now more widely available.

Computers make searching and viewing Candlestick formations an easy process. The development of excellent search programs provides an invaluable service. Candlesticks can be located and learned in a rapid process.

Fortunately, the same human emotions that the signals exploit—fear and greed—act as the best learning catalyst. Our own greed for making gains will instill the effectiveness of the signals into our mind. Learning the signals has been one of the major reasons that investors have not taken advantage of Candlesticks. It has been thought that understanding and remembering each signal was too much of a task. In addition, until now, there have been few places or people to confer with to verify whether one is understanding and learning the signals correctly.

This book, as well as Web sites such as www.candlestickforum.com provide the Candlestick student with places to refer to when trying to master this trading technique.

Following a basic premise of the Candlestick system, common sense, some of the processes for learning the different signals become simple: Where is the best place to buy? At the bottom, of course. Where is the best place to sell? Obviously at the top. When trying to learn the signals, most investors begin with this basic thought process. *If the signals are effective, then they should be easily seen at the turns.* This may sound too elementary, but it is the most effective method for remembering the signals.

Learn as though you would never be able to master it; hold it as though you would be if fear of losing it. Confucius

The desire to be in a position at the lowest point and selling at the highest point produces a quick method for identifying the signals. As you read at the beginning of Chapter 2, the "Signals" chapter, you were advised to become *familiar* with the signals on the first go through. It was not necessary to *memorize* them all from the start. There was good reason for that advice. Seeing the signals or what you may think you remembered as a signal, at a turning point, will ingrain itself into your memory much faster than trying to memorize them.

Learning the Signals

The process for learning and remembering the signals is much easier than most people expect. The following process is a step-by-step procedure for becoming acclimated to the signals in a very short period of time.

Step one is easy. On your computer, go to a Candlestick chart. Most software services provide them as an option along with bar charts and line charts. If you do not have an investment information provider, there are free charting services. www.bigcharts.com is a good chart provider. Once you have pulled up the candlestick charts, most charting services allow you to customize indicators. Set stochastics to 14, 5, 5. Or 12, 3, 3 for the swing trader, with two to five day holds.

Now the learning process becomes as easy as viewing and studying the charts. Look at the bottom reversal points. Is there a signal there? If some formations look familiar, leaf back through Chapter 2, the "Signals" section to see if you can locate them. Also take notice of the location of the stochastics. You will find that a vast majority of the reversal signals occur when the stochastics are in the oversold or overbought area.

Notice the easy-to-see oscillations in the Dell chart in Figure 5.1? Dell is an example of a good chart to trade, based on the Candlestick signals. If you run through the chart history of Dell's stock movement, it is easy to see the reversal signals. Most of the signals coordinate with the stochastics at the bottoms and the tops.

Through this exercise, you have now learned two important lessons. First, you will quickly remember what signals appeared at points that you wish you had bought (the greed factor once again). If your purpose for reading this book is to make money, then remembering those signals becomes an automatic process. It is much easier to remember what occurs at a bottom or a top when it results in money in your pocket. Secondly, witnessing a buy signal, occurring at a bottom, when the stochastics clearly indicate that the stock was oversold, will dramatically start changing your investment psychology. Why buy a stock when all the stars do not line up?

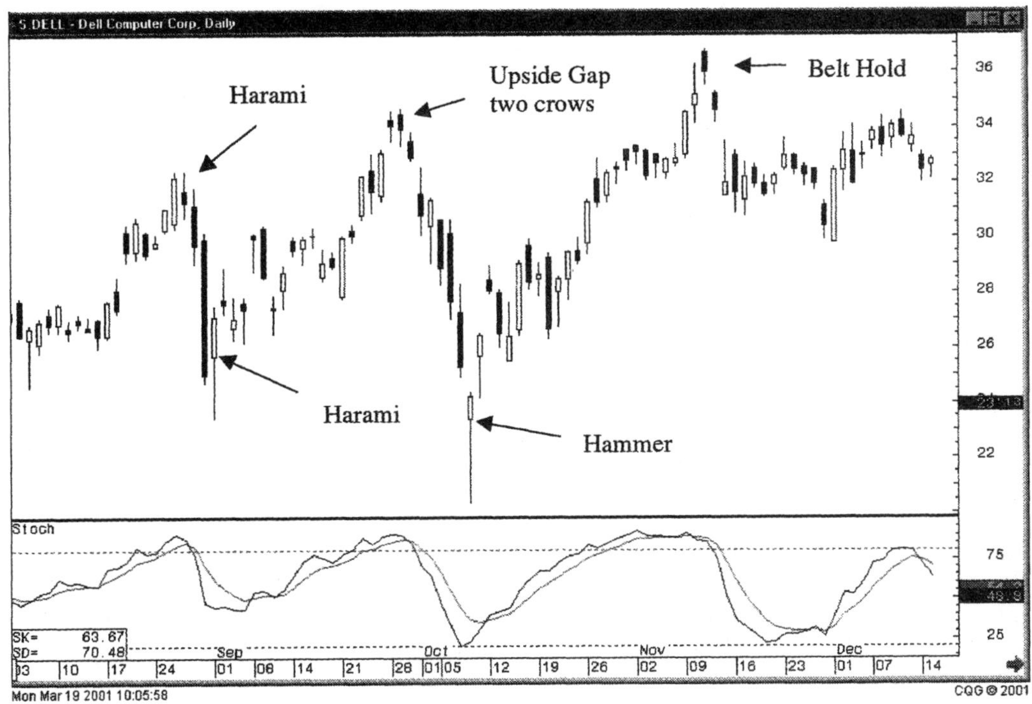

Figure 5.1 Dell Corp. trades in conjunction with the stochastics.

Fortunately, the number of signals you need to learn for successful investing is small. Of the thirty or forty Candlestick signals, approximately six to 10 of them will be more than what you need. These signals provide enough supply of excellent buy or sell positions each day.

The major signals that you will most often witness are as follows:

- The Doji
- The Hammer and Hanging Man
- The Shooting Star
- The Bullish Engulfing Pattern
- The Bearish Engulfing Pattern
- The Dark Cloud Cover
- The Piercing Line
- The Harami

These signals probably provide more than 75 percent of all the reversal situations. They are also the obvious Candlestick signals—obvious in the sense that they visually depict a change of direction. The Engulfing Patterns have a different colored body that stands out against the color of the current trend. The same can be said for the Dark Cloud Cover and the Piercing Line.

The Doji is unique in itself, a cross, with shadows as its predominant feature. The Hammers, Hanging Man, and Shooting Star have long shadows that make them stand out. Anytime a long shadow or shadows appear, investors should pay attention.

The remaining signals can be learned at a less aggressive pace. They will not occur as often; however, when they do occur, 400 years of statistical study has verified that they will probably produce a change of direction. Nevertheless, the learning process remains the same. Simply identify what happened at the reversal point. Is it a signal? And what was the status of the stochastics?

To reiterate, you will discover that the Candlestick signals can be observed an inordinate percentage of the time at the reversal points, with some qualifications. Not all stocks or trading entities will have clear trading patterns. Some are just "junky" traders. Leave them alone. There are thousands of stocks, commodities, and futures that work extremely well as far as providing good Candlestick signals.

For example, you can see in the Capital Federal Financial chart in Figure 5.2, there is absolutely no reason to be trading this stock. All stocks, no matter how volatile, will go through dead periods. If a chart starts going flat, leave it alone for awhile. There will be plenty of other places to put funds.

If you come across a chart that is hard to evaluate, skip it. There are 10,000 stocks to trade. You will have more excellent signals than you can handle. Go find those stocks and eliminate the sloppy trading stocks.

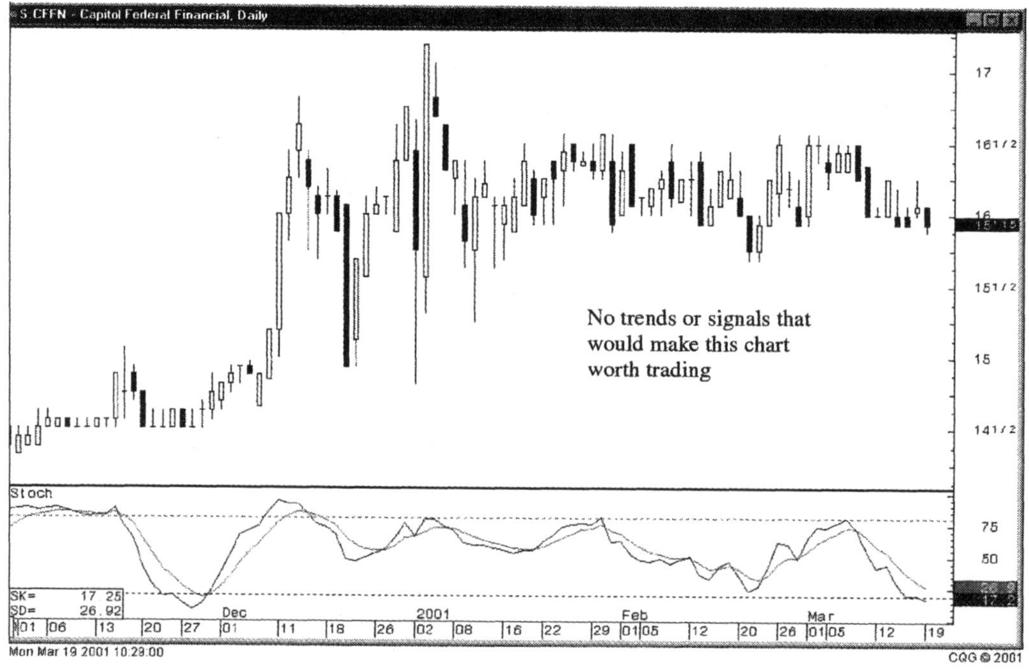

Figure 5.2 CFFN, not a trading chart.

As you study the charts, the stocks that have easy-to-read reversal signals will become evident. Put those stocks on a list somewhere. Some investors may use the Candlestick signals to trade a limited number of stocks, going long or short, at well-defined signal reversals. This style of trading eliminates the extra few minutes each day doing searches for new buy or sell positions. Becoming well versed in the trading habits of a few select positions has its advantages. Support and resistance levels are better identified. Correlating Candlestick formations with these levels produces an extremely high prospect of profiting from pinpointing the reversals. The positions can be exploited both ways—by bullish moves and bearish moves.

You will be pleasantly surprised at how quickly you recognize and remember the important signals. Learning the signals can take as little as a couple of hours. A couple of hours of reviewing past reversal points on your charts will help you retain the signal's formations. That forceful emotion, greed, produces the impetus for retaining the signal images. The process of remembering the signals is now driven from the desire of producing profits, not a mechanical exercise. Wanting to remember what will make money produces a strong motivational factor.

The visual identification is the important aspect of learning the signals. Knowing the name of the signal or the psychology of why the formation works is not a necessity for using the signals profitably. However, eventually knowing the name and becoming more knowledgeable about the psychology behind the formations gives the investor more confidence. It aids in the evaluation of whether a trade is in trouble or not, after you have put a trade on.

Search Programs

Using search programs has two major functions. First, using a search program allows the investor to dissect the formations as a function of formulating the search parameters. It will implant the elements of each signal firmly into your mind. There are a number of excellent search software service companies: TC2000, Telescan, and Trade Station 2000, just to name a few. All have excellent search capabilities. The second function of a search software program is the fast execution for creating a list of the best possible trades.

The best software program for providing an easy-to-use format at a reasonable monthly fee is TC2000. It doesn't bog down your system, and it is easy to customize for Candlestick searches. It allows you to download all ten thousand or so trading symbols. From that list, the best buy or sell formations can be cultivated in a matter of minutes. Additionally, TC2000 has dozens of pre-formulated technical processes already built into its program. This permits the investor to tweak the searches for optimal trades by using the best combinations of technical parameters. TC2000 makes finding those eight or 10 highest-profit probability trades amazingly fast, once the search parameters are in place. Spending an hour formatting the signals, the ones most likely to produce the best profits (that is, the major signals), is the best procedure for learning the signals.

Putting a signal's pattern formation into formula descriptions creates the best method for mentally understanding each signal. TC2000's customizing process is simple to use. It can be set up to search the total universe of stocks or customized to search specific industries or sectors. It can eliminate all the small capitalization stocks or all the large capitalization stocks, depending upon your personal preferences.

The following is a method that has been most effective in searches for the best possible trades available with no industry or sector preferences. Not all stocks fit necessary basic parameters, which can be established for all searches. These basic paramenters are simple.

First, liquidity needs to be addressed to be able to get in and out of trades. A small account might include the parameter that the daily average volume is greater than 200,000 shares per day. A larger account or an institutional account will probably eliminate all stocks that have less than a certain number of shares—for example, 500,000 shares to 1,000,000 shares per day. This will allow them to get into or out of a stock position without affecting the price radically.

The next parameter is the price range that reflects the investor's comfort zone. Because most brokerage firms do not margin against stocks trading less than $5.00 per share, you might make that a minimum parameter. Other traders make excellent profits trading stocks in the $2.00 to $5.00 range. They would set their parameters lower. Yet other traders are more comfortable trading stocks in the $20 to $70 price range. The parameters can be set to each investor's preference.

On the other hand, if you know that you will rarely buy stocks greater than $150.00 per share. Why bother evaluating those charts? Put on a maximum price parameter.

Once these basic parameters are put into the search function, you have reduced your universe of potentials down to approximately 3,600 stocks. Next, the search is oriented toward looking for longs or shorts. TC2000 makes it simple to segregate those stocks. If looking for potential long positions, a customized stochastics parameter is added. The TC2000 search program permits you to add or eliminate stocks by the level of the stochastics. In the case of searching for long positions, the search would be limited to all stocks that have stochastics below 20 that day. If you wanted to get more specific, it could be set up as stochastics below 20 *and* heading up. For the purposes of most searches, that extra tweak is not required.

Implanting the Signals in Your Memory

The exercise that will ingrain the signals into your memory is the next step. Describe each signal in formula terms. Going through the process of creating the formula for each signal is easy. The actual process of creating the formulas will make the development of each signal very clear. For example, how is the Bullish Engulfing pattern formed?

First, the open of today is below the close of the previous day. That formula would set up as:

$$0<C1$$

AND the close of today is greater than the open of yesterday:

$$C>01$$

That is easy. Once you have done this simple process, visualizing a Bullish Engulfing Pattern should be clear from now on. It is now in your search program. You can name it "Bullish Engulfing Patterns." To further enhance the search criteria, you would add the stochastics parameter to find all Bullish Engulfing signals that occur in stocks where the stochastics are below the 20 level. Every time you update the data (depending upon the speed of your computer, this takes from one minute to three minutes), the scan list will show you how many stocks showed up in that particular search.

All the signals can be dissected this way. The Shooting Star would have the opposite parameters. Stochastics would be set to find stocks with the stochastics over 80. The open and the close are within the lower 33 percent of the daily trading range. This would make the upper shadow twice the size of the body. Obviously, it will not take more than a couple of times to pull up the Shooting Star search results to recognize a Shooting Star. The same can be done with all the signals.

Time and effort? With the simplicity of TC2000's system, it should not take any longer than 15 minutes, at most, to formulate each signal. In less than three hours you should have a search program that spits out all the major signals every day. At that point, your job will be to evaluate the best of the best signals.

Summary

Learning the signals is easier than what the public's perception has been. The number of important signals, or the signals that are most often observed, is less than 10. The remaining signals should be studied, but the time spent upon them is a function of keeping them in the back of your mind. When one of the other signals appears, you want to be able to recognize that it *might* be a signal. After a few times identifying and verifying a signal (reviewing the signal pages), the formation will remain with you.

Today's computer charting services make analyzing past charts an easy exercise. Recognizing the Candlestick signals at the reversal points of past price movements reinforces the memorization of the signals as well as confirming to the investor the frequency with which the signals occur. Not being familiar with the signals is the major reason for such a large percentage of investors not taking advantage of them.

The motivation of making profits will be the best stimulus for the learning process. Do not let the task of becoming educated on the signals be a deterrent. For the few hours required to become acclimated to their identification and meaning, the profits developed from their use will be expediently massive.

Profits are made easier when identifying Candlestick signals in a common pattern. Wouldn't you like to be able to prepare for the next potential trade setup? Knowing approximately when a Candlestick signal should be appearing, due to a common technical formation developing, multiplies your investment opportunities. Powerful investment fund allocation strategies can be properly scheduled. Trade implementation can be optimized. Your entry and exit decision processes will be reinforced when recognizing successful formations. Chapter 6 introduces you to a number of common patterns. Being able to perceive profitable trades, with proven results, increases the chances of timely trading strategies.

Chapter 6

COMMON PATTERNS

Never believe on faith, see for yourself! What you yourself don't learn you don't know. Bertolt Brecht

Analyzing charts has residual benefits. As described previously in this book, finding the perfect signal becomes like finding that bright, shiny, new golf ball in the rough or the historic gold coin that washes up on the beach. When you see it, it jumps out at you. That instant exhilaration hits you, knowing that you have found something of value.

Whether perusing the charts is either a chore or pleasant exercise, it has beneficial side effects. Successful trading patterns eventually become easily recognized. Witnessing profitable combinations of signals, price moves, and stochastic positions provides an inventory of mental images. These images, just as the Japanese rice traders accumulated them over the centuries, become part of your arsenal for recognizing profitable trade situations.

To speed up the recognition process, this chapter illustrates a number of common patterns. These patterns are a combination of Western chart patterns with the Candlestick signals incorporated into them. Unlike Western chart analysis that anticipates a reversal occurring and waiting for the confirmation, the Candlestick signals add another valuable dimension. Identifying the formation of a Western chart pattern provides alerts for the Candlestick investor. When a potential reversal point is ready to be tested, the conventional chart watchers are waiting to see if a level is going to hold and reverse the trend. The added information embodied in the candles offers a two- or three-day head start for the Candlestick trader. This may not sound significant, but if a trade has a 10-percent return possibility, getting in before the rest of the crowd is important. The Candlestick signals are valuable for being aware when a longer-term formation is setting up.

The Importance of the Number Three

The number three has great importance in the Japanese culture. Their emphasis on the number three is important to their method of analyzing.

Double tops and bottoms and quadruple tops and bottoms have the same weighted importance as a triple top or bottom in Western analysis. Formations with three in them receive special attention in Candlestick analysis. If you study the amount of Western charting functions that use the number three, you discover that it holds a predominant position also. The head-and-shoulders pattern is the same as the Three Mountains Pattern in Candlesticks. Examples illustrate over and over how the number three influences investment analysis. There are three classifications of trends: major, secondary, and minor. The Japanese culture, in premodern times, associated the number three with mystical powers. Their saying, "three times lucky," is an extension of that belief. Threes are apparent in the descriptions of the reversal signals: Three White Soldiers precede a market rally, Three Black Crows forewarn of a market decline. Three Rising Method, Three Falling Method, Three River Bottoms—the number three is evident throughout the Japanese descriptions.

The number four, however, has foreboding overtones. This is due to the Japanese pronunciation of the number four being the same as the pronunciation of the word death.

Windows

An important gauge for detecting a direction and the magnitude of a trend is revealed through *windows*, the Japanese term for gaps. Western terminology is expressed as "the filling of a gap" whereas the Japanese call it "closing the window." A window is created when there is a gap between the high point of one trading day and the low point of the following day in an uptrend. The reverse occurs during a downtrend. The low trading point of the first day has a gap between the high trading point of the next day.

The appearance of a window has significant implications. It demonstrates a strong buying or selling presence. The Japanese say to go in the direction of the window. Windows also act as support and resistance levels. The appearance of a window in an uptrend signifies further move in that direction. It then acts as the support or floor on any pullbacks. If the window gets closed by the pullback and continues, the previous uptrend is negated. Conversely, a window to the downside strongly indicates that the trend will keep going in that direction. Any rebound of prices in that downtrend should run into resistance or a ceiling at the window. "Closing that window" means the rally continues and the downtrend has come to an end.

All windows eventually get closed or all gaps eventually get filled. Rarely will a window be left open. You can test an open window and use this information to your advantage. In an uptrend, the window can be used as an area to buy on pullbacks. If the pullback does close the window, it can now be used as a spot to short. The opposite strategy can be applied with a window in a downtrend.

The best place to use a window is at the point that a strong buy or sell signal is coordinating with the stochastics. As illustrated in Figure 6.1, representing Serologicals Corp., a trend started with a gap up after a Candlestick Morning Star signal. The window reveals that the buying is pronounced—a good sign to see. This is a case where the window may never be closed or at least not for a good while. The additional factors that make this a convincing trade is the stochastics starting to curl up. This is not a scenario plucked out of thousands of chart illustrations to prove a point. Do your own research. Review charts from the past, looking for the point where the gap up and stochastics coincide. It will not take long for the evidence to convince you that this is a high probability trade. Additionally, it will not take long to discover that this is not an isolated example. Chart patterns resembling this example appear almost daily in the universe of stocks.

The Japanese put great significance in windows occurring right after a congestion area or at a new high. Again, the status of the stochastics becomes important when analyzing the situation. A window to the upside, after a congestion area, has probably allowed the stochastics to gain more upside push. This would be a relatively safe time to buy, using the window as a probable support area after the next leg of the rally started.

Note in the Universal Display Corp. chart, shown in Figure 6.2, how the price was traded in a range between $8 and $10 for a few months. Apparently

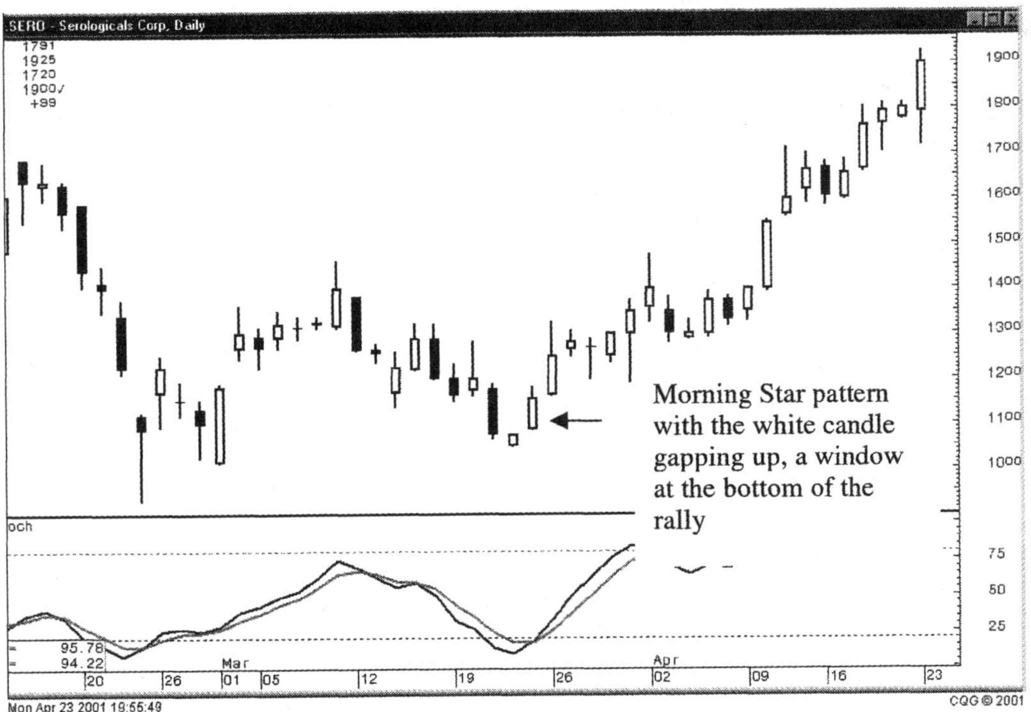

Figure 6.1 Windows or gaps at the beginning of an upmove indicates very strong buying presence.

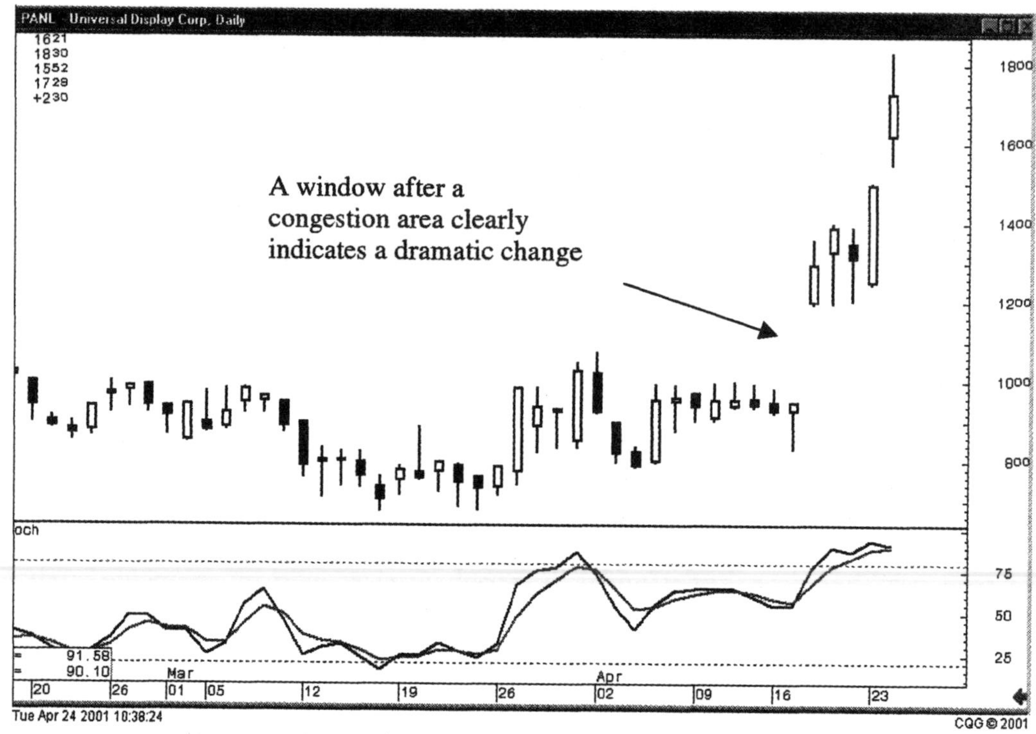

Figure 6.2 A large window reveals a new strong buying sentiment in a price trend.

something occurred to gap the price up to the $12 area. From that point, the upmove started to head higher, after testing the window area twice. The fact that it gapped up from a persistent trading range would have been the first alert. Having the knowledge that a window was created would have provided the confidence to commit investment funds at these new high levels.

A window appearing at new highs requires quick analysis. Is it occurring after a strong rally and with the stochastics well into the overbought area? Or has it recently hit a new high, backed off for a period, and is coming back up through the recent highs? The first description could be an exhaustion gap. As mentioned earlier, a trend that has been in existence for a period of time builds the confidence of investors. This confidence builds up to the point that the exuberance creates a gap up in price. If the selling does not start that day, more than likely, in the next day or two, the selling will become evident.

Figure 6.3, representing Methode Electronics Inc., illustrates a different situation at the new highs. Close scrutiny is needed to see if the buying is going to continue after the gap up. Usually after a big move to the upside, some immediate profit taking will occur. There will be a nebulous period after the stock opens.

Will the sellers start selling immediately, such as is the case in Figure 6.3, or will there be a short period of profit taking and then the upmove resumes?

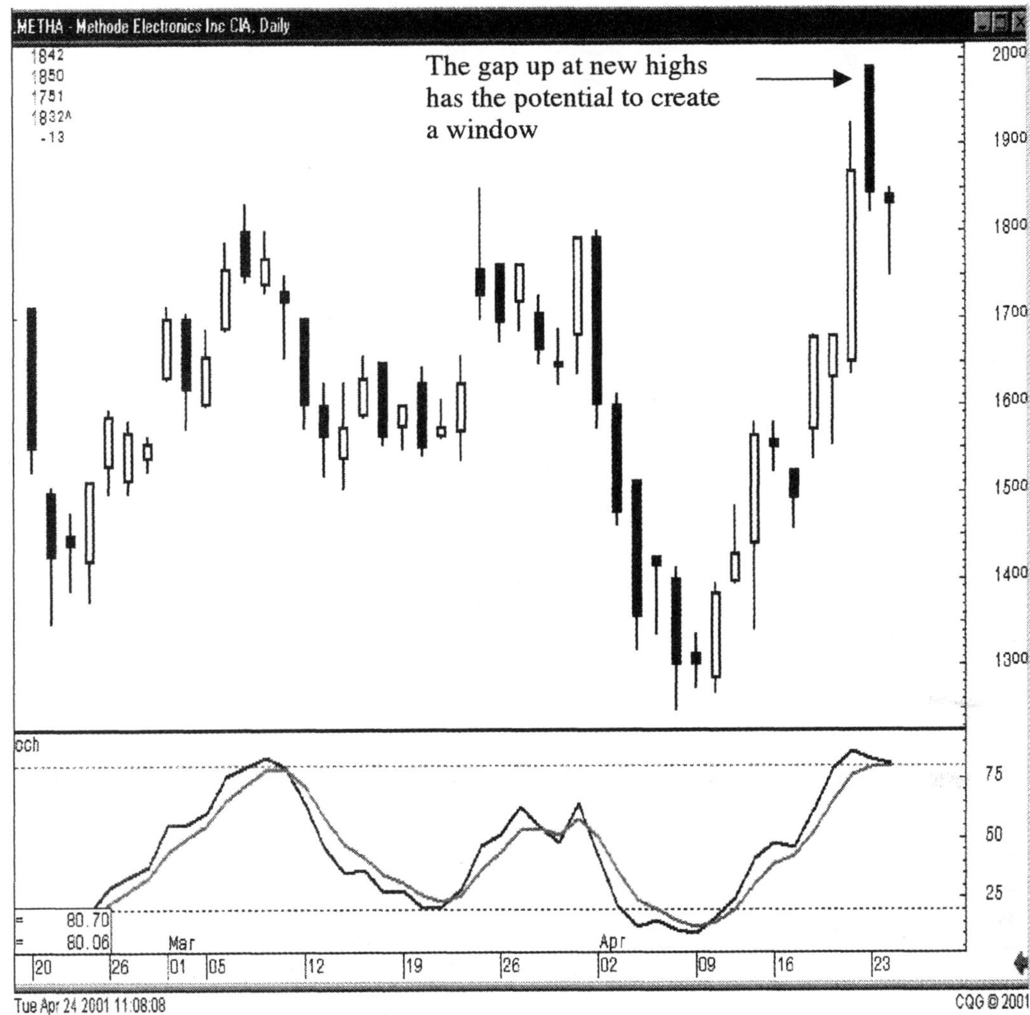

Figure 6.3 A gap up after a long uptrend is most likely an exhaustion gap, start taking profits.

That is what will have to be analyzed during the initial minutes of the trading day. However, knowing the status of the stochastics creates a tremendous advantage for being prepared. After a straight run up, as in this example, the stochastics indicate that this could be an exhaustion gap. Figure 6.4, representing Adobe Systems Inc., demonstrates how the stochastics suggest that more upside is available after the window.

Notice that the status of the stochastics were not into the overbought area yet in Figure 6.4. When the window is formed, the stochastics appear to have more upside potential available. That analysis should provide some impetus to remain long or to go long on this trade.

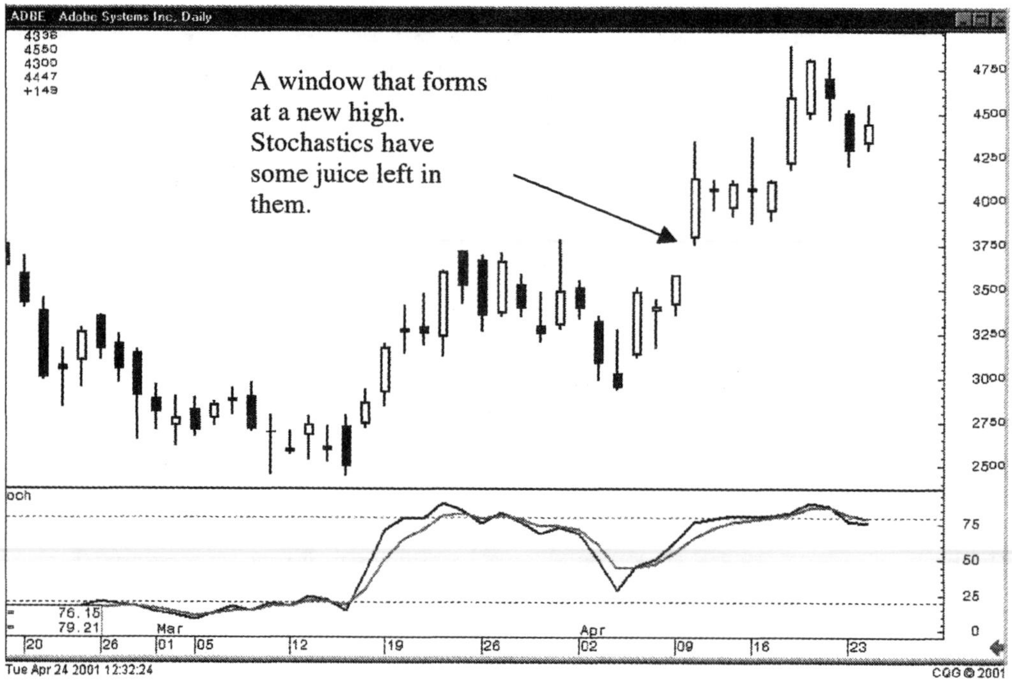

Figure 6.4 A window forming at a new high demonstrates strong bullish sentiment that should remain for a while.

High-Price Gapping Play

After a sharp move to the upside, it is normal to see a few days of consolidation. This is usually indicated by a Harami or small-bodied trading days. A group of small-bodied days reveals that the market is undecided. After a period of indecision, a window to the upside demonstrates that buying strength is coming back into the stock. The Japanese call this a high-price gapping play. It is named from the fact that the prices remained near the high end of the trading range before gapping to the upside. During this period of consolidation, the stochastics have usually had time to pull back and gather more steam for the next leg up.

Note in the Pulte Corp. chart, shown in Figure 6.5, that after a sharp upmove, the price consolidated for three days at the top range of the new high. The gap up after the consolidation period was a good indicator that new levels were going to be breached.

Low-Price Gapping Plays

The low-price gapping play pattern is the counterpart of the high-price gapping play. After a severe down day, a Harami signal and/or a series of small-bodied days trade at the lower end of the big downmove, showing price stability for

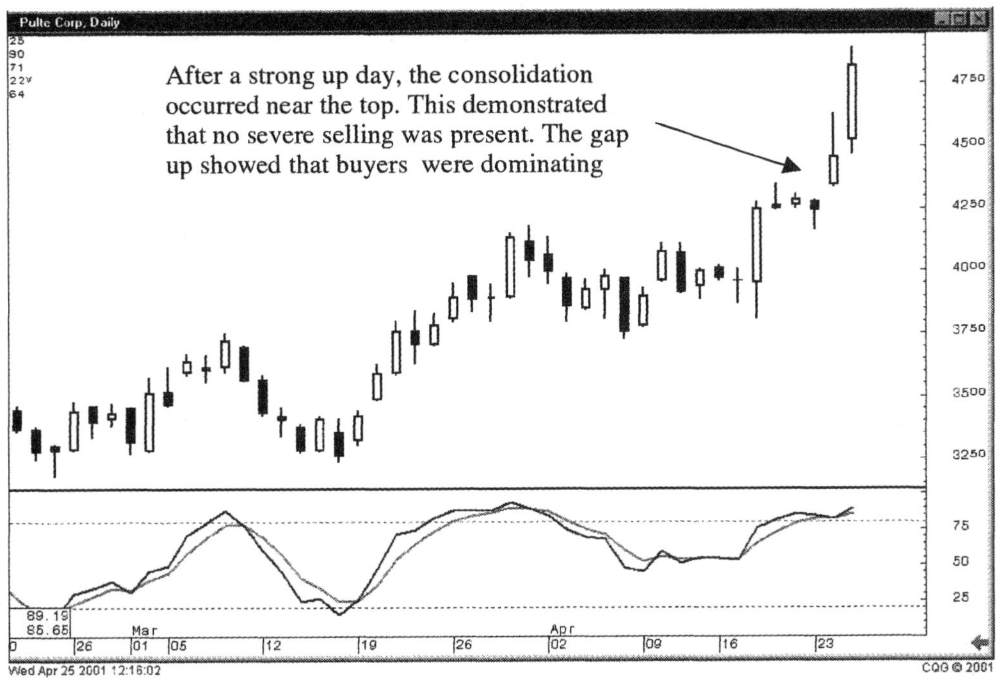

Figure 6.5 Gapping away from a high level, where the bears could not knock prices down, indicates strong investor sentiment.

a period. This initially gives the bulls hope that a base is forming. When the price gaps to the downside, the hopes of the bulls are dashed. More selling pushes the price down further as despondent bulls start bailing out.

The Safeco Corp. chart in Figure 6.6 illustrates the low-price gapping play. After a severe downmove, the downtrend is stopped by the appearance of a Harami. For the next few days, the bulls try to move prices back up. The bears are able to keep prices from advancing past the one halfway point of the last big black candle. The Doji indicates the bulls and bears at equilibrium. The weak open after the Doji would have alerted the Candlestick investor that the bears were in control.

Windows at Critical Points

Witnessing a gap over an obvious trend-line gives a good signal that a new trend may be developing. Figure 6.7, showing the NASDAQ index during early April 2001, reveals a breakout from the existing trend. The gap up from a few days prior during the bottom Morning Star formation, as well as the direction of the stochastics, were good indications that a breach of the trend-line was quite possible. Seeing this setup and witnessing a gap open above the trend-line would have provided the Candlestick investor ample opportunity to load up the portfolio.

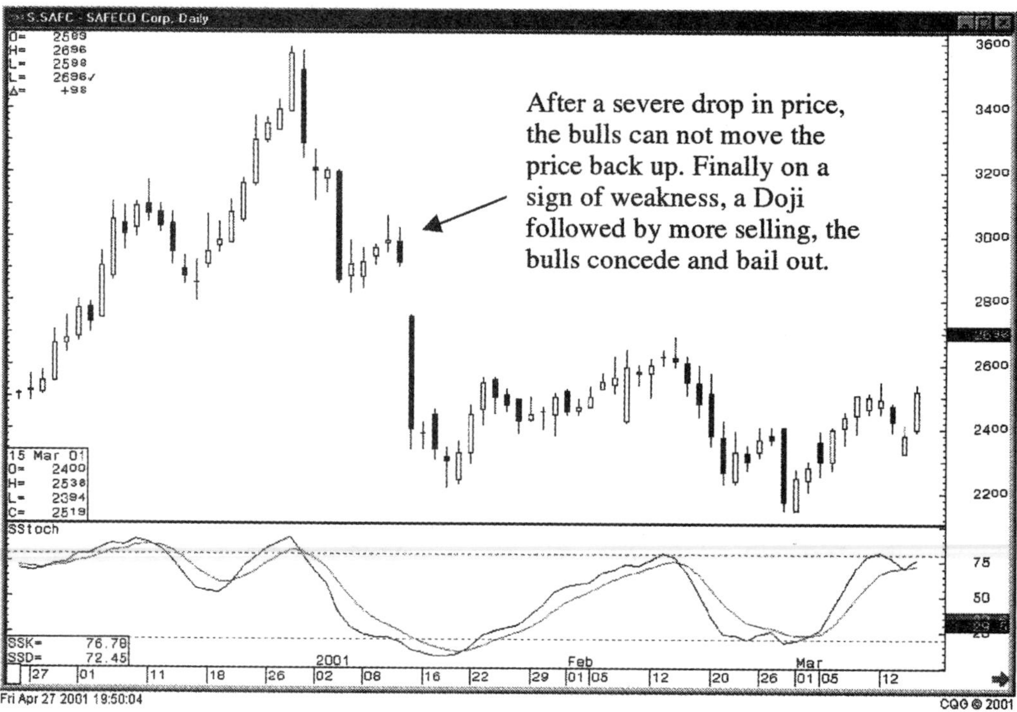

Figure 6.6 A gap down, after the bulls could not get a major upside move started demonstrates a strong selling impetus.

In this example, the trend-line became an obvious resistance area. All chart watchers would have been acutely aware of its presence. The fact that buying was enthusiastic at the point of breaching the trend-line and gapping up above the line, demonstrated a significant change in investor sentiment. The window, formed by the gap up, illustrated an obvious change that could be clearly viewed. This should have alerted investors that a new dynamic had come into the market.

Dumpling Tops

A Dumpling Top, which is formed by a convex series of small bodies, has obvious features that visually prepare investors (as shown in Figure 6.8a). The rounded top provides a clear indication that the buying is waning. As prices start declining, a window forms, demonstrating that the selling has picked up some strength.

As can be seen in the Clayton Homes Inc. chart in Figure 6.8b, the volatility of the stock price diminishes greatly compared to its previous trading ranges. The stochastics move into the overbought area as the bodies of the candles become small. The rounding top demonstrates a gradual change in

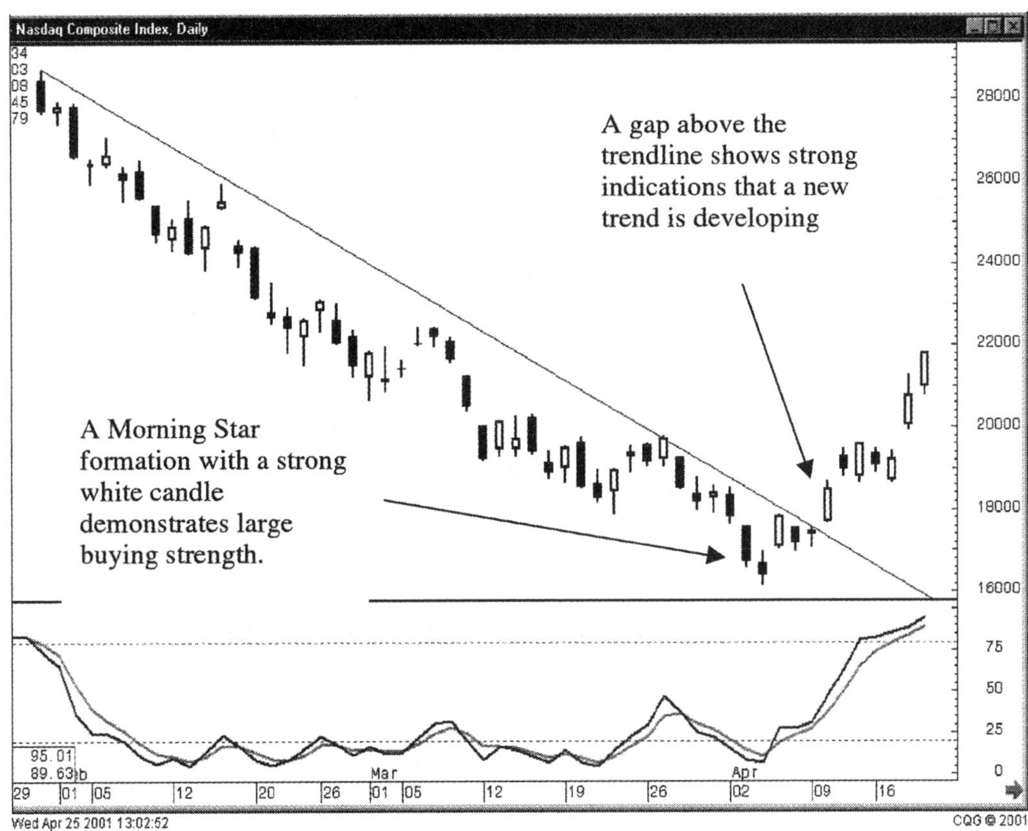

Figure 6.7 A window forming at a crucial trend-line means that the significance of the trend-line is not going to interfere with the strength of the buying.

investor sentiment. As the price starts its decline, a gap to the downside is indicative of the bearish sentiment starting to pick up steam.

Fry Pan Bottoms

The opposite pattern of the Dumpling Top is the Fry Pan Bottom (as shown in Figure 6.9a). Called a rounded bottom in Western charting, it has a convex formation. The small bodies provide a clear visual picture of buying slowly coming into the price. A gap up, as the ascent starts, shows the buying is coming into the price with some force.

The New Focus Inc. chart in Figure 6.9b is a good example of the Fry Pan Bottom. The magnitude of the daily price ranges contracts and the price shows a slow consistent rounding bottom. After a week or two of bottoming, the upside is started with a small gap. This reveals that the strength of the buying is stepping up the pace.

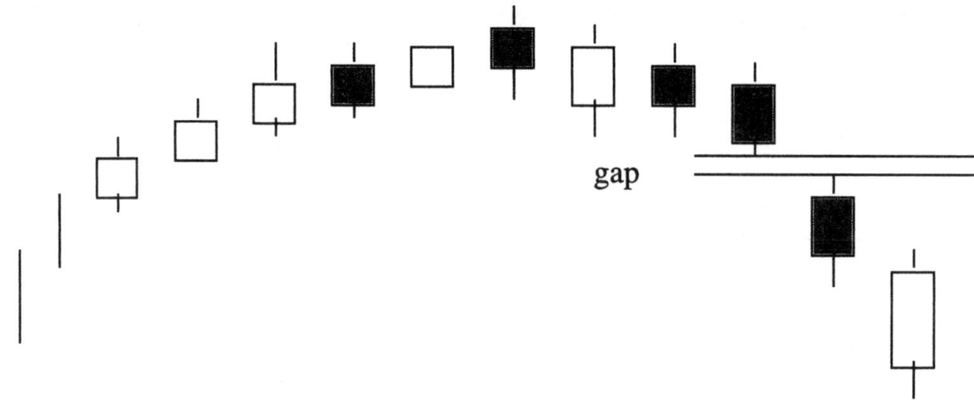

Figure 6.8a Dumpling Top.

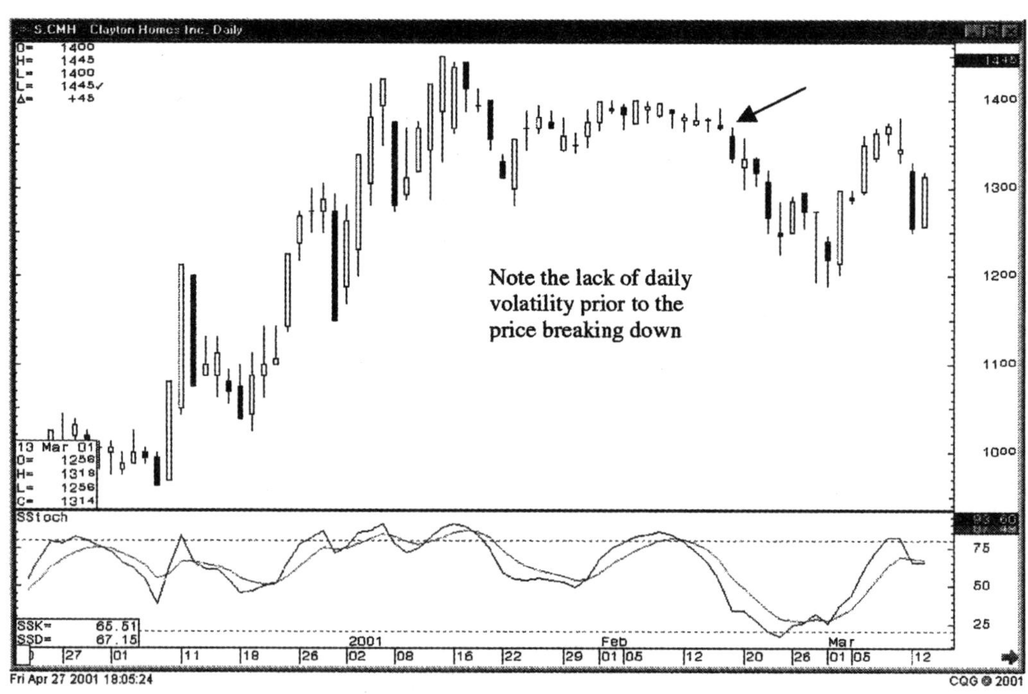

Figure 6.8b The gap in a Dumpling Top Formation is the evidence that the sellers are now in a rush to get out of the stock.

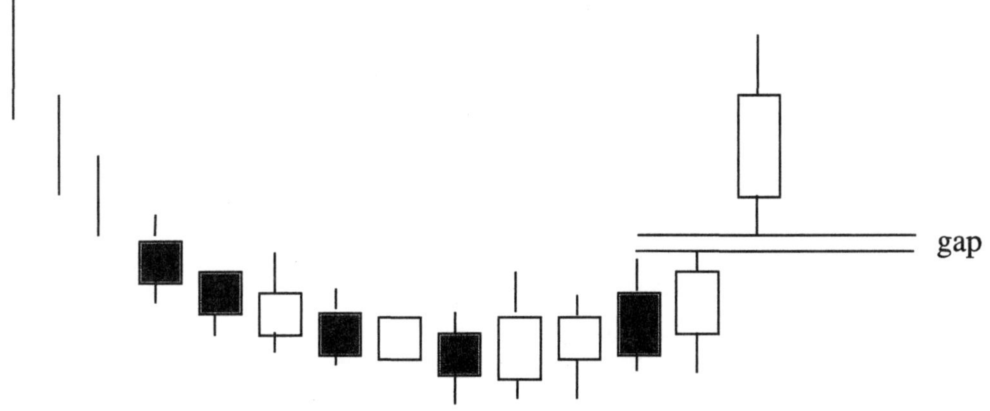

Figure 6.9a Fry Pan Bottom.

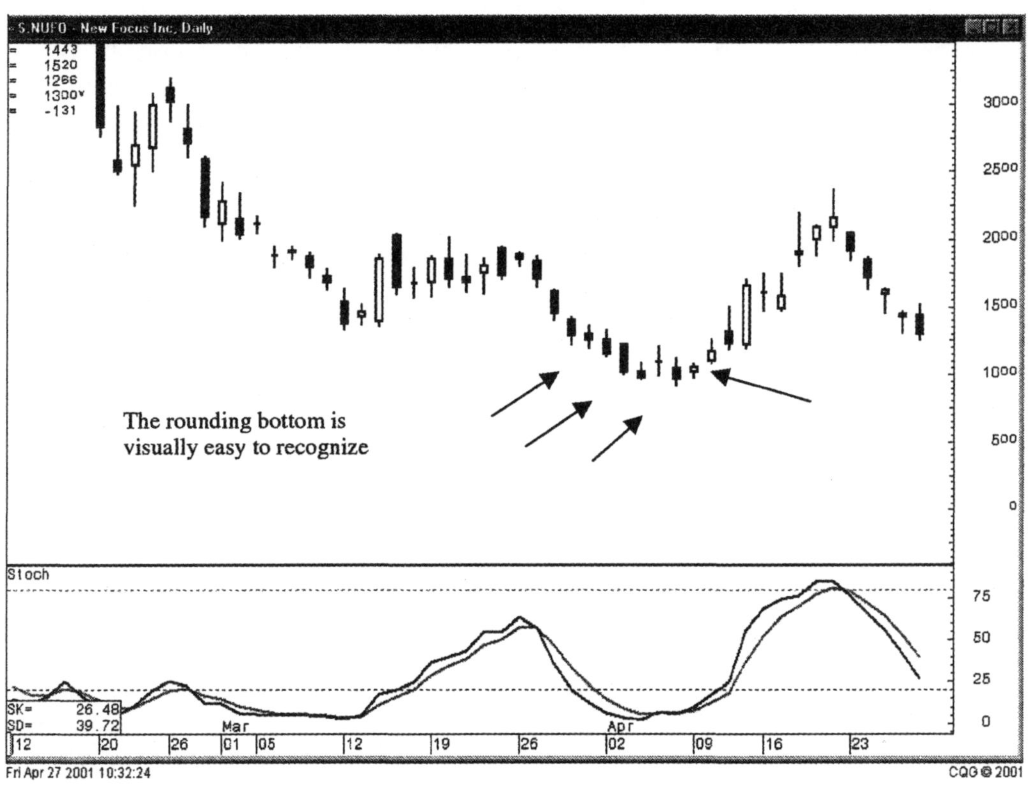

Figure 6.9b A gap to the upside indicates that the buyers are now coming into the stock with some force.

J Hook Patterns

A pattern that somewhat resembles the Fry Pan Bottom, but has more energy to it is the J Hook pattern. This pattern develops when a stock price has a strong upmove and then starts backing off. A Candlestick signal usually identifies when the initial upmove is over. The stochastics turn back down, confirming the downtrend. After a few days, the downtrend starts showing some signs of waning, either from candlestick bullish formations or the stochastics trajectory begins to flatten out. Signs of this occurrence should alert investors to closely monitor the price action over the next couple of days. The appearance of a strong bullish signal although the stochastics are still in the upper or middle range warrants investigating the chart further. If the stochastics begin to curl back up, a J Hook pattern is likely to appear.

The J Hook pattern has all the same elements of the cup portion of the Cup and Handle pattern. The difference is that the action is much faster than the Cup and Handle pattern. Where as the Cup and Handle pattern may take three or four weeks to develop, The J Hook may take only a little over one week. As seen in Figure 6.10, representing the JNI Corp., the recent high acts as the pivotal level. Candlestick signals will indicate whether the recent high

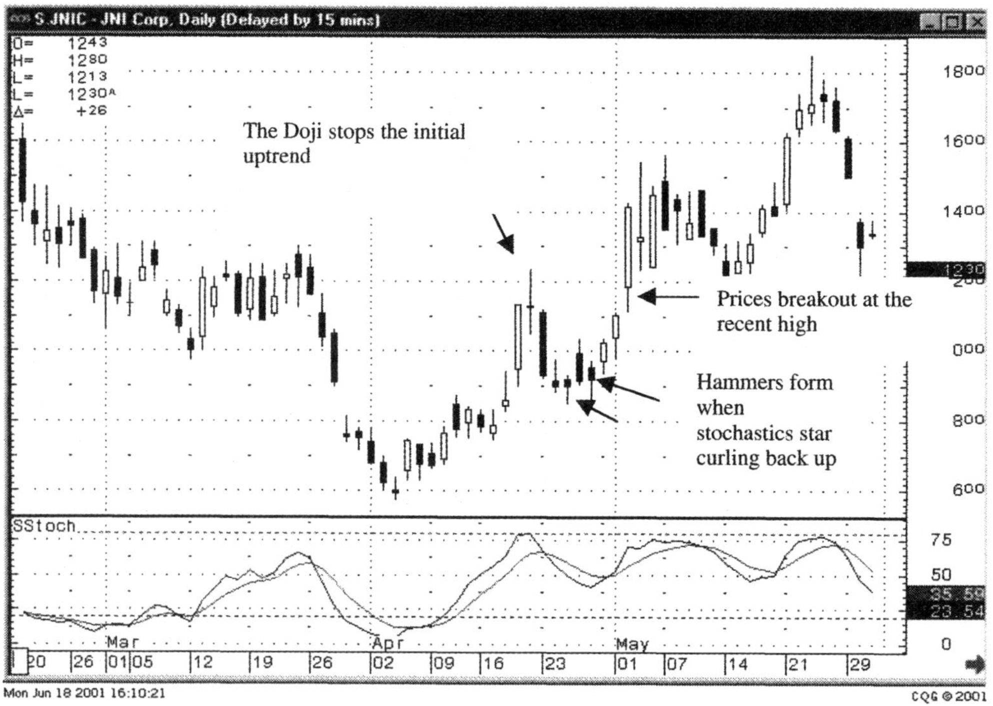

Figure 6.10 A J Hook formation is just a pullback. More profits are made when it breaks out to new highs.

will act as the resistance point or if prices can head to higher levels. The advantage of being prepared for this trade is the breakout aspect. Once prices breakout to new highs, the resistance disappears. Going above the last resistance level has everybody guessing. Where is the rally going to end? How high can it go? The bears step out of the way allowing the price movement to gain momentum. Use these trade set-ups and you'll find them profitable.

The recent high also acts as an alert. Notice in the Intel Corporation chart, shown in Figure 6.11, that the recent high now acts as a resistance level. Technical analysts, following other technical methods, are watching to see what is going to happen at the previous high. In the case of Intel, it tested the high and pulled back to form a Doji. This represents indecision at a crucial level. The Doji would have alerted the Candlestick analyst to take profits on the close. The other technical followers would not have confirmed the lack of strength in pushing through the resistance level until a substantial percentage lower. Having the additional foresight as to whether a rally or decline is going to persist can save significant profits. Being able to save an extra 3 to 5 percent on each trade adds up quickly. Turning funds 20 times a year would equate to an extra savings of 60 to 100 percent.

Figure 6.11 A J Hook pattern that showed weakness at the previous high. Take profits and go elsewhere.

Tower Tops and Tower Bottoms

Tower Tops and Tower Bottoms are clear reversal patterns—clear in the sense that they are easily recognized by a quick glance at a chart. The Tower Top is formed after the market has been in an uptrend.

In the Telecomp PCS Inc. chart, seen in Figure 6.12, a long white candle or a series of white candles appear. The long white body or series of white bodies form an upmove that is substantial and distinguishable from the rest of the advances and decline slopes of the normal trends. When the ascent slows decidedly and signs of selling appear, the Tower Top is completed with large black candles taking the prices down hard. The formation of long candles resemble a tower structure, thus the name. Some Japanese writings refer to the Tower Top as a Turret Top.

The Tower Bottom is obviously the opposite scenario at the bottom of a market trend. After the appearance of a long black candle or series of long black candles, the descent flattens out. Then one or more white candles appears. There are long candles on the way down and on the way up. Again, as in the Tower Top, the Tower Bottom formation stands out compared to the normal trading. It is a noticeable pattern. As seen in Figure 6.13, representing Tripath Imagining Inc., the long black candle and the long white

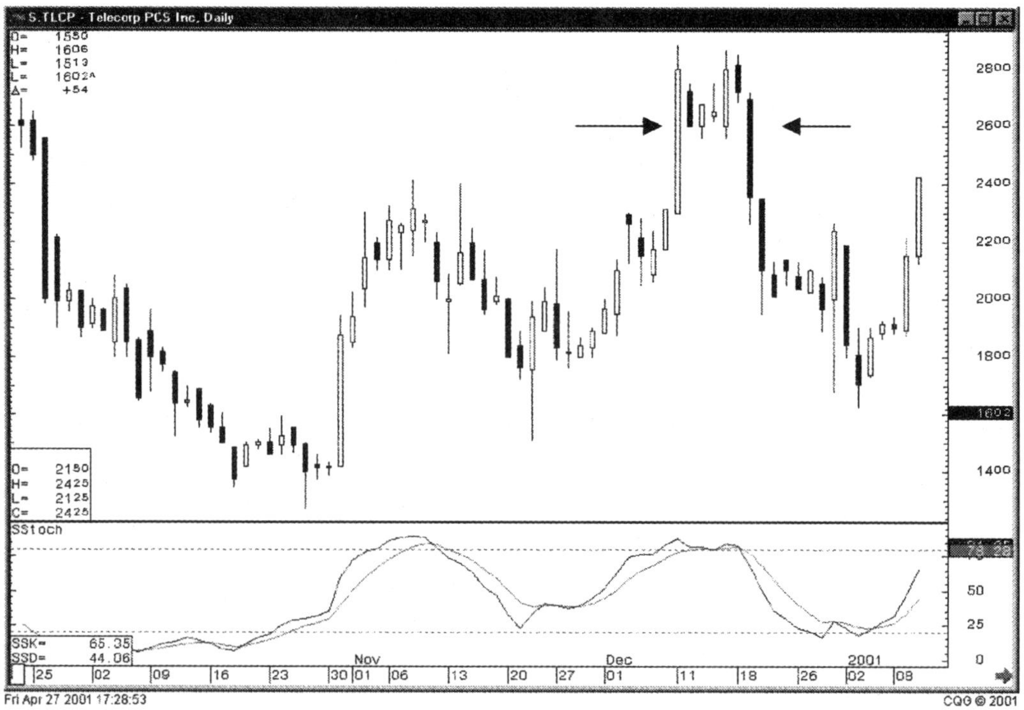

Figure 6.12 Tower Tops are easily visualized; they make great profit patterns.

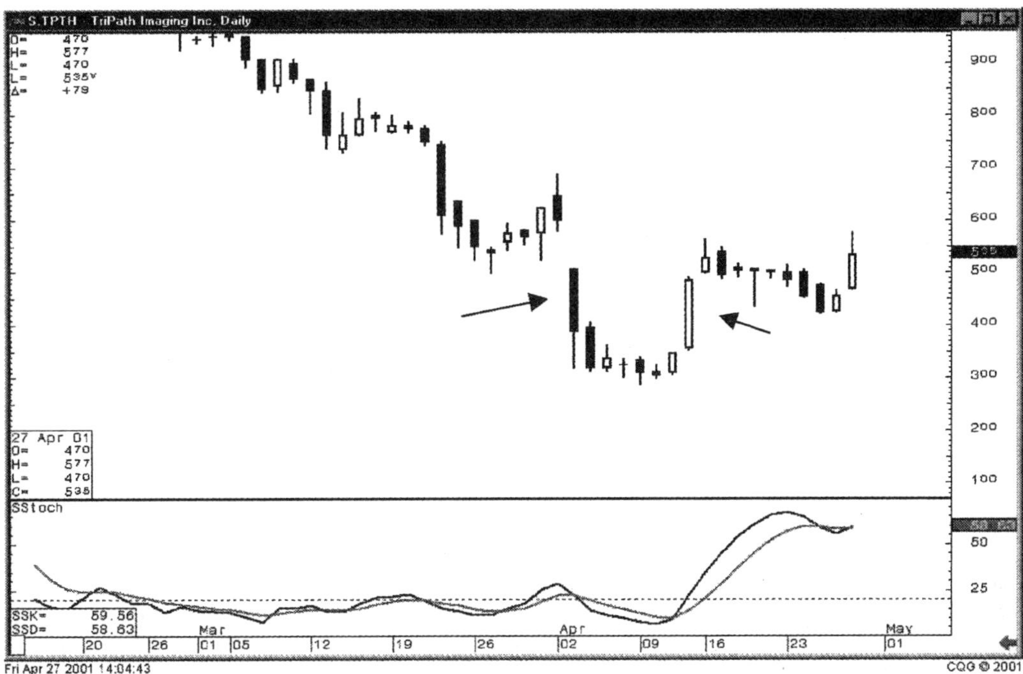

Figure 6.13 Tower Bottoms demonstrate an obvious change in investor sentiment.

candle are approximately the same length. Both are substantially longer than the normal daily trading range. This formation is extremely useful for the long-term investor. A monthly chart having this formation has a great probability of being at the bottom of a long uptrend.

Cup and Handle Formation

A common formation, sometimes incorporating the Fry Pan Bottom, is the Cup and Handle Pattern. This pattern is a Western charting pattern. However, the setup for its formation is visually clear after it has occurred. The Candlestick analysts can profitably exploit this formation, benefiting early in the formation's development. The Western chartist is waiting to see if the price breaks through the handle's peak to commit funds into the trade. Upon breaching that level, a breakout should occur. The Candlestick investor has double potential from the same formation. Upon witnessing the forming of what could be a handle and seeing that the downward trajectory of the next decline is forming a bottom, the Candlesticks provide a valuable tool to gain two sets of profits from this set up.

First, if it appears as if a bottom of the cup portion is forming, Candlestick buy signals will identify when the cup formation is starting up the other side.

The returns can be easily calculated. If a purchase is put on at the bottom of the cup, the level of the first major resistance will be the peak of the handle. That move could produce a return of 8 percent, 12 percent, or more. Not bad for a two-week investment. As the price approaches level that would act as the resistance or the breakout, Candlestick analysis provides additional indications of profit potential. Examination of stochastics indicates how much buying force remains at the point of breaching the resistance area. If stochastics are well into the overbought region when approaching that point, one should be prepared for signs of a Candlestick sell signal. Any sign of weakness can get the investor out at the best profit-taking point. Should the stochastics have strength remaining when approaching the critical price level and no Candlestick sell signals are appearing, this produces an additional profit situation. Knowing that a new burst of buying will occur when it breaches that level gives reason to add to the position.

The chart for American Medical Systems Holdings Inc., seen in Figure 6.14, illustrates the Cup and Handle formation. As the price moves up after bottoming in the cup portion, the targets become the peaks of the handle. Candlestick formations, correlated with the stochastics, provide the information needed to decide whether the past peaks are going to act as resistance levels or not. Note how the candle, before the candle that breaks through the first level, does not give any indication of weakness. Stochastics show no signs of turning back down even though they are in the overbought area. The candle that does break through the most recent peak, Point B, forms another strong candle formation with no signs of selling. This makes the next higher peak, Point A, the next likely resistance. As seen in Figure 6.14, that level is blasted through. The strong candle created from that breakout level indicates that price will go much higher.

The chart of ITXC Corporation, seen in Figure 6.15, demonstrates a fizzling at the Handle peak. A close above Point B wasn't as strong a close, even though it had a run up that day. Stochastics appear to be getting stretched. The Shooting Star of the following day does show weakness in the trend, indicating that the bulls had run out of steam at a well-watched area, Point A, at the peak of the handle. The fact that this weak signal was forming near the end of the trading day could have gotten the Candlestick investor out at a good exit point, the close that day. Other technical trading methods would not have indicated a failure of the trend until the open the next day or even lower.

Scary Moves

There are some common price actions that occur during trends. Not being familiar with them can scare you out of profitable trades. Learning how prices react once the trade and/or trend have started will keep you from being juked out of good trades.

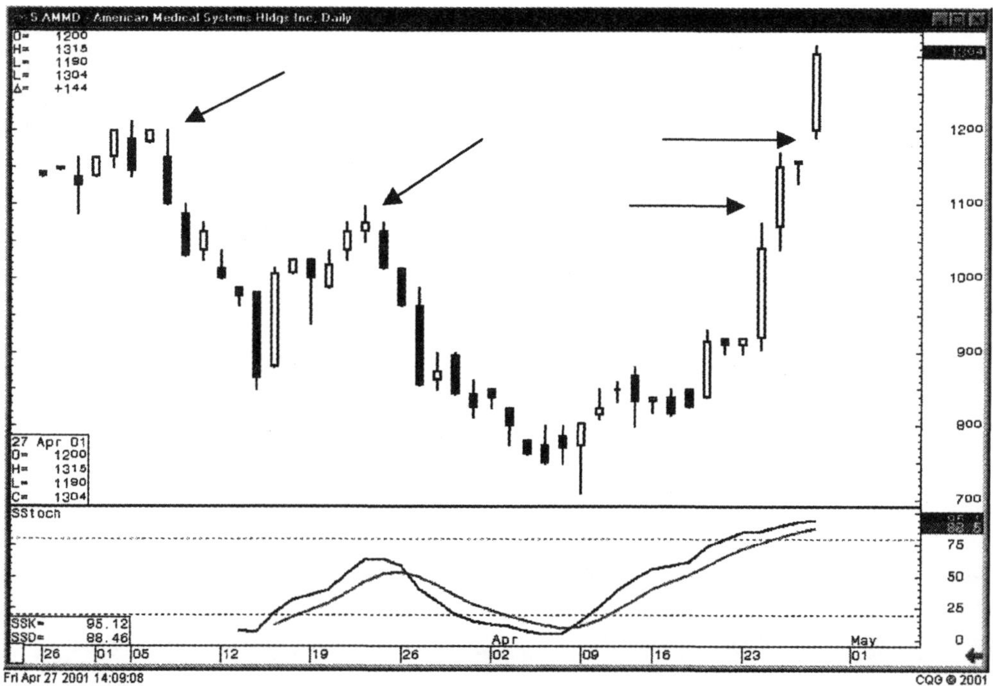

Figure 6.14 Previous high points of the handle make easily seen projected targets coming out of the cup side of the formation.

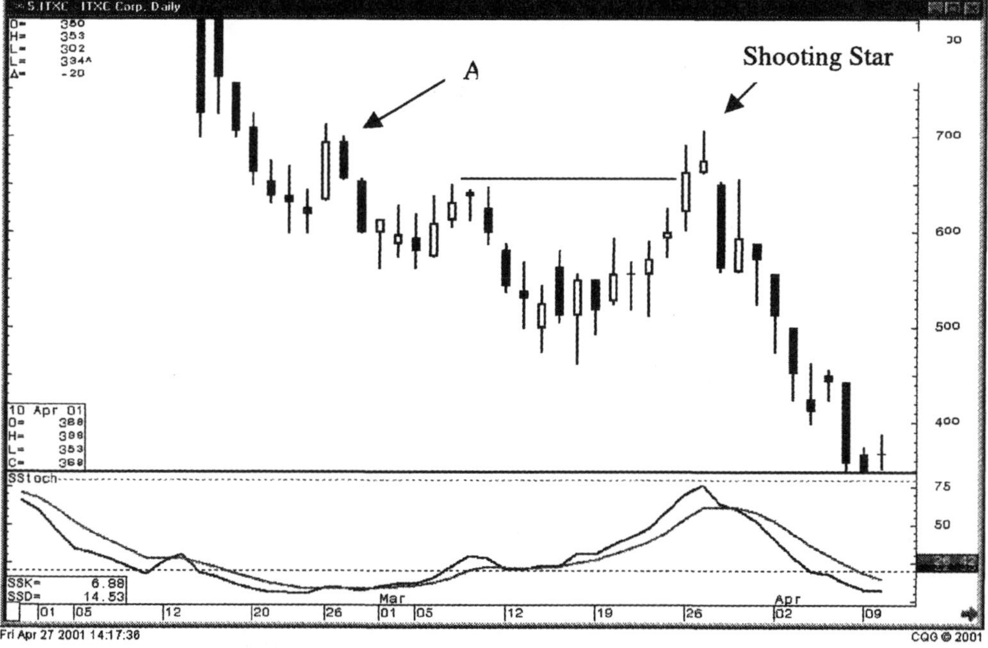

Figure 6.15 A Shooting Star shows buying weakness at a critical level indicating that prices will not move up past this point.

One common occurrence is the "last-gasp" buying day. This is seen after the third or fourth day of a reversal in a trend. Notice in Figure 6.16, representing Infosys Tech Ltd., how strong buying came in three days after a relatively solid sell signal. The top was identified by the Spinning Top. The next down leg was instigated by the lower open after the Hanging Man signal. This would have been a comfortable short in view of the stochastics direction. If the short position had been established on the open the day after the Hanging Man, notice how the second day after that would have been a testy period. Prices had come up through the entry point.

If the analysis has been performed, you've witnessed the signal, and you saw the downward movement of the stochastics, the best investment strategy is to wait it out. As scary as it will be, a basic rule for Candlestick trading is to let the end of the day form the signal. What happens during the day should not influence the trading decision. The Japanese spent many years identifying the results of the signals. The percentages are in your favor by honoring the indications of the signals.

Figure 6.16 Scary moves against a position can be mollified when analyzing the location of the Stochastics.

Waiting to see what the formation will be at the end of a time period is important. Figure 6.17, representing Integrated Circuits System Inc., demonstrates exuberant buying at the top. The Harami the next day shows that the buying had stopped, confirmed by the black candle the following day. But notice the third day after the Harami how the buyers brought the price back up to the top of the second black candle. This eats up a major share of the profits. However, the stochastics are in the middle of their downtrend. The buying is a function of the last gasp bulls thinking that the price had moved back to bargain prices. They run it up before the weight of the dominant trend pushes the prices back down.

Keep these occurrences in the back of your mind. The nimble Candlestick investor can take advantage of these fast moves by using smart stop and

Figure 6.17 The signals give an early verification of whether a trend-line is going to hold or not.

reentry points. For example, if a short position has been established and has a day or two of good profits, be ready for a reaction bounce. Being prepared for the bounce drastically reduces risk. Once any buying is observed, a safe method to stop out is placing a stop one-half way up the black candle of the previous day. The logic here is that if the price is brought up to that level, the buyers are present and will probably take the price higher. This protects some of the profits. Now a couple of reentry strategies can be put in place.

First, if the price advances a good amount higher and starts to hover at that high point, it may be time to short again. The reason is this: If the price had already moved up an inordinate percentage that day, how much further could it go? If it didn't start backing off before the end of the day, the trade could be liquidated with minor losses.

Second, once the price has gone through the buy-stop point and continued to higher levels, a sell-stop could be placed at or near the original buy-stop. If price came back down through that level, it would be demonstrating the lack of buyers to hold the price up. The downtrend should be continuing. This strategy stops out the trade as it moves up, protected the majority of the profits. If the upmove continues, no harm is done. On the other hand, if the bounce were nothing more than a bounce, as the prices came back down through the sell-stop, the trade would be reestablished. The cost of this protection was two commissions and maybe some slippage.

Trend-Lines and Trend Channels

Observe the obvious! Clear patterns can be seen on charts. They are easily seen by the inexperienced investor as well as the trained professional. Everybody that is observing them will have the same conclusions. If a support level holds, it is time to buy. If a resistance level holds, it is time to sell. The crucial word in these statements is *if*. Having the insight of the trend strength (stochastics) is an advantage. Witnessing a Candlestick signal at the point of support or resistance provides the head start to get in before the rest of the technicians. This extra lead time can make the difference between a good trade and a mediocre trade.

Anytime the obvious is going to work in your favor, use it. The trend-lines will not be evident in the early stages of a channel, but the early peaks and valleys create an opportunity for a good trade or two at the end of the channel. As illustrated in Figure 6.18, representing Johnson and Johnson, a trade situation would not have become obvious until close to the end of the channel. Yet it produced a safe short trade.

Note in the Credence Systems Corp. chart, seen in Figure 6.19, how a trend-line drawn across the tops when the Spinning Top buy point would have created a parallel line to form at the bottom. This pattern, in conjunction with the Spinning Top occurring at the stochastics turn up point would have produced a credible reason to commit funds to the trade. Additionally,

Figure 6.18 Strength or weakness can be seen at trendline levels, giving the Candlestick investor an advantage.

a short position starting from the top trend-line, a few weeks later may have reentered the short side after the pop-up near the lower trend-line. The appearance of the Doji and Shooting Star with some downside juice left in the stochastics would have given more downside profits.

The play at this level would be to estimate that there was enough downside left to possibly breach the lower trend-line. If the lower trend-line did not hold, as in this example, a sharp downside move would have been anticipated. This is due to everybody watching the trend-line selling or shorting when they see that line did not hold.

Learning Technical Patterns

Having knowledge of some of the basic technical patterns is an added benefit. Though not necessary for pure Candlestick trading, being able to incorporate the criteria that many other technical investors are using to make their decisions enhances the effectiveness of the Candlestick signals. Wouldn't you like to know that a reversal has occurred while the majority of investors are anticipating that a reversal has occurred, getting in before the crowd adds that much more positive potential to your position. Once you have identified successful patterns, initiated by your recognition of

Figure 6.19 Seeing a Candlestick formation that does not indicate any importance at a critical support level usually means that level is not going to hold.

Candlestick signals, it becomes easy to remember them. You will remain familiar with potential pattern set-ups due to the best stimuli available, *profits*.

> **I hear and I forget. I see and I remember. I do and I understand.**
> **Chinese proverb**

This chapter has exposed you to a few highly successful technical patterns. A more in-depth list and description of technical patterns can be found on the Web site (**www.candlestickforum.com**). The more you study charts, the more you will become proficient in visualizing how profitable trades set up.

Having the knowledge of what formations precede a profitable move, enhanced with the appearances of Candlestick signals, produce a combination of investment insights. These insights will revolutionize your investment thought process. In-depth signal dissection illustrates investor sentiment. The Japanese added an element that the most sophisticated computer programs are not capable of performing: analyzing the **thinking** that produced the signals. You receive the fruits of an exclusive research methodology. Where else have you studied the thought processes of the investor? Elliot Wave and Pattern Recognition methods touch upon the fact that investment psychology produces oscillations, thus cycles in price movements. Fibonnacci numbers demonstrate a way to measure the amplitude of the waves. But rarely will you find an investment method that breaks down each formation and describes what was occurring between the bull's camp and bear's camp. This information rewards the Candlestick investor with revolutionary investment advantages. The conventional investment methods become mundane. You will be provided with the ammunition to perfect investment strategies to maximize returns. You will use these skills for the rest of your life. You will take advantage of opportunities never presented to you before, mainly due to the fact that few in the U.S. investment community know how to extract the opportunities themselves.

Permanently Alter Your Investment Abilities

Your investment thought processes will be permanently altered—not because you have been exposed to a revolutionary new investment concept, but because you have been exposed to a revolutionary old investment program. Tested. Proven. Successful. And just now being properly taught in this part of the world. As mentioned earlier, this trading program was not being hidden from the masses. The Japanese never refused explanation of Candlesticks. The masses never asked to be taught. Your reading this book indicates that the wealth of conventional investment advise and programs are not fulfilling your expectations and you want more.

Chapter 7 illuminates investment basics that are inherent to the Candlestick signals, practices that are easily stated but never incorporated into most investor's disciplines. Adhering to the Candlestick lessons will produce profitable investment results that dissuade you from ever going back to the mediocrity of most investment programs.

Chapter 7

REVOLUTIONIZING INVESTOR PSYCHOLOGY

A man has no ears for that to which experience has given him no access. Nietzsche

A basic truth about candlestick signals is that they represent the results of 400 years of continuous research. This research studied and interpreted a well-known and common human weakness: emotional involvement with investment money. The studies themselves delved into the depths of two contradictory thought processes: logical reasoning and emotional speculation. Logical reasoning, pertaining to our investment decisions, can change into a fear-related response almost instantaneously. It is easy to look back at a bottom point on a chart and rationalize that we would have established our positions near that area. However, when that same scenario recurs, our rational evaluation is suddenly overcome by emotional speculation. When a stock is getting clobbered from a sell off that has been knocking down the price day after day, logic tells us that it is time to buy. Even with the appearance of a clear buy signal, the untrained investment mind allows a multitude of other factors to creep in. More than likely, during a stock's decline, analysts have begun their endless rhetoric. The company is having problems or the industry is changing for the worse. We watch the talking heads on CNBC or the Bloomberg channel express their opinions, stating all the reasons not to be in that stock or industry.

At the same time, our charts or whatever other indicators we follow are telling us that it is time to buy. We have analyzed our charts and indicators for hours, days, months, and even years. This same pattern or set of indicators has demonstrated over and over that an excellent buy situation is occurring. Our signal says to buy. But what does the normal investor do? He or she listens to all the emotional detractions. "What-if" the analysts are right this time and the stock/industry is heading for much worse? "What-if" my signals are wrong this time? "What-if" there is more bad news coming out about this company? It is not unusual to hear even the experienced, professional investors state: "All my research told me that I should have bought, but I just couldn't pull the trigger." The emotion *fear* can cripple the profit production of most investors.

How often, as a stock broker when recommending a stock near the bottom, would I hear, "I want to see what the stock price will do before I buy." In other words investors want to see a stock move convincingly upward before they get in. Try to figure out how to describe that logic in a disciplined investment program.

Fear is sharp-sighted, and can see things underground, and much more in the skies. Cervantes

When prices are going through the roof, how little convincing it takes to get investors to commit their investment funds. Your brother-in-law tells you to buy No Asset Corporation tomorrow on the open. It has already gone from $10 to $18 over the past three weeks. The buy-out is going to be announced at $32 a share in the next three or four days. Most investors, upon receiving the information, have two elements of emotion working against them, greed —a huge easy profit to be made in the next few days—and *embarrassment*. If you act prudently and do not buy the stock, how stupid you are going to look to your brother-in-law. What if this is finally the stock tip that does work. How foolish you are going to be trying to tell your source that you decided not to buy. Emotion overrides all investment planning and you buy the stock. Emotion is a predominant factor in most investment decisions. Note in Figure 7.1 how emotion knocks all value judgments out of the picture.

The best research in the world takes back seat when emotion overrules. A few years ago, the stodgy dead company, K-TEL, announced that they would be selling records and tapes through the Internet. Everybody should remember K-TEL. For years you would hear their ads on late night television. The stock price had traded between $4 and $6 for years. In a matter of one week after the announcement, the price had skyrocketed to $60 per share. Investors could not get their hands on the stock fast enough.

Figure 7.1 illustrates what happened to Homecom when they announced that they were going to sell insurance over the Internet the day after K-TEL made their announcement. In three days, the stock price went from $2 to $18. Investors were climbing over each other to get into the skyrocketing stock. Who was selling the stock at the $18 prices when the future appeared to be so "wonderful"?

Why do stocks go up after bad news? Notice what happened to Fifth Third Bancorp., shown in Figure 7.2. The smart money probably knew the news was coming weeks before. That can be seen in the selling that started occurring well before the news came out.

The advantage created by the candlesticks is obvious. At point B, conventional analysis would not have the clear evidence that the price opened at the bottom and started up. This indicates that the sellers washed out at the lowest levels. The buyers were waiting for the volume at the bottom to

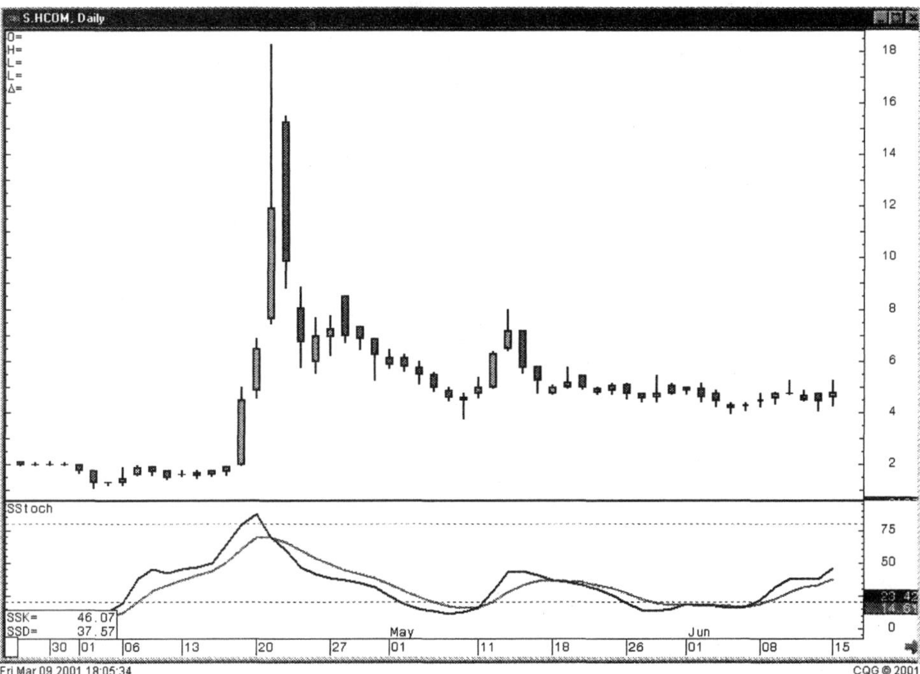

Figure 7.1 Homecom spiked because they announced selling insurance on the Internet, the day after K-TEL announced they would sell records over the Internet.

Figure 7.2 The "in-the-know" money was selling at A anticipating news and buying at B after the news was out.

put on their trades. Seeing the bullish candle gives an indication that the bad news was built into the price of the stock ever since point A.

Learn How *Not* to Invest

Knowing how the average investor thinks creates tremendous profit opportunities. Keep in mind that the candlestick signals are the graphic depiction of investor sentiment. Each candle formation is the front-line illustration of all the investor decisions pertaining to that stock during that time period.

Let us evaluate how most investors think. That should not be hard. Most of us have had plenty of experience thinking like "most" investors at some point in time. Analyzing how the normal investor thinks is a major step for preparing ourselves to profit from those reactions. Investing isn't any different that any other activity that requires calculated assessments. Rescue teams practice rescues; baseball players practice simulated plays; and military units practice combat maneuvers. Practice instills the correct mental processes to perform at the time of pressured execution. The same is needed for successful investment decisions.

Fortunately, this practice will be an inherent part of the daily search function. Using TC2000 provides the visual opportunity to evaluate hundreds of charts in the matter of minutes. The constant exposure to the customized criteria for finding the best possible trade situations provides an excellent platform for being visually prepared for future developing chart formations. Experience gained by this procedure will rapidly make you aware of whether the recent price move warrants putting your investment dollars to work, even when the biggest Wall Street analysts are recommending the stock.

Investment Brokerage Firms—Who's Side Are They On?

Understanding the role of the investment brokerage firms provides more insight into why most investors think and act as they do. Investors have one major misconception. They think brokerage firms are there to help them make money. That is only the brokerage firm's secondary goal. The primary goal of a brokerage firm is for the brokerage firm to make money. And their customers are the instruments to facilitate that purpose. For many years, the adage was "When the public is getting into the market, it is time to get out." And for many years, that was reasonably true.

But look at the dynamics that were in place to make that true. The investment professionals had all the information sources, the general public had very little. After their "wise" interpretation, recommendations were given to the public through their conduits, analysts and stock-brokers. Prior to the mid-eighties, investment information was not widely accessible. When the public was getting into the markets, it was largely due to the fact that the major brokerage firms were recommending that they do. So who was putting the common investor "in" when it was time to get out? You guessed it, the brokers.

There is another subtle implication from this arrangement. It assumes that the general public needed investment advice from highly skilled professionals to understand the available investment information. However, in recent years, the profits from the market has had a noticeable shift away from "professional investment institutions" to the average investor. This was occurring at the time when investment information was made readily available to everybody via the Internet.

Having the knowledge of what the Candlestick charts are telling you will illuminate obvious questions when following large brokerage firm recommendations. It has been noticeable over the years that rarely will analysts recommend stocks at or near the extreme bottom of a price move. As illustrated in Figure 7.3, representing Dell Corporation, the stock price bottomed and made a relatively strong advance. At the level indicated by the upper arrow, a major brokerage firm recommended buying Dell. This leads to a couple of questions. First, if a full-time, highly paid analyst liked the stock at $44, what happened over the past week or two that made the analyst like Dell at that level and not three weeks prior when it was 25 percent lower at $36?

Figure 7.3 Who was buying at point A? Why were brokerage firms recommending buying at point B?

The suspicion that evolves out of a situation such as this is obvious. A highly paid analyst, with mega-tools at his or her fingertips, having his or her ear to the most credible sources on Wall Street, doing analysis of hundreds of different factors for making a decision about a company, didn't like the stock at point A, $36. Yet with access to all the knowledge that an analyst should have available, Dell all of a sudden, became a great long-term buy eight days later at point B, $44?

Next, if the analyst has only now discovered that the company was a great buy, who saw that fact at $38, $40, or $42? Or could it be that a major brokerage firm, informed by their analyst that he or she is going to recommend Dell, starts to accumulate a large position of Dell stock—this being done under the guise of "protecting their clients." It can easily be assumed that the day a recommendation comes out, the volume is going to be many-fold greater than normal. However, if the "concerned" brokerage firm has accumulated millions of shares at lower prices, they can sell the stock to their client base during the high volume demand to keep the stock price from skyrocketing that day.

How nice of them! They kept the price stable for everybody to get in! In the process they made $1.2 million on commissions that day! And an additional $20 million from accumulating a stock position that they knew they were going to sell into their own client base. This is one reason that the general public will never be put into stock prices at the bottoms.

A thief passes for a gentleman when stealing has made him rich.
Thomas Fuller, M.D.

Being able to analyze the Candlestick charts provides an additional advantage. You may like the stock that your favorite brokerage firm is recommending. But now you will have the ability to analyze whether this is the time to get in or is there a pullback possibility that will make better sense. This is the ultimate second opinion.

Fortunately, there have been comments recently directed to the function of investment analysts of major firms. In entertaining yet critically pointed reporting, CNBC's morning Squawk Box crew, David Faber, Joe Kernan, and Mark Haynes, have poked fun at the credibility of the high-paid analysts on Wall Street. The one repeated phenomenon is the number of analysts who downgrade a stock the day that company comes out with the report of lower earnings or the warning of lower earnings. Are there not millions of investors aware that the role of the analyst is to analyze? Shouldn't the analysts be able to reasonably evaluate what will happen to earnings before the earnings are announced?

These analysts are the minds that are directing a vast portion of investment dollars nationwide. The same investment counseling recommended high-flying high-technology stocks at $120, but lowered expectations when the same stocks were trading back down in the $10 range. Again, the CNBC

Squawk Box crew should be commended. At least they have the insight to report the lack of effectiveness of this highly paid analytic portion of Wall Street's investment community. Yet, millions of investors will allow their portfolios, funds that they have spent a lifetime to accumulate, to be influenced or even managed by firms that have noneffective analytical departments running the show.

Who Has Your Best Interest at Heart?

This brings us to a major premise of this book. *There is nobody more interested than you when it comes to the management of your own investment funds.* With the accessibility provided through the information format of the Internet, investment knowledge accumulated through the years is now at your disposal. Candlestick analysis is a beneficiary of the computer age. What would have taken hours and days of analytical time is now made clear in a matter of seconds.

As touched upon in Chapter 1 of this book, most people do not have a defined learning process on how to invest successfully. The minute number of investors who immediately begin building a successful track record usually have an element of luck—not luck in respect to hitting the right trades early in their investment career, but luck in figuring out the right mental evaluations for successful investing. This is a small number of people. Why? Because successful investing includes developing correct investment planning. But more importantly, it involves controlling one's mental discipline.

Mental Discipline—A Built-in Candlestick Advantage

Once an investment position is implemented, the mental process renders a whole new set of disciplines. These disciplines are not required in most other decisions we make during the normal course of our daily lives. Hence, there is no prior way to exercise the proper investment mental conditioning. Mastering our own mental state takes practice. Unfortunately, that practice involves exposing financial assets to risk.

For the investor just starting out, it is suggested that there is a period of paper trading. This practice is good for identifying and establishing a trade. However, reality can be a shocker when the same scenario is attempted when real money is involved.

No schools teach the proper mental posturing. You can attend seminars to become familiar with disciplined investing, but the real test comes when your own money is on the line.

The Japanese Candlestick methodology has built-in advantages when it comes to the mental state of investing. Psychological thought processes are interpreted in the signal's development. Knowing how the signal is formed creates the advantage. Learning how the market action sets up the signal's credibility provides better insights on how the "losing" investor thinks. Initially that knowledge whams us in the side of the head. It makes us realize that we know the basics of investing, yet disregard them when we invest our own money.

Candlesticks Force the Basics Back into the Thinking Process

The basic principle of investing is: buy low and sell high. So simple. But is that the way most people allocate their funds? Far from it. If it is not a hot tip from a friend of a friend, it is because the investment news stations are reporting that the oil sector, or the semiconductors, or whatever sector has been moving up strong over the past few weeks. We then move our money to stocks in that sector. The problem with that approach is that a strong moving sector should have been bought when it first showed signs of a reversal. By the time everybody has noticed the move, the major portion of that move has been made.

Note in Figure 7.4, representing Allen Telecom Inc., that the signals can easily be observed when the stochastics are in the overbought or oversold area, or where the Stochastics are turning over.

Buy low. Sell high. Knowing what to look for lets you take advantage of buying at or near the bottoms. And the computer age has simplified

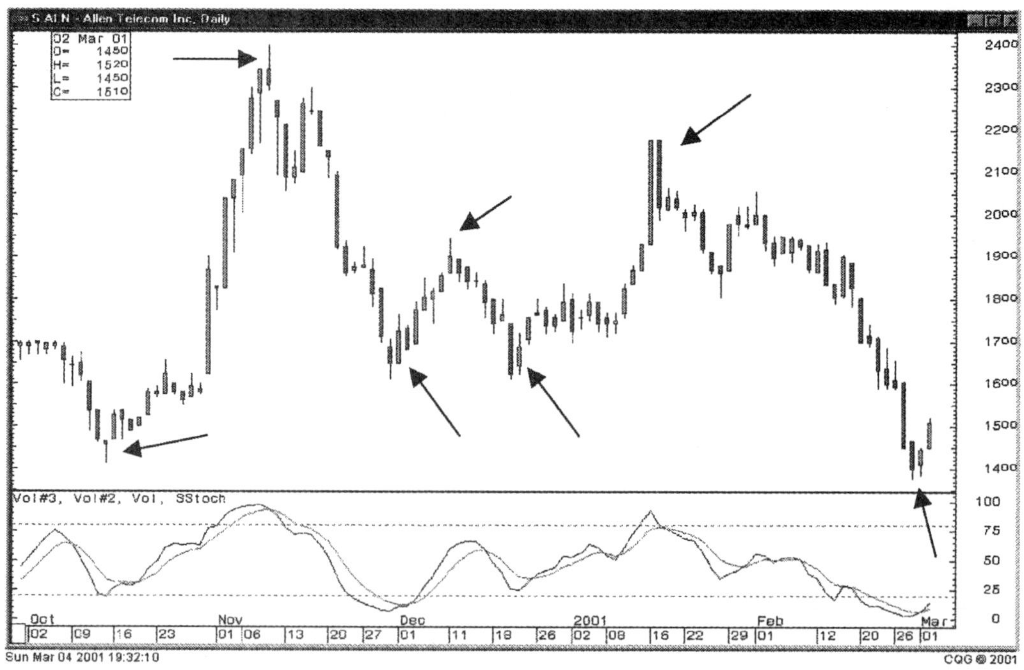

Figure 7.4 Simple observations, signals are prominent at the turns.

Candlestick reversal identification. Finding indicators that alert the investor to a potential reversal situation is now fairly easy.

Nothing Goes Straight Down or Straight Up

Note on the Adamai Tech Inc. chart in Figure 7.5, its decline was not a linear event. There were short-term rallies that produced additional return opportunities. Acknowledging the fact that prices move in waves and oscillations can dramatically enhance investor returns. Instead of sitting through a wave, investors have the opportunity to take advantage of the move going the other way or they can move their funds to another trade opportunity, and then come back to this trade. This greatly enhances the returns. Funds are kept in situations that maximize profit potential versus sitting through periods of negative returns.

Waves or oscillations create the high-profit potential that investors can exploit. This is evidenced by the existence of numerous wave-oriented technical analysis techniques such as the Elliot Wave method, the Fibonacci retracement number technique, the relative strength index (RSI) method, the moving average convergence divergence (MACD) technique, stochastics, Blake's pattern recognition method, and others. All of these technical

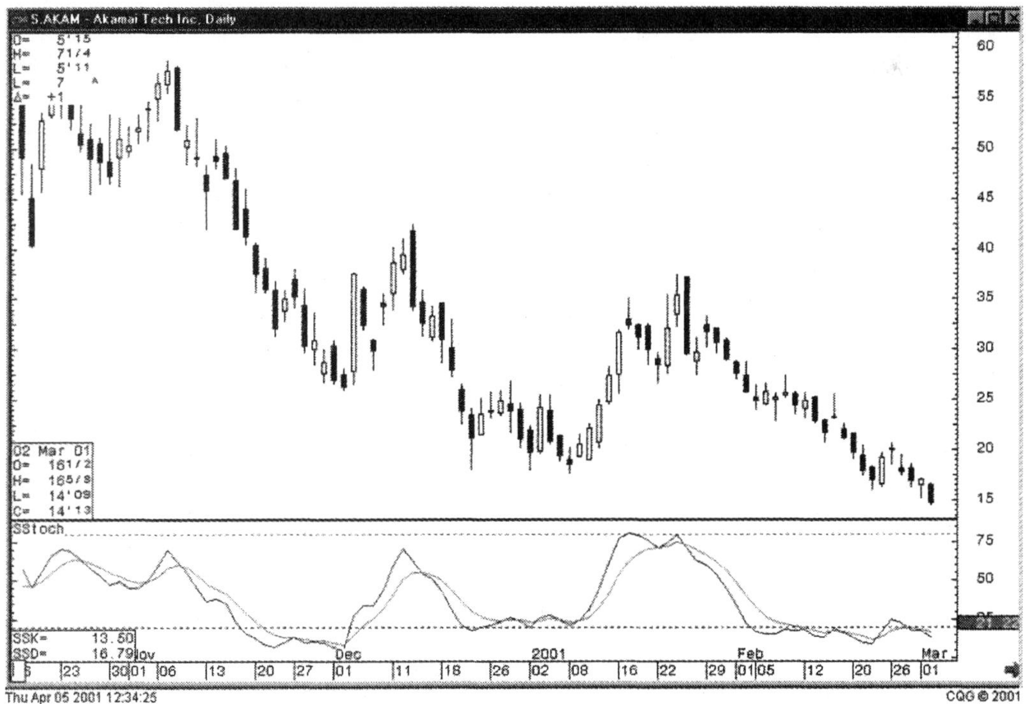

Figure 7.5 Declines and uptrends usually move in waves.

methods result from the recognition that there are wave-like patterns in price movements.

Although Japanese Candlestick Analysis is the preferred technical analysis tool, these other methods have some utility in acting as an alert for an investor to be ready for a Candlestick signal to occur. Having the knowledge of why Candlestick formations occur provides the mental preparedness for acting on those signals. Other technical methods, such as looking for support levels or resistance areas, involve passive analysis. Passive analysis is the *estimation* of where the investment community might see a reason to buy or sell. Candlestick signals identify the immediate direction and effects of emotional change.

Knowing the background of what makes a Candlestick signal highly effective also educates the investor on the psychology of price movements. In the process of learning the signals, recurring price movements should have become apparent. Windows and gaps help identify potential signal setups. Dojis at the top of a run produce obvious results.

The following examples illustrate a number of basic price moves that the Candlestick investor should be practiced at identifying.

Greed and Fear—Exuberance and Panic

The ability to identify Candlestick signals can be the most valuable investor resource. Learning the thought process of the unsuccessful investor and knowing how the unsuccessful investor thinks can be an immense advantage when capitalizing on the opportunities they create. Being aware of how investor sentiment is reflected in the market is the key to exploiting price movements. Dissecting chart patterns synthesizes a signal's vital observations. Understanding how a signal is formed makes recurring circumstances more obvious.

Let's see some historical price movements. Note in Figure 7.6 that after a number of declining days, the black candles (price movement) start to exaggerate. What is the psychological breakdown of this move? The stock is selling off. The further it goes down, the more concern it is creating for investors. As it keeps dropping, the pain of owning this position starts to get bigger. More selling occurs. More pain, more panic. The further the price drops, the more sellers get panicked. Fear is at its greatest just before the bottom.

This is an often seen phenomenon. Remember it. It is not unusual. It will recur. What is it that makes this pattern occur over and over for decades on end? It is simply the masses of investors who do not have control over their investment emotions. Will that ever change? No! Never. There is no universal educational forum that teaches investors how to deal with emotions. There will always be profits for the disciplined investor. Knowing why a price move is happening furnishes time to prepare for a money-making opportunity, the appearance of a reversal signal.

Figure 7.6 Panic and fear starts exaggerating the price move the further a decline continues.

Observe the same phenomenon in the uptrending price movement of the Wilbros Group Inc, seen in Figure 7.7. Note how the uptrend gets moving faster at the end of its move. Think like the normal investor. A stock keeps going up day after day. Soon, the investment sentiment gets more and more confident. Now the analysts are giving it brilliant future prospects. CNBC reports on how great the industry is doing. This stock/industry is going to skyrocket! But the charts show stochastics as being overbought. The price has already moved up 30 percent over the past few days. Thinking like the average investor, things look great. Even though the price is up 30 percent, the future sounds great. It's time to jump on the gravy train.

What creates exuberance? Greed. Conflict. The charts indicate that it is time to sell, but the world looks too good. It's got to be the time to buy. Logic versus emotion. What to do? Look back at Figure 7.7 and remember this pattern. In late January, this stock was trading at $6 to $7 per share. On March 8, a day after the Doji, it was in the $9 range. Over the next three days, it was up over 50 percent. The average investor is now getting confidence to buy. Each day that it goes up, that confidence gets stronger. Knowing that exuberance is now coming into the stock gives the Candlestick investor the foresight to become wary.

What should be expected? Under those circumstances, the Candlestick investor will start watching for a reversal signal. Stochastics are in the overbought area. Unless this company had recently announced that they had

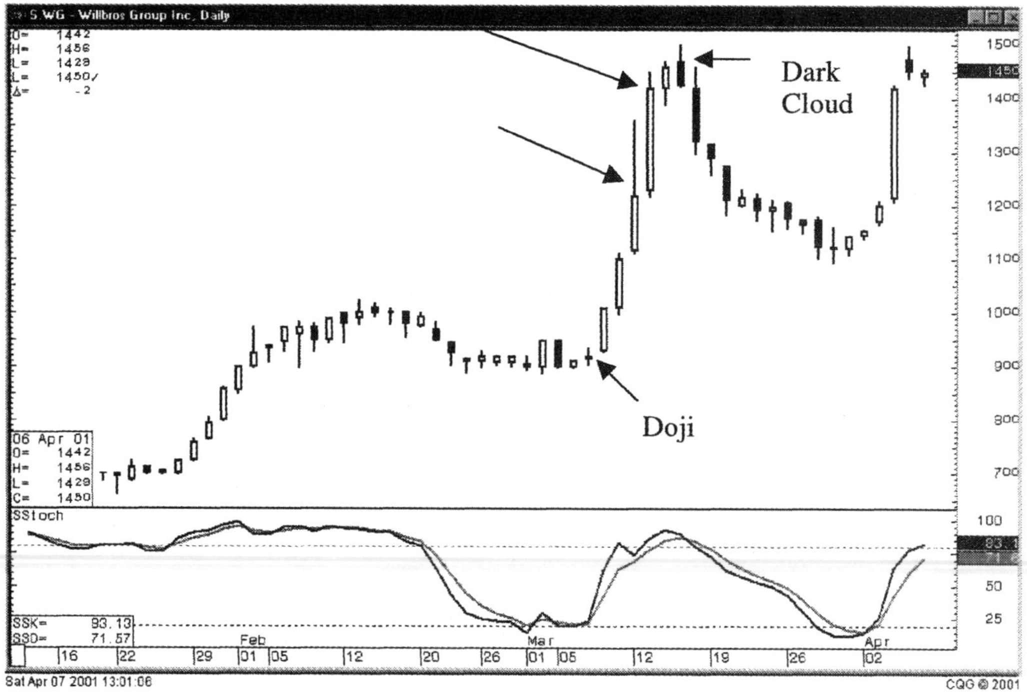

Figure 7.7 Exuberance grows as an advance continues.

developed a concept or product that was better than the proverbial sliced bread, caution is warranted. Knowing that exuberance may now be coming into the stock allows the Candlestick investor to prepare for the potential reversals. Prices do not go up forever. Prices do not go down forever. They ebb and flow. Sentiment changes. Profit taking occurs. These factors are predominantly evident in the existence of Eliot Wave theories, Fibonacci numbers, support levels, and resistance levels. These technical methods were created to exploit the oscillations of investment vehicle prices.

The Japanese Candlesticks eliminate grabbing for the skyrocket. The Candlestick investor would have been alerted to buying the stock the day after the Doji. If emotions had overwhelmed the investor and he or she bought during the exuberance, at least the Dark Cloud Cover would have been the alert to start getting out.

Candlestick Educated = Mentally Prepared

The Candlestick investor is mentally prepared to move contrary to the emotional flow. The most important element of investing comes into play: *Probabilities*. We invest in particular situations because we will *probably* make a profit. The next chapter demonstrates how the Candlestick signals can put all the probabilities in the investor's favor. The signals are still being successfully used, after hundreds of years of refining, for one specific reason. The probabilities of the signal yielding a profitable trade warrants acting upon its presence. Otherwise, it would not have sustained its credibility. The results keep making the signal important.

The Candlestick methodology prepares the user for high potential trades. Being able to recognize the potential set up for a reversal gives the investor the edge. Being mentally prepared is as important as having the operation requirements in place: funds available and execution points established.

Utilize the Best Tools Available

An important confirmation indicator of the Candlestick signals is the stochastics. Again, referring back to probabilities, the assumption has to be made that existing technical indicators have to have statistical credibility. Otherwise, they would not be a part of today's technical universe. Track records have to produce noticeable results through the years or they would not be used today. Combining a well-tested confirmation indicator with a well-refined reversal system creates a high probability combination. The function of stochastics is to provide a valuable input into the investment decision-making process. It compels the investor to buy in the low-risk (oversold) areas and sell in the high-risk (overbought) areas. This function is magnified due to the nature of the signals. A buy signal does not have the credibility in an overbought condition as it would in an oversold condition. Conversely, a sell signal, presenting itself at the end of a downtrend, does not have the same importance as it has at the top of an uptrend.

Step One to Changing Your Investment Psychology

Patience. Our past investing habits, such as jumping into hot stories that we hear about, can be explained somewhat. Prior to the past decade or so, getting specialized research information was hard to come by. Any hot news tip was usually more news than we had access to most of the time. Being able to research industries, let alone individual companies, was almost an impossibility. If we had excess investment capital, any investment news was something to take advantage of. Computer access has dramatically changed all that.

Buy low, sell high. It is much easier to abide by these simple principles provided that the tools to analyze them are available. Today they are. It is probably safe to say that the universe of stocks that individual investors can follow has jumped from an average of 20 stocks, 10 years ago, to 200 today. Ninety-nine hundred companies—that is the rough total of companies that investors can reasonably expect to be able to invest in—include Dow Jones,

S&P, NASDAQ, and Russell 3000. This does not include the many hundreds of penny stocks available on the pink sheets. This does not include the thousands of mutual funds or foreign companies available.

Patience and the mulberry leaf becomes a silk gown.
Chinese Proverb

Today, we have a multitude of research capabilities. Candlestick analysis is available on every charting service on the Internet. Fundamental research is accessible all over the Internet. Instead of having to move on the limited amount of investment information that was at our disposal years ago, our investment universe is now dramatically expanded. Each individual has the ability to analyze and compare from a multitude of investment sources. As recently as 10 years ago, information on the vast majority of companies was hard to get. Today, however, all company information is at your fingertips in the matter of seconds.

So how does patience fit into the scenario? Evaluate Figure 7.8, showing the Spectrasite Holdings Inc. chart. As shown in Figure 7.6, selling days get

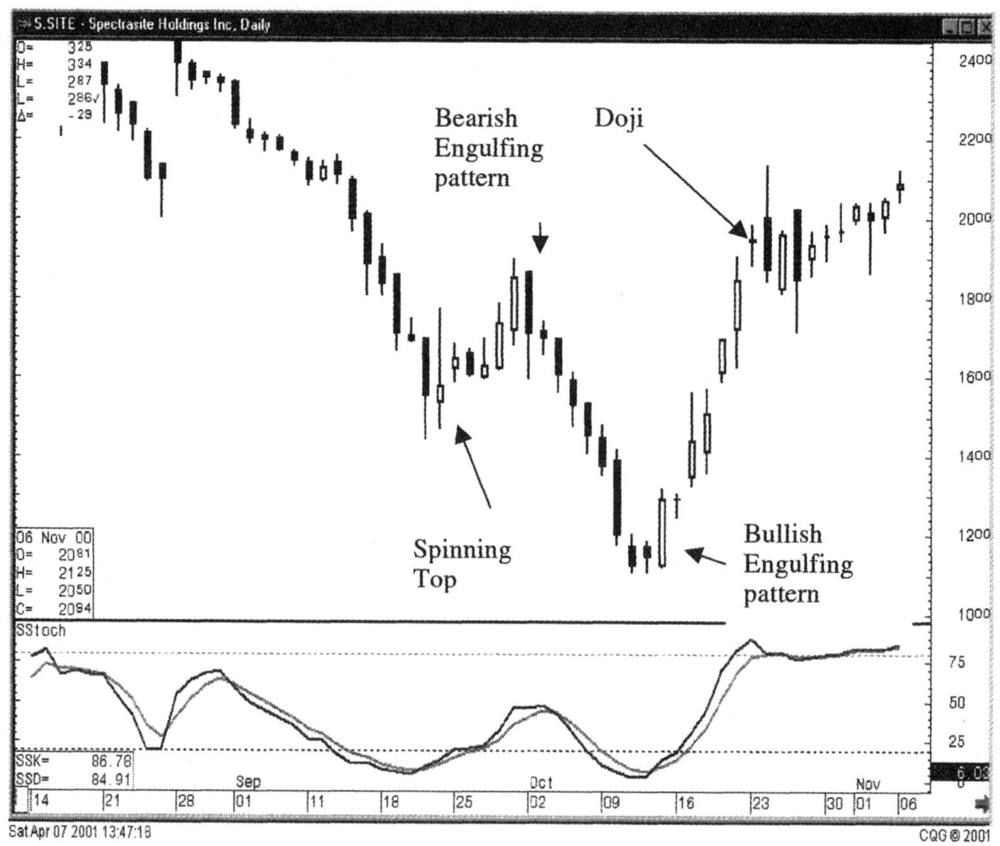

Figure 7.8 Signals pinpoint high-profit moves.

bigger as it nears the bottom. This provides the insight that the bottom is getting close, but when is the most profitable time to get in? When do you grab the falling knife? A Candlestick signal eliminates that problem. Buy when a signal tells you to. Will you get the absolute lowest price? Not necessarily. But you will be buying when the trend is now moving in your favor.

The Spinning Top, followed by an up day, indicated the downtrend had stopped. However, a week later the bearish Engulfing Pattern told the investor that it was time to get out. A worthwhile trade? Not really. But look at the results: a trade that didn't work well but at worst it broke even. At best it made 3 to 5 percent. Still not too bad for a nonworthwhile trade!

Two weeks later the falling knife has stopped, and a bullish Engulfing Pattern appears. Stochastics are oversold. Remember, the Japanese say to always sell when a Doji appears at the top? That trade, closed at the Doji, provides a good return. Bought on the close of the bullish Engulfing Pattern or on the open of the next day at $12.95 and sold on the close of the Doji at $19.50 returned 50 percent.

This is an excellent example to illustrate how Candlesticks tell you when to get in and when to get out. Some may argue that the Doji was not the ultimate top; that another Doji formed at the $21 price. The answer to that should be part of the Candlestick thought process. Why remain in a trade that was in the overbought area and had potential sell signals forming, for an extra 7.6 percent return after a 50 percent profit had been made in less amount of time? Take the profits and go find a low-risk trade situation.

The Ultimate Investment Criteria

The old subliminal investment rationale was "Is this the best possible place for my investment dollars, considering the time and effort required for exploring more possibilities and hunting down additional research to compare it with what I know now?" Considering the difficulty of obtaining any research years ago, most investment decisions were based upon placing funds in positions where the research was already available.

Today, both fundamental and technical research can be viewed on our personal computers in a matter of seconds. This dramatically alters the investment rationale. With no restrictions on available information, the investment program should be "Is this the best place for my investment dollars?" This creates a much more powerful investment stratagem.

Identify the stocks that fit the best possible risk/reward potential. For the investor who is anxious or impatient to have his or her money at work, Candlestick analysis satisfies that need. If you are buying, searches can be conducted in the matter of minutes to find the stocks that meet the strongest buy scenarios. Software programs have been written to find the positions that best fit the description of the low-risk, high-return chart pattern.

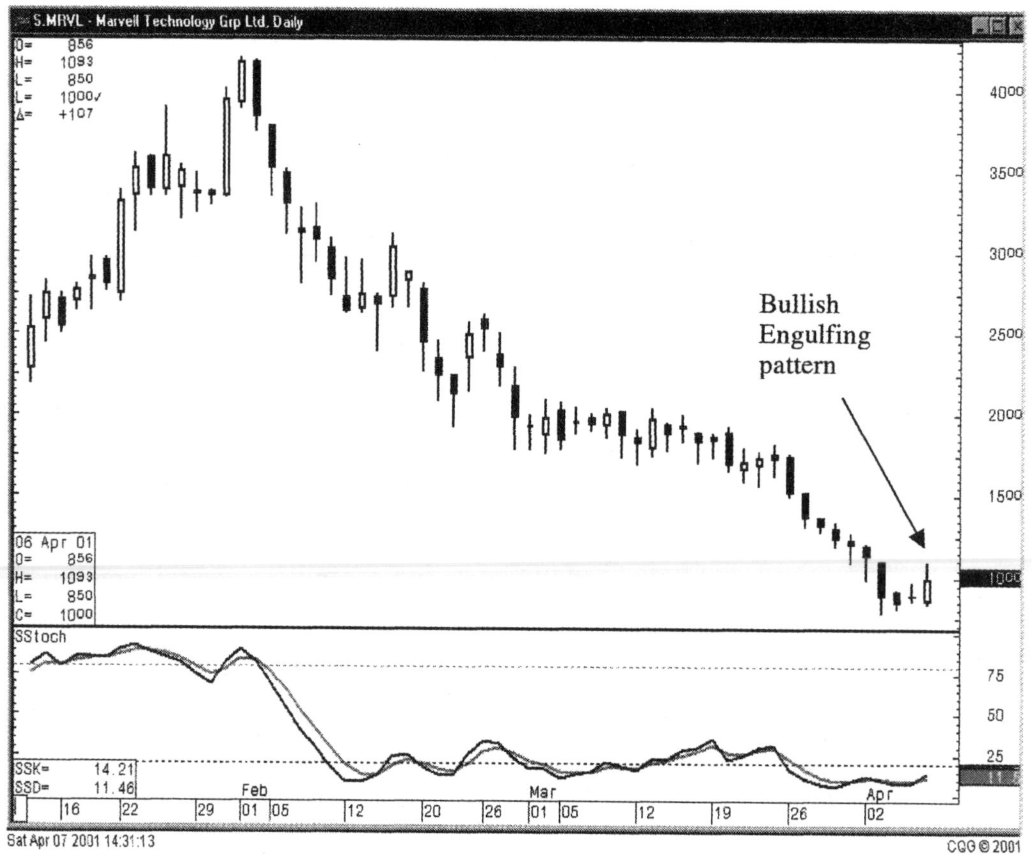

Figure 7.9 An excellent low-risk, high-potential trade set up.

Figure 7.9 clearly illustrates an excellent trade potential. The stochastics are in the oversold area. Common sense visualization sees a couple days of the decline flattening out. A Doji indicates indecision between the bulls and the bears. The next day forms a bullish Engulfing Pattern, showing that the buyers were stepping in. Further investigation would reveal that the volume was up dramatically. A look at the MACD may reveal that it just crossed the midline. Or analyze any other indicators you might want to use.

On any given day there will be many potentially excellent trades such as this one. The probabilities all point to this being a good trade. Why risk investment funds elsewhere? You may never have heard of this company before, but who cares? Without massive research expenses for finding out what is going on in a large number of companies, the Candlestick signal informed you that buyers were starting to buy this stock for some reason.

For those who may take longer to trust the pure technical indication of a reversal move, learning about a company's fundamentals does help the confidence level. You have the best of both worlds. If a Candlestick search finds a perfect buy signal, the fundamental background of the company can be researched online in the matter of minutes. But do not mistake this as a recommendation. Incorporating fundamental research into an investment stratagem is purely for making investors more comfortable with placing a position based upon what the signals are telling you. Fundamentals do not move stock prices in the short run.

Investor sentiment is what moves stock prices. A stock price that moves up 5 percent from one day to the next did so not because the fundamentals changed. The price moved because investors perceived that the company was worth more today than yesterday. *Why* does not matter. Being able to profit from that move is what matters.

The investment universe has over 9,900 possibilities. A search with all the right ducks lining up properly will probably produce between 10 and 100 good prospects each day. Even on the worst days there will be at least five prospects to choose from. The ease of Candlestick searches will always produce more opportunities than most investors can handle. That means an investor can afford to be patient and wait for the best possible investment situation to appear. No more running after hot stocks when they have already moved a great percentage. No more moving funds into mediocre positions due to the lack of research accessibility.

Knowing that high probability reversal moves are always appearing each day, the investor can reduce his or her risk by buying at the bottom in oversold situations. The same is true for the opposite end of the investment spectrum. Candlestick sell signals provide a format for taking profits or going short. Knowing the signs of a top and the investor psychology for setting up a sell signal allows the investor to hold until the probabilities dictate taking the maximum profits for the risk. This takes into consideration the risk/reward opportunities being presented every day through the searches. Why hold a position that has good profits in it while the upside potential is being overweighed by the possibility of a pullback? Those same investment dollars can now be moved to a chart signal that has low downside risk and high upside potential.

Take Control

Japanese candlestick investing will dramatically change your investment psychology. All the elements for high-profit investing are available. The signals themselves represent fully researched, high-probability occurrences. That alone puts probabilities in the investor's favor. Once you become familiar with the consistent results of the reversal signals, you become the director of your own results. Candlestick investing eliminates hoping for good trades or not being completely sure of what to do with portfolio positions. Every aspect of producing greater profitability will be established before the trades are executed. Coping with and eliminating losing trades becomes a mechanical function. Emotions will be out of the equation.

The following chapters demonstrate how to cultivate the good signals from the false signals. Descriptive illustrations prepare you for managing your own emotional weaknesses. These same weaknesses being exhibited by other investors provide profits to the Candlestick investor.

The investment strategies that follow range from using the simple common sense applications that are easily understood to the overlaying of Candlestick signals on Western technical analysis, directed toward the experienced investor. Whichever end of the spectrum you feel that you fit into, do not be concerned. Japanese Candlestick signals provide basic investment truisms that greatly enhance every level of investing.

Inherent benefits are produced from the detailed research of the signals. Basic human traits are identified through graphic chart formations. Understanding the emotional input that creates the formations provides tremendous profitable advantages. Eliminating them from your own investment reactions produces a platform of sound and controlled investment judgments.

When you learn how to utilize the signals to their fullest extent, your investment acumen will improve beyond your expectations. You take control of your own financial future. Your investment abilities need not be anything more than being able to identify a signal, knowing what that signal represents, and acting upon it in a disciplined approach. Extensive research is not required for placing a trade. The fact that the signals illustrate what is occurring in the stock price and being able to interpret that information eliminates the need for hours of laborious research. The hours of investigative efforts are made apparent in how the stock price is acting. The best use of your time is to find out what stocks are able to produce an investing profit. *Why* a stock price is moving is not important. Researching stocks that *should move* does not increase your assets. The Candlestick signals are only concerned with what is moving or has a high probability of producing profits in the next day or so. This is the truism stated in Will Rogers' investment philosophy: Buy a stock that is going up; if it doesn't go up, don't buy it.

Putting Candlestick analysis together with common sense disciplines produces what every investor is searching for: profitable trading programs. Signals simplify the basic concept of investing: buy low and sell high. Candlestick analysis is the roadmap to achieve those ends. The following chapters incorporate the elements of the signals into logical investment trades. The visual aspect of candles provides a clear insight into the direct and the force of a trend. Improve your investing abilities substantially by experiencing the insights the remaining chapters reveal. You are among the first to receive tested successful trading practices. Read with the mindset that these few programs can be easily adapted to your specific interests. The frameworks illustrated in each program will expand your investment horizons.

Chapter 8

ANALYZING PROFITABLE TRADES

Success consists of a series of little daily victories. Laddie F. Hutar

What should be the main objective when investing funds? A simple enough question, with an equally simple answer. To maximize profits with the minimal amount of risk! But if you were to ask investors to describe their parameters for maximizing profits, 99 out of 100 of them would not be able to explain their investment parameterization. As previously discussed in this book, most investors do not even have an investment plan. At best, individuals go to a money management consultant and establish an overall investment plan. This plan involves setting aside so much for retirement, college funds, estate planning, and so forth. That is all well and good for the people who are satisfied with severely moderating returns for the sake of not having to worry about devoting time to investing. People spend more time planning how to get the kids to soccer practice each week than they do working at developing financial security. The shame of it all is that financial security would require much less time than "kidpooling." However, as someone who is reading these words right now, you have gotten to this point due to your desire to optimize your investment capabilities.

What does it take to create a consistently profitable investment program? Candlestick signals provide a major element in the answer to that question. Being able to identify reversal signals is the heart of any successful trading strategy. That knowledge can be further honed to put every aspect of probability in our favor.

Searches, built with specific parameters, can be designed to find the optimal trade situations. As discussed in Chapter 5, prospects found in the search can be further screened to find the trade situations that have the maximum potential for profitability, the highest probability of succeeding, and the least amount of downside risk. This may sound like a tall order, but it is not. The search capabilities of today's software packages perform this process in a matter of minutes.

This chapter is oriented toward equity traders. Using Candlesticks for individual commodities, bonds, or currencies requires less evaluation. Sugar,

British Pounds, and Thirty-Year bonds, to name a few examples, have a smaller number of outside factors that move prices. Stocks seem to have more outside influences affecting their direction, such as market direction, industry concerns, competition, management problems, supply factors, and so forth.

Common Sense

With that in mind, it is best to exploit all the information available. The more positive or negative the factors that all line up at the same time, the more effective the signals become. As stated in earlier chapters, the signals exhibit an extremely high degree of accuracy. But to get accurate trades, a minimal amount of preparation is required. This preparation requires nothing more than the basis for candlestick signals: common sense! Simple logic is integrated into the evaluation process. Common sense factors generate the best probabilities for producing profits.

This may sound simplistic, yet, it is the common sense approach that most investors *do not* follow when they hear about a good investment situation. Broken down, the evaluation for establishing a position is logical. Once the step-by-step procedure becomes common practice, an investor can evaluate the best possible trades in a matter of minutes.

Steps for Establishing the Best Trade Probabilities

Following a few simple steps pinpoints the most profitable trade potentials. This process will become second nature. Time expended upon this process can be condensed down to a few minutes each day:

- Identifying the signals
- Analyzing the stochastics
- Analyzing volume
- Reviewing other technical indicators
- Reviewing past actions
- Applying conventional charting techniques

The Anatomy of a Signal

Understanding the significance of the signals can be summarized in one statement: *The signals are created by the cumulative knowledge of all the investors participating in that stock during that time period.* If you don't remember anything else about Candlesticks, remember this statement. Stated another way, the price movement of a stock is directly influenced by the total knowledge of all investors of what was happening in that company, the industry, market indexes, politics, world affairs, and/or the weather in Nome, Alaska. Every person who acted on that stock in that timeframe, did so based upon the information that he or she had access to. That is the reason the Candlestick signals are extremely informative. They reveal information that would not otherwise be available to the common investor.

The signal is the culmination of all active investor knowledge during a time period. Understanding the ramifications of this statement produces invaluable insight. If a stock has a strong buy signal on a day when the market index, the one most closely associated to that stock, is crashing, the stock will have significant ramifications. Investors were buying that stock despite the fact that the market index was declining. That indicates that other factors influenced investors to get into that stock that day. Again, that signal was created with the cumulative knowledge of all the buyers and sellers that day, and part of that knowledge included knowing the direction of the index.

A Candlestick signal is the first true indication of a reversal. All other technical analysis can now act as alerts that a signal may occur or confirm the appearance of a signal. Using as much information as is available enhances the probabilities of implementing a successful trade.

The Analysis of the Stochastics

As discussed in Chapter 5, stochastics play an important part. They are vital for assuring the identification of low risk/high potential trades. Their function is important for establishing the credibility of a signal. It is easy to determine the validity of a buy or sell signal when the stochastics are in the extreme overbought or oversold areas. A buy signal does not mean much if a stock price is already in the overbought area. Conversely, a sell signal does not have great importance when the stochastics are in the oversold area.

When trading off of the stochastics alone, traders consider the optimal buy or sell time is when the fast and the slow stochastics are crossing. This method works reasonably well. However, there can be a good amount of slippage in this method of trading by not getting in at the optimal point. Combining stochastics with Candlestick signals pinpoints when a reversal has occurred.

Note in the Dell Corporation chart in Figure 8.1 that the Hammer signal could have had the Candlestick investor in on October 8 whereas the crossing of the stochastics would not have had the pure stochastics trader in until October 10—over 17 percent higher.

What happens when a buy signal occurs when the stochastics are in a downward trend and are *almost* or *just going* into the oversold range? The same question for a sell signal when the stochastics are *almost* up to the overbought area.

Using the parameter that the signal carries 80 percent of the investment decision and the stochastics carry 20 percent of the investment weight, you

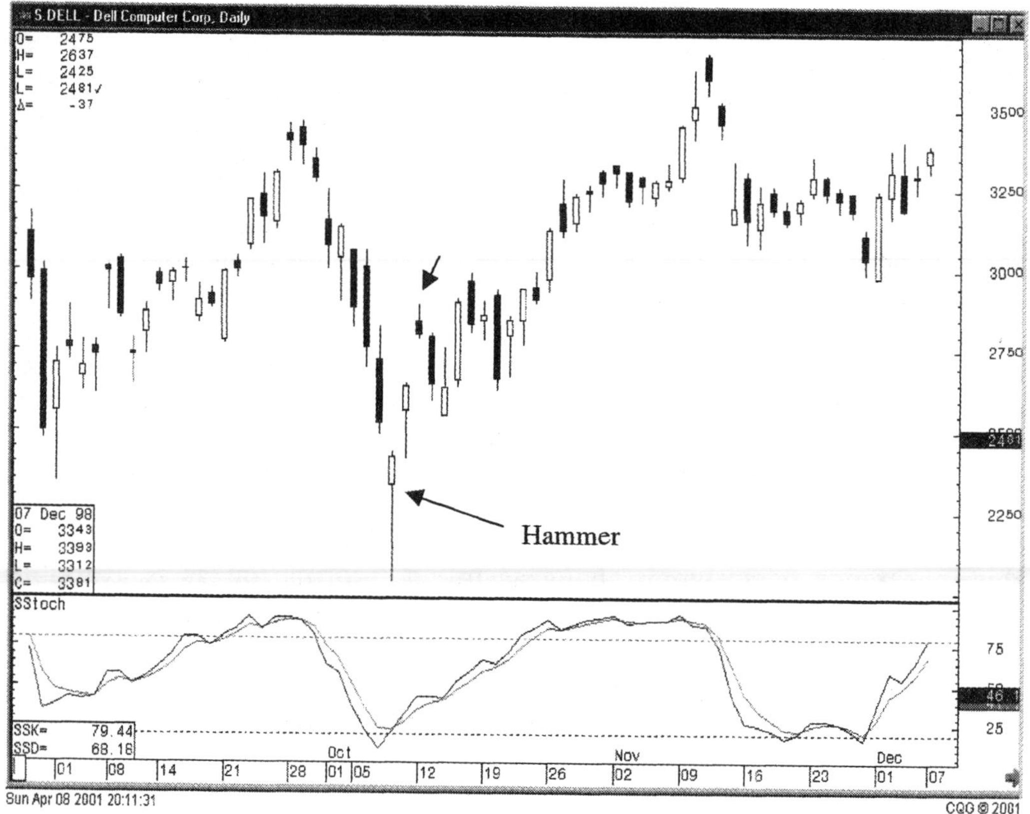

Figure 8.1 A strong buy signal corresponding to the location of the stochastics produces high profit potential.

will have to exercise subjective analysis at times. This subjectivity comes into play when the signal and the stochastics are not in synch. Of course the best reversal points are when the Candlestick buy signal occurs and the stochastics start to curl up from deep in the oversold area.

A few simple observations can be made to determine if the signal is a true signal. The first analysis is a simple review of how the stochastics have acted at the reversal areas in the recent past.

Note that in the Elizabeth Arden Inc. chart, shown in Figure 8.2, the stochastics have had a recent history of turning back up before they go into the oversold area. This chart makes it apparent that the stochastics did not have to get to the oversold area. It becomes obvious that there are Candlestick buy signals occurring when the stochastics curled up before. In each case, the uptrend continued. What does the current scenario imply? Under these conditions, the *probabilities* are that an uptrend has started.

Analyze the results. When a candlestick signal occurred, whether the stochastics were in the oversold or near oversold area, what was the result? If prices went up from the buy signal, then the probabilities say they will do

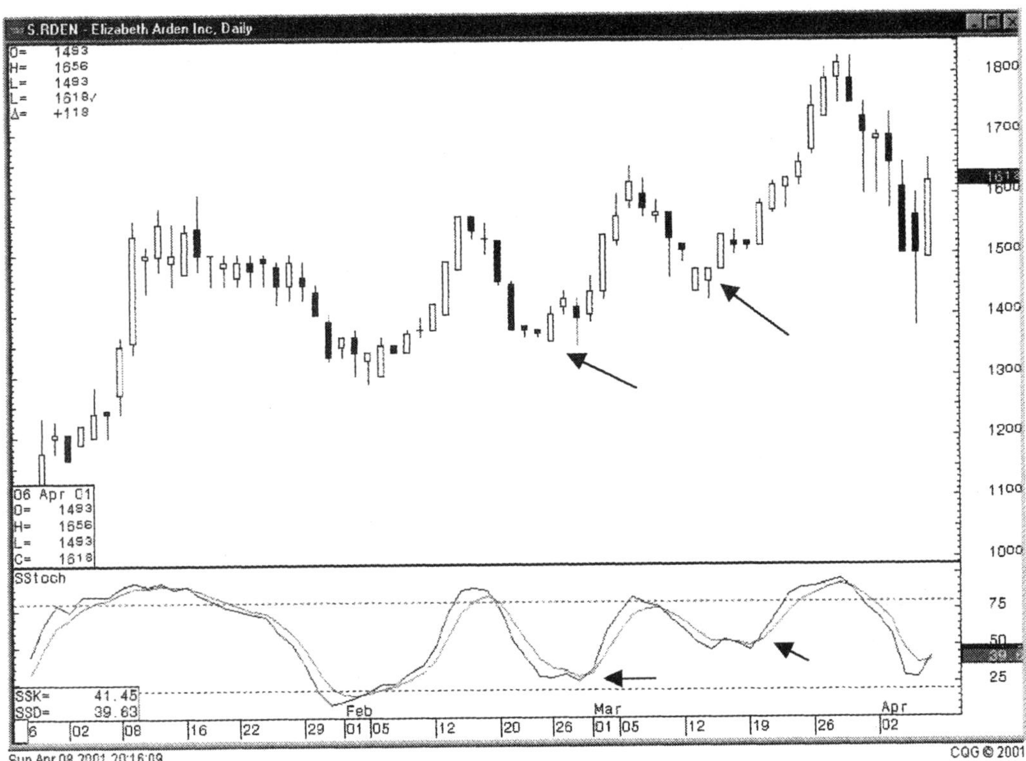

Figure 8.2 The signals themselves will over-weigh the stochastic position when an identifiable trend is observed.

the same from here. If there is a doubt, why chance it? Either wait for further confirmation or wait for better signals from the next search.

What happens when a strong buy signal occurs when there is still a strong downmove in the stochastics? A few situations can be anticipated. The buy signal could continue prices upward, curling the stochastics up. Or the uptrend could immediately fizzle with the stochastics continuing their downward move. However, going back to the premise that the signal is the buy indication, experience says that the price might be bouncing up in a downtrend. If a long position is put on, be prepared to be nimble. Be alert to the price moving up for two or three days before the next sell signal shows up. Then expect the prices to back off again, moving the stochastics down into the oversold area.

Note that in Figure 8.3, representing Cephalon Inc., the Inverted Hammer, a bullish signal, appeared well before the stochastics got near the oversold range. This is a case where the signal is the overriding influence. The Health Management Association Inc. chart in Figure 8.4 provides an illustration of a price moving up from a bullish Engulfing Pattern. After a couple of days, a Hanging Man fizzles the rally. The aggressive Candlestick trader would have

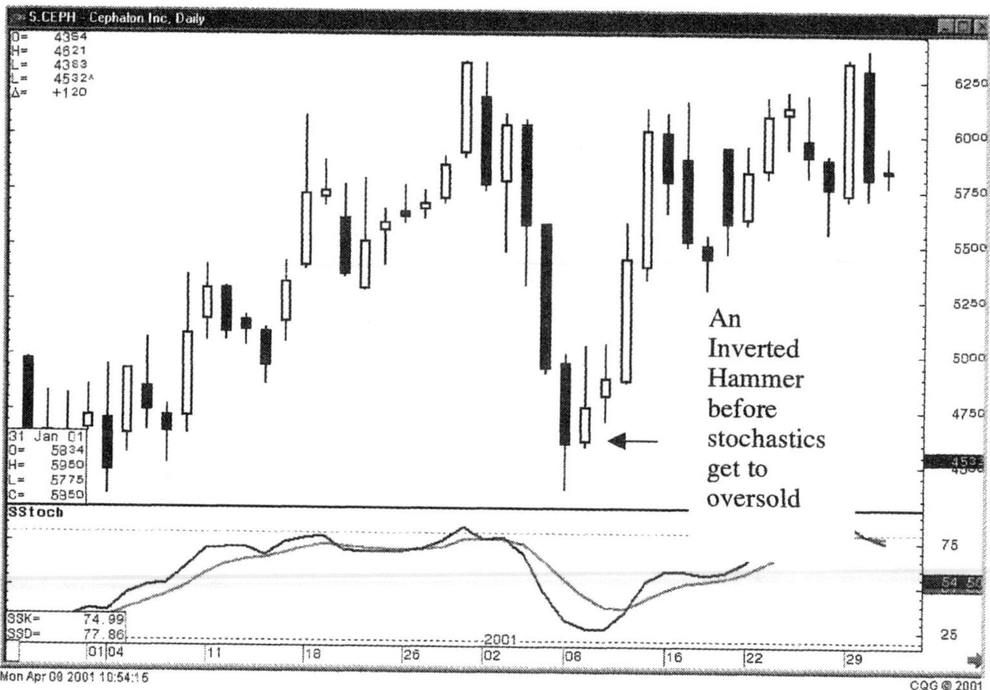

Figure 8.3 Another example of the signal having more importance than the location of the stochastics.

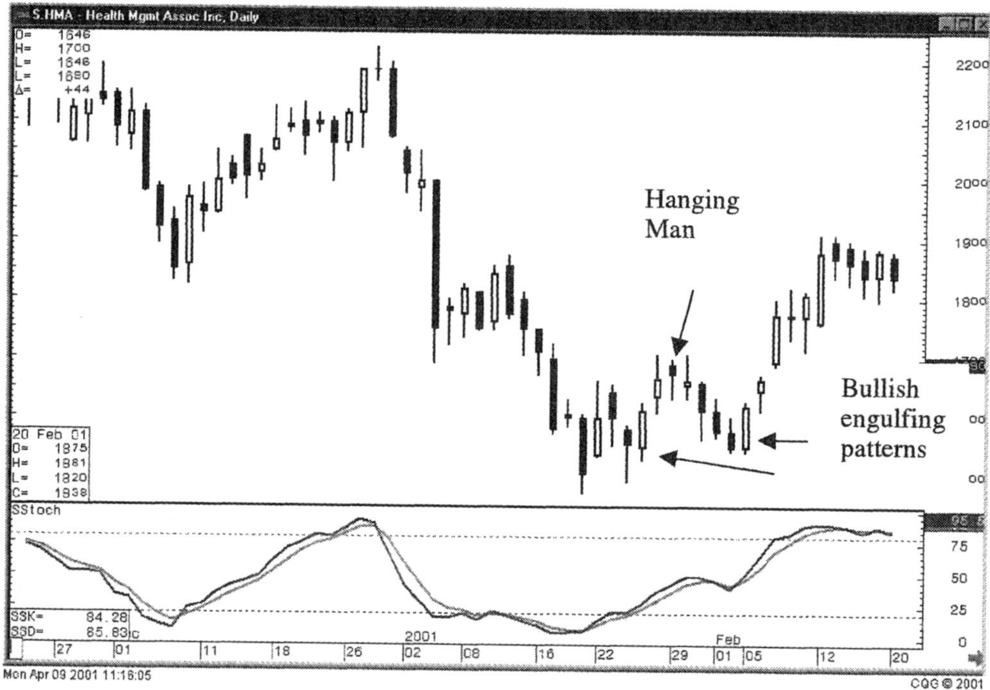

Figure 8.4 A second buy signal at the bottom of a downtrend has much more credibility, increase the long position.

made 4 to 5 percent on the trade. The next bullish Engulfing Pattern provides the opportunity to another 18 percent on the next run up.

Being prepared for this type of situation prepares the investor for multiple profit opportunities. If the buy signal precludes the stochastics getting to the oversold range, it may be setting up for a double bottom formation. The fact that a buy signal has occurred indicates that buyers were showing interest at these levels. If after a day or two the upmove appears to be fizzling, a sell signal appears and the stochastics have not made a clear move to turn up, take a quick profit.

Figure 8.5 shows a potential buy situation at the first set of Spinning Tops. The stochastics are just getting to the oversold area but are not quite there yet.

When the price does back off from there, this stock should be put on the ready-alert list. It has already been revealed that buyers have been stepping in. Since the predominant trend had been controlled by the sellers, prior to the bounce up, the sellers who didn't feel that the trend had finished are now stepping in again. They push the price back down to where the buy signal appeared at the bottom. Remember, this was approximately the price range where buyers were stepping in before. If the stochastics did not turn up significantly during the bounce up, they should be getting closer to the oversold condition as prices move back down. The big white candle following the Spinning Top confirms that the buyers were coming in with force.

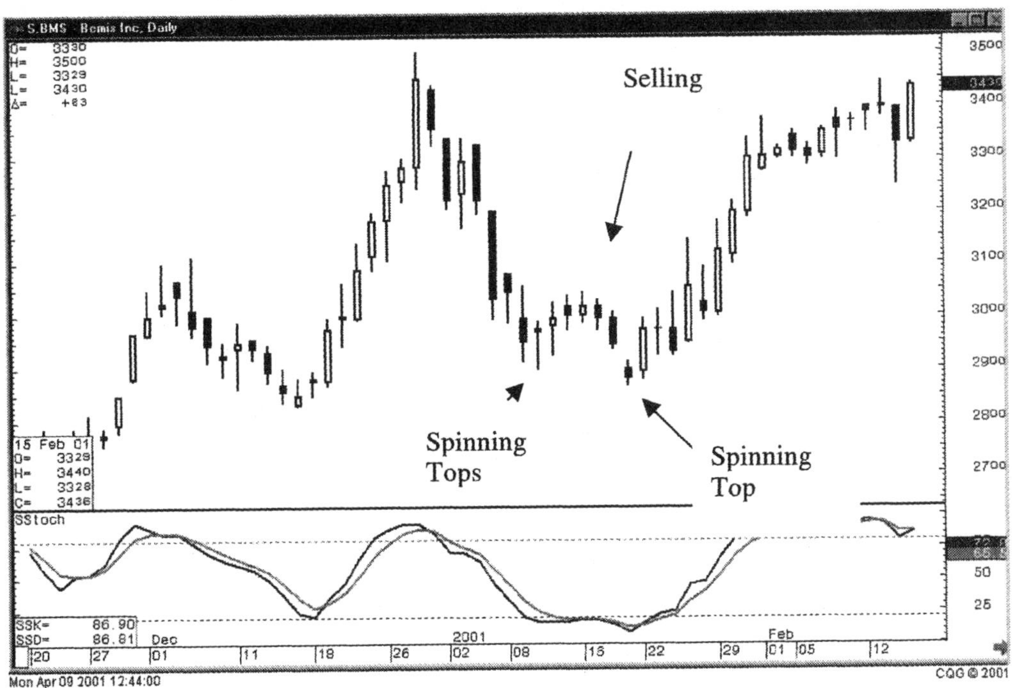

Figure 8.5 Double bottoms make excellent profitable trades.

What was the risk of this trade so far? A buy signal appears but the stochastics are not confirming. The trade was put on, with the investor being prepared for a possible quick fizzle. If the move had continued, the stochastics would have curled up and a good profit would be accumulating. If the move fizzled, a slight gain, a break-even, or a slight loss might have occurred. At worst a slight loss would have occurred, in keeping with minimizing losses.

Now what are we left with? The Candlestick signal has indicated that buyers were present a few days before near or slightly below these levels. This becomes a time to watch for another buy signal to appear. This time the stochastics should be at better levels. If a strong buy signal occurs before they get down to the lowest level of a few days ago, that becomes a positive sign. If the prices come back to the exact point of where the previous buy signal occurred and another buy signal forms, that has positive implications. The investor can reestablish positions at these levels.

Again, as illustrated in Figure 8.6, Avnet Corp., the second buy signal has stronger ramifications to it. First, the double bottom will start becoming

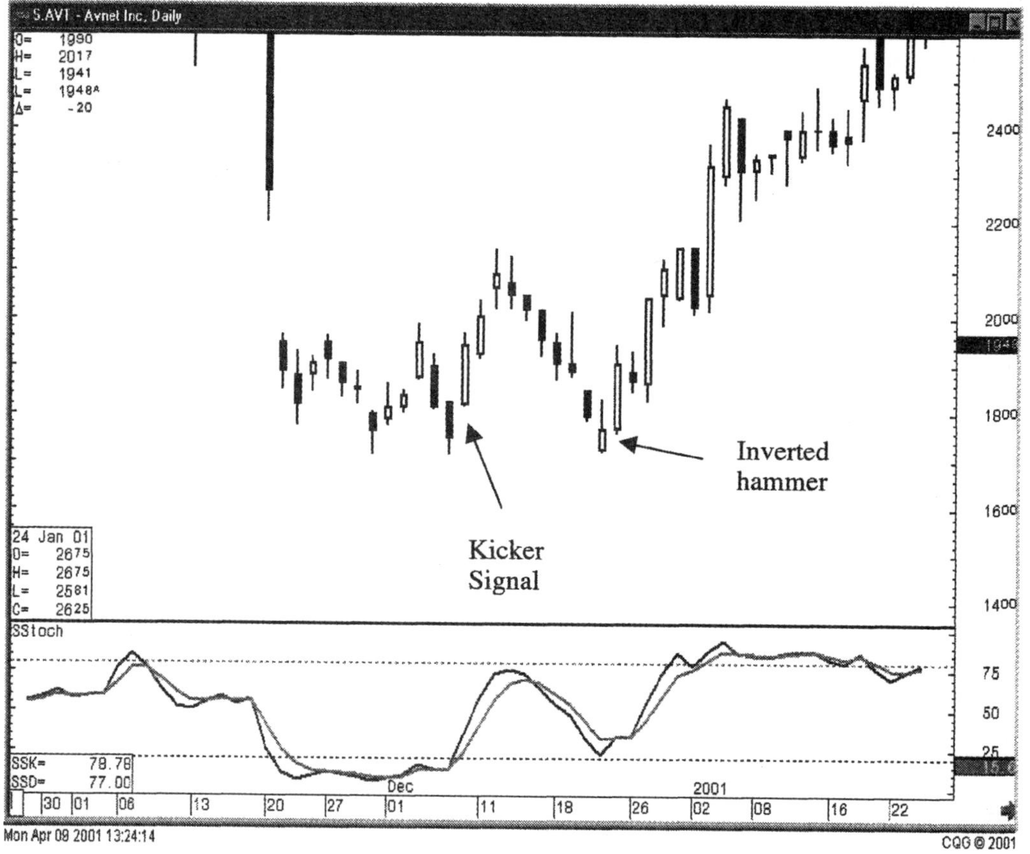

Figure 8.6 Buying at the previous low acts as an excellent buy point when another Candlestick buy signal appears.

obvious to the conventional chart watchers. They should start committing funds to the position. Second, if the second buy signal occurs at or close to the previous low point, a stop loss can be put at one level below that point. Finally, if the buy signal represents the start of the next up move, the bears become less certain about the downward trend and start holding back. This gives the bulls more of an opportunity to take control.

Stochastics provide the confirmation for the signals. They are initially used for searching potential trades. They are also used for determining the appropriate timing of trades. This function is not restricted to only the stochastics. With the development of new software and indicators over the past couple of years, more accurate combinations of indicators may be available. However, through years of testing, the stochastics offer an extremely high degree of credence for confirming successful Candlestick trades. This is a good indicator to experiment with for those of you who like tweaking the systems.

The Analysis of Volume

Volume is not a major indicator when evaluating the signals. However, it is useful for adding credibility to a trade decision. Though not a necessity

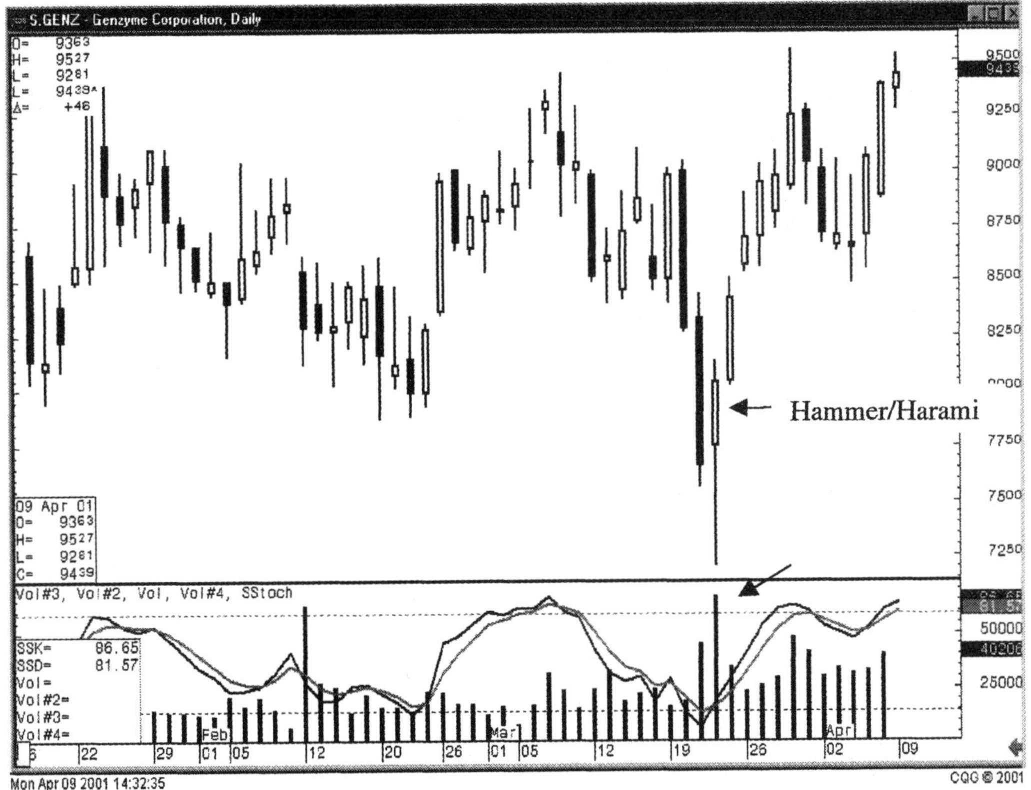

Figure 8.7 Expanded volume is a good confirmation of a buy signal.

determining whether to commit funds when the Candlestick signal appears, volume does help confirm a signal. A volume spike during a one-day signal formation is a good indication that the blow-off has occurred. A two-, three-, or four-day formation could have a volume spike occurring during any one of those days. The fact that a large amount of shares have changed hands during the reversal period has great implications. It usually means that the panic of the sellers or the exuberance of the buyers has moved shares from the emotional crowd.

Note in Figure 8.7, representing the Genzyme Corp., how the volume expanded during the panic selling at the bottom.

Knowing that the buy signal was formed, the stochastics were in the over sold area, and the volume indicated a blow-off day, the investor can commit funds with a high degree of confidence. In Figure 8.8, representing the Claret Corp., the volume increased dramatically on the day of the Doji in the three-day Morning Star signal. The reversal was more convincing when the white candle day gapped up on even greater volume.

This example illustrates that the major exchange of shares does not always have to occur on the bottom day. The signal was the stimulus for

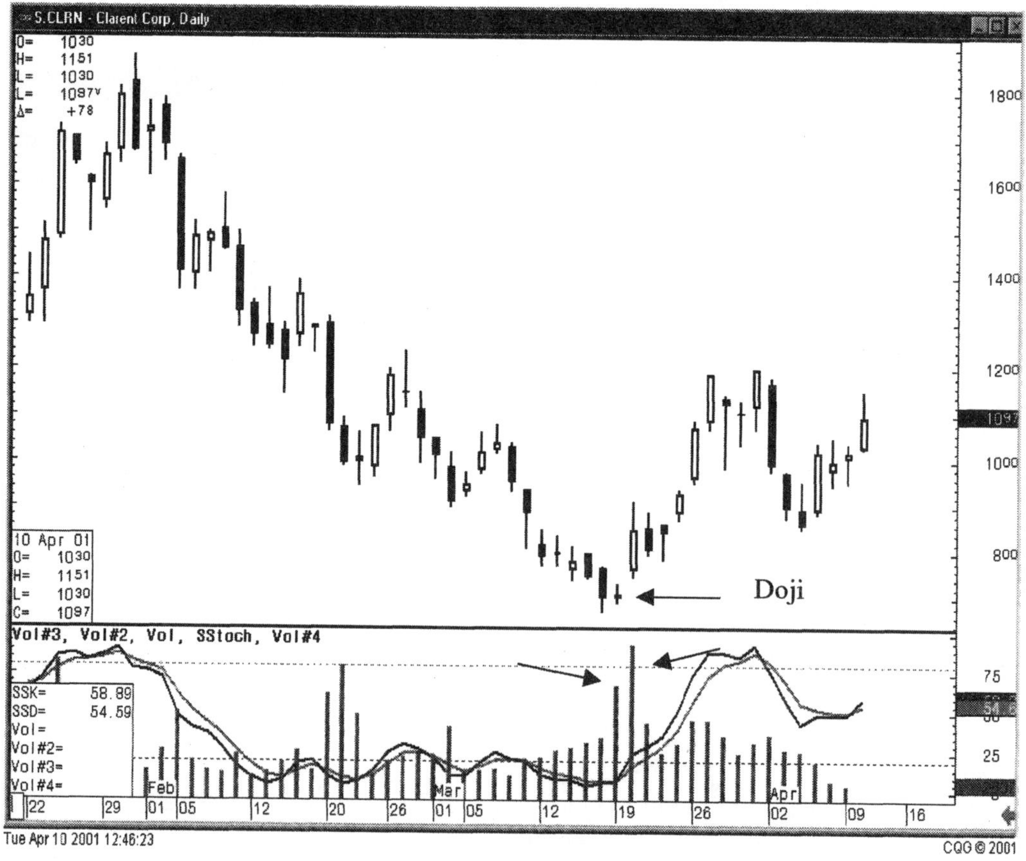

Figure 8.8 Massive volume, along with a gap up, is one of the best buy formations.

doing this trade, the stochastics confirmed it, and the volume spikes added extra credence.

Identifying the False Signals

One of the most often voiced reasons for *not* learning the Candlestick signals is the risk and consequences of observing signals in places where they do not demonstrate reversals. This is false reasoning. As discussed early in this book, not all Candlestick formations create a reversal signal. Additionally, not all reversal formations mean that a turn is going to occur. So how do you tell the difference?

As discussed in the stochastics section, observing where the signals appear in conjunction with the stochastics level is essential. Many formations require confirmation. For example, a Hammer formation appearing at the bottom of a long downtrend requires a white candle (or a bullish confirmation) the next day. Analyzing the signals, the location of the stochastics, and the most current formations, provides common sense insights as to what the investment market is thinking. This analysis is easier than it sounds. The Candlestick methodology was developed through the simple observations of human nature. The operative word is simple. There are no complicated, intertwined analyses that have to be interpretive. A Candlestick signal is most effective at the right place and the right time.

The majority of what are considered false signals is the mis-evaluation of the signal's potential when the confirming indicators have not aligned. Understanding that the probabilities are *vastly* in the investor's favor upon identifying a good signal has appeared also incorporates the fact that it is not 100 percent foolproof. Whatever the percentage (68-, 74-, or 83-percent correct), it still has the potential of being 17-, 26-, or 32-percent incorrect. Being prepared for the incorrect possibilities allows the Candlestick investor to maximize upside potential.

An incorrect signal can be identified and liquidated quickly. Examples of a strong signal fizzling are demonstrated in a Harami formation occurring after the long white candle of a buy signal. Figure 8.9, representing Aspect Telecommunications Inc., shows a strong buy signal appearing in the form of a Morning Star pattern. Stochastics are in the oversold area. The next day it forms a Harami, definitely not the sign of the buyers still coming into the stock. Two days later, another Morning Star set up. Again, a Harami demonstrating that the buyers were not stepping in with force. In both instances, only small losses would have been incurred, had the Candlestick investor observed and interpreted the signals correctly.

Applying the definition of the signals that they are the cumulative knowledge of all the investors that participated in that stock that day creates a cushion for keeping "bad" surprises from occurring in your portfolio. That is not to say that false signals do not occur. Surprises happen. Earnings warnings, analyst downgrades, executive resignations, or S.E.C. investigation

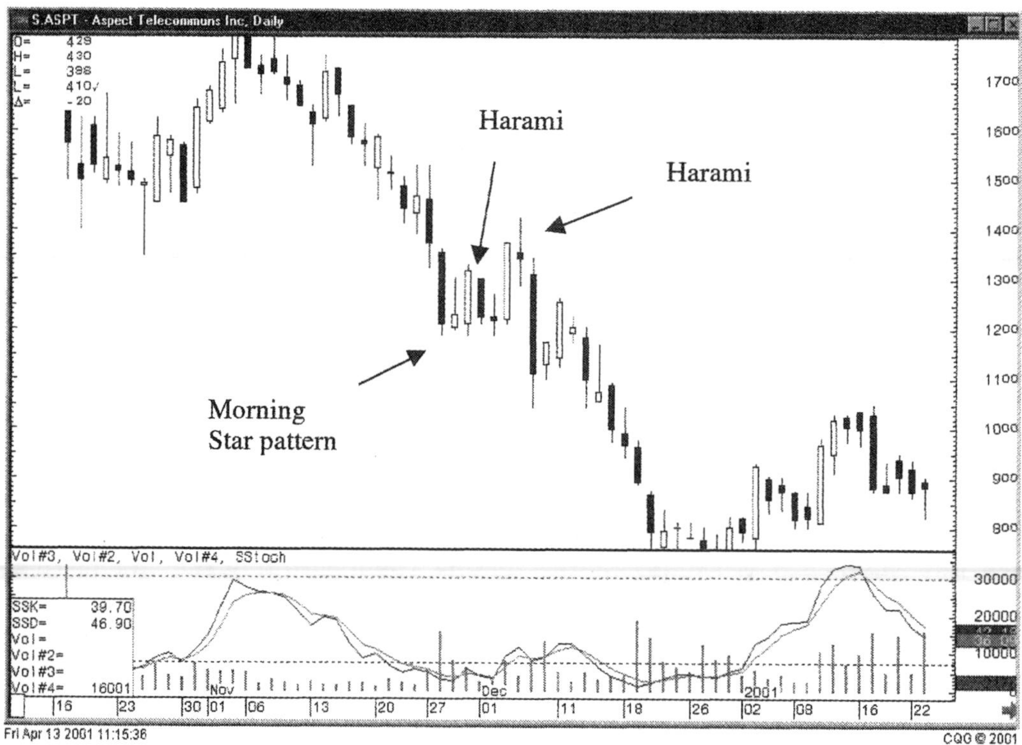

Figure 8.9 A true buy signal has evidence of continued buying, a false signal shows evidence of sellers the next day.

announcements can slam a stock price whether you do technical analysis, fundamental analysis, or buy and hold investing. There is no way to protect against that type of occurrence. But that brings us back to the aspect of probabilities. A certain percentage of signals are not going to work. However, the vast majority of the trades that do not work can be quickly identified. Approximately 98 percent of the time, the Candlestick analyst will be able to exit those trades with a small loss, breakeven, or—not unusual—a slight gain.

The remaining 2 percent of the "false signals" will be circumstances that are going to be total disasters. Buying a stock with a strong buy signal, even having all the confirming indicators in line, could still be affected by a negative announcement before the next open. The stock opens down 20 percent the next morning. There is nothing that you can do. So liquidate the trade and go on to a chart pattern that is putting the probabilities in your favor.

As shown in the Celeritek Inc. chart in Figure 8.10, a Morning Star signal occurs the day before an earnings surprise. But for every surprise against the signals, there are three or four positive trade surprises that are the result of the signals. Expect these losses occasionally. Do not worry about them. Remember, the Candlestick signals are putting the probabilities in your

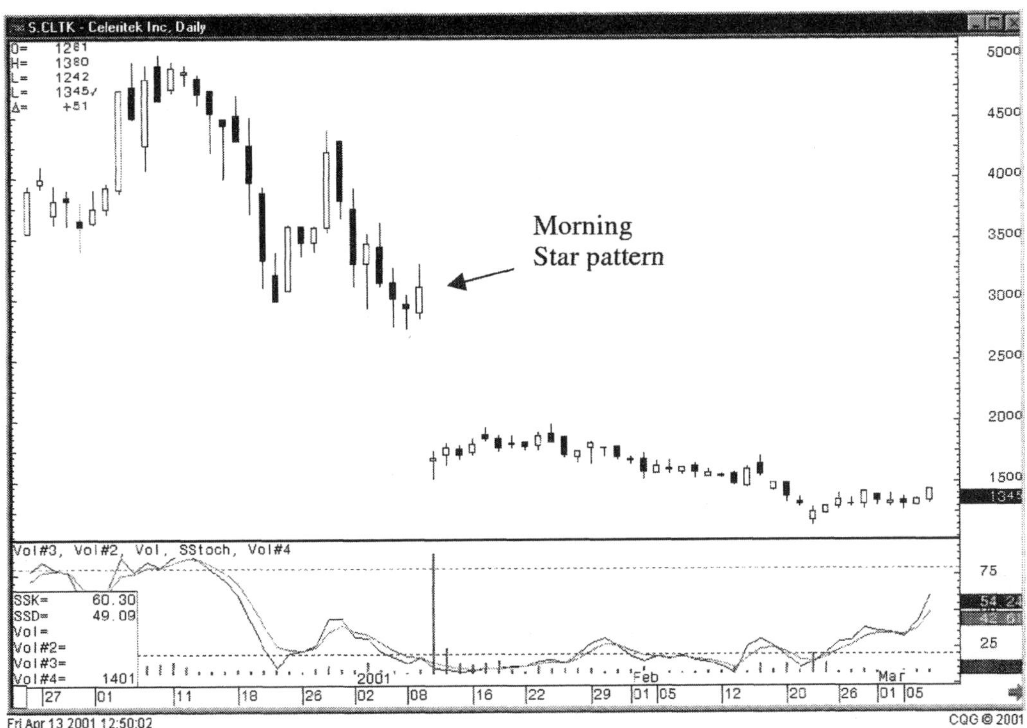

Figure 8.10 Bad surprises can be avoided by analyzing what the rest of a sector is doing.

favor. That means you will profit from most of the trades you put on. You will be in trades that you only take slight losses, breakeven, or, at best, make a slight profit. Then occasionally, you will get hit with a surprise.

Figure 8.11, showing the CLNT chart, demonstrates how the accumulation of stock leads to a surprise to the upside after a Candlestick buy signal. Note how the price remained relatively flat during the decline in stochastics.

Fortunately the function of the signals is to moderate the pain of the big hit. Back to the basics, the signals are formed by the cumulative knowledge of all the investors that are participating in the trading of that stock that day. That boils down to the concept that if there is aggressive buying going on in a stock, the probabilities are extremely high that something positive is going to be announced. For every big negative surprise that occurs from a Candlestick signal, it has been offset by three to four big positive surprises.

The Doji is a prime example of a signal that can be misinterpreted as a false potential. They can occur anywhere. But if you remember the rules for a Doji, all the false signal potentials disappear. A quick refresher, when a Doji observed at the top of a strong upmove, the Japanese advise to sell immediately. A Doji found at the end of a long downtrend means bullish confirmation is required. The weight of the market can still press prices down.

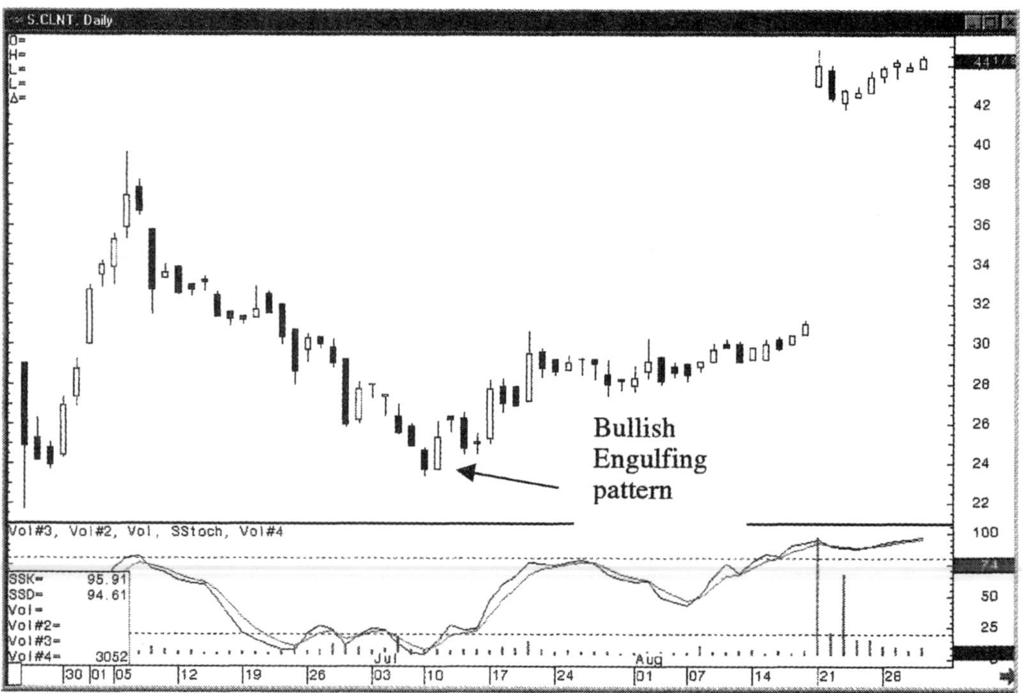

Figure 8.11 Probabilities favor good things happening, confirmed by the evidence that the signals convey.

Figure 8.12, representing the Dell Corp. illustrates a couple of Doji examples. How does one evaluate Dojis when they appear in what could be considered midrange? To restate an earlier point, the Japanese traders say you should always pay attention to Dojis—no matter where they occur. The trading definition of a Doji is that there is indecision going on between the bulls and the bears. Always take notice of this formation.

The Doji at the top is a clear sell signal. Four days later a Morning Star setup occurs. Is this the beginning of another run up? The stochastics are not in the optimal place, a downward bias is still intact. The prudent action is to see how it performs the next day after the big white candle. Another Doji/Harami occurs, giving indication that the bulls are not involved with force. The Morning Star signal is now not interpreted as a false signal but as a bounce that was immediately identified by the appearance of the Doji/Harami.

Notice in Figure 8.13, representing Juniper Networks, how the first Gravestone Doji was confirmed by a strong white candle the next day. However, a Shooting Star/Harami showed weakness. The Dark Cloud of the following day would have provided more evidence that the bulls were not following through. At that point, close the position and find a better place to put the funds.

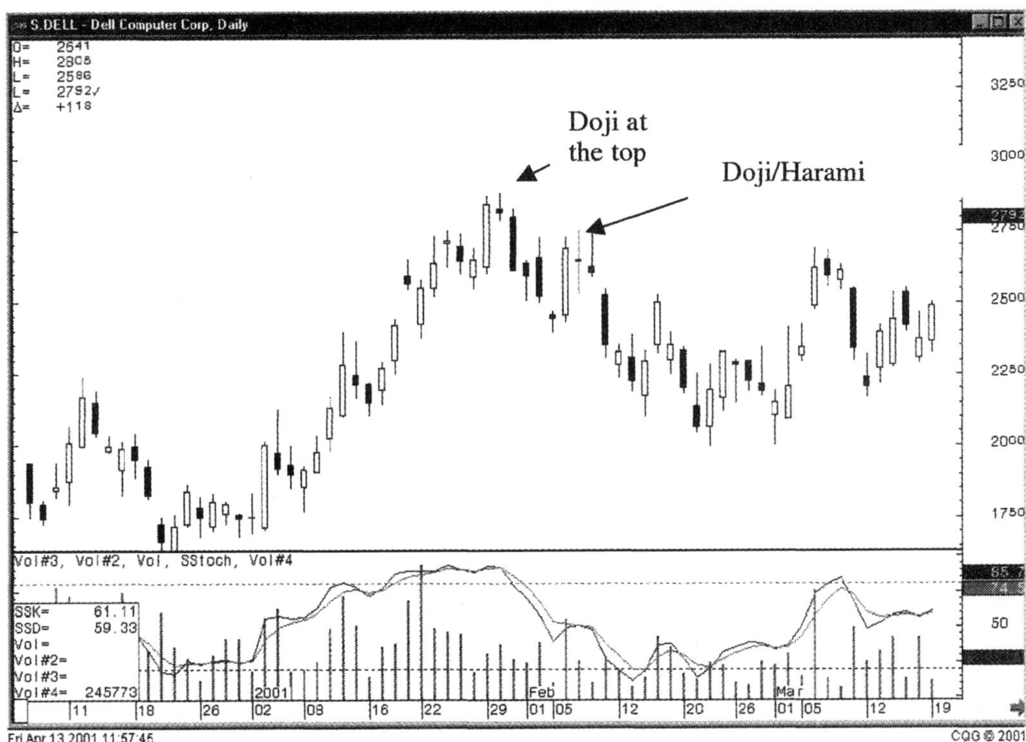

Figure 8.12 A Doji should always be acknowledged. It represents indecision, a possible change occurring.

The second Gravestone Doji in this example illustrates how a Doji requires confirmation to be an effective reversal signal. In this case, there was no buying to demonstrate that the bulls had taken control. These evaluations do not detract from the statement: *The signals are the cumulative knowledge of all investment decisions related to that stock that day*. But if there were indecision in the stock price that day, common deduction says to try to analyze *why* that may be. If there is an obvious answer, such as the NASDAQ was off 150 points today and looks like it could go lower the next day, the Candlestick investor is slightly prepared for the next day's possibilities.

Signals that occur at less than optimal places still warrant evaluation. A strong buy signal appearing near the bottom, but not quite in the oversold range, should get consideration. It may not be the time to step in now, but the signal indicated that buyers were starting to come into the stock. That acts as an alert. The price is getting close to price levels that attract buyers' attention. Keep this stock on close observation. A major reversal may be occurring soon.

False signals in the Candlestick method are a phenomenon created by those who have not taken the time to fully understand how to use

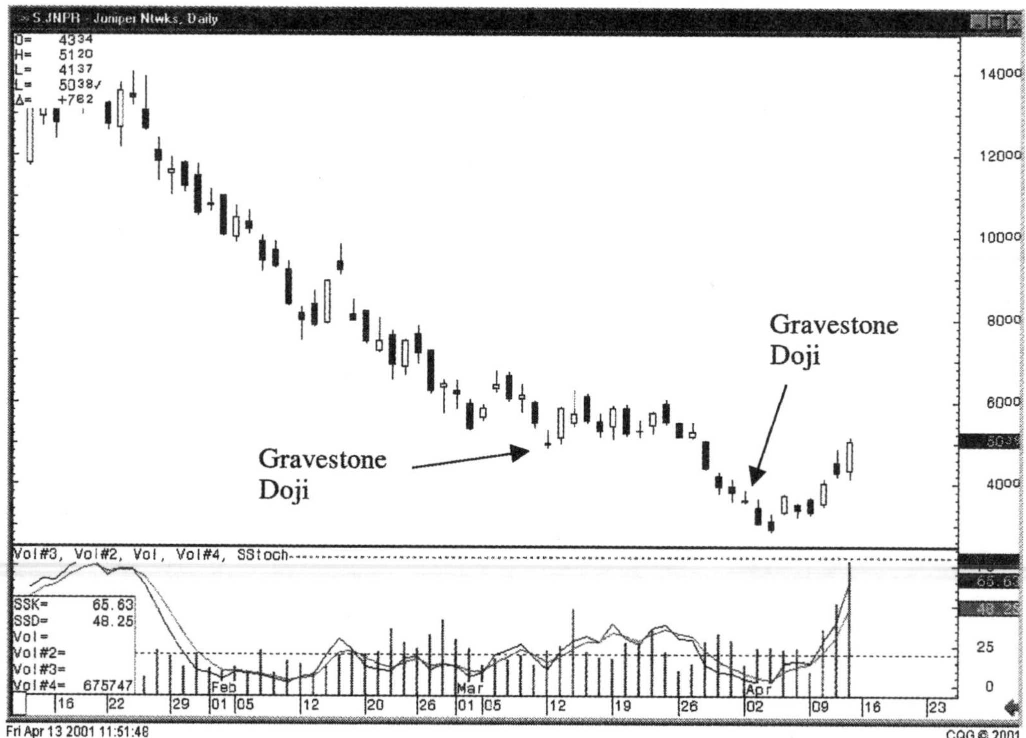

Figure 8.13 When a signal is followed by a number of opposite signals, get out and put your money in better places.

Candlestick signals properly. Once you have learned how to evaluate what the signals are telling you, the aspect of false signals will disappear.

Apply Simple Western Chart Techniques

As you read in Chapter 6, there are some simple techniques that can further enhance putting the probabilities in your favor. **Observe the obvious.** That is what the majority of chart watchers will be doing. If there is a pattern on the chart, use it to further confirm a buy signal or sell signal. Trendlines or trend channels are simple tools. If you can see where a trendline is obvious, that means others are witnessing the same thing. The advantage the Candlestick investor has is the additional knowledge of what a price action is attempting to do at that level. Others are waiting to see what will occur.

It is fairly apparent in Figure 8.14, representing Transocean Sedco Forex, that a trading channel has been established. A Spinning Top, followed by a black candle with stochastics in the overbought area, would be enough evidence that the price had topped out and was turning down. The additional fact that the Spinning Top had just touched the trendline provided additional

Figure 8.14 Candlestick signals fine-tune the buying and selling trends at crucial points.

impetus to sell longs and/or going short. History did bear out that the price retraced to the bottom trendline over the next couple of weeks.

Putting Everything in Order

Taking the proper steps to evaluate a trade puts the odds of success overwhelmingly in your favor. Each step consists of common sense evaluation. The process is simple.

1. Candlestick analysis with over 400 years of fine-tuning, provides a viable platform for identifying reversals.
2. The signals, correlated with stochastics, further enhance the probabilities that a true reversal is occurring.
3. Monitoring the progress of the trend to find signals that would indicate whether the buying or selling forces are continuing the trend allow profits to run and close fizzled trades with minimal losses.
4. Use other technical methods to further confirm the decision for establishing a position. The advantage investors have today is the availability of numerous technical tools on computers. M.A.C.D. coming up

through the neutral line, the crossing of moving averages, volume spikes, relative strength indexes, and lunar statistics are all confirming indicators that can be incorporated into your analysis.

Taking these simple steps will provide the resources to eliminate all but the highest probability trade potentials. With this knowledge, an investor has the capability to analyze all trading entities. The implementation of these factors enables the Candlestick analyst to quickly and accurately analyze the direction. To further enhance the potential of profitability, Chapter 9 is intended to instruct you on how to add more elements to the evaluation process to insure the most profitable trading.

Chapter 9

MAXIMIZING PROFITS

Unless you enter the tiger's den you cannot take the cubs.
Japanese Proverb

Now it is time to make bold statements. In the professional investment field, being correct on trades 55 to 65 percent of the time is considered extremely good. In commodity investing, being correct 55 percent of the time will make you a fortune. Knowing how to identify the Candlestick signals is just part of successful investing. Knowing how to use the signals profitably creates powerful investment results. Candlestick analysis, performed properly, and coordinated with simple, but disciplined trading rules, results in an investment program that can produce a correct trade ratio close to 80 percent.

Bold statements do not mean a thing unless they can be proven. This chapter will describe the ingredients that produce these results. To restate, the major advantage the Japanese Candlesticks provide for the investor lies in determining probabilities. Proper evaluation of a Candlestick signal, aligned with confirming indicators, produce extremely high probabilities that a reversal is occurring. Although this chapter is directed toward equity traders, commodity traders can benefit as well. Using Candlesticks for individual commodities, bonds, or even currencies requires less evaluation. Sugar, British Pounds, Thirty-Year bonds, and so on have a smaller number of outside factors that move prices. Stocks seem to have more outside influences affecting their direction: market direction, industry concerns, competition, management problems, supply factors, and many more too numerous to mention.

The examples demonstrating how to maximize the Candlestick's potential have one important element: common sense! As seen in the descriptions of the signals themselves, the Japanese use one common denominator. The explanations of their formation are all with simple rationale: no sophisticated formulas, no deep-rooted psychological underpinnings. After hearing what the explanation is for each signal, it is easy to think, "Yeah, that makes sense." Each of the cultivating elements, for producing the highest probability trade, embodies the same approach. Basic common sense will be evident through the whole process.

With that in mind, it is best to exploit all the information available. The more positive factors that line up at the same time, the more effective the signals become. As stated in earlier chapters, the signals exhibit an extremely high degree of accuracy. But to get successful trades, a minimal amount of preparation is required. This preparation requires nothing more than the basis for candlestick signals. Common sense! Simple logic is implemented into the evaluation process. Common sense factors generate the best probabilities for producing profits.

This may sound simplistic; yet, it is the "common sense approach" that most investors do not follow when they hear about a good investment situation. Broken down, the evaluation for establishing a position is logical. This evaluation should include:

1. Which direction is the market moving in general? Market being defined as the indices NASDAQ, Dow, or S&P.
2. Which direction is a sector moving?
3. Which stocks have the best upside potential in that sector, with the least amount of risk?
4. How does the stock open the next day?

Following these simple steps vastly improves the possibilities of putting on correct trades. However, before dissecting each step, there are two important elements that need to be established before a successful investment program is formulated:

- Your investment capabilities
- The condition of the markets

As mentioned earlier in this book, most investors do not have a well thought out investment program. Each investor should evaluate his or her particular investment capabilities. Investment capabilities do not refer to investment abilities. Capabilities refer to the time and energy that each investor can allot to investments. When the investment resources were dispensed solely through the brokerage firms years back, individuals were limited to how actively they wanted to invest. Fortunately, the advent of the home computer has provided investors with many additional tools that were not available a decade ago. How you invest your funds now has a whole new dimension. Investors have much greater control over their investment future. Greater scrutiny should be put into the investment approach that each investor would prefer to take.

Today, each investor can decide how much time and effort to put into his or her investment program. Having access to live quotes opens a wide range of possible investment plans. These plans range from day trading all the way to the buy-and-hold strategy. Computers provide the opportunity to keep in constant contact with the markets. Checking the evening paper for closing quotes has progressed to being able to view live quote prices on the computer screen all day.

Plans get you into things but you have to work your way out.
Will Rogers

Each investor needs to establish an investing program that fits his or her schedule. If getting to a computer screen once a day is difficult, a longer-term holding period should be considered. If your job provides constant access to the computer screen, a two- or three-day swing trade program can be considered, or even a day-trade program can be effectively maintained. Conversely, trying to do day trades when the computer is not always accessible is not going to be the most profitable trading program.

Once you establish an appropriate investment schedule, you can implement procedures to maximize profits. Every investor should mentally establish the trading program that he or she feels will best use his or her time capabilities.

The second major element for maximizing returns is the analysis of the market conditions. This procedure dramatizes the need to break away from customary investment planning. Most investment programs are directed toward long-term holding periods. What dictates a long-term holding period? The IRS! How many people do you know who will watch an investment price drop 20 percent from where they should have sold to save 8 percent on their taxes? The market conditions should dictate how long an investment should be held—not artificial investment criteria. If it is obvious that sectors are moving from peak to valley every five months, why hold onto a stock that may back off 40 percent before it turns back up? Is it not more logical to pay taxes on a 40-percent gain at the higher tax rate than pay the lower tax rate on a 12-percent gain? Candlestick signals provide an accurate method for seeing the tops and the bottoms. Why knowingly watch profits disappear? If the markets are demonstrating that the best profit potential is in 90- or 30-day holds, develop a trading strategy that produces the greatest amount of returns using those parameters.

Another major misconception is that money cannot be made when the markets are going down. That thought process negates a vast potential for making profits. With Candlestick analysis as the investor's tool, the direction of the markets in general can be projected easily. Take advantage of that benefit. For instance, Candlestick indicators may show that the market will be in a decline for the next two years. You can put a trading strategy into action to exploit that knowledge. In that case, shorting stocks may be the best possible trading strategy. Why let profits slip away when they can be easily captured?

Shorting Stocks

The concept of *shorting* stock is not a clear or comfortable concept with the majority of investors. "How do you sell something that you do not own?" is the most asked question. If you are not clear or comfortable with shorting stock, please read this section carefully.

The idea of shorting stock is sometimes portrayed in some way as being un-American. There seem to be bad connotations associated with shorting. In actuality, this has been the message usually conveyed by stockbrokers. The simple reason for this is that it means extra work for the broker. The broker could not just write a ticket and put it in to the order room, but instead they had to have another person check with their stock position division to see if certificates were in a margin account of one of the firm's clients. If so, then it could be borrowed and lent to you to sell short. If they did not have the certificates, the back office could check with another brokerage firm and ask to borrow some of that firm's stock certificates, a practice common on Wall Street. But as you can see, this is a lot of extra work compared to just writing a simple buy ticket or sell ticket. To eliminate this extra hassle, stockbrokers would rather discourage their customers from shorting. However, when a stock is running up too fast, you can bet that the brokerage firm floor traders are shorting into the exuberant buying.

If you analyze the concept of shorting, you will realize that it goes on all the time in every day life. When you walk into the local Cadillac dealership, put in an order for a car with specific colors and options because they didn't have it on the lot, they have just shorted you a car. When you order a birthday cake at the grocery store, to be made and picked up tomorrow, they have shorted you a cake. (Where do you think the term "short cake" came from?)

The market goes up and the market goes down. Then it goes up and down again. And again. Why restrict your opportunities to make a profit? Is there anybody who would not have liked to short the high-technology stocks when they were selling at $125 in March 2000 and be buying them back at $15 in September 2000? Buy low and sell high is the method for making money in the stock market. It does not matter which order it is done. This concept is easier for commodity and futures traders. Going long and short is the accepted standard business practice for investing in those markets.

Alternatives to Shorting Stocks

If shorting still makes you uncomfortable, there are alternatives. One method is to put extra effort into finding rising stocks in a declining market. As imagined, the pickings are going to be slim. However, to paraphrase the basic premise of the Candlestick signals: The signals are the cumulative knowledge of all investors participating in the investment decision process pertaining to that stock during a given time period. That means that if a stock is showing a buy signal during a declining market, the buy signal was formed by the actions of all investors that day. Those investors, both buyers and sellers, affected the stock price. They created a buy signal, while knowing that the market was in a downtrend. Finding those opportunities may be few and far between. When they do appear, the high probability is that something company-related, not market- or sector-related, is moving the stock. The number of trade possibilities may be greatly diminished in a declining market, but the probability that something good should be happening in that stock may warrant more investment funds allocated to fewer positions.

Some investment accounts, such as retirement accounts, are restricted from shorting stocks. This obstacle, however, can be circumvented easily. Some of the mutual fund companies have funds that are short funds. This means you can buy a fund that is short stocks. The buying of such a fund will provide a vehicle to profit from a declining market or sector. Having this capability greatly enhances the magnitude of profit potential. The direction of the market does not inhibit the opportunity for making a profit. The degree of accuracy from Candlestick analysis, for determining the general market direction, will induce measures to find and participate in investment vehicles that take advantage of downside moves as well as upside moves.

Maximizing All Probabilities

With money in your pocket, you are wise and you are handsome and you sing well too. Yiddish Proverb

What direction is the market moving? This is the million-dollar question for most investors. But as demonstrated earlier, the Candlesticks are efficient for identifying investor sentiment. They work as well with indices as they do with individual stocks. Performing the same evaluation on an index, Candlestick signal identification and the status of the stochastics provide a relatively high degree of directional accuracy.

Logic would dictate that if a market that has advanced for a certain number of days, weeks, or months, and is now showing Candlestick sell signals, then we would want to consider whether or not the markets are overbought —especially if the stochastics are in the overbought area! As illustrated by the major reversal of the NASDAQ in March 2000 (see Figure 9.1), simple visual analysis identifies a Shooting Star, confirmed the next day, producing all the requirements to warn the Candlestick investor that a top was put in. Further visual analysis identifies a second sell signal approximately two weeks after the first signal. It was also confirmed that the bears were taking over the controls.

Candlestick signals work effectively for illustrating a general change in investor sentiment. Using this knowledge gives an enormous advantage for establishing profitable trades. It is obvious that if the market indices are

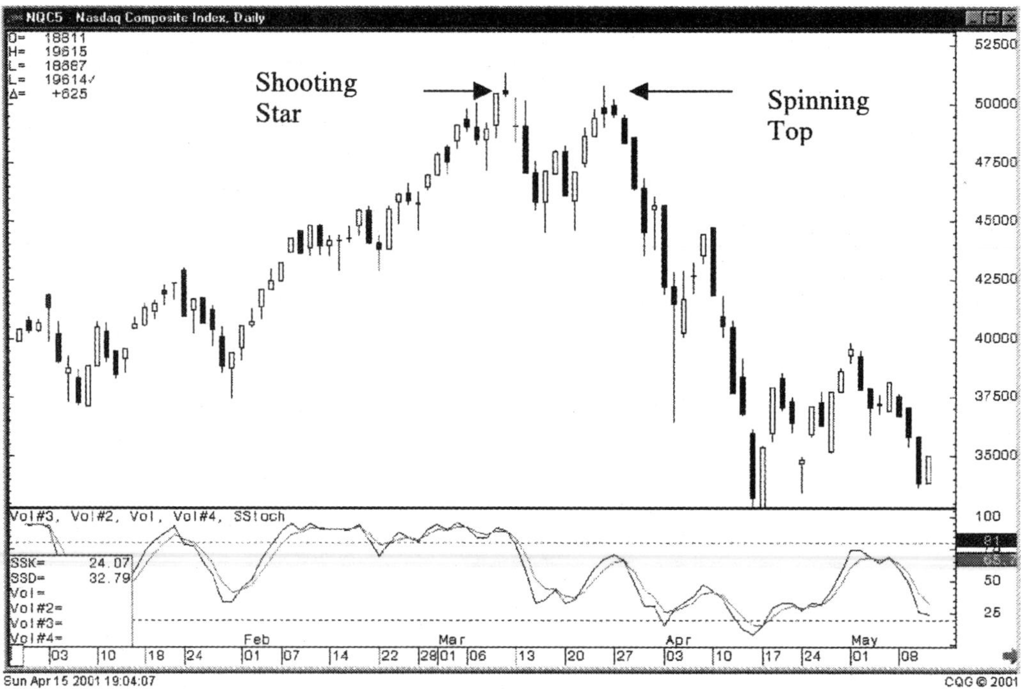

Figure 9.1 The signals can provide a clear illustration on where markets are heading in general.

showing overbought conditions, the majority of the stocks involved with forming that index should show similar conditions. Probabilities should favor looking for short signals.

Another relevant method for identifying market direction is using the results from software signal searches.

Computer Searches Help Confirm Market Direction

Logical deductions can be made when confirming the market direction. This input is derived by software searches. An efficient search program is marketed through TC2000. This program has a number of aspects that make it invaluable to an investor.

TC2000 can run a search for the best possible Candlestick trades available on all exchanges—DOW, NASDAQ, and S&P. This software program can scan the entire universe of stocks, approximately 10,000 possibilities, almost instantly. It can be programmed to scan for your personal parameters, signals that you can customize, as well as provide dozens of technical indicator searches that are built into the program. For the price of an inexpensive dinner for two each month, TC2000 can save you hours upon hours of time.

A directed search fulfills two important functions. The first is that of identifying the best possible Candlestick potential trades. The second is that it produces valuable information on where investment funds are being placed. Distinguishing where investment funds are flowing to and from furnishes the investor with extremely profitable opportunities. The parameters of a search can be developed to identify the best potential long positions and the best potential short positions. The results can project and/or confirm what you have identified by viewing the index charts. If a search, with equal parameters for both long and short positions, produces more potential situations for one direction versus the other, it can be logically deduced that the market is going to move in that direction.

For example, you have established parameters for the best potential Candlestick trades. After scanning the universe of stocks (or the universe that you developed as tradable stocks), the results of the search produce common-sense information. If 400 stocks fall into the category of being overbought and have potential for creating sell signals and 100 stocks show to be oversold and have the capability to produce buy" signals, it becomes obvious that four times as many stocks are ready to turn down. If this information is correlated to a chart that has been in an uptrend for a period of time, it should make you wary that the market is about to reverse and head down. Four hundred potential sells in markets that are ready to start a decline are better probabilities than 100 potential buys.

The market trend does not need to be timed perfectly. A top or a bottom could take one day to make itself apparent or it could take weeks, maybe months of volatile, choppy consolidation before the trend reveals itself. As long as you can produce a rough evaluation of the market's direction, the probabilities of successful trades are enhanced dramatically.

Logic dictates that a portfolio of stock positions will not perform tremendously well if it is positioned opposite the major market trend. That does not rule out the potential of long stocks that are going up during a downtrending market, but the probability of that happening is not as high as the alternative. Use whatever cliche you prefer—"The trend is your friend" or "Don't try to swim upstream." Why place investment funds into positions that do not provide the highest probabilities of making money? If the charts tell you that the general market trend is down and the sell potentials greatly out number the buy potentials, put the majority of your investment funds into shorting stocks.

The Candlestick signal is the most important factor in technical analysis. It reveals that buyers were coming in during unfavorable surrounding conditions. The strength reveals that other factors had to be affecting the movement of the stock price. One such possibility can be the "investor consensus" pertaining to a specific industry.

Revisit the previous example where the index signal appeared to indicate a top and the search produced 400 good sell signals and 100 good buy signals. Despite the fact that there were four times as many short potentials as there were long potentials, *long potentials were still available.* Depending upon each individual's investment plan, specific results of the search will benefit investors with different investment goals. These 100 stock possibilities produce valuable information. For instance, it might reveal that a large percentage of these 100 stocks, showing excellent buy signals, are coming from one or two industries. This valuable information can be identified quickly. These industries should be looked at closely. Something fundamental may have occurred to make a large number of stocks in a particular industry move up while the rest of the market was moving down.

In Which Direction Is Each Sector Moving?

TC2000 also has the ability to search individual industries. These searches can sort the industry indices from the most overbought to the most oversold. The same visual analysis can be applied to industry indices as they can to individual stocks. Has a Candlestick signal been identified? What is the status of the stochastics?

Note that in the OSX Philadelphia Oil Service Index chart, shown in Figure 9.2, a confirmed Harami reveals the start of a rally. If this occurred when the rest of the market was declining, the open of the first day after the Harami signal would make it obviously apparent to the Candlestick analyst that strength was coming into this sector. It may take another day or two

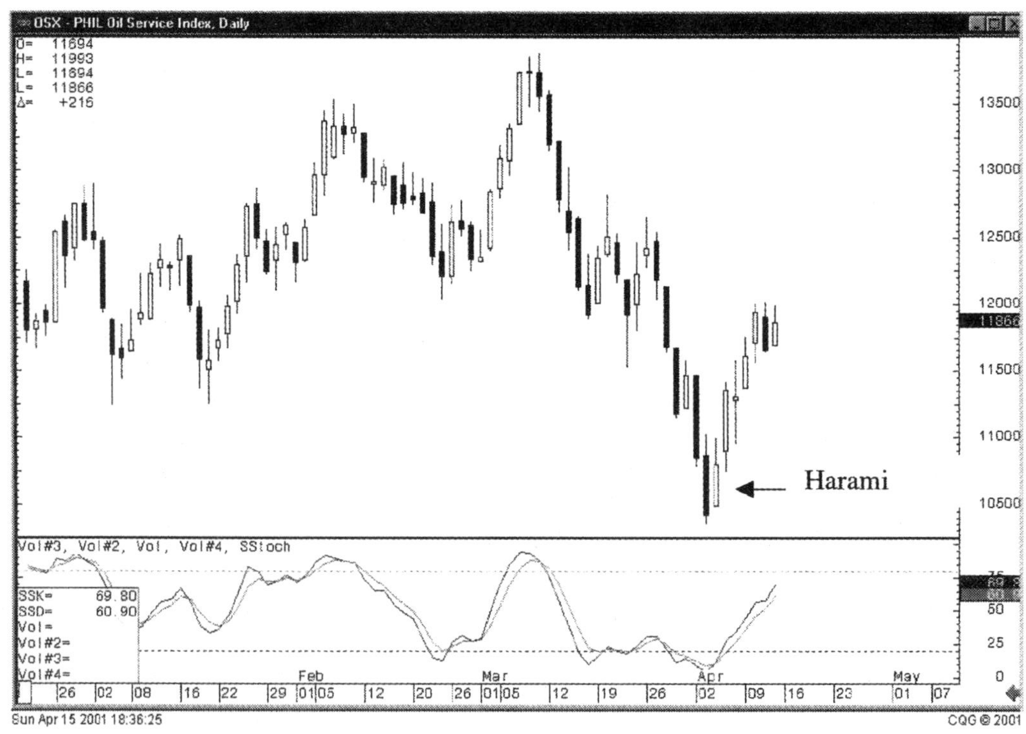

Figure 9.2 Each sector can be analyzed.

for the conventional Western chart analyst to pick up that there had been a reversal in this particular industry.

The short-term Candlestick trader will be alerted to where the funds are flowing. Even in a down market, long trading opportunities can be identified. The short-term trader has something to trade in a down market. The long-term investor may have discovered the beginning of a major uptrend for an industry. If the weekly and the monthly charts correspond with the daily chart, the long-term investor has identified where to place funds for a long-term hold. The option trader may have found a good option-buying situation. A steadily declining market should have greatly reduced option premiums. Identifying an industry or group of stocks, prior to the majority of the investment community, at the beginning of an upmove, produces highly profitable opportunities. In a nutshell, when the best probabilities are on the short side of trading, longs can still be found. Of course, the opposite is true. There will be good short opportunities during roaring bull markets.

Back to putting all the probabilities in our favor. Our analysis is that the index most associated to the stocks that we trade has an observable trend. Use the following scenario as an example. The markets have all had clear reversal signals. It is time to go long. The TC2000 search produces 500 excellent buying opportunities and only 60 good sell opportunities. You are only looking for two long positions for tomorrow's trading. How do you narrow down which stocks have the greatest upside potential?

The next TC2000 search can be for specific industries. Which industries have had the greatest percentage decline during the previous downtrend? Which industries appear to have the strongest buy signals developing? Which industries have the lowest stochastics that are now starting to turn up? These are all parameters that can be applied to a TC2000 search. The results are produced instantly. These results now direct the investor to the highest profit potential groups. For example, the TC2000 search narrows the best potential trades to three industry groups. These industries had the most pronounced declines during the downtrend. They are now showing the strongest buy signals. Within these industries, the field of great potentials is narrowed down to 50 positions. From that number, the investor can evaluate which are the four or five best potential trades.

Which Stocks in That Sector Have the Best Upside Potential and the Least Amount of Risk?

The objective of any investment program? Producing the maximum return while minimizing risk. How does Candlestick analysis accomplish this? Back to the basics: common sense! How is the potential field of 50 great prospects narrowed down to three or four?

Let us review. To get to this point, the Candlestick charts visually illustrated the direction of the market. Then an excellent buy signal presented itself on the index chart. The TC2000 search program verified the beginning of a new direction with over 500 excellent long possibilities, compared to 60 sell potentials. A further TC2000 search identified the best potential industry groups. The combination of these groups provided 50 excellent prospects.

What parameters are used to pick the best of these excellent prospects? Each industry index is comprised of a number of these stocks. If the evaluation of the index resulted in recognizing that a buy signal had appeared, and the stochastics were in the oversold area and turning up, it can be assumed that the stocks representing that index will have somewhat the same appearance. However, there will be differences in each stock chart. Some did not decline as fast in the downtrending market. Others were extremely oversold. Some may have started to climb a few days or a few weeks ago. These stocks now have less upside potential because a portion of their upside has already been expended.

The best picks are derived from finding the stocks that have the best parameters aligned that day. Which stocks have produced a strong buy signal today? Or yesterday? Or will be confirmed by the correct opening the next day? Our evaluation is to determine the strongest signal, confirmed by the stochastics being in the optimal status. That does not diminish the potential of the 45 positions that were cultivated out. They are still excellent situations. The evaluation process is to maximize profit potential. Each parameter that fits our evaluation process increases the odds in our favor.

Effective Stop-Loss Placement

Along with obtaining maximum upside, consideration has to be given to minimizing the downside. The Candlestick signals make it easy to establish stop-loss levels. This process is based upon pure common sense. If the buyers start stepping in at a particular level, and that signal forms a Candlestick reversal signal, the probabilities (confirmed over the past four hundred years) are relatively high that the trend has changed direction. What made that buy signal? The buyers created an environment that started to overwhelm the sellers. An easy concept from which an easy stop-loss strategy can be implemented. Refer to Figure 9.3, the Marvell Technology Group Ltd. chart, for an example.

The first obvious signal, the bearish Engulfing Pattern, clearly illustrates that the sellers started showing their colors at the $42 range. Break the signal down to the elementary points. At the $42 price level, the buying stopped. The next day, sellers took over, creating the bearish Engulfing Pattern. The following day, with its evidence of more selling on the open, would have been the logical entry point for establishing a short position at approximately $37¾.

What is the *stop-loss* level? If the signal resulted from the sellers making their presence known at the $42 level and demonstrating that they were

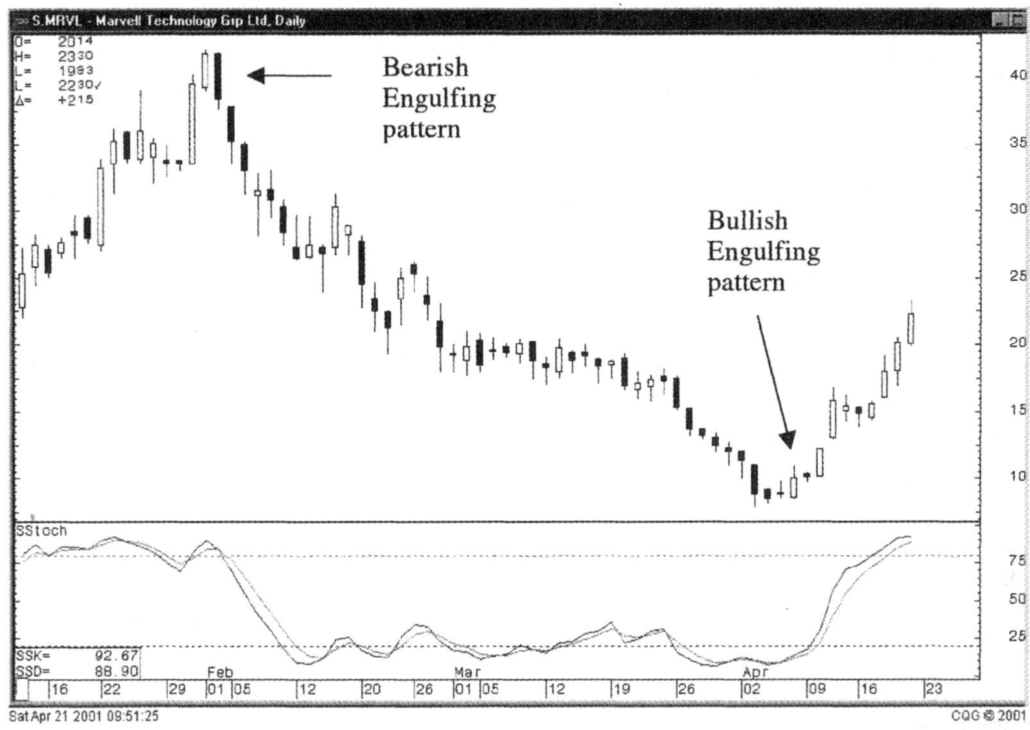

Figure 9.3 The open price of the Bullish Engulfing pattern becomes the obviuos stop-loss level.

controlling the price, logic would tell the Candlestick investor that, if the price got over $42⅛, the bulls were still in control. Shorts should cover. Will this happen often? The probabilities say no. The fact that the signal was formed put the probabilities in the favor of the downside. The stochastics, being in the overbought range and turning down added to those factors. Could prices go back up from the entry point of $37¾? Of course! But as long as the price movement didn't negate the sell signal, the downside would be the bias.

A sell-stop at $42⅛ closes out a position where selling caused a signal but the bulls gained back control. How much further can the bulls move up the price? Who knows, but why risk it? Take the money and find a signal that has high probabilities of producing a profit. However, don't forget about this stock. What has been disclosed by the signals that was not evident to the conventional chart followers? One major element: The sellers stepped in with force. Keep this information in the back of your mind. The aspects of a profitable trade have already presented themselves. Stochastics show this stock to be overbought. Sellers have been evident at these levels. It is not unlikely that the buying gets hit again by the sellers. Unless the buyers can take the price up to new levels, be alert for another sell signal in the near future. A second sell signal usually creates a greater potential for the move to persist. The first signal started creating doubt in the current trend advocates. The second signal convinces those trend advocates that the trend has now been reversed.

The same logic could be applied to the buy side. The bullish Engulfing Pattern illustrates that the bulls have taken control. Stochastics have turned up out of the oversold range. If the bulls demonstrated buying pressure at the bottom of the white candle that day, it should be apparent that if the price came back down through that level, that the bears were still in control. The stop should be set one tick below the open price of that day.

Notice how the Morning Star pattern formed on the Fidelity National Financial chart in Figure 9.4. Two days after the signal, the trend had a dramatic reversal. If the gap open to the downside didn't make you close out the position, a stop at the bottom of the white candle of the Morning Star pattern should have been the final exit point. Was this an unprofitable trade? Of course! But the loss was minimal and the time spent having money tied up in a bad trade was also minimal. The Candlesticks are quite efficient for letting you know when to get into a trade and when to get out.

Find the obvious level that indicates that the move did not work. Always keep in mind the interpretation of the signals. A reversal of the previous trend has occurred. If prices go below the signal level, then it is obvious that the trend did not reverse.

Figure 9.4 Placing stop-losses becomes visually obvious.

How Does the Stock Open the Next Day?

What constitutes a strong reversal signal? The Candlestick definition states that there is a change in investor sentiment. That is as complicated as it needs to get. The signal itself represents the presence of investors doing the opposite of what the existing trend was doing. The two exceptions in the Candlestick signals would be the Inverted Hammer and the Hanging Man, as explained earlier. Where the price opens, the day after the signal appeared, has an important role in how strong the new trend will move. Also, it can determine whether the new trend will develop at all.

Consider the strong buy signal evident in Figure 9.5. The assumption is that the bulls are now taking over control. What should be expected the next day? More indication that the bulls are still around. The sellers should be backing away. The next day should demonstrate the presence of continued buying strength. The price, at least, should not show any great amount of weakness. The fact that the signal occurred in the first place provides proof that there were a lot of buyers. Strength should be demonstrated in the next day's opening. Opening near or above the closing price of the prior day assures

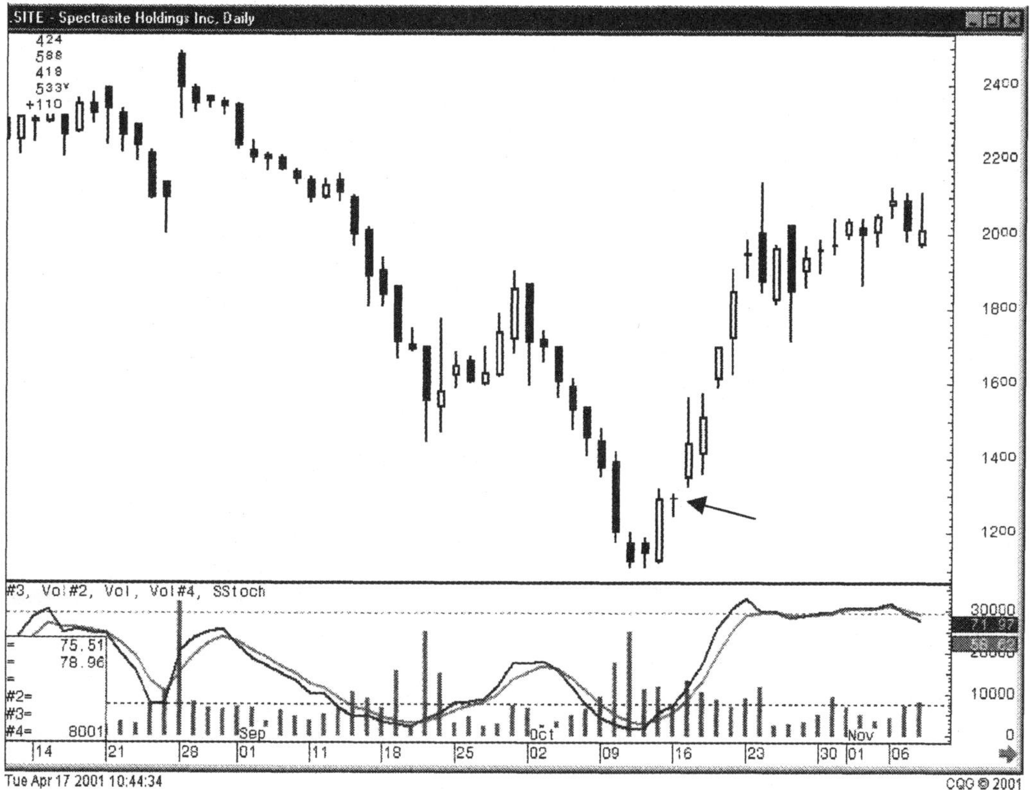

Figure 9.5 Stops at obvious points allows the investor to move on to positive trades.

the bulls that buying is still present. A gap up is the best bullish indicator. It portrays that the buying is getting aggressive.

If the price had a big day on its signal-producing day, a Doji or a small-range trading day near the upper end of the previous day's range is not a terrible sign. There will be a reasonable amount of profit taking or non-convinced bears still putting in trades. A consolidation day is expected. Figure 9.5, representing Spectasite Holdings Inc., notes how the second day showed a little indecision. But it did not show signs of weakness. The gap up the following day would be good evidence that the bulls were still around and in force. To increase the probabilities of being in a good trade, observe the obvious. A Candlestick signal indicates that a change of investor sentiment has occurred. If so, the next day should not negate that fact. Simple logic! If the buyers are now taking control, then that should still be evident the next day. Figure 9.6, representing Powerwave Technologies Inc., illustrates the apparent lack of buyer participation the very next day. A Morning Star pattern fizzles the next day. A good rule of thumb is that if a position were put on at the opening and if the price comes back down to the fifty percent level of the previous days white body, liquidate the trade. The reason-

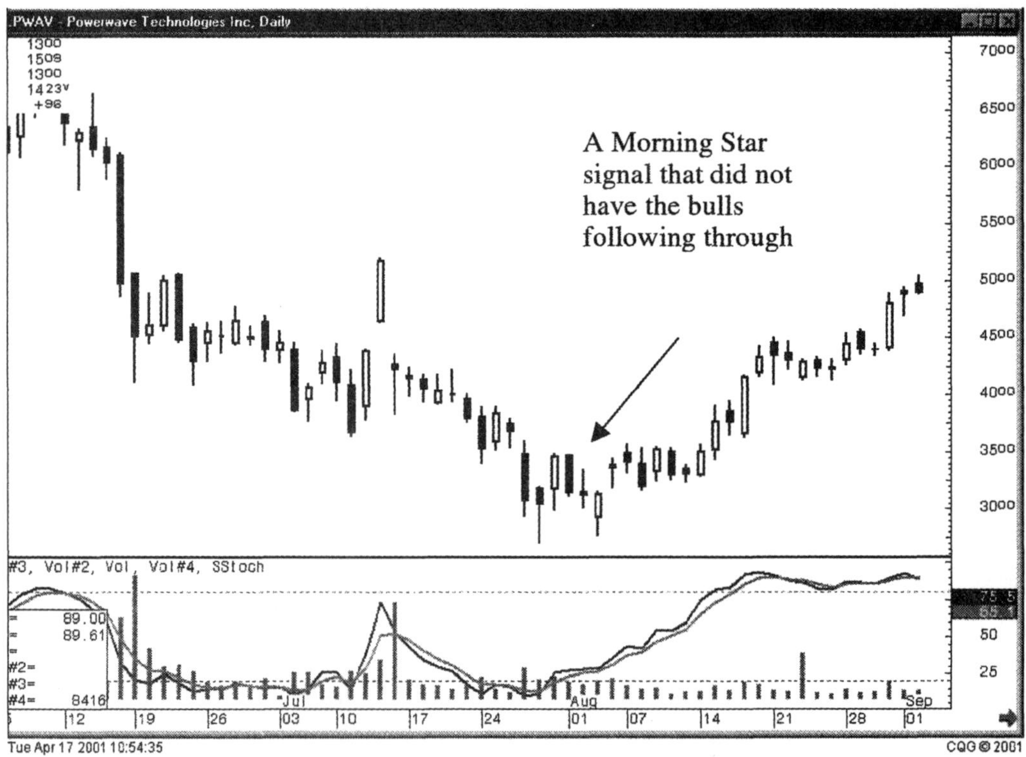

Figure 9.6 The opening price the next day provides valuable decision making elements.

ing behind this is if the bulls were actively involved, the price would not be backing off that far.

Prices opening at the lower end of the signal day's white candle body does not represent buyers showing strength. It illustrates that the sellers were right back in, controlling the price movement.

In Figure 9.7, the next day forms a Harami. What is the significance of a Harami? It tells you that the current direction has probably been stopped. Where the Harami closed versus the trading range of the previous day is important. Visually, an investor can easily interpret the investor psychology that underlies what occurred. A Harami, closing at the lower end of the previous day's candle body, signifies a severe lack of bullish ambition. Be prepared for more weakness.

The higher the Harami closes on the previous day's candle body, the less enthusiastic the sellers appear. A Harami closing at the top end of the previous trading range will usually indicate one to three days of flat or slightly lower trading before the upmove resumes.

A weak open, after a strong buy signal does not eliminate that stock from being a potentially good trade. It does alert the investor that the upmove is

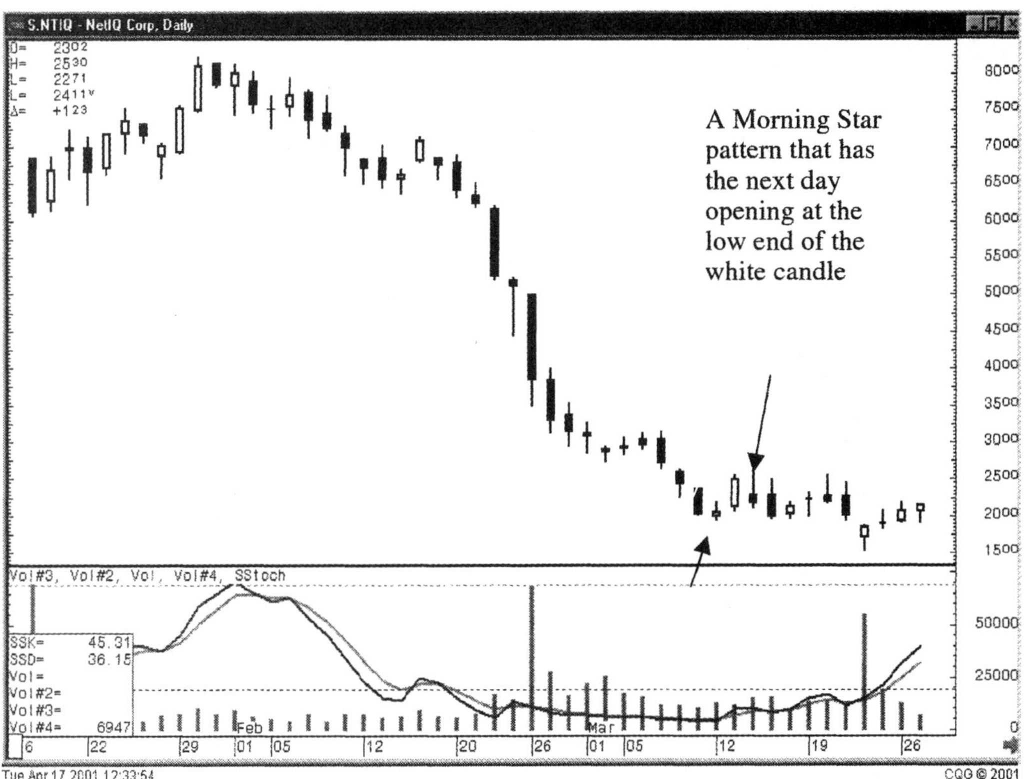

Figure 9.7 The signals tell you immediately what investor sentiment is doing.

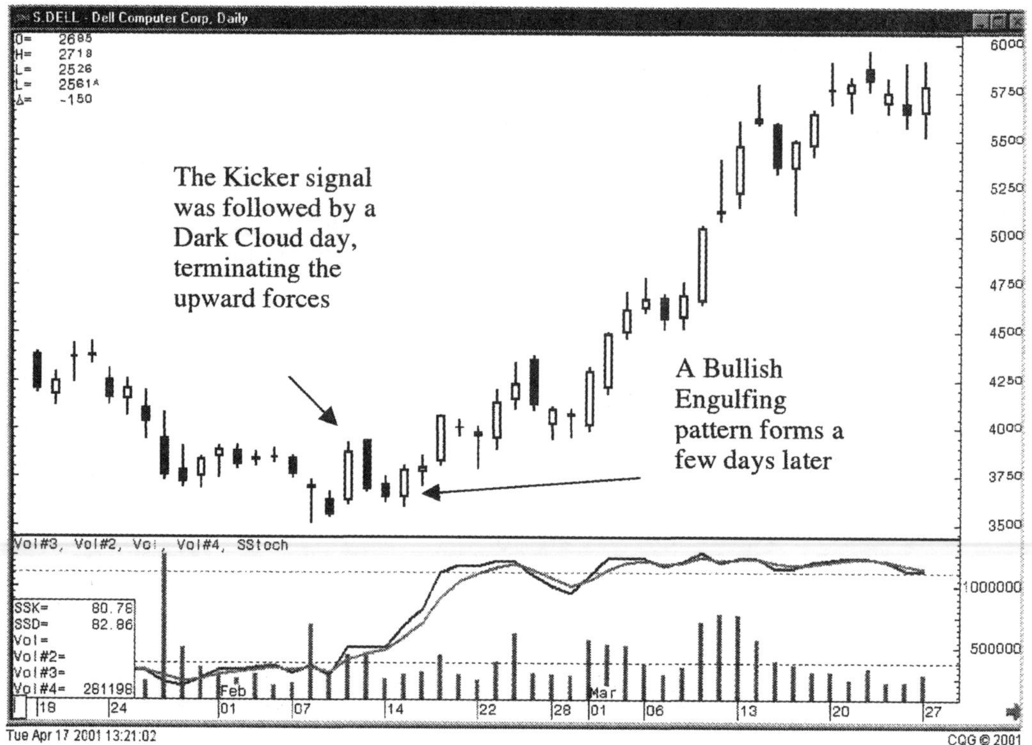

Figure 9.8 After a strong buy signal, a selling formation warns of lack of conviction.

not happening now. This gives the investor the opportunity to put investment funds elsewhere to maximize profits. The presence of the buy signal should make the Candlestick investor aware that buying did start in this stock. Keep it on close monitoring. Note that in the Dell Corp. chart, shown in Figure 9.8, the first signal fizzles but the second signal provides the impetus for a strong rally. If the stochastics are already in the oversold condition, a second buy signal may be developing within the next few days.

The establishment of the trade itself can greatly enhance the probability of a successful trade. It boils down to a simple question. Is the opening of the stock consistent with the scenario of the buy signal? In other words, is a buy signal being followed up by more buying? A gap up demonstrates profound buying demand. An open at or close to the previous day's close indicates that the buyers are still around and are sopping up any selling or profit taking from the day before.

Use this simple procedure to cultivate the best trade situations. There will be times when the research process provides more trade possibilities than what is needed. That provides the opportunity to take advantage of the positions that are opening in the manner that demonstrates continued buying pressure.

Simple Cultivation Process

Putting the probabilities in your favor is a relatively easy process. Fifteen additional minutes of analysis each week will produce a highly efficient evaluation process. This is a process, however, that most investors either don't understand or don't take the time and effort to do.

Analyzing the Candlestick signals through visual interpretation and search results creates a well-founded basis for finding profitable trades. Emphasis is put on investing in the direction of the market trend. Why try to swim upstream? Specific sectors and industries perform better at certain times than others. Search programs find where the investment funds of Wall Street are flowing. Candlestick signals alert the Candlestick analyst when this process is starting, well before the rest of the investing community notices the change.

Once the industries are identified, searches cultivate the best individual stock situations. The cultivation process reduces potential candidates down to a number that can be closely analyzed. From this group, each potential position can be scrutinized to the fullest. The most powerful reversal signals can be found and correlated with the status of the stochastics.

The final group of candidates may still number more than the positions required to be put on the next day. Those positions should be evaluated for minimizing the downside possibilities. Stop-losses should have obvious levels. This process may not reduce the number of candidates for the next day. It should prioritize which stocks would be the top candidates.

The final stage of the cultivation process can narrow down the trade choices. The opening prices of the next day. To verify the signals implications, that a reversal had occurred, the opening price the following day should continue the same message. Hopefully at least two stocks opened the next day confirming the previous days buy signal. If more than two open and confirm the buy signal, you now have the subjective option of picking the positions you feel have the most upside potential.

If less than two confirm the signal, the previous list of candidates that you used to narrow down the final four or five picks, can be analyzed to see if any of them opened in a manner that warranted upgrading their potential. The final candidates exhibited all the makings of being the best candidates. But that did not mean that the other candidates weren't excellent possibilities. If the final candidates do not pass the final test, go back to the previous broader list of candidates. The manner in which some of those stocks open may provide the proper trade.

If you follow all these steps, you will dramatically improve the probabilities that the majority of the positions placed in your portfolio will be profitable. Not only does this provide good profits, it creates a comfortable peace of mind. Gone are the doubts about whether you got into a stock too late or too early. If a trade does not work out, emotion is not involved. The Candlestick investor should have the presence of mind to realize that a trade that did not work is just a cost of business, part of the probabilities. The attachment to that trade becomes nothing more than saying, "That was a bad one, now get out and find another trade that shows good probabilities." Once this mental process has been established, bad trades will have minimal losses and good trades will produce gains until the next reversal signal appears.

The following chapter will describe in more detail how to implement a trading program that maximizes profits, minimizes losses, and eliminates all emotional influences.

Chapter 10

TRADING PROGRAMS

Perfect discipline requires recognition of infallibility. Infallibility requires the observance of discipline. George F. Kennan

A disciplined trading program is important for producing consistent profits. Without it, maintaining profitability becomes extremely difficult. Just by having established a program, the initial step for successful investing has been accomplished. You had to put the effort into investigating methods or procedures for producing favorable results. Logic says an investor would not put together an established program from losing trade statistics. Everybody wants to develop a trading method that creates positive results. The results now become a function of how that program is maintained.

Unfortunately, other elements interfere with maintaining the proper discipline to achieve success. Once a trading program is altered, deviating from the discipline required to minimize losses and produce gains, it is hard to achieve the desired results of the trading method. Once the parameters for entering or exiting a trade have been circumvented by human intervention, the framework of the trading program disappears. Human emotions have an enormous influence on the completion of the trade. Emotions are the biggest hindrance for most investors to stay the course. These emotions, once controlled, become the source for producing profits from others who do not control their emotions. It was from these flaws of emotional control that the Candlestick trading method was developed.

If the downfall of most investors is fear and greed, and Candlestick analysis exploits those emotions, how can these emotions be redirected into a program that takes advantage of them? This is not a rhetorical question for the development of a perfect trading program; this is a question to eliminate the weaknesses that most investors experience.

The following investment program was developed over a 15-year period. It incorporates the knowledge of the Candlestick signals and the procedures described in the past few chapters. Use the rationale for the setup of this trading program to develop the trading program that best fits your schedule and investment capabilities. This chapter and the following chapters describe investment programs that use the advantages of Candlestick analysis to the fullest extent.

Optimal Trading

Trading on a consistently proactive basis and not on a reactive basis requires eliminating human emotion from the decision-making process. Maintaining a disciplined trading program, based on calculated investment procedures extracts much greater profits from the market than undisciplined or unthought-out methods. Having a method to produce consistent profits provides a compounding effect that extensively outproduces the buy-and-hold method, or the method of buying the next tout from your broker and hoping that it will turn into a big win while not having any exit program for the last four touts that he or she gave you.

The first step for developing a successful trading program is having confidence in the methodology. Assuming that the statistics quoted earlier in this book hold true, at least three out of every four trades are going to be successful. Following the profit maximization steps can push those statistics up to four out of five. With those statistics as the backdrop for putting on trades, you can reasonably expect a monthly return of at least 10 percent. Does this seem like a bold statement? Follow the logic and the process for obtaining these returns.

The optimal trading program requires a few basic elements for a successful outcome:

- Easy access to a computer screen during the day
- A discount brokerage firm with low commissions
- Subscribing to a search software program
- Access to a live trade feed

Know Your Trading Schedule

The trading strategy that optimizes the following procedures requires that the investor have reasonable access to the computer screen each day. Being able to use a computer is important. It provides the medium for researching the best trades and executing orders. The discipline described incorporates trades that exist for an average of two to five trading days. Fizzled trades that are liquidated the same day are included, as well as, trades lasting up to 10 to 14 days before a viable reversal signal presents itself. Having a search software program, such as TC2000 or Telescan, simplifies the search process down to a matter of 5 to 10 minutes a day. Both programs also provide the ability to customize searches.

There will be periods in all market cycles where one set of formations is working better than the others. This does not pertain to the Candlestick signals specifically. It is directed more toward the conditions of the market. For example, after the indexes have had a period of uptrend followed by a period of pullback and are now resuming the uptrend, J-hook patterns may be producing better gain potential versus stocks that are in their initial bottoming stage. Having the ability to analyze each area of formations in the matter of minutes creates a clear comparison of which group of stocks to be concentrating on.

Research can be done anytime before, during, or after market hours. But access to the computer screen during the first 15 minutes of the market open and the last 15 to 30 minutes before the market close is vital. This will be explained further when discussing trade executions.

Low Commissions

The advent of the discount brokerage firms furnishes a mechanism for trading the number of times required to achieve maximum returns. As discussed in Chapter 9, it is expected that when a trade does not confirm a Candlestick signal, liquidation is executed immediately. There will be periods of choppy or reversing markets when entering and exiting trades a multitude of times prior to a direction is established. The lower the cost of getting in and out, the less effect that it will have on the equity of the account.

Do not be lulled into thinking that there are not significant costs associated with entering and exiting trades, even at $8 or $12 per trade. The investment brokerage industry is set up to try to profit from every trade that is made. Slippage will be present in every trade that you do. That is the case whether you are paying low commission rates or high commission rates. You can reduce severe execution slippage by exercising common-sense practices when getting into or out of trades.

Expect the slippage. It is part of reality. The Candlestick method of trading has been developed to reap excessive gains from the market. A bad fill on a trade should not be the criteria for making or not making a trade. The potential gain on a trade should have been analyzed to produce at least a 10-percent potential return—or the trade should not have been made in the first place.

Fund Allocations

Once everything is in place for putting on trades, the account is funded, access to a research software program is established, live feed for viewing the market movements and stock prices is in place, and it is time to allocate funds to positions. For the sake of this example, a $100,000 account has been established. What is the best way to allocate funds for each trade? The optimal number of positions on at any one time is between 7 and 10. Any more than this number starts to diminish the time needed to evaluate each position daily and keep a clear mind when executing trades. Any less than this reduces the probabilities of being positioned in a trade that moves dramatically in the direction that the signal indicated.

For example, start with an eight-position portfolio. The trade positions should be allocated to $12,500 per position or reasonably close. Buy lots of stocks that round out to the nearest 100 shares. If buying 900 shares of a stock costs $12,800 or $11,300, go ahead and execute that amount. You do not want to be waiting around for odd lot orders just to keep the dollar amount exactly at $12,500.

What is important is not to have some positions skewed too large while others are too small. The reason is simple. When all eight positions are implemented, all with fantastic signals, the probabilities still will produce mostly winners and a few losers. Nobody can predict with 100-percent accuracy which of the signals will produce a big winner and which trades will fizzle. Over-weighting one position over another allows the element of emotion to creep into the investment decision. The fact that more funds were put into one position and not another implies that your investment prowess stated that one stock was going to do better than the less invested position. If you are that good, you didn't need an investment plan in the first place.

Divide positions as evenly as possible. A bad trade will thereby be offset by a good trade elsewhere in the portfolio. Having equal positions keeps the decision-making process as mechanical as possible. The historic statistics of putting on Candlestick trades will provide positive results scattered across evenly funded positions. There is no need to put yourself in a situation of having to second-guess yourself.

Starting the Positioning

Producing above average returns embodies some simple compounding facts. It is easier to compound returns from a base amount plus additional funds (profits) than it is from a base amount minus funds (losses). This may sound elementary but it is usually not taken into consideration by most investors starting out. The compound effect is dramatically altered by how the initial funds are used. In our example, the account is starting with $100,000. The rate of return is based upon the profits produced from the inception of the trading program.

How the first transactions perform has an immense effect on the total return down the road. For instance, all the steps have been taken to establish trades. As described in Chapter 9, you have analyzed the market direction, analyzed the sectors that showed the best potential, found a multitude of excellent Candlestick buy signals, and are ready to commit funds. The next morning, you buy eight positions that all open in the manner that demonstrates continued buying. However, at 1:33 P.M. that same day, Alan Greenspan crosses his eyes the wrong way in front of the House Ways and

Means Committee hearing. The market turns around and heads south. By the end of the day the account is down $8,000. Not your fault and not the signals' fault—just one of those facts of life. Even though the results of the positions that were put on were statistically in line, three were up slightly, two were flat, but three were down big, the results are that the account is down. No great concern. Liquidating the bad positions and/or putting on new positions, long and short over the next period of days, weeks, or month makes up the losses. But the make up of those losses has to be done from a smaller base of investment funds; $92,000 of equity had to make back the $8,000 to get back to even.

Two dynamics were at work that slowed down future gains. First, it took a higher return being produced to gain back the losses. Secondly, once the account was back to even, that time had been expended. It does not seem like that should be a big deal, but in the calculations of compounding, it can have large ramifications out in the future. The following illustration demonstrates what a one-month delay in profits cost the investor 12 months down the road.

$100,000 Compounded 12 Times

The effect of a one-month delay cost this account $28,531 at the end of one year, the difference between Month 11 and Month 12. A more conservative approach can be taken when initiating the beginning positions. Of the best positions, put on three trades the first day. If an unexpected surprise crunches the market that day, losses should be minimal. The positions can be reevaluated and the next day adjusted to the new indications of the market. More than likely, if everything followed the expected results of the day, hopefully two of the three positions showed profits and the third showed a slight loss. The account over all was up. That could lead to adding another one or two positions the next day. Theoretically, the majority of the positions should show profits each day. Some of the profits will be offset by the losses in a minority of the positions. This should produce a net profit the majority of the trading days. After a few days, all eight positions should be on. At that point, a daily cultivation process keeps the best possible profit situations in the portfolio and eliminates the weak ones.

Cultivating the Portfolio

Once the investment funds are fully allocated, the portfolio can be maintained with an effective profit-maximizing process. Each position should be evaluated daily. Some of the positions may have been on for one day, some on for two, three, and so forth. Each position is evaluated as far as what is the remaining upside potential, what is the downside risk, is there any indication of weakness showing up in the move (that is, weak candlestick formations), and what is the condition of the stochastics? The evaluation process may show that Position 3 is getting toppy, and Position 7 would be a sell if it opens weaker the next day. And/or Position 6 has run up 14 percent over the past two days, indicating it might be preparing for a profit-taking pullback. The remaining positions all look solid for further profits.

The evaluations are now compared to the results of the latest search. Two signals may have been found that are compelling buys under the current market conditions. The availability of a constant supply of excellent trade situations creates the opportunity to shift funds from a good trade potential to a great trade potential. If the evaluation of Position 3 is that it has already made a good move and still has the possibility of continuing a few more percentage points, the decision might boil down to whether it is worth sitting in this position to make another 6 percent after moving up 12 percent or should the funds be moved to a new position where the upside appears to be 15 to 20 percent. This is a good problem to have. When the search program produces a constant supply of excellent trade situations, existing positions constantly have the capacity to be upgraded.

This supply of excellent trade situations is the stimulus for a basic rule for this style of trading. When in doubt, get out. If there is a situation where staying in a position has some doubt to it, get out. If there isn't a good place to put the funds immediately, there will be the next day. The search software programs, able to scan 10,000 stocks instantly, will always produce at least one or two high-potential trade situations each day. Why expose investment dollars to any questionable situations when they can easily be moved to low-risk, high-profit probability situations? An illustration of this situation is demonstrated in Figure 10.1, representing Marvel Technology Group Ltd., and Figure 10.2, representing Bell Microproducts Inc.

If Marvel Technology Group Ltd. was bought at the bullish Engulfing Pattern, it would have more than a 100-percent gain. Stochastics are in the overbought area. The question has to be how much more upside potential is left. There have not been any signs of selling. This chart should now be compared to what the latest search produced, Bell Microproducts Inc. Stochastics are just coming up out of the oversold area. A Morning Star signal appeared followed by continued buying. This looks like a good buy situation. But the account is fully allocated.

This is the dilemma that the Candlestick investor wants to always have. Now the decision boils down to which is the best place to have your investment dollars. The evaluation becomes simple. What is the upside potential of both positions? Marvel could keep heading higher. Bell seems likely to be able to fill the gap of a few weeks ago, taking the price up to $10, approximately a 25-percent gain from the $8.25 price. Could Marvel hit $26.50 to $27 in the same amount of time? Maybe, but at this point the chart on Bell Microproducts appears to be much more compelling chart. The first logical target seems to be $10, with $12 not being out of reach. To be stated more

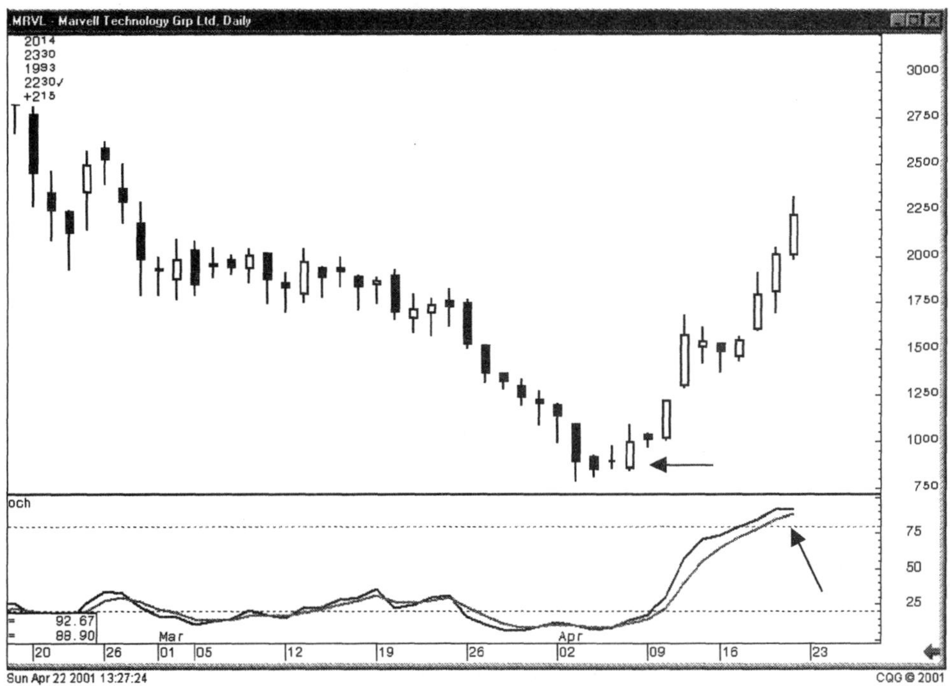

Figure 10.1 What is the risk and potential of this stock at $22.50?

Figure 10.2 What is the downside risk and upside potential of this stock?

simply, "If there were money available to invest today, which position would I invest in?" That should be the primary question each day.

This process will dramatically alter the investor's mental state. Having an abundant supply of potential profitable trades each day creates the opportunity to eliminate emotional attachments to any one trade. This line of thinking, combined with the single-figure portfolio management practice (discussed in the following section in this chapter), will eliminate emotional involvement in investment decisions. The decision to stay in or get out of a position is not predicated upon how much higher can the existing position go. The important question remains "Where is the best upside potential weighed against the downside risk?" It directs the Candlestick investor to analyze the best potential for producing the maximum profit for the account versus maximizing profits from specific positions. The effect of this cultivation process is always having funds placed in the best potential positions. The risk of squeezing out the last profits from a good trade, being exposed to elevated prices, and the possibility of extensive pullbacks is dramatically reduced.

Single-Figure Portfolio Management

Along with fear and greed there is one more major emotional element each investor has to deal with. Ego! Not the ego that everybody wants to go out and boast about how great an investor he or she is. It pertains to the self-analysis that each of us goes through when putting on a trade. Nobody likes a losing trade—not so much because it lost money, but more that it went against our analysis. Being we each know that we are smarter than the average person, our egos get dashed when a stock purchase goes down. Our superior intelligence analyzed and decided that a stock was a good buy, but now we are *wrong*. Our egos step in. We are too smart to be wrong. This stock will come back. As it goes lower, our ego gets that much more out of whack.

At that point, the investment strategy becomes one of holding the position until it gets back to breakeven, and then selling it. The first question is why does this stock have to ever come back up to where you bought it? This is a prime example of most investors not having a credible investment program. This trade was put on for one set of reasons and it was kept on for a completely different set of reasons. The major reasons losing trades are held is because of ego. Unfortunately, holding on to losing trades does not maximize profits.

Implementing a discipline to maintain a set number of positions with an equal dollar amount allocation is the first step to eliminating emotions in investment decisions. The way to completely take emotions out of the process is to use a *single-figure portfolio management program*. That one figure is the bottom line. At the end of the day, there should be only one concern: What was the value of the portfolio? What was the total net gain or loss for the day?

This method of analysis eliminates the concern of the performance of each individual stock. At the end of each day the cost basis for each position held at the close becomes that day's closing price. This procedure eliminates any ego hang-ups. Emphasis is now directed to how the total portfolio did. If the concept of Candlestick trading holds true, the majority of the positions should have been up, a lesser number of positions down, producing an overall gain for the day.

The total value of the portfolio is calculated upon the gains or losses incurred on each position held, up or down from the previous closing price. Any stock positions bought or sold are calculated against closing prices. Stocks that were bought during the day are showing a profit or loss from where they were purchased compared to that day's closing prices. Any stock sold during that trading day will be calculated against the previous night's closing price.

This process removes the stigma of what the purchase price was for each position. On a nightly basis, each position can be objectively evaluated based upon the Candlestick signals, stochastics, and its status pertaining to its recent price movement. What was originally paid for the position becomes irrelevant. The important criteria becomes, "What is this position going to do tomorrow or the next few days to benefit the single-figure?"

Embarrassment

Analyzing all the factors, visually evaluating the probable potential of positions on the charts, helps eliminate another emotional trauma. Having a format for when to put positions on or take positions off alleviates the self-embarrassment process. As touched on in the introduction of this book, how most investors trade is predicated on what if somebody found out that I did this faux pas or that faux pas?

Why do investors stay in trades too long? Because it would be embarrassing to have somebody find out that Marvel was sold at $22 and proceeded to run up to $64. Or on the other hand, how you bought XYZ Corporation at $20, took your losses at $18 and it turned around immediately and went to $48. This embarrassment is usually self-inflicted. In the total scheme of things, who is ever going to know other than yourself?

Using the Candlestick signals helps in two ways. It forms a basis for putting on trades or taking off trades. If Marvel (as seen in Figure 10.1) is sold at $22, it is based upon the best investment decision for that particular time. If it proceeds to $64, the right decision was made for the right reason when it was liquidated. Too bad that a good run up was not fully exploited. However, the probabilities made better sense to take profits at that point and move the funds to another trade. There is nothing that can embarrass a person if he or she did the right thing at the right time. Another Candlestick rule is not to look back. The program is not to maximize profits on each trade; it is to maximize profits for the account.

Secondly, whether taking profits or cutting losses, the Candlestick signals tell you when to get in and when to get out. If XYZ Corp. was shown as a buy at $20 and then looked bad, getting you out at $18 might have you back in at $21 on a better signal. Again, this could cause the ego/embarrassment dilemma. How hard it is to repurchase a stock that has recently given you a loss. Remember the single-figure does not care. A good trade signal is a good trade signal. Do not shy away from a stock just because it fooled you the first time. Remember, 99.9 percent of all the trades that you put on in your account will never be seen by anybody but yourself. Don't let your emotions be your own worst enemy.

Market Direction

As described in Chapter 9, knowing the direction of the market is important for placing correct trades. The majority of the time a trend will be obvious. However, there will be times when the markets are choppy and a direction is hard to decipher. Fortunately, this is the atmosphere in which the Candlestick signals will outperform other trading programs. The innate function of the signals is that they demonstrate where investment funds are flowing. In a nondirectional market, this becomes a priceless barometer.

Sometimes the markets just get too sloppy to trade at all. For example, if the market is oversold and still in a slow decline, every strong up-day may appear as a reversal signal. Longs are put on only to witness more downside the next day, producing small losses. If you cannot get a feel for the market, go to cash for a few days, until a better set of signals becomes evident. This does not happen often but it does occur from time to time.

Despite this type of action, there will still be good trades produced by the signals. Analyze the market action. This may be a period where successful trades are one or two days long versus three to five days long. It could also highlight a sector more clearly. If prices in general have been bobbing up and down, a sector may stand out due to a consistent move in one direction. Study that sector. Allocate investment funds according to procedures.

Identify the Sectors

The advantage of identifying a sector, moving in a particular direction, is twofold. First, it greatly reduces the search process each day for potentially profitable trades. Even though the search software can pinpoint many good trades in the matter of minutes, there is additional credence in finding good trade situations in a sector that is attracting investor attention. Secondly, the universe of the search is greatly reduced. What appears to be a redundancy in benefits has an underlying benefit. The knowledge that investment money is coming into a particular sector creates more time to fine-tune the analytical process for identifying the most compelling Candlestick signal.

Sector searches contain some double confirmation aspects. Being able to see where the big investment money is flowing produces strategic clarity that few investors use. This amplifies the practice of putting investment dollars in the most profitable situations. In a rising market, knowing which sector has the greatest upside potential enhances profit opportunities. All boats are raised in a rising tide. Identifying the Candlestick signals in sector indexes allows the investor to maximize profits. A strong signal during the rising market trend targets the sector that has an inordinate amount of investment dollars coming into it. This provides the opportunity to exceed the "rising tide." The more obvious benefit comes from being able to identify buying coming into a sector when the general market direction is down. Candlestick signals stick out like sore thumbs in this environment. If shorting stocks does not fit your investment profile, then identifying the sectors that can produce profits in a declining market atmosphere becomes an excellent supply of opportunity.

A residual benefit of participating in a sector trend is the further elimination of the false signal surprise. The news that affects an industry or sector is the result of fundamental elements that have made the sector attractive. The probabilities of a surprise adverse announcement is reduced. And by rare occurrence, if there is a surprise announcement that could greatly affect a stock price, the enthusiasm about the sector in general will moderate the price reaction.

Locating Candlestick signals in sector indexes is useful for maximizing long-term investment profits as well as pinpointing short-term trades. Candlestick signals on the weekly and monthly charts clearly illustrate when longer-term trends are changing.

Long-Term Investment Programs

For those investors who do not have the time or inclination to trade their portfolio daily, weekly, or even monthly, the Candlestick signals can be used effectively. As described earlier, the signals are the depiction of investor sentiment during particular time durations. Whether the time frame is one minute or one month, the signal created is the measurement of investor psychology during that time frame. A bullish Engulfing Pattern witnessed at the bottom of a monthly chart, corresponding with oversold stochastics, should act as the same alert to the Candlestick investor as the same conditions seen on a daily or minute-by-minute chart. The only difference becomes the time factor.

As seen in Figure 10.3, representing Stewart Industries Inc., the long-term trend was down for over one year. After trading flat for over another year, the long white candle, after the three months of indecision signals, along with stochastics coming up through the 20 line, gives a good indication that the long-term trend had changed. The appearance of a bullish candle when the stochastics have come up through the 20 line provides the long-term

Figure 10.3 Monthly charts can work in conjunction with short-term charts.

investor with a valuable timing tool. To confirm the reversal, the weekly chart can also be used to verify the change in long-term sentiment.

This use of the Candlestick signals enhances the Warren Buffet method: accumulating companies and industries that are in the unwanted stage and holding them for three years or longer until the cycle makes them the hot companies. Having the ability to see when the crucial buying is starting to come into companies or industries greatly multiplies earning potential. It reduces sitting in a stock while the price is in its bottoming stage. In the example of Stewart Industries, the Harami of mid-1999 indicated that the selling had basically stopped. However, there was about a year and a half of bottoming before the price started showing upward movement. Buying anytime before the first of the year 2000 would have resulted in flat returns. An accumulation period is fine if you are a wealthy client in the Warren Buffet program, but if you are trying to maximize returns, the timing aspect plays an important role.

You as an investor can use the Candlestick formations to enhance the establishment of a long-term position. You can put a simple procedure in place. Analyzing the monthly charts, as seen in Figure 10.3, will identify those stocks that are coming off bottoms. These bottoms can be the long gradual bottoming formations or the hard decline followed by an obvious

Candlestick buy signal. The advantage that the Candlestick signals provide is clear indications that buying sentiment is visually apparent. A signal on a monthly chart can be confirmed by corresponding signals on the weekly chart. Once you make the decision to commit funds to a long-term position, the daily charts provide a format for accumulating positions during the short-term pullbacks.

Intermediate Investing: Buying Bad News

The longer the term of a trading-hold period, the more important the company's fundamentals become. As with all companies and industries, some economic environments are favorable and some are unfavorable. Rarely will the price history of a stock be straight up. Companies experience growing pains, some getting too big too fast. Or management changes. Or faulty management decisions are made. Yet, the one major analytical factor that most investors fail to consider is the ability of management. It is this factor that Candlestick signals help to exploit for producing extraordinary profits.

When a company is going through a bad period, it has usually been made evident by the reduction in the stock price. The further the stock goes down, the more emotion is brought into the price. The smart money got out of the stock at the beginning of the decline. They foresaw the results of what current economic factors or management decisions would do to the stock price down the road. The more complacent investor rode the decline all the way down. They got tidbits of analysts' opinions as to why the stock was going down by watching clips on the financial stations. Finally, the bad news is announced. An earnings warning, a loss of a major contract, the loss of market share—the reason for the suspected price decline over the past three months is finally made public. The investors who held their position through the decline finally acquiesce and throw in the towel. What has been publicized on the financial stations for the past month is apparently true. The stock price gaps down 25 percent on the open.

Is this the time to be buying or selling? The Candlestick formations created can answer that question. The particular candle formed on the day of the gap down holds an immense amount of information. It gives a clear signal indicating if and when that stock should be bought. It is a common phenomenon to see the price of the stock come back up to and exceed the price level of where the huge gap down occurred. It usually does so within the next three months if not sooner. The result is 25-percent gains or better in a three-month time frame. Those are not bad returns for any investment program.

Why does this program work? Emotion. The bad news has been speculated through the financial mediums for weeks and months. All the news is negative. The bad announcement knocks the price down dramatically. Nobody wants this stock anymore. *Except*, who is buying this stock when everybody is selling?

The buyers are the investors who anticipate the effects of good management. A company does not and will not remain in existence if there is not good management at the helm. Management is not a static function. Mature companies have qualified decision-makers. They did not get to upper management by chance. The term *mature* is crucial. Growth companies have the potential to succeed because of their product or service. The uniqueness of the company can sustain growth for a period despite the lack of management skills of the founders. As it matures, getting competition or expanding into less developed markets, management becomes more important. A well-managed company does not stay static in its thinking.

The same adverse factors, that induced the smart money to get out at the highs, should have been evident to top management. These factors should have set alert management on a course of corrective action. Even though there might not been anything that could be done to avert the negative news, changes would have been developed to solve the problems. When the bad news was announced, corrective actions were probably already well underway. The future should be different from the recent results. That is why somebody is buying the stock that the panic sellers are providing at a deep discount.

Candlesticks provide the optimal time for accumulating the discounted stock. The formations created by the panic selling reveal valuable information. As illustrated in Figure 10.4, representing Plantronics Inc., the news that

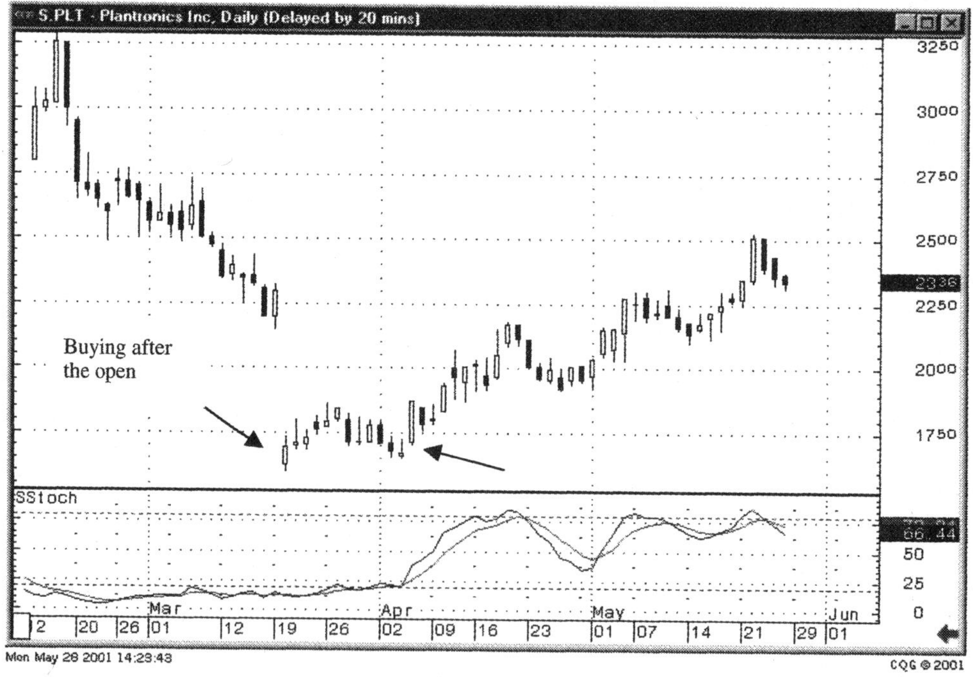

Figure 10.4 A white candle after major negative news reveals that some buyers feel that the price represents a buying area.

produced the big drop was met with immediate buying. The white candle indicates that the extreme selling was done on the open. The subsequent buying was based upon somebody evaluating that the selling was overdone. It was time to look ahead to future possibilities. The white body illustrates that more buying than selling occurred after the opening price. In most cases, the low of that trading day when a white candle forms acts as the support level for future trading. Note that two weeks later an Inverted Hammer followed by a strong white candle creates a second opportunity to accumulate more stock. Approximately six weeks from the gap down day, the gap is filled and then exceeded. Buying stock in the $17 area produced a 27.5 percent return when the gap was filled on April 19—an acceptable return for a six-week investment.

The white candle formed on the day of the big percentage move down provided the Candlestick investor with a valuable insight. Buyers were stepping in after the stock price opened that day. This provides the knowledge that the selling is being soaked up, unlike the signal illustrated in Figure 10.5, representing Dollar Tree Stores, where after the open, the sellers were still dominating. This clearly illustrates that despite the big drop in price, the bad news was apparently more involved than what the market was expecting. A black candle reveals that the sellers overwhelmed any buying after the open.

The black candle is a clear signal that all the selling is not finished. In this example, the buying signal did not appear for another five trading days.

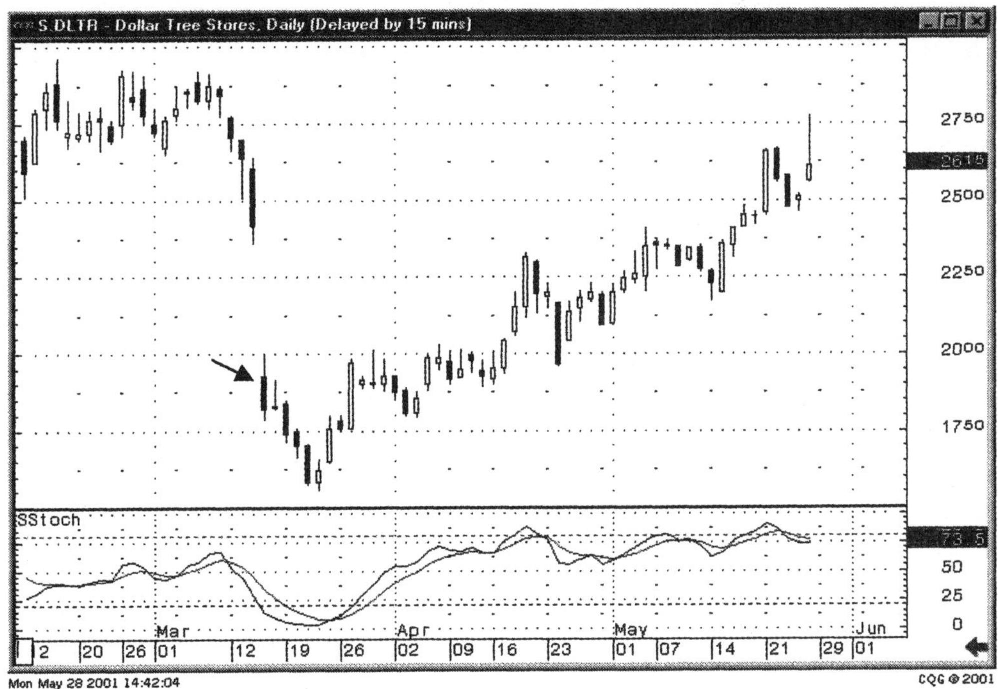

Figure 10.5 A black candle after bad news reveals that all the negative implications are not yet realized.

The Harami indicated that the selling had stopped. The strong open the next day illustrated that the buyers were continuing their presence. Buying Dollar Tree Stores at the $16.50 to $17.00 area would have resulted in holding the position for seven to eight weeks before getting back to the levels where prices gapped down. May 4 filled the gap at $23.63. Holding to that date produced approximately a 29-percent return. The appearance of a black candle on the gap down day provided the awareness to not commit to this trade yet, more selling was evident. Identifying the buy signal a few days later, under the circumstances, made for an excellent, relatively low-risk transaction.

Finding these trades does not require a great amount of time expenditure. If one's schedule permits an investor to get to a computer screen once every week or two, this method of investing becomes a good program. The search programs can be formatted to identify these situations. The search parameters can be easily established:

- Stock prices that have declined X percent from their highest levels within the past 30 trading days.
- Stock prices that have gapped down greater 20 percent during the past 7 trading days.

These searches will produce enough situations, out of the universe of stocks, to keep six or eight positions fully funded at any one time. This type of trading program makes for low maintenance investing. The probabilities are extremely favorable that profits will be made. This is derived by simple rules. Fundamentally, companies work to get mistakes and/or bad economic factors corrected. Technically, the stock prices are usually in oversold conditions when the bad news is finally reported. The gap formed will eventually be filled. Using Candlestick buy signals pinpoints when buying starts coming back into the stock. The low point of any buy signal can be used as sensible stop-loss points. Again, the common thread of successful invest logic is incorporated into this trading program. The investor who does not have much time to devote to position analysis can produce excellent returns by holding trades for 3- to 16-week periods. The positions can be identified with 30 minutes of research every week or two. It does not take a rocket scientist to realize that positions that produce 20 to 30 percent returns every month to four months, rolled over into the next position, creates an exemplary compounding effect.

The visual aspects of Candlestick formations supplies investors with a powerful advantage for developing profitable trading programs. The program can be customized to fit every schedule. The most dominant aspect is the proficiency of the signals to recognize the change of trend direction. Whether that trend is months or minutes does not alter the function of the Candlestick signals. The signals measure investor sentiment occurring in the specified time increment.

Day Trading

The advent of the Small Order Execution Systems (SOES) trading was the result of the one-day market crashes over the 15 years. The SEC ruled that small investors should be able to have access to the markets on days that dramatic moves in the market make it impossible to get through to stockbrokers. The crash of 1987 was a good example. The Dow-Jones crashed over 500 points in one day. The phone lines to the brokerage firms were jammed. Only the institutions with direct lines to the floor traders were able to execute their trades. The average person had no way to facilitate an order.

That lack of access is what started opening up the trading options for the average investor. New avenues of getting orders executed were implemented. This created a new form of investment trading, day trading. The development of online investing expanded greatly with the new electronic trading capabilities.

SOES trading firms produced a few years of flurry about the SOES bandits. Media hoopla investigated the aspect of the bandits creating new volatility to the markets. In actuality, the ability for day traders to cut into the hefty profits of the market makers led to the market makers getting favorable rulings for backing away from trades. This new flexibility was the cause of more volatile price movements. But that is neither here nor there. How to make money using Candlestick signals is the important subject.

The basis for most of a day trader's profits are the results of quick arbitrage situations or scalping short-term trend movements. Candlestick signals applied to a 1-, 3-, 5-, and/or 15-minute chart create excellent successful trade conditions. How the charts are used can enable a trader to develop multiple of successful trading programs. The most basic program for the trader who can constantly monitor each trade, the one-minute chart, can produce dozens of high-probability trades every day. As seen in Figure 10.6, the same parameters found in the daily charts are applied to the one-minute chart. A buy signal appearing when stochastics are in the oversold area represent a high probability of a successful trade.

In this case, the trade may last 3, 5, 7, or 10 minutes. Note that the arrows point out clear Candlestick formations, Morning Star signals, Evening Star signals, Bearish Engulfing Patterns. These formations can be acted upon with a high degree of confidence. This requires having fairly fast trade capabilities. It also requires a trading entity that is constantly liquid. Excellent trade signals become less valuable if the trading entity is difficult to get in and out of, the bid/ask spread is too large to overcome, or the slippage (execution price) is too exaggerated to produce profitable trades. The NASDAQ futures, the Standard and Poor futures, or the Dow-Jones futures provide the liquidity for successful day trading. They all have constant liquidity that makes immediate entry and exit of trades easy.

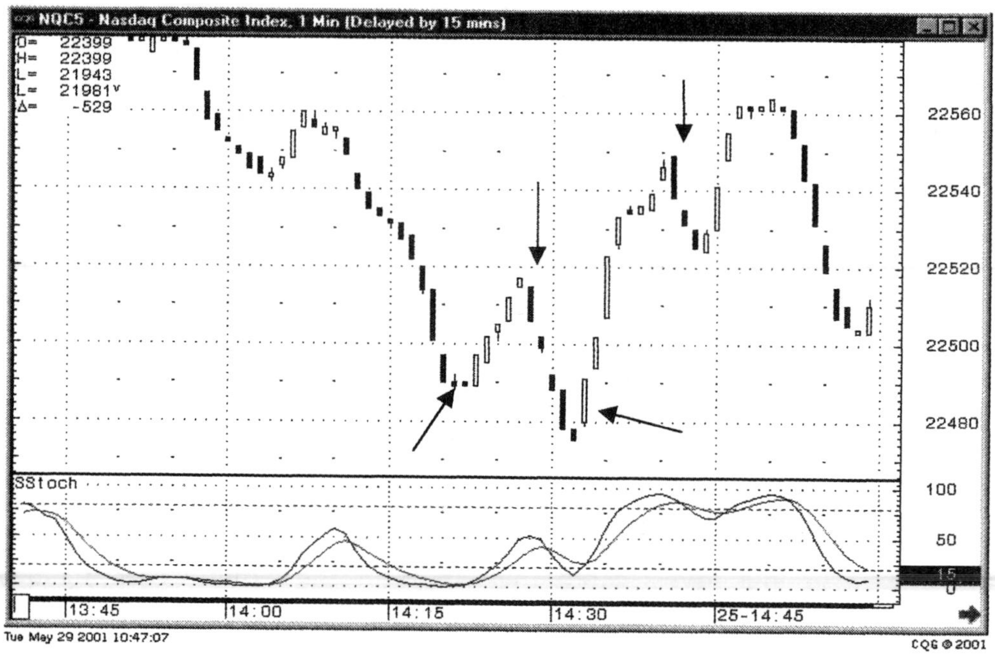

Figure 10.6 One-minute charts produce excellent trading set ups for day-traders.

Note how the 15-minute chart, seen in Figure 10.7, was forming a Morning Star signal. This indicates that the longer-term daily trends may be changing. An analysis of the five-minute chart, shown in Figure 10.8, reveals that the trend is showing a few candles that indicate strength. The information conveyed by both of these charts would lead to the one-minute chart. The next bullish formation would act as a safe entry point for a trade that should last from 45 minutes through the remainder of the day, depending upon the appearance of a sell signal.

The day trader who can't or does not want to be tied to the computer screen every second that a trade is in place has alternatives. Statistical studies are easily implemented for longer day trading programs. For example, fewer but better success probability trades can be put in place when the 15- and the 5-minute charts both show Candlestick buy signals along with stochastics being in the oversold area. When both of these charts correspond, the one-minute chart can then be used to put on the trade at the most opportune time. Figures 10.7 and 10.8 are showing bottoming formations at the same time. This offers an opportune trade development the next time the one-minute chart produces a Candlestick buy signal corresponding with the stochastics being in the oversold condition. This trade now warrants a hold period until the 15- and 5-minute charts show a sell signal at the same time. A trade of this nature may last for a few hours at a time.

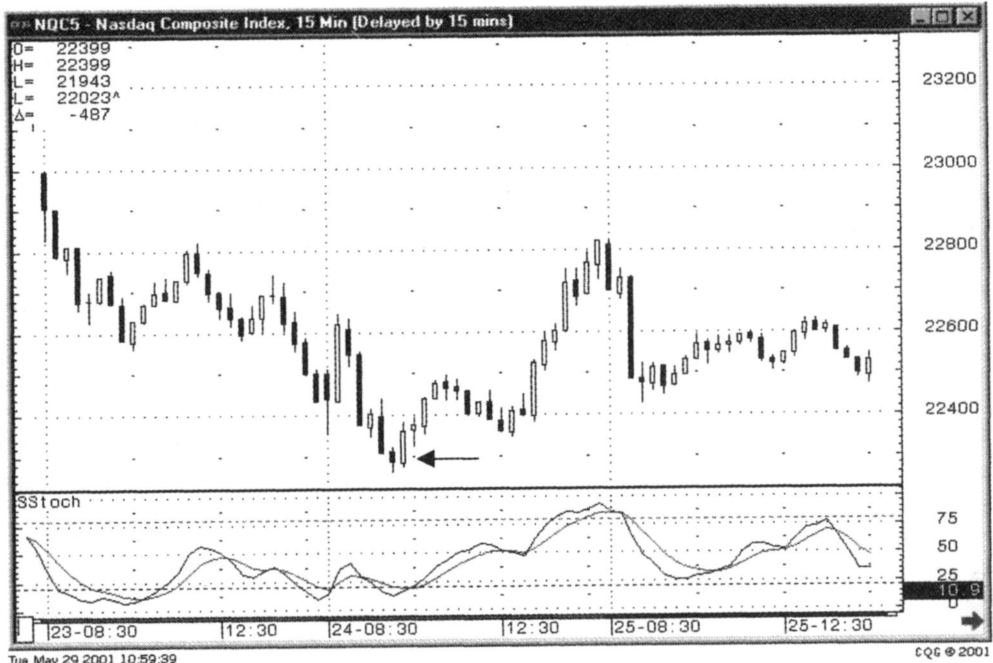

Figure 10.7 The NASDAQ 15-minute chart.

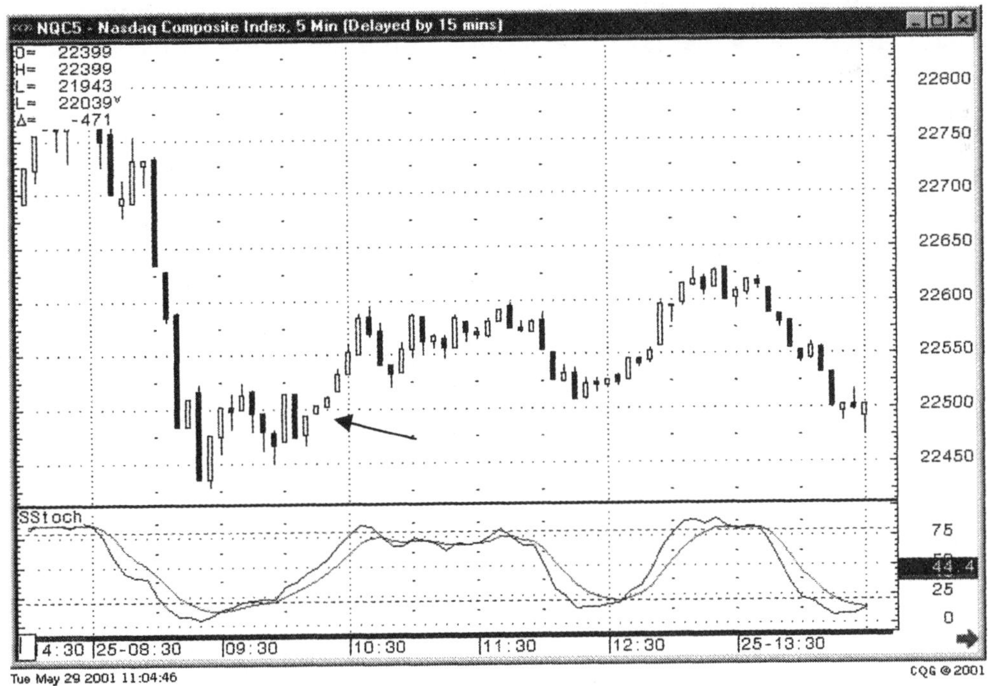

Figure 10.8 The NASDAQ five-minute chart

The length of trades will be a direct function of successfully combining chart patterns. Back testing may discover that the 3- and 10-minute charts acting in conjunction produces profitable trades 73 percent of the time while the combination of successful trades in the 5/15 combination works 67 percent of the time. Whatever statistical testing is done, the Candlestick signals provide a basis for testing. The signals act as the catalyst for effective testing. The favorable probabilities of a successful reversal is a built-in factor of the signal. This element, applied to other successful result characteristics, creates a trading program that makes identifying short trend changes visually easy and quick. The speed of recognizing a trend change in a day trading program is important. Executing trades after a trend has started and exiting after a profitable trend has shown a reversal will greatly reduce the potential profit. The position needs to be put on at the first signs of a reversal and exited upon the first signs of the trend ending. The Candlestick formations or the set up for a Candlestick formation allows the Candlestick day trader to anticipate when those signs may be forming. Getting in or out prior to the majority of the traders moving en masse greatly reduces the slippage generated when a trading entity is moving extensively in one direction.

Using the signals to establish trades reduces the guesswork of when a trade is about to reverse. Establishing a trading discipline using the signals as the framework for putting on a day trade gives the trader the statistical advantage. Knowing that a set of corresponding buy signals has a much greater probability of producing a successful trade induces the trader to move quicker, gaining execution advantage over the momentum traders. The visual clarity makes the day traders trade implementation an easy function of the trading program.

Chapter 11

USING CANDLESTICKS TO IMPROVE ELLIOT WAVE ANALYSIS

What we want is brand-new ideas that do not upset our old ideas.
Peters Almanac

Elliot Wave analysis is one of the most widely used analytical tools in the financial industry. It is estimated that 80 percent of all institutional investors incorporate Elliot Wave into their trading programs. This tends to move markets in unison because all investors are reacting to the same set of parameters. This chapter should be read from two different perspectives.

If you are not extensively familiar with the Elliot Wave concept, do not spend a great deal of time trying to understand or learn the following information. This chapter describes the history and basics of the Elliot Wave program. It takes a great amount of time to fully understand and become proficient at Elliot Wave analysis. This is not the correct book for achieving that purpose. More importantly, it is not important for being successful in Candlestick investing. However, knowing the simple basics will help in identifying when all the Elliot Wave followers are expecting a reversal. Also, the fact that Elliot could reasonably identify wave movements in investment vehicles adds to the argument that oscillation occurs constantly in investment markets.

The main purpose of this chapter is to benefit the existing proponents of the Elliot Wave concept. The combination of Candlestick signals, incorporated into Elliot Wave analysis, makes Elliot Wave analysis less subjective. The subjective aspect—being able to identify the direction of a trading entity — is a major difficulty of Elliot Wave analysis by itself. Candlesticks eliminate the variables of such interpretation.

Elliot Wave Background

Ralph Nelson Elliot formalized his discovery of the wave concept in the early part of the Twentieth Century. His assertions were relatively simple. Price movements contain a five-wave upmove, followed by a three-wave corrective downmove. As illustrated in Figure 11.1, waves 1, 3, and 5 are called *impulse waves*. Waves 2 and 4 are considered *corrective waves*. The same analysis holds for a downtrending market, as seen in Figure 11.2. The impulse waves represent the declining slopes, while the corrective waves are the upward bounces against the dominant trend.

Elliot has to be commended for the research that he did. Whole books are devoted to the concepts that he developed. Backdated information on the Dow was difficult to obtain up until just a few years ago. Its collection and interpretation had to have been painstakingly difficult back in the 1930s.

Elliot's assumptions have contributed long-lasting attributes to investing. He asserted that everything moves in the same pattern as the tides. Because the market in its truest form remains constant, time is not an affecting element. To fully understand the importance of Elliot's work, it is important to understand the concepts that he produced:

- Nature's Law
- The "Secret of the Universe"
- The wave principle
- Interpretative market letters
- The use of Fibonacci ratios

In Elliot's writings, he states, "Nature's Law embraces the most important of all elements, timing. Nature's Law is not a system, or method of play-

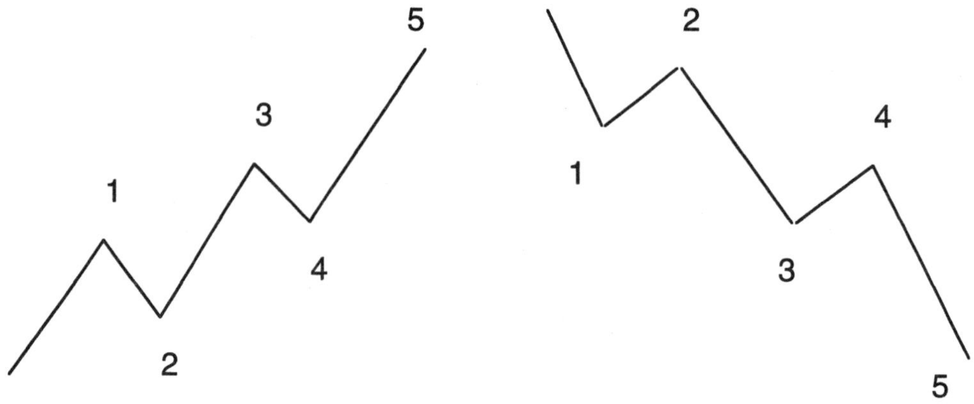

Figure 11.1 Elliot wave for uptrending market.

Figure 11.2 Elliot wave for downtrending market.

ing the market, but it is a phenomenon which appears to mark the progress of all human activities. Its application to forecasting is revolutionary." His discoveries are based upon Nature's Law. He said, "This law behind the market can only be discovered when the market is viewed in its proper light and then is analyzed from this approach. Simply put, the stock market is the creation of man and therefore reflects human idiosyncrasies." This parallels the concepts revealed in Candlestick signals. Human emotions are the overriding elements that move markets.

His independent conceptualization came close to touching on what the Japanese had discovered over hundreds of years of studying human nature. As implied by both Elliot Wave and Candlesticks, the price action of stocks has predictable movements. Price is based upon the psychological sentiment of investors. The fluctuation between fear and greed creates the oscillations in the markets. The mainstay of the Elliot Wave analysis is the ability to anticipate the magnitude of a move. The weakness of the Elliot Wave analysis is determining direction. Mastering the Elliott Wave concept takes years of experience. The reason? The vast amount of subjectivity in determining which "wave" is in effect. The degree of accuracy that is revealed in Elliot Wave analysis has been convincing for many years, provided that you have the skill to analyze wave count status correctly. As logic would dictate, if there were no credence to its abilities, it would not be in existence today.

The ability to forecast into the future is the motivation of all investors. Elliot made major strides in projecting the future. He stated, "All human activities have three distinctive features, pattern, time, and ratio, all of which observe the Fibonacci summation series." This led to his interpretation of the waves, forecasting future price movement and magnitude, through the identification of patterns. This projection method relied on the Fibonacci ratios. This declaration goes against the once popular Random-Walk theory that states there are no patterns in trading entities.

Mastering the Elliot Wave technique affords some highly successful trading. However, mastering this method takes years of analysis and experience. And for good reason. The basic concept would be fine if the five-wave patterns were consistent and easily definable. One of Elliot's most important statements is, "A cyclical pattern or measurement of mass psychology is 5 waves upward and 3 waves downward, totaling 8 waves. These patterns have forecasting value—when 5 waves upward have been completed, 3 waves down will follow and vise versa." (See Figure 11.3.) This is one of the few times that Elliot gave a definitive rule with forecasting value. The market exhibits patterns that adhere to this formula an inordinate amount of the time.

Consistent with Elliot's analysis, the end of the fifth wave is an extremely safe area to invest funds. Occasionally, an extension to the fifth wave circumvents this safety cushion. (See Figure 11.4.) Fortunately, this is the perfect criterion for using the Candlestick analysis. It can verify or negate the probability that a change of direction has occurred.

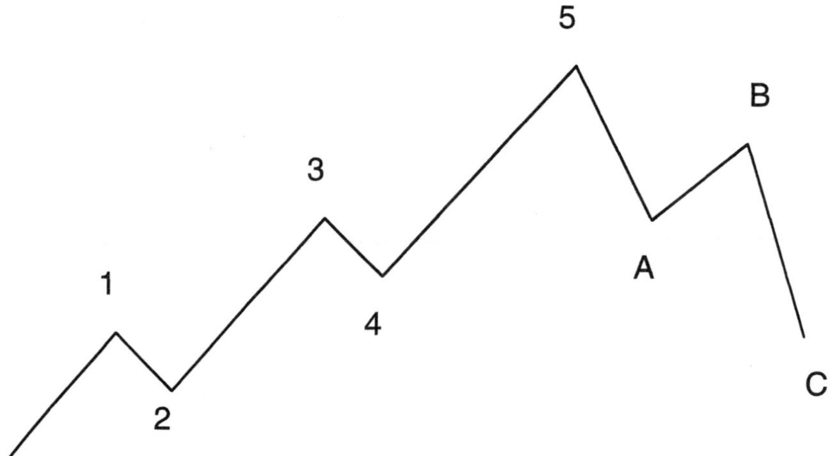

Figure 11.3 Five waves up, three waves down.

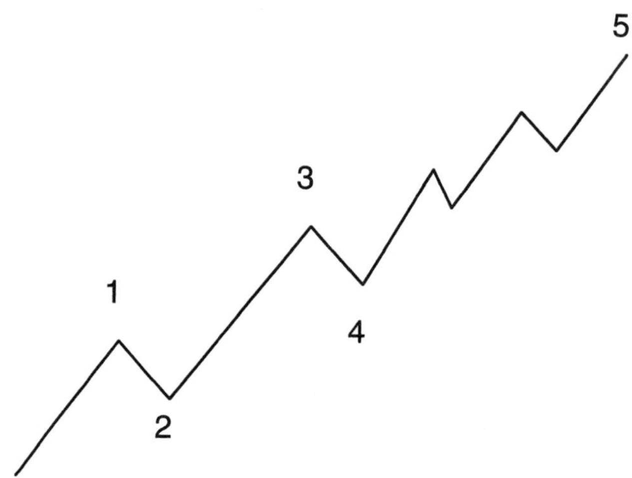

Figure 11.4 Five waves with the extension in the fifth wave.

Time periods do not affect the observation of the waves. You can see in chart analysis whether intraday, daily, weekly, or monthly. Elliot made three general rules about the five-wave movement:

- Wave 5 appears very similar to wave 1 under most circumstances.
- Probabilities indicate that wave 3 is going to be the longest wave.
- Wave 4 should not touch or breach the top of Wave 1 in the uptrend.

Fibonacci Numbers—Predicting the End of Wave 5

The Fibonacci ratios play an important part in projecting the end of an up trend. The two critical numbers are 1.618 and .618. Price goals can be calculated, but before that can happen, the swing size has to be defined.

The continuous movement in one direction is called the *swing*. In any trend, prices are going to oscillate in small increments. The magnitude of those increments has to be defined. A small move in the opposite direction has to be clarified as either a reversal wave or just part of the movement in the current wave direction. Small opposite direction movement does not need to be acknowledged. Developing criteria for establishing what constitutes a move helps eliminate the "noise" of a trend analysis.

Candlestick analysis has definite rules that greatly reduce the worry of calculating insignificant pullbacks. Not every zig and zag will have a Candlestick signal involved. Observing a short-term pull-back, during an uptrend, when no identifiable Candlestick reversal has become evident *and* if the stochastics are not in an area that would signify a reversal, the Candlestick analyst can have confidence that this is a temporary pullback, not a reversal.

The Fibonacci Ratio 1.618

In applying his analysis to the markets, Elliot rarely gave definitive rules. However, rules have been established through the years to make the concept easier to trade. When a three-wave pattern has been established, the top of wave 5 can be calculated. The peak of wave 5 should be .618 times higher than the total move from the beginning of wave 1 to the top of wave 3. What defines the peak of wave 3? First, wave 3 has to be longer than wave 1. Secondly, in an uptrend, wave 4 should not breach the bottom of wave 2. (See Figure 11.5.)

The main problem though, is that there are few regular five-wave swings. Elliot, In order to fine-tune his concept, Elliot tried to illustrate all the possible wave patterns. These included: zigzag, flats and triangles, double and triple sideways, and waves with extensions. (See Figures 11.6, 11.7, and 11.8.)

Wave patterns could be completely changed when prices move past certain expected resistance points. Being a proficient Elliot Wave advocate requires a great amount of subjective interpretation. Candlesticks, overlaid on the Elliot Wave analysis, provide a more powerful analytical tool.

The Basics of Elliott Wave

According to Ralph Elliot, "All human activities have three distinctive features, pattern, ratio, and time, all of which observe the Fibonacci summation

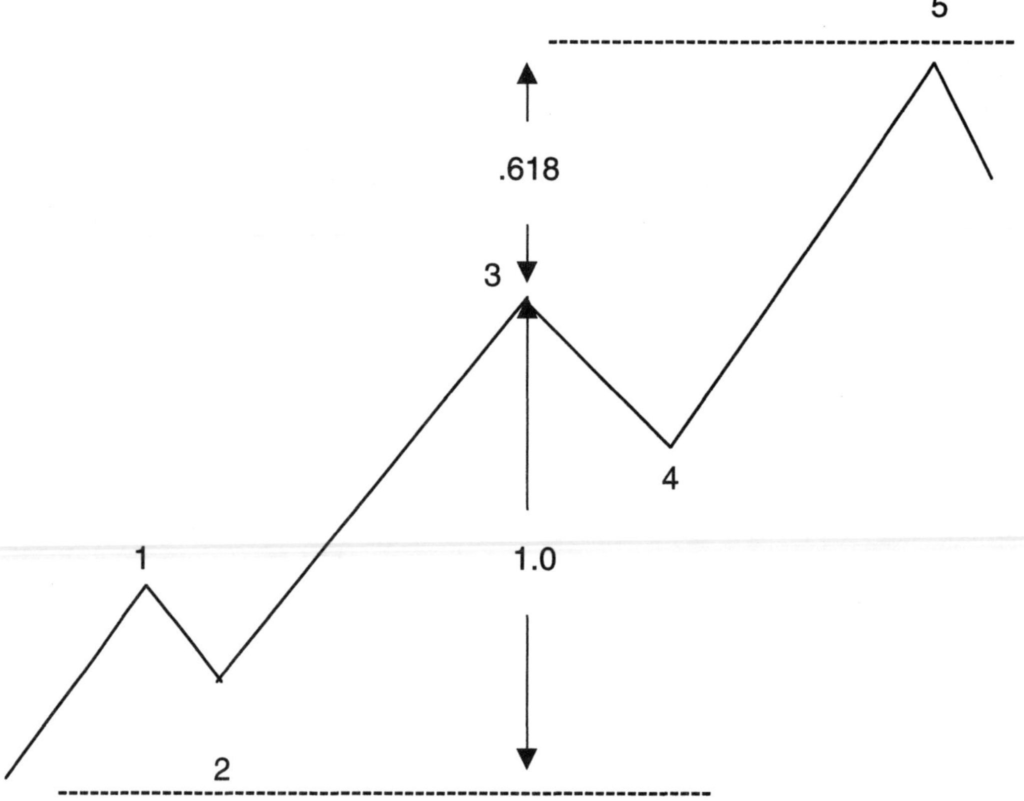

Figure 11.5 The Fibonnacci ratios in use.

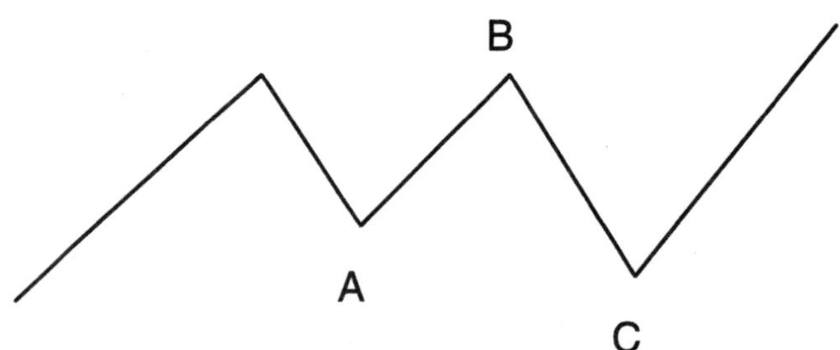

Figure 11.6 Minor correction of three waves.

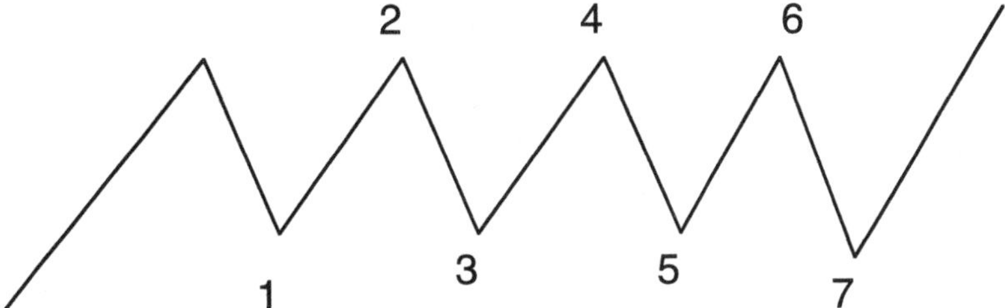

Figure 11.7 A double sideways correction with seven waves.

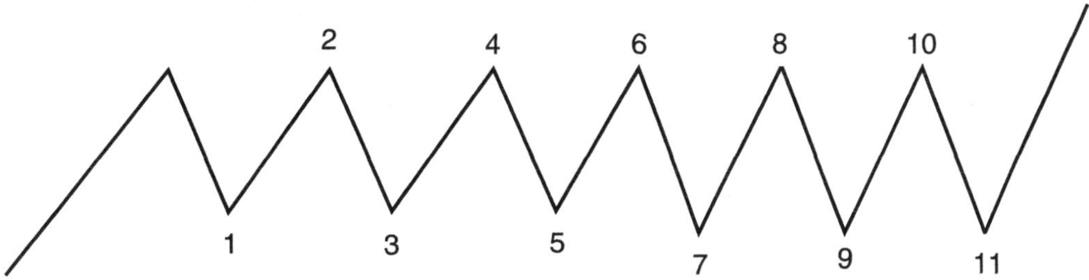

Figure 11.8 A triple sideways correction with seven waves.

series." He contended that a wave pattern is always in progress. He was quite specific when he introduced his wave concept, describing the market cycles as bull market and bear market.

A bull market is divided into five *major waves*. Major waves 1, 3, and 5 of a bull market can be subdivided into five *intermediate waves* each. The intermediate waves 1, 3, and 5 can be further subdivided into five *minor waves*. A correction consists of three waves: A, B, and C. As you might notice, this starts to create a possibility of some subjective interpretation. What wave of what wave is being portrayed? Are we in the A wave of a correction or the third or fourth wave of an uptrend? The major problem over and above this interpretive problem is that the five-wave swing has little regularity. The perfect five-wave general market formation is the exception, not the rule. To account for this dilemma, Elliot produced a series of market patterns intended to take care of almost every situation.

The Five-Wave Swing

In a regular market rhythm pattern, wave 2 cannot pull back below the beginning of wave 1, and wave 4 cannot pull back below the top of wave 1. If it does, the wave count has to be refigured. (See Figures 11.9 and 11.10.)

Corrections

Corrective waves 2 and 4 can each be subdivided into three waves of smaller degrees. Waves 2 and 4 alternate in their patterns. If wave 2 is a simple pattern, wave 4 will be a complex pattern. Conversely, if wave 2 is complex,

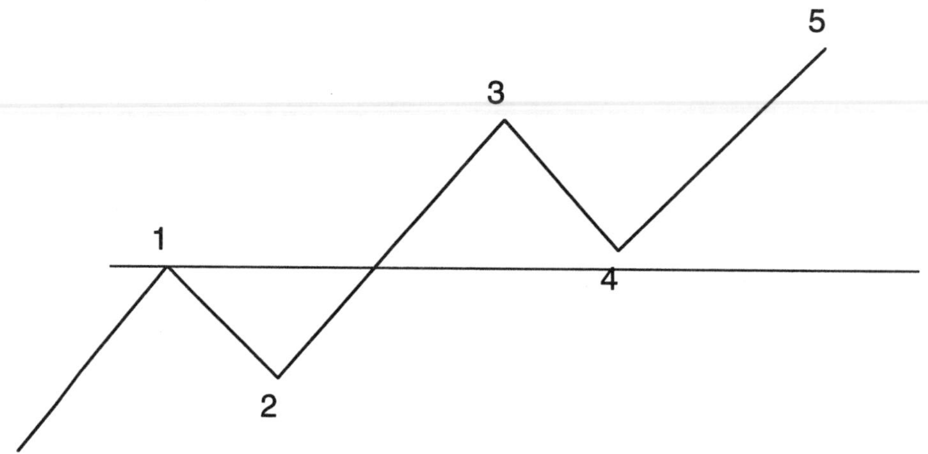

Figure 11.9 The correct wave count.

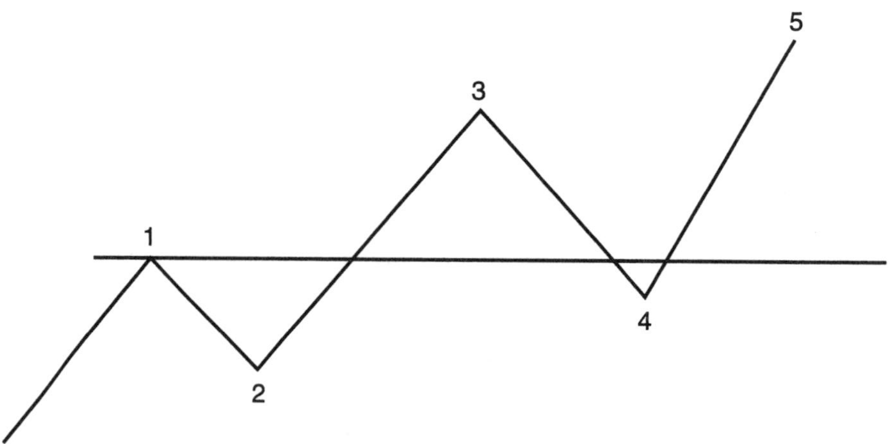

Figure 11.10 An erroneous wave count.

wave 4 will be simple. Elliot, through these observations, connected Nature's Law with human behavior. The pinecone and the pineapple have spirals that alternate by first turning clockwise, then counter-clockwise. The same pattern alternation repeats itself in the corrective aspects of wave 2 and 4.

Even Elliott described some of the patterns as difficult to use for forecasting future price moves: "The student cannot be certain that a triangle is forming until the fifth wave has started," he commented, regarding the uncertainty involved in triangle interpretation. He noticed that the standard types of corrections did not cover all the possibilities of market actions. This caused the addition of illustrations for more complex corrections.

Once again, this left the determination of a breakout, of a market move, in a rather nebulous area. Elliot did state that "It is possible however to know when elongated wave C will occur by understanding the rule of alternation." Yet, it is not clear from his deductions that wave C can be forecasted with any degree of accuracy. Is a minor-, double-, or triple-wave pattern being formed, and which way will the trend move at the end of the wave action?

As mentioned earlier, the multitude of wave count variations takes years of study in order for the analyst to gain a feel for prospective setups of market moves. As illustrated in a few pages, the simple five-wave pattern can have hundreds of variable possibilities. Subjective interpretation is necessary at every turn in direction.

How are these pages of illustrations beneficial to the novice? Most important is being aware of what the Elliot Wave advocates are watching for. If you know at what price points a large contingent of investors are anticipating a possible change of direction, then you can be prepared to anticipate and move in the direction of the masses. If everybody is buying at the same points, it then becomes a self-fulfilling prophecy. Despite all of Elliot's nebulous wave count considerations, he did provide a few rules that should be remembered. His basic principles about wave movements are reasonably reliable:

- An impulse or corrective market cycle has at least three waves.
- Wave 3 is normally the longest.

Elliot Wave interpretation has the disadvantage of the loose parameters that were initially established by Elliot. Instead of having a concise set of rules for identifying wave counts, it appears that new rules were added when the simple patterns did not perform in the manner that was expected. This kept expanding the number of possibilities of how a wave pattern could move, thus expanding the amount of subjectivity required in the analysis. Fortunately, in this age of sophisticated computer software, there are many excellent software services that provide the Elliot Wave interpretation. Using the reversal points as targets for watching when potential Candlestick signals may appear adds another viable reversal point criterion.

The optimal use of Candlesticks, overlaid onto the Elliot Wave evaluations, provides the direction of the most recent trend. This allows the Elliot

Wave analyst to get a better look at the potential wave setups. An excellent example can be illustrated in the much-used Fibonacci retracement levels. The retracements have three possible levels: the 38-, 50-, and 62-percent areas that are high probability reversal points. However, at which one will a price move reverse? This question is easily answered when applying the Candlestick method.

Having the knowledge of how and when a Candlestick signal will occur, allows the Elliot Wave follower to pinpoint which level will act as the reversal point. If stochastics are moving toward the oversold area when prices approach the 38-percent level, you should be alert for a Candlestick reversal at the level to be prudent. Conversely, if the stochastics appear to have more downside push and there are not any signs of potential reversal signals developing, it can be assumed that the 50- and 62-percent levels will be tested.

Note in Figure 11.11, representing Elantec Semiconductor Inc., how the upmove stopped exactly at the 38-percent level. The Candlestick investor would have been alerted to take advantage of the move to almost the maximum profit point. The stochastics demonstrated that this stock was well into the overbought area. After an uptrend over the past four weeks, the price gaps up. This should have been a vital warning indicating that the end of the

Figure 11.11 A candlestick sell signal is occurring at the first level of retracement, indicating this is the area to take profits.

uptrend was near. Having that knowledge and being able to see where the 38 percent level would be a point that other Elliot wave followers may be taking profits provides a good scenario that the price does have enough strength left to try and test the 50- and 62-percent levels.

The Carbo Ceramics Inc. chart in Figure 11.12 shows how the price was going to go up to the 62-percent retracement level without stopping at either the 38- or the 50-percent level. Let's analyze the stochastics. At the 38-percent level, the stochastics were not showing any signs of turning down despite being in the overbought area. On top of that, the price closed above the 38-percent level. This provided the insight that the 38-percent level was not a retrenchment level, and that the 50-percent level should be the next level to watch. Another factor that would have kept the position on is that the window occurred at the same level about a month previous. Assuming that most windows are closed and it was partially filled when closing above the 38-percent level, it should be reasonably assumed that the gap was going to be completely closed the next day.

Figure 11.12 No candlestick signs of weakness until the 62 percent retracement level.

The next trading day took the price almost up to the 50-percent level. Again, neither the stochastics nor any Candlestick formation gave any indication that the sellers were stepping in. However, this was definitely the area to be alert as to the action of the stock price. The next day opened at or slightly above the 50 percent level. At this point, one should have been ready to be nimble. As the price moved up away from the 50-percent level, you could reasonably assume that the 62-percent level would be an important resistance level. Of course, two things could have occurred at that level. It either stopped there or had other things in mind by breaking through that level and continuing higher. In this case, seeing that the high of the day stopped right at the 62-percent level should have been a convincing sign. If that was not enough to confirm that the 62 percent was the final point, the fact that the next day went up to that level again and backed off, producing a Tweezer Top, should have provided the incentive to take profits.

Notice the other aspects of Candlestick observations incorporated in this chart. Note how the magnitude of the daily trading ranges expands at the end of the trend move. Also, note the double bottom. Keep in mind that a severe trend move does not reverse all of a sudden. It usually takes a couple of bobs to convince the other camp—bulls or bears—to get out of the way.

The Candlestick signals can alert the Elliot Wave follower as to when the current trend has fizzled. Note in Figure 11.13, the NASDAQ Index, how the projected points may not be obtained at point 3. A Doji occurring at the same time the stochastics are turning down gives the indication that the trend is about to turn down. Point 4 should be the next target. Using the Elliot Wave points is one method of projecting the magnitude of a move. In analyzing this chart, a window is present at the same level as point 4. This should add extra credence to the move reaching that area.

From the level that the turn appears to be occurring, a new set of points will have to be calculated. The two point 5 projections may have new values with wave 3 not getting as high as originally projected. This early alert gives the Candlestick investor the advantage. A shifting of positions by the Elliot Wave followers may provide a short-term powerful move. Having the Candlestick signal forewarning produces more opportunities to exploit that knowledge.

Summary

The combination of the two methods produces a powerful investment platform. Elliot Wave analysis works well in projecting the magnitude of a trend move. Candlestick analysis works extremely well in identifying reversals and direction. Implementing the two together greatly enhances the probabilities of executing successful longer-term positions. You get the best of both worlds. As time goes on, the incorporation of computer analysis can hone

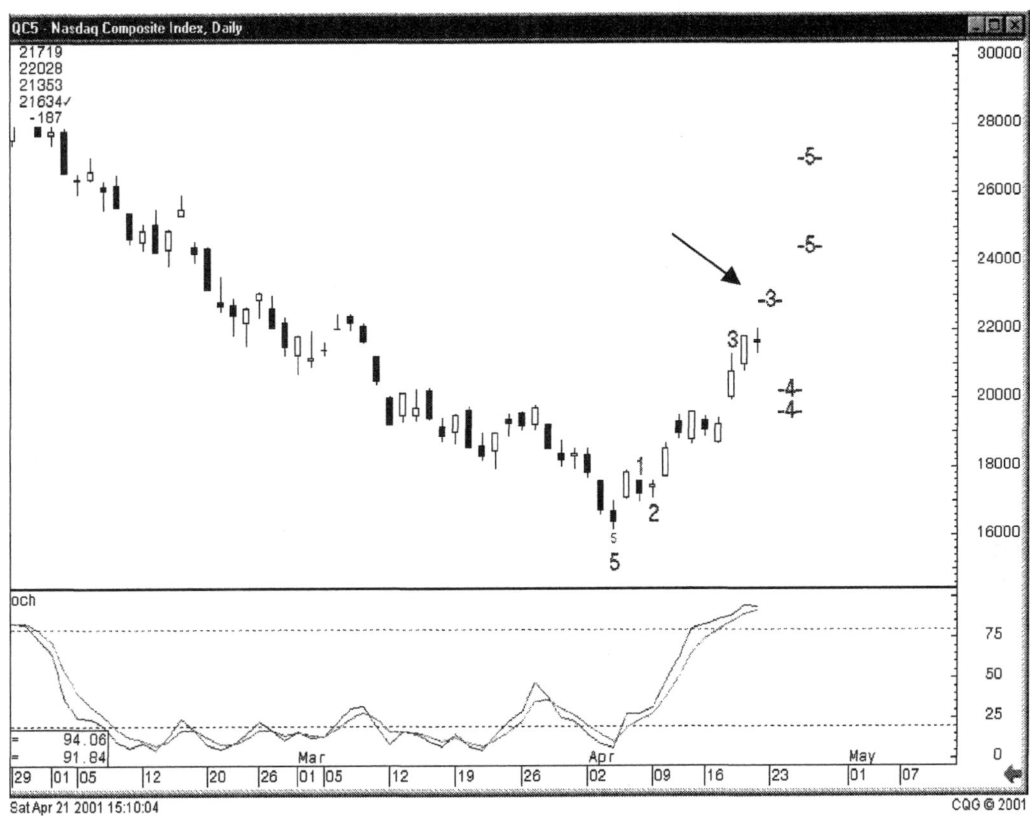

Figure 11.13 Knowing simple Candlestick trading rules provides information that maximizes profit-taking procedures.

this trading combination to an even greater degree. Improving the directional calculations provides the Elliot Wave advocate a valuable tool. Profits can be improved by knowing which levels are going to be hit and which wave count is being prepared for a change. The attributes of each method can enhance an investor's ability to vastly improve portfolio returns. Currently, additional statistical testing is being performed to further perfect the trading returns using the combination of these successful methods.

Chapter 12

OPTION TRADING REFINED

**If you want to succeed, you should strike out on new paths rather than travel the worn paths of accepted success.
John D. Rockefeller**

Options are the high-risk investment vehicles—or so it is thought by the majority of investors. Why are options considered high risk? Simple. Most investors lose money in options. Statistics show that over 80 percent of all option trades lose money. Why is this so? Because the odds are stacked against winning from the start, due largely to three factors:

- First, as with all investments, the direction of price movement has to be correctly analyzed. This procedure alone is a major hurdle for the vast majority of investors.
- Next, the magnitude of the price move has to be correctly calculated—another procedure that has not been perfected by the average investor.
- On top of all this, being correct as to the time element is added.

The combination of these three essential factors is extremely difficult to access correctly. And to add insult to injury, a premium is built into the option price. This premium reflects the speculative fervor of the market participants who think prices will move in their direction. The highly leveraged method of participating in the move creates a parasitic premium that is added to the true value of the option.

How do Candlesticks turn disadvantageous probabilities into advantageous trading profits? The signals that have been described to this point can be applied to align the elements of success, namely, signals, stochastics, market direction, and so forth. A few simple processes can be employed, that will exploit the same factors that make other investors lose money and put money in your pocket.

Direction

As you study Candlestick signals, you will discover that the improvement in accuracy will be quite noticeable. Under certain circumstances, the accuracy probability becomes extremely high. When all the essential indicators line up for a successful stock trade—for example, the signal showing strong buying, the stochastics below the 20 line, further confirmed by a bounce off a trend-line, and overall market direction, and so on—an option trade can be executed.

As in all the equations for producing a profit, direction is the first consideration. Obviously, a clear and decisive signal is the reason for considering the trade in the first place. Knowledge of the reversal signals creates a huge advantage for exploiting short-term market moves. Especially profitable is the ability to pinpoint absolute bottom signals. Not only is there the benefit of purchasing an option at the ultimate lowest price, the premium or speculative fervor is also at its lowest point. This creates a double upside reward. As the price of the stock goes up, the option price goes up and the speculative enthusiasm expands the premium. Along with direction, the potential magnitude of the move has to be determined.

Magnitude

An analysis of a stock trade incorporates the potential magnitude of the price move. To briefly review, this involves analyzing where the next resistance or support might occur. Speed and magnitude of the previous move that is reversing is one factor. Congestion levels above the reversal area is another. Trend-lines and Fibonacci retracement levels are more considerations. But most importantly, the signal itself dictates how strong the move could be. A major reversal signal, compounded with a gap up, will substantiate a much stronger advance than a secondary signal. The status of the stochastics should indicate how long the upside move can potentially be maintained. The analysis of the upside is going to dictate the ultimate trade strategy. And this has to incorporate the final element: timing.

Timing

The weakest area of analysis for most option traders is the evaluation of time constraints. This is the area where human weakness is mostly like to be involved. The direction and the magnitude not only have to be correct, it has to be correct in the proper time frame. For every day the trade is in existence, time is working against the profits. This is experienced in two ways. First, the potential of the opportunity of a big upmove lessens as the time for it to occur lessens. Secondly, as time diminishes, so does the investment fervor. Premiums also diminish as time passes away.

Time also becomes a major determinant in the type of option trade that should be established. Three weeks remaining before expiration has a different trade strategy than one week remaining. A two-month option has different strategies than a two-week option. The length of time to expiration dictates how to position the trade.

Emotion is the major culprit causing trades to lose money in 80 percent of option trades. Most call option buyers purchase the call due to some reason they think will make the stock go up big. For example, let's say the time frame is two weeks before expiration date. After the commitment of funds to the trade, the price does move up. Unfortunately, it does not move in the magnitude or speed to offset the diminishing premium built into the option price. Being correct in the direction of the move feeds the ego. The trade was correct. But if the magnitude of the price move was not great enough to offset the cost of the option premium, an emotional dilemma is created. Should the trade be liquidated or will the price move further, significantly more than its norm, between now and the remaining time to expiration? Gone is the original trade expectations and in comes hope for a positive resolution to the trade.

Establishing Profitable Trades

Even after evaluating direction, magnitude, and time, options still contain aspects that work against producing profitable trades,the bid/ask spread. Even with ultra-low commission fees, the cost of entering and exiting a trade can be substantial. This amplifies the necessity of executed trades that have high probabilities of being correct. The percentage loss, on failed trades, exacts a greater price than seen in other trading entities. As illustrated in the following example, failed trades take a toll on an account rapidly.

For example, a stock trading at $65 bid and $65.30 ask has three weeks to go before expiration date. Currently, the $65 strike price is trading at

- $4.10 Bid
- $4.30 Ask

The purchase is put on at $4.30. The speculation is that the stock price can go up at least 10 percent to approximately $71 in the next three days. This should take the price of the options up to $8.50 or so; however, nothing happens to create that move. The stock pulls back slightly to $64.75. Essentially the trade did not work. It is time to get out. Now the price of the option is

- $3.65 Bid
- $3.95 Ask

Exiting on the bid side, this fizzled trade cost $.65 on a slightly depressed price action. The price of the option reflects the loss of stock value as well as the loss of time premium. This creates a loss of over 15 percent. It does not take a lot of bland stock price moves to deteriorate a substantial portion of an option trading account. This should emphasize the benefits of placing as many controllable probabilities in your favor before a trade is established.

Using the steps for putting on a successful stock trade becomes all that much more critical when putting on an option trade. Each step needs to be scrutinized. Especially the final step, watching how a stock price will open. If you followed the other steps—analyzing market direction, evaluating the sector chart, identifying a strong Candlestick reversal signal, and seeing the stochastics in the proper area—then the final evaluation becomes an important element of the whole process: How is the stock price opening? The reason this step is vitally important is due to the time constraint on the trade.

A strong reversal signal followed by a Candlestick formation that would indicate a day or two of consolidation is crucial if there are only twelve more trading days to expiration. Three days of consolidating will dramatically diminish the time value of the option price. The open of the trade day should demonstrate strong buying presence: a slight gap up or at least opening in the same price range as the close of the previous night. The further away the option expiration date, the less critical it becomes. But common sense would ask, "Why put on the trade if a weak signal appears the next day?" Wait a couple of trading days to see when the consolidation is over and the new buying comes into the stock price. If it still appears to be a good trade, you should be able to pick up the opens at a lower price, the time premium having reduced.

As illustrated in Figure 12.1, the opening price demonstrates that the buying is still present after the bullish Engulfing Pattern signal. This is an indication that price is not weakening due to the lack of buyers.

An option trade has better probabilities of succeeding, in the time frame available, when the signal shows continuous buying after the signal. Figure 12.2, representing Maxim Integrated Products Inc., gave a warning that the buyers had stepped away by its weak open. A Morning Star formation followed by a lower open the next day reveals that the buyers stepped away. This led to the consolidation for the next few days and then the buying resumed. But for an option trade, witnessing the lower open the next day creates an extensive risk element. Even though the Morning Star formation created a high probability that the trend would be up, the weakness of the next open clearly demonstrated that the signal was going to be effective after some waffling. Valuable time and option premium would have been used up.

The image of option trades is usually the high risk, homerun-hitting returns from a highly leveraged investing. Just the mention of options scares most investors. However, options do have their advantages in certain situations. The most dramatic illustration would be buying 1,000 shares of a $37 stock. It is targeted to hit 45 over the next 6 trading days. The call option,

Figure 12.1 The open price will produce the impetus to put the option trade on.

Figure 12.2 A weak open following a strong potential buy signal reveals that the buying is not still present, a time-oriented option trade should be held back.

strike price $35, is trading at $5.50. Its expiration date is 21 days away. Buying the stock put $37,000 exposed to the market to make $8,000, a 22-percent return in just over a week. Not bad. Buying 10 options costs $5,500 exposed to market risk. If the stock price hits $45 in the projected time period, the option price goes to $11.50 in six days. A 110-percent profit in six days, quite a bit better. Depending upon the analysis of market conditions, the option trade may be the safer of the two trades. If the market in general is in the condition of crashing prices on bad news, owning the stock may carry the bigger risk. An unexpected earnings warning, in certain market atmospheres, can crater a stock price. The stock could gap down the next morning to $25. This would have resulted in a $12,000 loss by owning the stock. The option would have lost what was put into them, the $5,500. In this instance, options were clearly the better play considering the market conditions.

Candlestick signals reduce the probabilities of being caught in a surprise situation. Unfortunately, it can still happen, but not nearly as often. When the Candlestick signals indicate buying pressures appearing in a stock price. The smart money is not often fooled.

Strategic Option Spreads

Using the known statistics to your advantage can produce large profit capabilities. It is known that 80 percent of the option trades loss money. Since that is the case, exploit that knowledge. The Candlestick signals provide clear directional information—the key element for establishing a trade opportunity. The magnitude becomes an evaluation process and the time factor is a known entity. If direction and time are established portions of the total equation, then magnitude becomes the unknown factor. How can the unknown factor be fully exploited? The target price of a move can be estimated by resistance levels from trend-lines, congestion areas, and Fibonacci numbers. These are projected target prices based upon having a high degree of probability that prices are heading in that direction.

Another known fact is that premiums are built into the price of options. The speculative exuberance is captured by the convenience of a leveraged investment vehicle being available. The greed factor—being able to take a little money to make inordinate profits—keeps options priced above their intrinsic true value. Knowing that investors are paying too much for a trade that loses 80 percent of the time adds a valuable dimension. Now there is a method to exploit the unknown factor.

Use the same example as above. A stock is trading at $37 a share. The $35 call option strike-price is $5.50. The difference in this example is the expiration date is eight trading days away. This changes the picture entirely. Before, when the price moved to $45 over a six-day period, there was still enough time until expiration for some of the premium to remain in the price of the option. Now when the price gets to $45, expiration will be within two days and no premium will remain in the option price. How can this trade be best positioned? What is the best risk/return formula?

Analyze the possibilities. The target is $45. The options are priced as follows:

- $5.50 $35 strike price
- $2.50 $40 strike price
- $ .95 $45 strike price

If the confidence level is high for hitting the target of $45, the following scenarios are what the average option speculator would evaluate. Buying the $35 call at $5.50 requires the stock price to go to $40.50 just to break even. Hitting the $45 price makes $4.50, or an 82-percent return.

Buying the $40 strike price at $2.50 requires the stock to hit $42.50 just to break even. Hitting $45 doubles the money invested. Buying the $45 for $.95 makes no sense if it is not targeted to go above that price. It will expire worthless and $.95 of exuberance will be gone.

This is the time to apply a spread trade. The more aggressive investor would shoot for the bullish spread. Buy the $40 calls at $2.50 and sell the $45 calls at $.95. The cost of this trade is $2.50 minus the $.95, a net outlay of $1.55.

$$\$2.50 - \$.95 = \$1.55 \text{ net outlay}$$

This improves the equation immensely. Now the break-even is $41.55, above the level of break-even of buying the $35 calls and below the break-even of buying the $40 calls. However, the upside percentages change dramatically. If the price of the stock is $45 or higher on expiration date, the net return will be $5.00. If the stock price goes to $47, the net difference between the two call option prices will remain at $5.00:

- Expiration Date − Stock price = $45 or greater
- $45 calls = 0
- $40 calls = $5.00

A $1.55 of investment exposure returns $5.00, a 322-percent gain. Different factors can be weighted in this example as far as downside exposure, including how much could have been lost if the price did not go to $45. The primary point is the use of selling call options to the optimists that are looking for the big leverage move.

The normal question is, "What if the price skyrocketed to $55? You have limited your gains to $5.00. What about all those potential profits that you gave up?" This is the logic that creates the large premiums in options: the hope of that big move that will produce the bonanza trade. Yet, keep in mind that more than 80 percent of option investors lose money. A spread incorporates the knowledge of a price moving in a direction during a set time frame. It also calculates the probable magnitude of that move. Buying one set of calls and selling the higher set of calls exploits the existence of the exaggerated premiums.

You can capture additional profits by taking advantage of the same exuberance that exists on the put side—in this case, depending upon the equity of an account, knowing that the direction of a stock is heading up, and selling the puts (writing puts) can add income to the account. Selling a call or a put requires special margin adjustments. Being able to use the Candlestick signals provides a strong platform for writing options.

Writing Options

It makes good sense for the aggressive investor to use all the profit potential available when finding a strong trade situation. All the reasons for buying a stock position can be transferred to evaluating the options—both calls and puts. A strong Candlestick buy signal that induced the purchase of a stock position might as well be further used for increasing profits on that trade. An analysis of all the factors, the strength of the buy signal, status of the stochastics, and the time remaining until the next expiration period creates the opportunity to put extra profits into the account without any more research analysis. Simple logic implies that if the stock has a high probability of moving upward, the put prices have a good probability of declining. Just as buying a call has a premium that can diminish rapidly as both time and stock price could work against it, the same is true for benefiting from the same factors.

The ability to convert ideas to things is the secret of outward success. Henry Ward Beecher

Every day that the price goes up, the price of a put diminishes, both from the stock price going against it and the time premium losing the enthusiasm of the bears. The same is true for writing calls against long positions. A long-term position does not go straight up. If an investor's program is to buy and hold, writing calls against the position can greatly enhance returns. As seen in Figure 12.3, representing eBay Inc., the chart illustrates that the stock price had advanced in late January 2001 to the point that a sell signal is occurring when the stochastics show an overbought condition. It is demonstrating a sell pattern, a bearish Engulfing Pattern formation. If the general market conditions collaborate by appearing toppy also, this would be a good time to sell calls against the position. If the probabilities indicate a pullback in the stock price, why not take advantage of that move?

Figure 12.3 Writing calls against a long position or buying puts after a major sell signal has high probabilities of producing profits.

As illustrated in the eBay chart, the sell signal is confirmed by the overbought condition of the stochastics. Additionally, the highs of the past few days have been right at $55. The lack of strength of getting through that level provides a price to consider selling options against the position. The $55 calls can be considered as the optimal strike price. The recent run up to this level should have the premiums at the most exuberant prices. The remaining time before the expiration will be a factor as to which strike price is the most likely to produce added income without getting the stock called away.

Options have many valuable attributes for enhancing returns. The aggressive trader can leverage the results of finding excellent high probability trades. Option trades can be structured to take advantage of the direction of price and time expanse to expiration. Using the option premium to exploit profits can be formulated by implementing spread strategies. Huge profits are not always made on hitting the big option trade, but the potential of megaprofits is what keeps the option premiums consistently overpriced. Trading against the optimism (greed) of the average option speculator creates the opportunity to extract consistent revenue from them. The consistency of those profits creates a compounding effect. Compounding profits will produce much greater returns, with dramatically less downside risk than hitting the big option trade once in a blue moon.

Conclusion

Trading options using Candlestick signals produces an extremely profitable element. Just the aspect of having a high probability of a price moving in a particular direction creates opportunities to manufacture huge profits. Calculations of the three major elements is incrementally expanded by having a handle on that key element. Time and magnitude can then be structured to exploit the correct directional moves. Stripping away one of the major elements variability improves the potential to achieve profitable returns on an expediential basis. More in-depth successful option trading criteria is available at the **www.Candlestickforum.com** Web site. Whether buying or writing, the Candlestick signals will modify the methods you use to make profitable option trades.

Chapter 13

CANDLESTICKS WITH COMMODITIES AND FUTURES

If skills could be acquired by watching, every dog would be a butcher. Turkish Proverb

Commodities and futures: the optimal use of leverage. Incorporating Candlestick signals into commodities and futures trading is of vital importance. Knowing when and where the shift occurs in bullish and bearish sentiment for leveraged investment vehicles is essential for successful trading. To foresee the potential change in price direction produces outstanding trading profits. This is not pie-in-the-sky rhetoric. The Candlestick methodology was developed for the purpose of exploiting profits from commodities trading. Four hundred years of proven results came about through trading rice. Putting the signals to use in fast-reacting markets is not new for Candlestick analysis. It is probably safe to say that Candlestick analysis is the oldest technical trading method in the history of investment markets. Its use has delivered unrivaled results for the Japanese rice trading houses for centuries. It is the ideal method for increasing profits on its own merits or for being overlaid onto existing successful trading programs. The combination of Candlestick reversal signals is the perfect complement to existing proven trading programs. Overlaying the two methods can be a useful filtering process for reducing and/or eliminating bad trades.

On its own, Candlestick trading delivers impressive results. Keep in mind, investor sentiment is built into the signals. The appearance of a signal is the result of change of sentiment. This furnishes instant data required by a trader to make decisions. Whereas other technical programs provide indicators that a change of direction might be occurring, the signals tell you that the turn *is* occurring, giving the trader the advantage of a head start.

The information conveyed by the creation of the signal informs the Candlestick analyst that the trend sentiment has been altered. That realization also acts as excellent stop-loss calculations. Note that in Figure 13.1, representing August Feeder Cattle, the Doji was the signal that illustrated

Figure 13.1 Candlestick signals in commodity trading make for clear, high-profit trades.

that the uptrend had come to a top. Stochastics confirmed the peak. The lower open the following day gave clear indication that the bears were taking control. Where should the stop-loss be placed?

Going back to basic logic, it can be easily surmised that if the Doji represents indecision at the top and a lower open the next day demonstrates that the selling has started, that would be the optimal point to short Feeder Cattle. All indications lead to prices going lower. Using the same line of logic, if the Doji were the sell signal, confirmed by the lower open the next day, prices had hit their high point in this rally. That rationale can be built into a logical stop-loss level. The high trading level on the day of the Doji was 92.05. A stop-loss can be set one level above the 92.05 at 92.10. If the Doji were the topping signal, it would be logical to say that if prices went above the top of the topping signal, then the top was not indicated by the Doji. Get out of the trade.

Most commodities and futures positioning, like equity investing, is based upon fundamental reasons. The word *positioning* is the functional word of this statement. Day-trading and short-term trading lean more toward technical analysis. Fundamental analysis for individual commodities and futures is subject to fewer outside factors that influence the movement of price. Agricultural products are greatly influenced by the weather. The projection of crop reports or feedlot numbers, price movements of related commodities, and acres planted are all factors for evaluating fundamental elements. Fortunately, with a small number of factors to evaluate, research is accomplished with fewer variables to affect a trend. This enhances the value of a trading method that accurately identifies a trend. You have to contend with less waffling or fluctuation. As seen in the Soybean chart in Figure 13.2, the trend persists for weeks on end, thus providing a long-term holding period that generates tremendous profits. Profits can be further enhanced with position management, increasing or decreasing the total position as the short-term Candlestick signals dictate.

Commodity traders or futures traders who are oriented toward fundamental research for the basis of their trades can find valuable attributes in Candlestick analysis. Fundamental research diagnoses what the correct direction should be by evaluating how all the known information should affect the price movement. Putting a trade on should be the conviction of that analysis. However, not all researchers have all the pertinent information available to them. Having Candlestick charts that show direction or signals that contradicts the researchers' analysis can act as a monitoring system. The Candlestick charts, showing a sell signal when all fundamental information warrants a buy, reveals that something may be wrong. If selling is coming into the price, there may be fundamental factors that haven't been

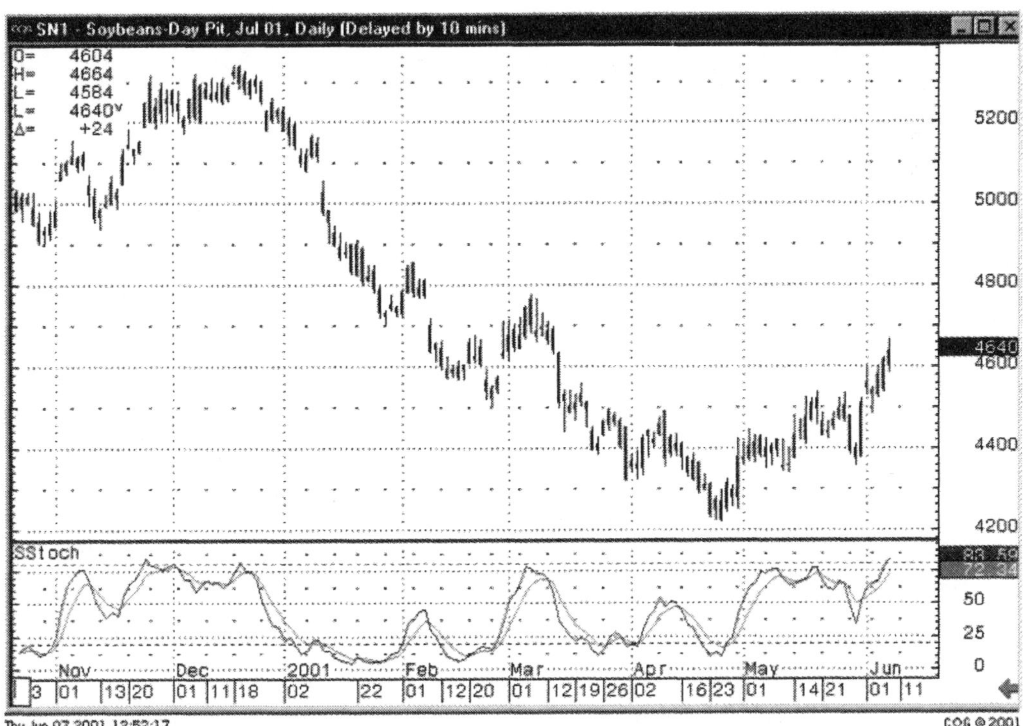

Figure 13.2 Soybeans trend in one direction for months at a time.

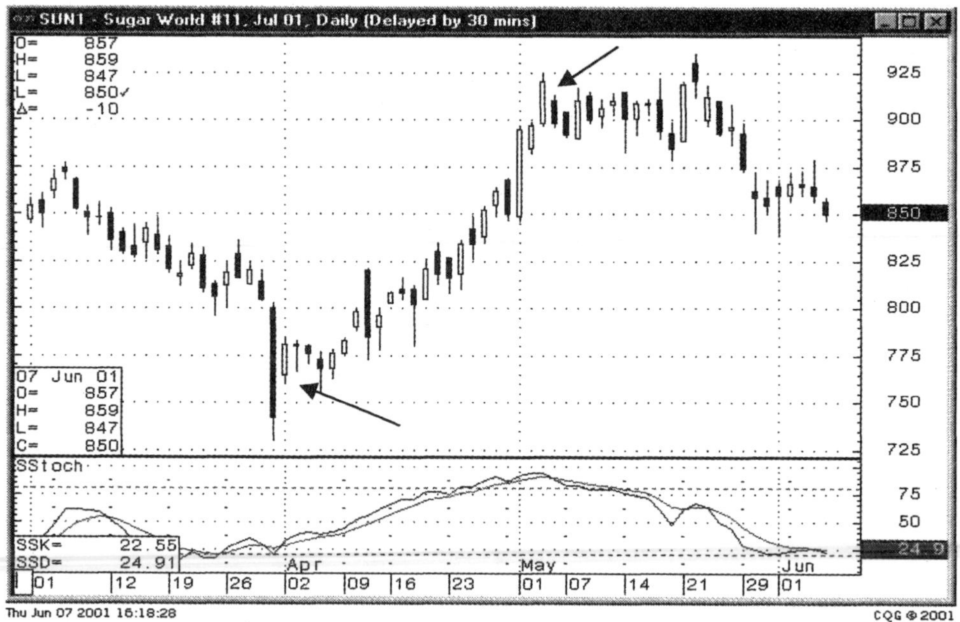

Figure 13.3 World sugar.

researched yet or existing information was not evaluated correctly. This information inconsistency should prohibit a major positioning mistake. The other possibility is that the fundamental research prognosis is correct, but it may not be factored into the price by the rest of the market participants as of now. The timing may be too early.

Whether trading grains, meats, currencies, or metals, the signals will be apparent in whatever trading entities have fear and greed involved. Note that in Figure 13.3, representing World Sugar, Haramis start the trend and end the trend. You need to adhere to trading rules more stringently when dealing in the commodities and futures market. A wrong move against a highly leveraged position can devastate equity quickly. Applying the basic rules and common sense analysis of the Candlestick signals puts the favorable probabilities on your side of the ledger.

Being able to view any chart has invaluable benefits for a full analytical investment program. Where is the NASDAQ going tomorrow? Where is the Dow going tomorrow? Knowing how surrounding factors and markets have an effect on particular trading entities helps you perform fast and interpretive analyses to draw conclusions on the entity that you are trading. As seen in the 30-year bond chart in Figure 13.4, a bearish Engulfing Pattern has just occurred. Stochastics indicate that they are turning down.

At quick glance, bonds should be selling off. If that information is added to the analysis of what affects what you are trading, it benefits you in having another piece of information that helps confirm the signal you are about to trade or thinking about continuing the hold of an existing trade. For exam-

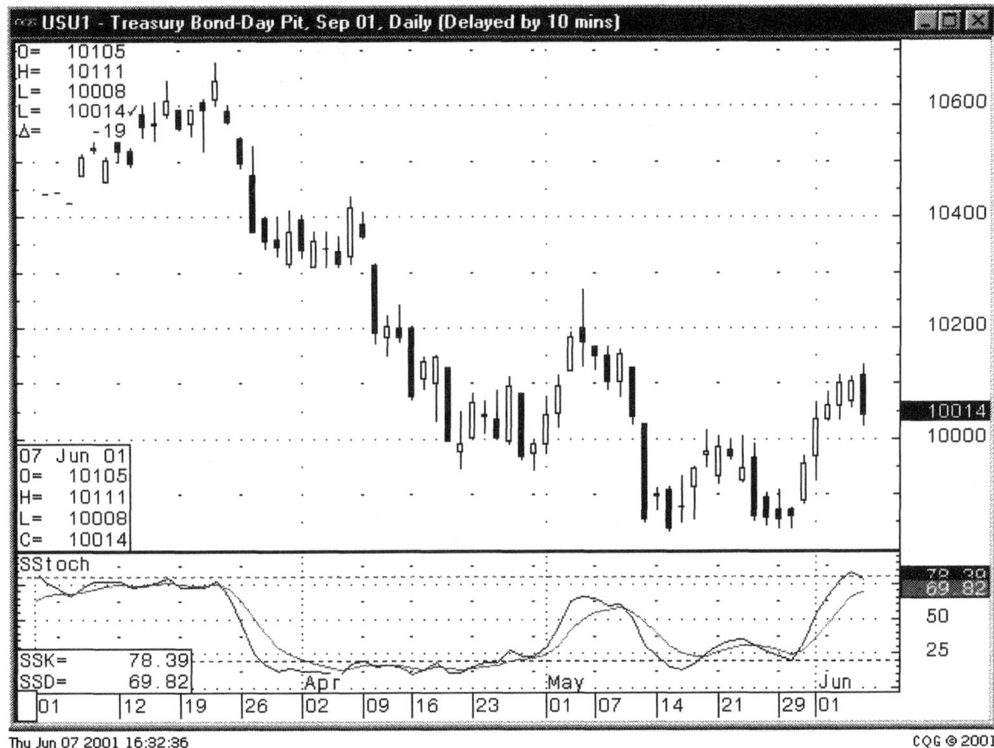

Figure 13.4 A U.S. 30-year bond is a good trading entity using candlestick signals. Knowing which direction the bond market will move adds insight on how the stock indexes will move.

ple, if it has been verified by past occurrences that the bond market going down, that is a good indication that money is flowing out of bonds and into equities, and it adds validity to a bullish trend on the NASDAQ or Dow chart if the bond market can be seen as turning down. Having the ability to see Candlestick formations provides another tool to quickly analyze an associated trading entity. Each factor that you line up to verify a trade is that much more information to put the probabilities in your favor.

Use the Candlestick signals for commodities and futures trading. Do not disregard the elementary rules for protecting capital. Using the Candlestick signals as a framework puts the odds of profitable trades greatly in your favor. Don't let the lack of verbage in this chapter act as an indicative barometer as to the importance of candles to trading commodities and futures. On the contrary, the signals act as a much purer indicator for entities that have fewer market considerations. An important adjunct for fundamental investors is the accuracy and ease with which the Candlestick formations illustrate when fundamental perceptions are not being embodied in the price. When all fundamental evaluation leads to crude prices going up, but the Candlestick signals show prices going down, you need to make a quick and thorough review.

Apparently there is a fundamental influence being projected into the price that you or your research has not taken into account.

Fortunes can be made in the futures market. Candlesticks are the closest technical tools to perfect short-term trading programs. Keep in mind, it was commodity trading that developed this method. Its credibility has already been proven. Using it properly is the bridge to success.

Chapter 14

THE ULTIMATE INVESTMENT PROGRAM

> **Life is like a play; it is not the length, but the excellence of the acting that matters. Seneca**

What is the definition of the ultimate investment program? The program that all investors are pursuing. The answers to this question most likely would include making massive amounts of wealth, with no risk, and without the use of large amounts of capital. Aren't we all looking for that program? The pursuit of large financial gains is the goal of the aggressive investor.

New inventions or concepts do not originate from the ground up. They are usually the combination of two or more existing inventions or concepts. The automobile was not an invention of unique ideas. It was the combination of existing transportation, the buggy, with a small gas-powered engine. The gas-powered engine was the combination of pistons powered by a gasoline mix being properly used. A carburetor created a gas mist that could be used to explode, forcing the pistons to move. Pistons moved in the proper order by attaching them to a camshaft. The carburetor was developed by using the same concept, a misty spray, as used in French perfume bottles. The automobile was not a unique development in itself. It was the putting together of many existing technologies to create a new product, a product that revolutionized humankind's transportation.

In much the same manner, putting together the ancient concept of Candlestick analysis with relatively new investment products creates the opportunity to greatly expand the wealth of investors. This can be done with a program that eliminates all risk minimal amounts of capital, relative to the returns that it can produce. Candlestick trading and the other program have absolutely nothing in common, yet when they are combined, they produce a wealth-building program that was inconceivable just a few years ago.

In recent years, with the advent of computers radically improving the sophistication of hedging calculations, an interesting loan program has been developed. This program was the offshoot of providing risk reduction for large institutional investment positions. To minimize a large long position's exposure to market corrections, hedging becomes an important aspect to risk management. Apparently, not many years ago, somebody came up with a brainstorm by modifying the hedging process to create a loan product for investors currently in stock positions that cannot be easily sold, such as taxes, restricted stock, and option positions.

The marketing target for this loan product is simple. There are many investors who have stock they can't sell. Either the cost basis is so low that the taxes would eat up a major portion of the holdings value, or the stock is restricted and cannot be sold for a specific time period. After a person works for a company for many years, the value of that person's company stock may be an inordinate percentage of that individual's financial assets. Diversification would be the prudent course for the individual's financial security, yet the sale of the stock is unadvisable. If the stock is sold, taxes immediately reduce the whole estate by over 25 percent. This puts that person in a quandary. If the stock price appears to be declining, and may do so for a large percentage reduction in price, is it better to sit through the pullback or sell and get hit with a horrendous tax bill? Many people are in the situation where the tax bill keeps too many of the eggs in one basket.

The new lending program eliminates that problem. The terms of the new loan product are usually structured as follows:

- The loan can be structured for 3, 5, 7, 10, or 15 years.
- The loan amount is 90 percent of the value of the stock.
- Interest annually will be 10.5 to 12.5 percent, depending upon the size of the company.
- Interest accrues until the end of the loan period. Dividends collected are credited against the interest expense.
- The loan is a nonrecourse loan.

This loan format acts as an excellent asset protection program. For example, Mr. Rich bought $30,000 of Dell Corporation stock in 1990. In 2001 that stock position is worth $3,000,000—a wonderful move and a great profit. Unfortunately, Mr. Rich's total net worth is $3,800,000. The Dell position represents about 80 percent of his estate. He is at the age that selling the Dell position is going to greatly affect his retirement funds. The taxes would reduce his total net worth by close to $1,000,000. However, he now has an alternative.

Mr. Rich can borrow 90 percent against the $3,000,000 position for a five-year term. The term of the loan can be structured to fit projected future life changes. If working now, in five years Mr. Rich may be retired, having a whole new tax bracket. Or a strategic gifting program may be devised to bequeath portions of the stock positions to relatives, greatly reducing the tax consequences. At worst, the question of taxes can be addressed and planned for over the next five years.

For now, the loan makes $2,700,000 available without any tax ramifications. These funds can be invested in other investment vehicles more suited for Mr. Rich in this stage of his life. He can diversify his portfolio or purchase real estate, whatever disperses his risk exposure over a broader array of opportunities. The eggs are not all in one basket anymore.

What are the costs and the risks associated to this loan situation? The most important element to the loan is that it is a nonrecourse loan. What does this mean? If the value of the Dell position falls from $3,000,000 back to $1,000, 000 over the next five years, Mr. Rich has a nonrecourse loan. This means all he has to do is say to the lender, "You keep the stock and I'll keep the loan proceeds you gave me five years ago." He keeps the $2,700,000 original loan proceeds, giving the stock (the collateral) to the lender. This decision, because of the non-recourse aspect of the loan, has no ill effect on Mr. Rich or his credit. Essentially, this loan acts as a 90 percent downside protection for the investor. This will trigger a taxable event but that is five years down the road and a lot of tax planning will have taken place.

At the other end of the spectrum of possibilities is that Dell's stock price has made the value of the stock position worth $6,000,000 at the end of five years. Mr. Rich has a couple of options at this point. First, he could pay off the loan plus the interest. Interest accruing at 10.5 percent compounded over a five-year period would make the loan payoff amount $4,450,000. This figure may initially seem excessive; however, remember the benefits derived from the loan. Hopefully it was reinvested where it was producing returns that provided monthly or annual cash flow. The time value of money enhances the benefit of receiving income at the present while paying the expense sometime out in the future. This provided Mr. Rich with money that could be spent on a current basis while not having to pay interest until the end of the loan period. On top of that, the interest expense was not a consideration unless the stock price was positive during that time frame. If the stock went down during the same period, giving up the stock to the lender negated the loan amount and interest.

The second alternative would be to renew the stock loan. Borrowing 90 percent against the new stock value would release an additional $950,000, the net difference of the original loan and accrued interest.

Original loan amount	$2,700,000
Accrued interest	$1,750,000
Total amount owed	**$4,450,000**
New loan proceeds	$5,400,000
Net new capital	$ 950,000

The process starts all over. Now the new downside protection level is raised to the $5,400,000 level. Initially, some investors may react to the amount of interest that is paid over the five-year period, which looks large compared to the amount of total proceeds received. What you need to remember is that the original $2,700,000 should or could have been reinvested into situations that offset part or all of the interest expense.

The important aspect of the loan program is that it did not leave the investor exposed to a dramatic change in total asset valuation due to the rise or fall of one stock position. Mr. Rich could sleep better knowing that the major portions of his assets were well diversified.

These types of loans have caused some controversy. Articles in financial magazines dispute the ethics of this type of loan. "Is it fair for top executives to create these loans on their stocks positions?" they are asking. A loan against stock is called a "collar." A top executive transacting this type of loan is not producing any sale. No sale, no reporting required by the SEC.

The controversy this produces is that while an executive has just greatly reduced his or her downside risk, maybe because he or she does not have confidence in the growth potential for the company, the trackers of insider selling do not get an indication that the insider has greatly reduced his or her exposure to the stock price. Fortunately this is a controversy that probably will not affect the existence of the lenders.

Viewing the loan transaction from the positive point of view, if an insider needs capital for other purposes, he or she does not have to sell stock. If the executive wants to buy a Rembrandt, stock does not have to be sold. Buying a Rembrandt does not throw panic into the rest of the shareholders, witnessing an insider dumping some of his or her stock. The executive wins, being able to buy the lifelong dream. The rest of the shareholders win, not having downward pressure put on the stock. No selling shows up on the radar screens of inside-trading watchers, maintaining the impression of confidence by inside executives.

Creating the Ultimate Investment Program

How does the combination of these two processes, Candlestick investing and 90 percent nonrecourse loan transactions, formulate the ultimate wealth-building program? Using elements of both programs creates a riskless transaction. Features of the loan program eliminate market exposure. Candlestick signals provide the moves necessary to consummate leverage exploitation.

Warren Buffet has become one of the richest men in the world by taking advantage of proper timing. He buys the stocks or industries that are currently out of favor. Fundamentally speaking, most industries have cyclical movements. Oil stocks have been observed to move in four-year cycles, following the basic movements of the commodities, such as crude oil, natural gas, heating oil, and wholesale unleaded gas. The funeral home business moves in six-year cycles. When times are profitable, the mom-and-pop funeral homes jump in, putting pressure on major players' profits. After a few years of stiff competition, the mom-and-pops go out of business or are merged into the bigger companies. Profit margins swing back up for the next few years. Things get good and the mom-and-pops start cropping up again.

Mr. Buffet made his fortune by having patience; long-term investors buy the down-and-out industries. When the cycle reaches its peak, he sells to everybody who is willing to pay top prices when everything looks rosy—a great investment strategy for those who can wait three years to find out the results of their investments. However, this method has its risks. A new innovation can make an industry obsolete. Your investment for the last three years may not come to fruition. Not only could you lose equity, but you lost three years of potential time to discover that the trade did not work. All those funds are committed to the trade, at risk for years, and may have nothing to show for the investment. For the wealthy, that may not sting a great amount. To the smaller investor or the money manager, three years of a poor result could have a great impact on living conditions or career status.

The ultimate trading program removes that possibility. It establishes long-term transactions carrying no downside risk nor extended capital exposure to a trade situation. The potential for maximum gains with no downside risk and no market exposure can be put into an actual trading program. As you have learned in this book, the Candlestick signals create high probabilities of profitable trades because they are the result of a change in investor sentiment *now*.

Having the ability to make a quick move on a stock price is the first ingredient for the ultimate investment program. This is accomplished by identifying the appropriate signals and market conditions. For example, the NASDAQ appears to be bottoming. At the same time Lucent has declined from the sixties to its recent low of $7.50. A Candlestick signal forms an excellent buy signal. The purchase price is at $8.20. Over the next couple of days the price moves up to $9.25, a gain of 12.8 percent. This creates a great opportunity. Where is Lucent's stock price going to go over the next three years? Who knows? Is it worth holding long-term? Again, who knows?

In this example, assume that the initial position was a $100,000 purchase or 12,200 shares at $8.20. (At this time, $100,000 of stock value is the minimum loan amount for this type of lending company. For some investors, $100,000 of stock may be stretching the financial purse strings, but that amount can be accomplished with $50,000 using margin.) The value of the position has increased to $112,800. If the position is moved to the lender for a loan, a 90-percent loan will free up $101,500 of capital.

The result of this transaction is that the investor, upon seeing an excellent potential move in a stock price commits funds to establish a position. The stock price moves up over 12 percent. Instead of taking a quick profit, the stock is used as collateral for a three-year loan. The loan proceeds $101,500 are returned to the investment account. The investor now has the original investment funds back in the account, ready to purchase the next buy signal situation. Additionally, the investor controls 12,200 shares of Lucent Technology. Because all the funds used to buy the stock is back in the account, there is no money at risk. The nonrecourse element of the loan structure means that there is nothing to lose on this trade. In three years from now, if Lucent stock price equals $78,000, the investor just walks away from the collateral. Nothing is lost, except the initial opportunity of taking the $12,800 profit when it moved from $8.20 to $9.25. On the other hand, if Lucent climbs back up to $60 at the time of the three-year loan term, the 12,200 shares are now worth $732,000. Subtract the initial $101,500 loan proceeds and the accrued interest of $35,000, and the net profit is $595,000 plus the $1,500 received in the initial loan amount over the $100,000 purchase price.

This appears good on paper—provided each and every trade worked out as planned. That will not always happen. The best approach is to put the probabilities in the investor's favor. This can be done by using the trading program described in Chapter 10. For example, assume that an investor has $400,000 to put into the trading program. This can be margined to $800,000 of buying power. Once eight separate $100,000 positions are established, the trading discipline is put in place. The expectation should be that one or two positions will fizzle and have to be liquidated and reinvested. Three to five of the positions should move positive over the next couple of days, anywhere from 3 to 8 percent. One or two positions may hit 10 percent or greater. Once one of these positions exceeds the 11-percent gain area, it becomes a candidate to be moved to the lender. At 11 percent or greater, the 90-percent loan proceeds will exceed the initial $100,000 investment. In some instances, a stock price will run 20 percent, 39 percent, or greater.

A stock price with a percent gain exceeding 11 percent can be used in two ways. The excess from the loan proceeds—that is, anything coming back over the $100,000 investment—can be thrown back into the account to beef it up a little, or the excess gains can be used to offset another position placed over at the lender at the same time. An example of this would be placing two stocks with the lender. One stock may have a 20-percent gain while the second stock only has an 8-percent gain. However, the combination of both returns exceeds the 90-percent loan amount that would cover more than the initial purchase price, $200,000. All the money to establish both of those trades, $200,000, would be back in the investor's account.

Also, it will be important to have both of those stocks collateralizing two individual loans, not one combined $200,000 loan. There is good reason for the individual loan set up. Each loan is established as a nonrecourse loan. Combining two positions could drastically alter the outcome of the profit picture. Consider what could happen in a combined loan. Stock A gains $90,000 over the next three years. Company B loses $90,000 over the next three years. The net result is that the value of the stocks is still at $200,000 when the loan comes due. With the accrued interest on the loan, you wouldn't make money and would walk away from the transaction with no gains.

Placing the two positions in two separate loans completely changes the profit picture. Company B, the stock that lost $90,000 over the three-year loan period, is a total write-off. You tell the lender to keep the collateral and you will keep the proceeds of the loan from three years prior. Company A on the other hand, is up $90,000 during the same time period. You are now ahead by $55,000, $190,000 of current market value minus the original loan amount, $100,000, minus the $35,000 in interest. Loan proceeds on Company A have nothing to do with the loan on Company B. Having two separate loans would put you $55,000 ahead.

Producing Future Income Stream

Structuring a disciplined trading program can effectively provide retirement income for the rest of your life. This assumption is based upon the consideration that the equity markets will fluctuate up and down, but the overall trend is always in an upward direction. Nobody can foresee where the market will be in three, five, or seven years. A reasonable assumption is that it should be higher than where it is today. Whether it is or not becomes less of a factor under the fully leveraged investment program.

For the sake of illustration, consider an investor who has $400,000 to trade. This can be margined out to $800,000 of purchasing power. The position target will be eight $100,000 positions. Depending upon the aggressiveness of the investor and the direction of the markets, it is reasonable to anticipate three or four positions moving up over 11 percent each month. Using the assumption that each trade will average three to five days in length and market conditions provide an environment that does not totally eliminate all buying, the search programs should find at least one 10-percent plus pop up in every 8 to 10 trades.

Using this scenario and trying to be ultra-conservative, anticipate placing one loan transaction every month. This process involves taking a profitable trade each month for the next three years. At the end of the three-year period, the amount of stock placed with the lender will be approximately $4,000,000 or 36 months of $111,000 positions. The cost of these trades is $3,600,000. The loan proceeds are $3,600,000. At the end of three years, the original $400,000 will still be in the account, provided the remaining trades during the three-year period were managed with the assistance of the Candlestick signals. The trades that did not fulfill the 11-percent price increase criteria still produced positive results, with most trades creating 3- to 10-percent returns offset by a minority of trades being flat or producing small losses.

On top of having the original investment funds in the account, those funds are responsible for controlling an additional $4,000,000 of equities. These positions are being controlled with no risk remaining. All the funds used to put on the trades are back in the account.

Month 37 becomes the first month that a loan comes due. For the sake of this example, let's assume that the markets in general performed in a relatively normal manner for the three-year period, oscillating but in an upward manner. If the purchase of Position One, bought three years back, had been in an unwanted, out of favor stock or sector, its cycle could be in the peaking stage when the loan comes due, essentially the same strategy Warren Buffet uses. Additionally, this trading program does not have the worry of a sector or stock not performing. If the value of the stock is below the break-even point (original loan amount plus accrued interest), it will not cost anything to walk away from the loan. On the other hand, if that stock is trading much higher than the initial transaction, a good chunk of profit could be coming in that month. In the meantime a new position is being put on in a stock that is currently in an unwanted sector.

This perpetual investing program has the potential to benefit from the upside gains while not participating in the downside losses. Where will the markets and/or a particular stock be in the next three years? Nobody knows. Will the market be acting strong or weak at the time a loan comes due? Nobody can answer that. However, the probabilities favor that if a loan is coming due each and every month from that point on, there will be periods when the market, thus the stock collateralizing the loan, will be hitting a high point when the loan terminates.

Hopefully, the stocks put into the loan program are bought based upon their low relative value compared to the rest of the market. This will put less importance on the condition of the market when the loan is due. If the stock has been moving up through the three-year period, due to that sector coming back into vogue, it should be substantially higher. Not having to offset gains with losses, the potential returns have a great advantage. All losing trades are flat. All winning trades are money in the pocket. The profit scenario becomes interesting. Without loses offsetting profits, a large percentage of profitable positions coming due each year are not required to produce a good annual income. The returns can be dramatic even under the scenario of 11 flat months and 1 month with a position that skyrocketed over the past three years.

Receiving the gains has an additional benefit. If a stock rose dramatically, producing a good profit upon the expiration of the loan period, profits can be reaped on a tax-free basis. The loan can be rolled over at the new market price of the stock. Renewing the loan at 90 percent of the current market price pays off the original loan, pays the accrued interest, and puts new tax-free loan proceeds in the investor's pocket. Now the downside is protected at the new higher level.

The upside to this program is obvious: large potential gains with no downside risk and no capital tied up for years to control a large equity portfolio. This program forces the investor to stay with a position from the bottom of a cycle to the top of a cycle. To get to these attributes, costs are incurred. The fact that at least a 10-percent gain was forfeited to establish full reimbursement from the loan proceeds is one cost. Approximately $10,000 a month or $360,000 could have been realized over the three-year period. On a $400,000 account, that would have been considered an excellent rate of return. That potential return has to be considered when evaluating the pros and cons of this program.

The cornerstone of this program is the effectiveness of the Candlestick signals. Investors can concentrate investment dollars into situations that are performing right now, whereas most investors, holding for long-term, do not gain any major benefit from short-term rallies with their funds tied up after a short-term move. This program exploits the short-term move by making the result of the move into a long-term benefit. The immediate gains achieve the needed criteria to establish fully leveraged stock positions.

Taxes are another consideration. You will have to pay capital gains at some point. Fortunately that point can be pushed out into the future, which means less valued dollars to pay taxes. Many advantageous estate-planning strategies can be developed using this program. You can formulate interesting gift packages with fully leveraged stock positions. You can implement better tax strategies when you know the exact selling dates ahead of time.

In the recent past, one of the cornerstones of the American auto industry has been fighting off the bad news. Ford Motor Company had trouble with their SUV sales due to bad tires. Ford's fault? Firestone's fault? Who knows, but who cares? Ford is not ready to go out of business. Nobody has a good outlook for the company *today*! The stock price is in the low twenties. It has a price-earning ratio of nine and pays out a dividend of over 5 percent. Is Ford's stock price going to always stay this cheap? Probably not. Will their problems last forever? Probably not. Is the management of Ford Motor Company stupid? Probably not. Here is the prime circumstance for buying a good company's stock while nobody likes it. Will the public have forgotten about the tire problems of Ford's SUVs in three years? Of course. More likely it will all be forgotten in six months. Will Ford resolve the problem and repair its image to the public? Probably. That's how any company stays in business. Will the stock price be higher in three years down the road? Who knows. But wouldn't it be an interesting play to buy the stock on a Candlestick buy signal, have it make a quick move, get all your money back out, then sit with Ford stock for the next three years without any capital tied up in it?

The Candlestick Charts provide the visual format for identifying when the long-term trend is changing. Figure 14.1, representing Ford Motor Company's monthly chart, shows indications of a Fry Pan Bottom forming. A Doji signal may be forming at the end of a long black candle in what appears to be a slowly ascending trend. If the daily and weekly charts appear to be bottoming, this would lend more evidence that the long-term chart may be in the lower portion of an uptrending trading channel.

Extrapolating how the weekly and daily chart movements will form candles on the monthly chart gives the long-term view a head start. As seen in Ford's weekly chart, shown in Figure 14.2, the stochastics are near the oversold range. If it were to reverse and become bullish, a white candle would be

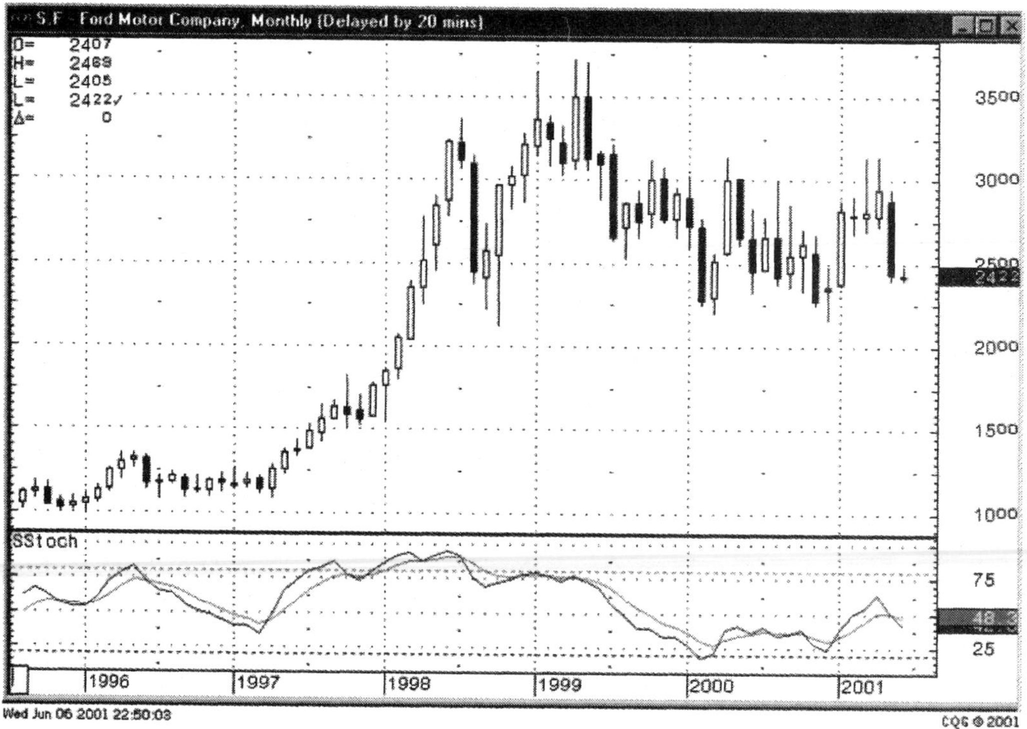

Figure 14.1 A chart can indicate a long-term pattern forming.

forming after a Doji formation on the monthly chart. The process from that point is to keep an eye on the daily chart, watching for a bullish signal.

Having the visual platform, while listening to all the bad news about a financially strong company, provides for the opportunities to get into good stocks while they are down. Having loan products that produce the method for owning a stock position for long-term without having capital tied up is the ultimate way to invest.

Conclusion

The ability to control a vast amount of equity with no money at risk can produce sensational increases to an investor's estate value. Candlestick analysis creates profits from ordinary stock price patterns. When it is combined with this relatively new lending product, inordinate returns can be realized. If you, as an investor, are going to spend time and effort to study the market to extract profits, why not use the fruits of those efforts to maximize your wealth potential. The products are there. The opportunities are there. The right combination, implemented properly, can advance your wealth exponentially.

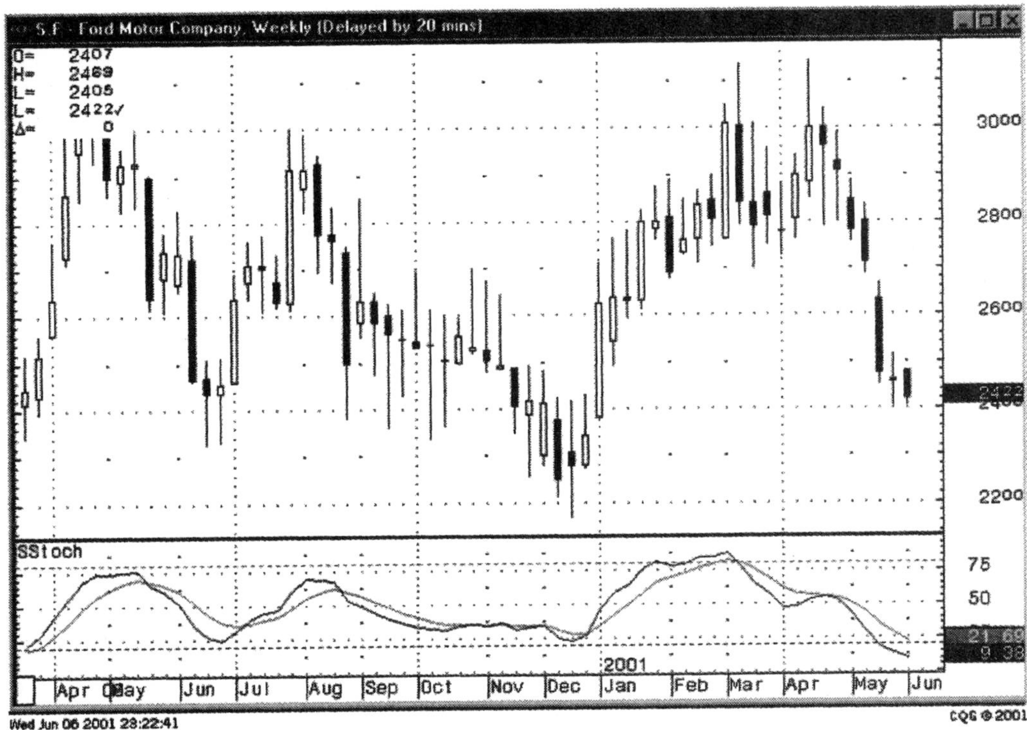

Figure 14.2 Ford Motor Company's weekly chart confirming what the daily chart may be revealing.

Using the Candlestick signals provides a profit capability not found in the vast majority of investment tools. Having the ability to pinpoint trades that are moving right now eliminates wasted return potential by not having to be in positions for lengthy periods. Quick moves can be exploited for huge profit potentials. The elements of the ultimate trading program can and should be implemented in a disciplined approach. Maintaining the proper discipline produces the opportunity to benefit from all the winning trades while not having to be concerned with any of the losing trades. How can you beat a trading system like that?

Chapter 15

CANDLESTICK TRADING RULES

Better one safe way than a hundred on which you cannot reckon. Aesop

Through the years, because of the inherent nature of the signals, some basic rules can help an investor maximize profits. These rules were developed because of profits, created by using the signals. Acting against the signals provides clear lessons on what not to do. Just as in Mom telling you not to put your hand on the hot stove, it becomes clear in your mind what she was saying the first time you do it anyway. In this case, a trading rule can be reinforced by watching how a trade would have performed whether you participate in the trade or just watch the trade results. Some of the rules are derived from the great alterations the Candlestick investing program provides for investment thinking.

When in Doubt, Get Out

The hardest aspect of investing is trying to eliminate the emotional element. Well thought-out decisions made under rational conditions disappear once our money is exposed to the trading environment. Emotional attachment creeps into a trade after the intellectual prowess expended to establish the trade. Using computer search software provides the investor with more opportunities than he or she could possibly handle. Having a bountiful supply of trade possibilities creates the maneuverability to place funds in a multitude of situations. Investing has the basic function of being a by-product of probabilities. We invest our funds in trade situations that have good probabilities of making money. the Candlestick signals have high probabilities of making profits, but not all signals are going to result in gains. Hopefully three out of four will be profitable; even four out of five is obtainable. But that leaves 20 to 25 percent of all trades should not workout.

You need to understand when one-in-four or one-in-five investment situations are not going to work. When these situations become apparent or if the analysis of a position does not have clear directional indications, get out.

Why stay in a trade that has questions surrounding it? Take that money and put it into the next batch of clear Candlestick signal situations. A questionable trade situation does not put the probabilities in your favor. Liquidate it. There will be a plentiful supply of signals waiting to be evaluated at the end of the day or week or whatever timeframe you are investing. When in doubt, get out. There will be many places to put investment funds that have the probabilities clearly in your favor.

Don't Look Back

How many times have we held onto a position too long because it was projected by somebody else or we wished for a price level much higher than where it was at the time? All indications show that it was time to sell but how stupid we would be if we sold at the first signs of weakness, only to see the price skyrocket later. As a consequence, the price backs down. We don't sell it now because we know that it should have been sold at the higher level. We will wait until it bounces back up to that level. When it goes lower, we now try to get out at the level that it just came from. This keeps happening until we've held the stock through a whole cycle. Not only does it not get back up to the initial level that we felt that was the right time to sell, that position has encumbered those funds that could have been making money elsewhere.

The only reason time and profits were wasted was the fear that doing what appeared to be right at the time, selling at the appearance of a sell signal, could have resulted in the price shooting up after we sold the position. Embarrassing. But embarrassing to who? Mostly to ourselves. How stupid we would feel to make a decision to get into a position, and then get scared out of the position only to have left the big profits on the table. The Candlestick signals provide the format to eliminate that trauma. Take it right back to the foundation of the signals. They are in existence today good reason. Hundreds of years of observations have proved that the signals demonstrated a reversal occurring. Why doubt it? If your observations and the best of your investment decision processing tells you to liquidate the trade, don't fight the percentages.

Investment decisions have to be made with the best information available at the time. If the price skyrockets after you have closed the trade, you still made the right decision with the information you had at the time. Disciplined trading programs involve making the decisions that follow the parameters of that program. If signs say that holding the position was a low probability situation, do what the trading program dictates.

If there is still a strong conviction that the stock price will go higher, there is nothing to stop an investor from monitoring the price action. If a buy signal reappears, buy back into the position. Otherwise, those funds should have been reallocated to a position that has better upside probabilities. If the original position does turn around and head back up, so you missed it. Your investment funds should have been working in another good trade situation.

Don't look back. Make the best decision you need to with the evidence presenting itself at the time. For every instance where looking back creates anguish, there will be a dozen times that you are thankful for taking the right action when you did.

Plan Your Trading

The identification of the reversal signals takes only a few minutes each evening. Having uninterrupted time to analyze which of the potential trade signals is the most promising is essential. Once careful study determines the order of the best potentials for the next day, keep that order. Slight changes should occur, depending upon how the stocks and the market in general open the next day. Rarely, if ever, will there be a reason to deviate from that list. If the top one or two stocks open in a manner that does not demonstrate the continued participation of what the Candlestick reversal signal was indicating, then look at the next best positions. If the market opens in the manner that makes all the potentials doubtful of being a good trade, just stay out. For example, if five excellent long positions were the best prospects for the next days open and the next days futures showed a major bearish open, then one of those stock potentials may be opening with the evidence of buyers still participating. They all are opening lower. If a strong bearish open was not what was anticipated for the next day, then keep your investment funds on the sideline. Do not attempt a shot at shorting.

To do nothing is sometimes a good remedy. Hippocrates

Attempting to find a good trade situation off the cuff does not have the structure of analysis needed to consider all the probabilities. Sit back and get ready for the next day. It is better to miss potential profits than to have to make up losses before being able to get to a profitable balance. There will be good trade situations the next day.

If a Trade Is Not Working, Move On

Not all trades are going to be instant winners. Always keep the probabilities in mind. A vast majority of the trades should work. Some will not. Some will be fizzlers, not doing much of anything. When a signal is observed and a trade is established, expect good results. Those results should involve some subjective visual expectations. The results of the trade can be visually interpreted at the end of each day. If a stock price does not seem to be confirming the signal, whether the next day or three days after the trade has been placed, do the same evaluation that should constitute the underlying premise of your investment program. "Is this the best place to have my investment funds?" If the bullish sentiment appears to be less than expected after a strong bullish buy signal, compare it to other opportunities. The three days after a trade was established may not have revealed any selling pressure, but it may not have demonstrated any significant buying presence either. A fizzler. Don't be apprehensive about liquidating that position and putting the funds into a current strong signal. However, if a strong buying signal had enticed you into making the trade in the first place, that illustrates that a buying force had existed for some reason. Keep the stock price closely monitored. It may produce another strong buy signal in the next few days. This would be evidence that the buyers were still interested. Then funds can be recommitted to the position, even if the entry point is higher than the original entry point.

The only important decision process should be whether this signal was going to produce a profit, not what happened with the position in the prior few trading days. As a rule, keep the investment funds in trades that have the best potential. If an existing potential is not performing as expected, move on to one that has that potential to maximize profits.

Don't Allow the News to Influence Your Trading Decisions

A major influence upon the investment world is the easy access to investment news. CNBC and Bloomberg are on all day long keeping investors bombarded with every piece of news. But this news fits into a specific category: reported news. Reported news is the actual reporting of the news that somebody has known about for days, weeks, or months. You make your investment decisions based upon the Candlestick signals. You are convinced that the formations are based upon the cumulative knowledge of all the investors participating in the buying and selling of that stock/trading entity that day. Do not make different investment decisions based upon the reporting of news. Unless an item comes to the public forefront that is a total surprise to the investment community, the reporting of the news is the consummation of what the stock price has been illustrating.

If you live by the sword, you may die by the sword. If you invest based upon the principles of Candlestick formations, then trust the formations to lead you to successful circumstances the vast majority of the time. To deviate from the basics of the probabilities demonstrated by the existence of the signals leaves the investor flopping around with no accounting procedure for tracking successes and failures. Stay with what the signals tell you.

Candlestick-Specific Rules

Being able to anticipate the development of a reversal pattern can result in getting into or out of a position before the rest of the crowd. For example, witnessing a Shooting Star at the end of a lengthy uptrend, when the stochastics are well into the overbought area, forewarns that the trend may be over. Upon seeing the price open weaker the next trading day, the Candlestick investor knows to take profits immediately. This is a situation that does not require waiting until the end of the day to view the completion of the candle formed that day.

Under different circumstances, the rule would be to wait until the end of the day to see what candle formation was making itself present. There will be a good many instances where a trade has been put on based upon the presence of a Candlestick signal. The stochastics are in an extreme range, confirming the signal. After the third or fourth day the price opens and makes an immediate move back in the opposite direct, eating up most of the trade's profits. The first inclination is to liquidate the trade before it gets any worse. If the indicators are such that it does not warrant considering that a reversal has occurred (for example, the stochastics are still near the range that it started), hold the position until the end of the day, if no news would suggest that the position should be liquidated. The reason is simple. The purpose for establishing the position was due to the Candlestick signal, a completed Candlestick signal. An early day pullback during a long position uptrend or a price bounce occurring during a downtrend can be normal buying and selling forces at work. The current trend does not change until a reversal signal appears. That reversal signal is formed by the close of a day's trading activity. Profit taking is apt to enter into the price movement of a stock at any time. What goes on during a candlestick formation time frame is not important. It is the final price of that time period that will demonstrate cumulative results of investor sentiment. An important rule is to make entry and exit decisions based upon the candle formations that present themselves at the end of the day.

The Doji at the Top

Always sell when you witness a Doji at the top. The signals are representative of successful trading formations. The Japanese did not come up with the rules for signals without a great amount of research behind them. Why play against the probabilities. The Japanese have witnessed many times over that indecision at the top of a sustained rally warrants selling the position immediately. Modern-day evaluation confirms that rule. If the Doji does not represent that exact top, which an extremely high percentage of the time it does, it indicates the existence of sellers at this price level. If prices do go higher over the next day or two, the price gain from the point of the Doji is not great enough to warrant the risk to obtain the last remaining profits. Money could have been placed elsewhere for the same, if not better returns, without the potential downside exposure.

Stay with the Rules

Always remember that the signals are still around after hundreds of years because the evidence of their success could not be ignored. Profits have been the result. Don't project the potential of a trade to the point that you expect it. Despite the fact that a projection exercise is needed to establish whether the trade is worth putting on, that projection should remain a guideline only. The signals are statistically accurate for putting on a trade. They are just as accurate for ending a trade. If a trade shows signals opposite the entry signal well before what you mentally projected to be the target, don't fight the signal. Get out. As stated in the first rule, when in doubt get out. Price movements don't care one iota what you think the price should go to. Always let the market (signals) dictate your course of action. A sell signal can always be followed by another buy signal. If so, get back in. However, the signals are formed by the change of investor sentiment. Why would you want to try to buck that reality?

Use the signals to your advantage. Maintaining simple rules always keeps results accountable. As long as you keep the playing field level, the results can be analyzed correctly. Keeping basic rules allows the investor to keep from letting emotional reactions interfere with disciplined trading practices. The statistics will be the guiding force of your discipline. Once you realize that the signals produce trades greatly in your favor, deviating from the rules that take advantage of those statistics leaves you out in the realm of investing with no improvable program. The Candlesticks are successful. Don't think fate or good fortune is going to come to your aid when ignoring the proven results.

Chapter 16

CONCLUSION

The conduct of our lives is the true mirror of our doctrine. Montaigne

This book was written for one purpose: to expose the ease of using the Candlestick method. The main deterrent for this methodology becoming a widely used trading program has been the perception that it was difficult to learn. My goal in this book has been to eliminate that impression. Learning how to use this program should be analogous to learning the alphabet. Once each letter (signal) is learned, it can be used to form simple words. Once those words are learned, their use can be put into more sophisticated structures (sentences). The same is true with the signals. Once they have been learned, trading procedures can be easily put in place to make the signals more effective.

Through many years of experience, it has been found that the Candlestick technical analysis furnishes a multifaceted benefit to investors. Being able to recognize reversal signals is only a portion of the beneficial aspects. This is an important part of an investment program, yet additional ramifications are a result of trading confidently using the signals. Being able to use them effectively has a dramatic effect upon an investor's investment psychology. Being influenced by outside news or hot tips becomes less prominent. Taking recommendations from professional investment advisory people is now done without blind participation. Investigation of low risk, high probability trading techniques is in your control. You are not restricted to the accepted forms of conventional investing any longer.

Once you have discovered the ease of using the Candlestick method, controlling the risk consequences becomes a self-refining process. Having control of why an investment is made has the added advantage of knowing when it should be ended. The bottom line is that your investment results are now in your total control.

The Candlesticks are excellent stand-alone investment cornerstones; however, more benefits are derived when they are used in conjunction with existing technical methods. Pinpointing the reversal points enhances your ability to develop profitable trading programs when overlaid on a technical analysis method. Each investor can benefit from the signals, whether a novice investor or a professional trader. Each market has its own trading characteristics, and particular signals may work better in one market versus another. Characteristics of a particular stock or commodity may demonstrate excellent reversal points using only one specific signal. You learn these traits through observation. Fortunately, the Candlestick signals provide the opportunity to perfect trading programs by being able to visually witness buy and sell points.

The severity of the losses experienced in the high-tech stocks from early 2000 to early 2001 brought many investors back to reality. The New Economy, once the buzzword, started to resemble Old Economy. For three years prior to that, the dynamics of fundamental research were skewed to fit the moves of the market. Analysts who were recommending stocks at $120 were re-recommending them at $10 three years later. "If I could only see the turn coming, I would have made a fortune on the short side" was an often heard exclamation from investors.

The truth of the matter is that you could see it coming. Candlestick formations decipher emotional rhetoric. Loudly proclaimed stock recommendations are visually scrutinized by the results of investor decisions. Being able to evaluate potential market movement frees investors from the idiosyncrasies of the accepted investment culture. A culture that dictates that you cannot outguess the markets. Listen to the experts who advise buy and hold. Obtaining a 10- or 15-percent annual return is the expected norm. That leaves the question, "How do people become rich from investing in the stockmarket if we all are best advised to obtain mediocrity?"

That is why you read this book. Do not let the "experts" influence your fate. To produce average returns, something must have produced good returns, others bad returns. The names of Buffet, Soros, Rogers and others would not be names of recognition is they hadn't figured out how to greatly exceed the expected returns the market relinquishes.

You may not want to be a famous name, but there is absolutely no reason that you can't extract inordinate profits from the same investment playing fields that everybody else has access to. This book should have made you realize that a system has been developed to fulfill that purpose. Use that knowledge. Eliminate emotions from investment decisions. Price movements are mechanical processes implementing emotional influences of the masses. Candlestick analysis has categorized those elements into visual formations. You can take advantage of that knowledge. Your formula for wealth is now indoctrinated with a profit-oriented methodology that has proven itself over and over. It takes our own human weaknesses and mirrors them to expose profitable opportunities.

Hopefully, the procedures explained in this book have helped you discover some aspects of your own aptitudes and weaknesses. Controlling emotion is the most difficult element of investing. Use the signals' probability factors to get accustomed to a new method of thinking. Put your toe in until the results produce the confidence needed. Fortunately, unlike years past, delving into this little known trading method does not have to be tested alone. Please use the Web site that can act as a backup for unanswered questions: **www.candlestickforum.com.** Experiencing trade situations does not have to be like reinventing the wheel. Profit from the experience of other traders. Providing insights into trades that are familiar allows the new Candlestick investor to gain profitable experience without having to participate in losing situations.

You now have the knowledge to control your own investment future. The probabilities are in your favor. The market is wide open for exploiting the signals. Make inordinate profits. Good luck.

To continue your education about Candlestick investing, use the expertise of the staff at Candlestickforum.com.

GLOSSARY

Western and Japanese Technical Terms

The following is a list of terms used in this book and in association with Japanese Candlestick analysis. Some terms are purely of Western origin; others are purely of Japanese origin. Many are used for description in both Western and Japanese techniques, becoming intermingled through the years. This glossary is not meant to be all-inclusive or detailed. The terms cover the common topics found in both methods.

Bar charts The conventional graphic depiction of price activity. The trading range is illustrated with a vertical line representing the high to low prices during a time period. Open price is shown by a short horizontal line attached to the left side of the vertical line, the close is a horizontal line to the right side. Price is represented on the vertical scale of the chart. Time is represented on the horizontal scale.

Blow-offs A topping or bottoming action. Occurring at the end of an extended move. Prices move sharply and rapidly in the direction of the current trend on high volume. If the price reverses direction after this movement, a blow-off has occurred.

Breakaway gap When prices gap away from a technically defined area, such as a congestion area or a trendline.

Breakout The movement that pushes through a resistance level or a support level.

Confirmation When a move or an indicator substantiates the anticipated action resulting from another indicator.

Congestion area Trading activity where the price movement stays within an observable trading range for an extended period of time.

Consolidation Trading in a range of the congestion area with the implication that the trend is resting and will resume the direction of the current trend.

Continuation patterns A pattern that has been observed to indicate that the current trend will continue.

Dead cross When short-term moving averages cross under the longer-term moving averages and a bearish signal is given.

Deliberation pattern Also known as a stalling pattern, prices are coming to a point of a reversal.

Divergence The disparity between indicators when a price action has made a move. One indicator confirms that the move was correct, the other shows the opposite. For example, if prices hit high and the relative strength index does not, a divergence has occurred.

Double bottoms An easily recognized technical pattern illustrated by a W-shaped bottom where prices reverse at approximately the same lows.

Double tops Price movement that resembles an M where the highs are approximately the same.

Downgap Prices gap down in the next time period to levels below the total trading range of the previous time period.

Downtrend Prices trading lower usually represented by lower lows and/or lower highs.

Elliot wave Ralph Nelson Elliot developed a system for forecasting price movements based upon oscillations in investor sentiment. The basis of the theory revolves around five waves in a general direction (five-wave upmove) followed by three corrective waves in the opposite direction (three-wave downmove).

Exponential moving average A moving average calculated by exponentially weighted input.

Fibonacci numbers The series of numbers that are derived by adding the two previous numbers to obtain the next number. That number added to the previous number results in the next number. The series of numbers produces ratios used extensively by Elliot wave advocates, 38 percent, 50 percent, and 62 percent.

Filling the gap A gap becomes filled when prices move back into the black area of trading. Candlestick terminology describes this as "closing the window."

Gap A price void where the trading range between one time period does not overlap with any price trading of the next time period.

Golden cross A bullish signal created by the short-term moving averages crossing above the long-term moving averages.

High-wave A group of candlesticks with long upper and/or lower shadows. This grouping of formations foretells a market turn.

Implied volatility A measure for the market to forecast future volatility.

Inside session This is a trading session where the high and the low of a trading period remains within the high and the low of the previous trading session.

Intra-day Trading periods that begin and end within a one-day time frame.

Islands A formation created at the end of a trend where prices gap away from the current trend, trade for two or more days at those levels, and then gap back in the opposite direction. This leaves an island of trading at the end of the trend. Commonly known as island reversals. Strong reversal indicator.

Locals Floor traders that make their living by trading a particular entity.

Lower shadows The trading range below the body of a candle.

Momentum Related to the velocity of a price move. The most recent close is compared to a specific number of closes in a specific time frame.

Morning attack A Japanese definition for a large buy or sell order on the opening that is designed to significantly move the market.

Moving Average Convergence-Divergence oscillator (MACD) A combination of three exponentially smoothed moving averages.

Neckline The level that indicates the lows of the head in the head and shoulders formation or the high points in an inverse head and shoulders formation.

Night attack A large order placed at the close to move the market.

Offset The term for closing trades. Longs are said to liquidate. Shorts are said to cover.

On-Balance Volume (OBV) A cumulative volume figure. If prices close higher than the prior trading session, the volume for the higher day is added to the OBV. Conversely, volume is subtracted from the OBV on days when prices close lower than the previous day.

Open interest Pertains to future contracts. It is the number of contracts that are still outstanding. It will be equal to the total number of long and short positions, however not the combination of the two.

Oscillator An indicator based upon a momentum formula that moves above or below a zero line or on a chart grid between 0 and 100 percent. They depict overbought and oversold conditions and positive or negative divergences; *r* measures the velocity in a price movement.

Overbought A term associated with specific oscillators to denote when a price has moved to far, too fast in an upward direction.

Oversold The same as the overbought definition except for it being in the downward direction.

Paper trading A popular method using real-life trade circumstances and trading with imaginary trading funds.

Petrifying pattern Another name for the Harami cross.

Protective stop An order placed to limit losses on an existing position. If prices move to that level, a trade is initiated to liquidate the position avoiding further loss potential.

Raindrop Another name for the star formation.

Rally Usually a strong upward price movement.

Reaction A price movement that moves opposite the current trend.

Real body (or body) The boxed area from the open to the close is what forms the body of the candle. When the close is lower than the open, a black body is produced. A close above the open causes a white body to be formed.

Relative Strength Index (RSI) An oscillator developed by Welles Wilder. It compares the ratio of positive closes to negative closes over a specific time period.

Resistance level A trading level where obvious selling keeps the prices from advancing any further.

Retracement The price movement in the opposite direction of the recent trend.

Reversal session After a move experiences a new high (or low), the next close is below (or above) the previous day's close.

Rickshaw Man A long-legged Doji where the body, although small, is in the center of the formation.

Selling climax After a move downwards, prices push sharply lower on heavy volume. If prices move higher from these levels, a selling climax has occurred.

Selloff The downward movement of prices.

Shadows The extreme price movement outside the body of a candle creates the shadows. The lower shadow extends from the bottom of the body to the low price of the day. The upper shadow extends from the top of the body to the high price of the day.

Shaven bottom A candlestick with no lower shadow.

Shaven head A candlestick with no upper shadow.

Simple moving averages The smoothing of price data where prices are added together, and then averaged. The term *moving* is included due to the fact that as each new day's information is added to the numbers, the oldest data is dropped.

Spring When prices break below a congestion area, and then spring right back above the broken support area, it has produced a bullish signal.

Star A small body that gaps away from the previous long body. A star indicates the reduction of force illustrated by the previous long candle. A star following a long black body is called a raindrop.

Stochastics An oscillator that measures the relative position of closing prices compared to the trading range over a specified period of time. %K indicates the fast stochastic, %D indicates the slow stochastic.

Support level An obvious level where buyers are shown to step in and hold prices above that level.

Tick volume The number of trades occurring during a specific time interval.

Time filter A price level that prices have to stay above or below for a specific period of time to confirm that a technical level has been broken.

Trend A price's prevalent directional movement.

Trend-line A line that can be drawn along a series of highs or lows. This requires at least two points for a line to be drawn. The more points that are associated with the line, the more strength the trend-line carries.

Trend reversals (or reversal indicators) Price action that indicates the high probability of a trend reversing its direction.

Tweezer tops or bottoms Highs or lows of a trend that are duplicated in back to back trading days or within the next few sessions. The name is derived from the price movement to those levels forming a tweezer-like visual. It is a minor reversal signal, however, its significance becomes greater if the highs or lows are touched with long shadows or if the identical bottoms are part of another reversal signal.

Upgap A gap in prices to the upside.

Upthrust The price movement that carries prices through and above observed resistance areas. If these new price levels do not hold and prices pull back under the breached resistance level, it is called an upthrust. It now becomes a bearish signal.

Uptrend Prices that are trading higher.

V bottom or top A sharp reversal forming a V pattern at the bottom of a trend or an inverted V at the top of a trend.

Volume The total number of shares or contracts trading in a given day on that trading entity.

Weighted moving average A moving average where the most recent data is given greater value that the oldest data.

Window The same as a Western gap. Windows can indicate the beginning of a strong trend as well as the end of a trend, exhaustion window. As Western technicians say that prices will always fill the gap, the Japanese expect to close the window.

Yin and Yang The Chinese name for the black (Yin) and the white (Yang). Good and bad, positive and negative.

INDEX